ATLAS OF WORLD HISTORY

This edition published in 1994 by Blitz Editions
an imprint of Bookmart Limited, Registered Number 2372865.
Trading as Bookmart Limited, Desford Road, Enderby,
Leicester LE9 5AD

Revised and updated edition 1994

ISBN 1 85605 221 4

Printed in Italy by Vallardi Industrie Grafiche S.p.A.
Lainate (MI) - May 1994

ATLAS OF WORLD HISTORY

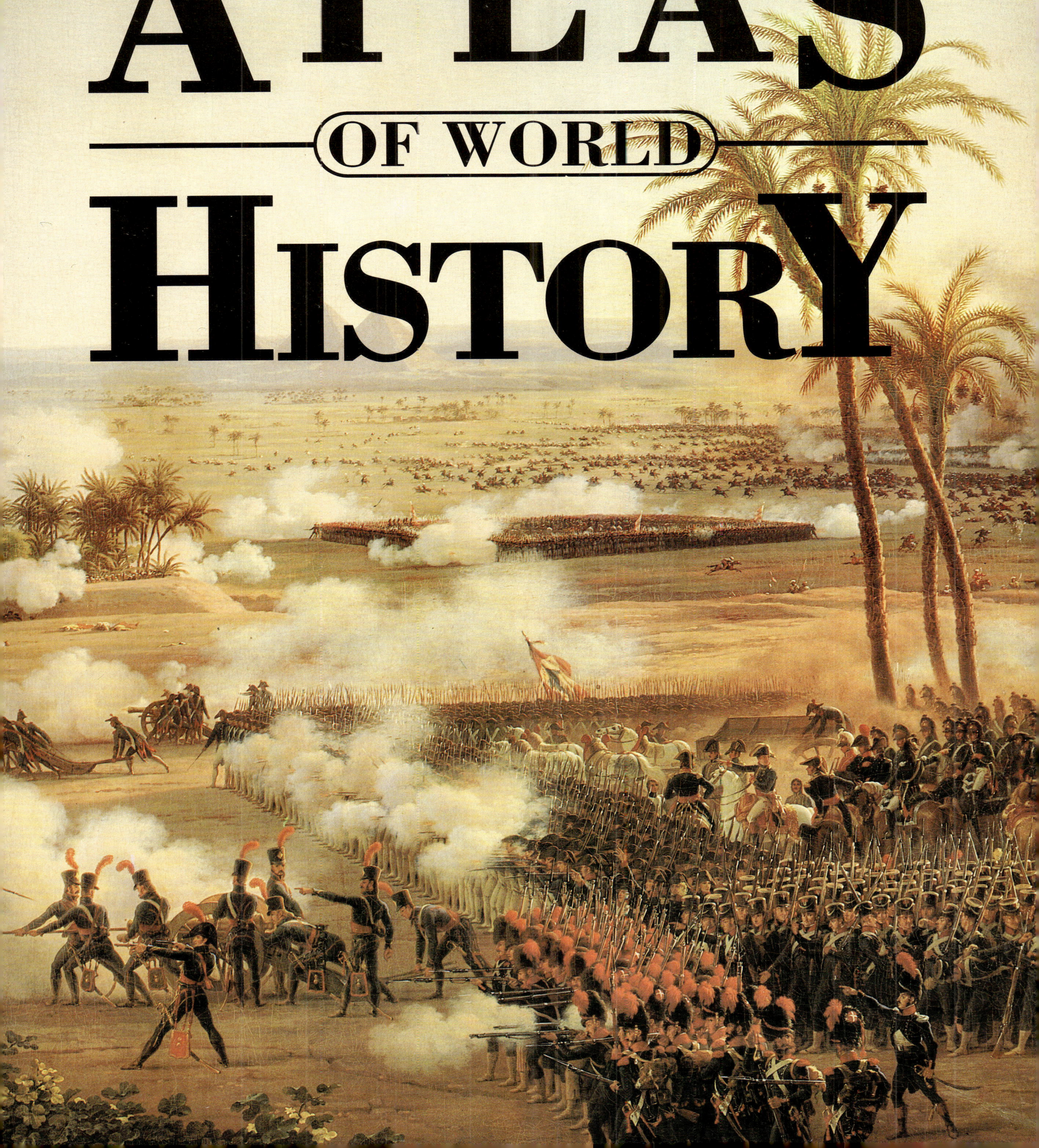

galia.
hispania.
ITALI
BAR
B
ARIA
Tingitania.
Libia.

Contents

THE ORIGINS OF CIVILIZATION

Age | Cultures, methods of working and human types

NEOLITHIC

Man developed a productive economy, based on agriculture and the domestication of animals. Ceramics and the techniques of smoothing stones appeared.

7,000 years ago

MESOLITHIC

MAGLEMOSAN
Located in Northern Europe. Remains of ships have been found.

TARDENOISIAN
Trapezoid-shaped tools of small size appeared.

AZILIAN
Small manufactures and painted stones.

10,000 years ago

PALAEOLITHIC — UPPER

MAGDALENIAN
Remarkable development of artistic skills and of working in bone.

SOLUTREAN
Objects of high technical and artistic quality were produced.

AURIGNACIAN
The first examples of figurative art and of objects made of bone appeared.

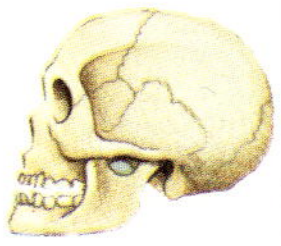

Modern man
Sapiens sapiens

30,000 years ago

PALAEOLITHIC — MIDDLE

MOUSTERIAN
This is divided into many cultures characterized by a greater variety of manufactures: fine points, knives and scrapers.

Mousterian scraper

LEVALLOISIAN
Stone objects with roughly pointed edges are typical of this culture.

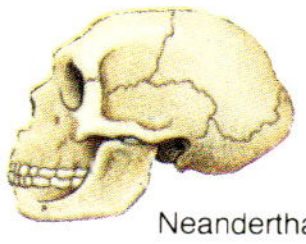

Neanderthal man

100,000 years ago

PALAEOLITHIC — LOWER

ACHEULIAN
The typical tool was the hand-axe, now more regular in shape and more sophisticated.

Acheulian hand-axe

ABBEVILLIAN
Appearance of hand-axes, bifacial tools with sharp and curved edges.

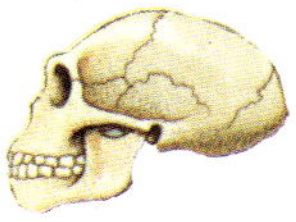

Homo erectus

PEBBLE CULTURE
Tools made from small lumps of stone or pebbles whose edges were sharpened for cutting.

2,000,000 years ago

The origins of man

The origins and development of the first man constitute a fascinating but difficult field of investigation. Only discoveries of fragments of bone, usually jaws and teeth, enable us to obtain some idea of the characteristics and evolution of the ancestors of man. Their emergence is lost in a time which, although geographically close, is historically almost beyond the possibility of analysis, dating back hundreds of thousands of years.

Modern science, following in the footsteps of Charles Darwin's theories as expounded in his *Origin of Species*, has recognized that the human species and the big apes in fact derive from common ancestors who lived between fifteen and twenty million years ago, but the origin of modern man is still largely shrouded in mystery. Even if it is well understood that the characteristics of the genus *Homo* make him similar to primates such as the gorilla and the chimpanzee, the genetic process which gave birth to the human species is still not completely known.

Among the most recent discoveries, those made in Ethiopia indicate that, more than four million years ago, a primate, today known as *Australopithecus*, had adopted an upright posture, a first step in the evolution of man. The first type classifiable as belonging to the genus *Homo* is the so-called *Homo habilis*, who lived in Africa between two million and one and a half million years ago. *Homo habilis* was the first creature to make stone tools.

About a million years ago *Homo erectus* appeared: his remains have been found in Africa, Asia and Europe, and his knowledge of the use of fire has been established by the discovery of burnt objects at fossil sites. Then, dating from perhaps 250,000 years ago, the first evidence of primitive types of *Homo sapiens* appeared, of which two sub-species have been discovered: Neanderthal man (*H. sapiens neanderthalensis*) and Cromagnon man who was already very similar to modern man.

The finds

Finds of pre-hominids (*Australopithecus, Ramapithecus*) are confined almost exclusively to the centre of Southern Africa, while numerous remains of creatures belonging to the genus *Homo* have been discovered in Europe. Of the latter, few examples have been found of *Homo erectus*, but numerous sites have yielded remains associated with the various sub-species of *Homo sapiens* (*Homo sapiens steinheimensis, Homo sapiens neanderthalensis* and *Homo sapiens sapiens*). Among the best-known locations are Olduvai in Africa, Neanderthal, Steinheim and Cromagnon in Europe.

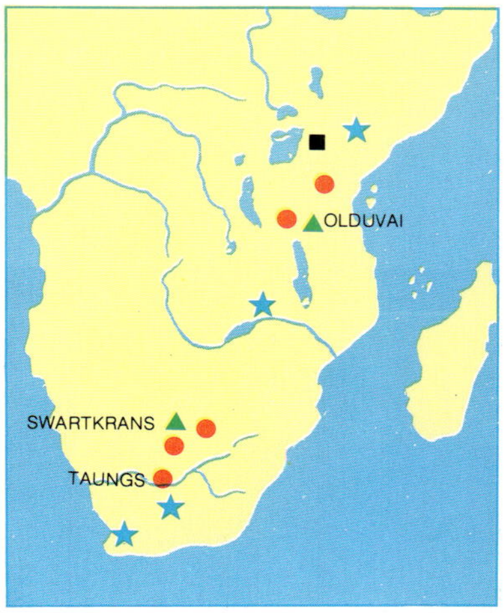

Ramapithecus | *Homo erectus*
Australopithecus | *Homo sapiens*

Hunters

Hunting and gathering were the main means of providing for survival in the prehistoric periods. Throughout the Palaeolithic Age, hunting was the only means of obtaining food, skins and bones, and it was only with the arrival of the Neolithic Age that man turned to animal rearing and cultivation of the soil to raise crops. The remains of animals found in Palaeolithic settlements show that, parallel with improvements in manufacturing techniques, methods of hunting also underwent development: it was now being practised in groups and with more sophisticated weapons. Pictures found in France and eastern Spain—as for example in Lascaux—document palaeolithic hunting techniques and also early man's skill in extracting colours from natural sources.

Venus figures

An interesting chapter in Palaeolithic art is the one which produced numerous small, female anthropomorphic statues, dating from about 20,000 years ago and often called "Venus figures" by palaeontologists. Made of stone, ivory and bone, they are normally between 3.5 centimetres (1½ inches) and 22 centimetres (8½ inches) in size, and are remarkably similar despite their varied origins. In these works, the artists pay particular attention to certain characteristics of the female body, emphasizing especially those connected with fertility and giving birth. Sometimes this means omitting arms and neglecting details of the face and head.

Zoomorphic representation

Numerous objects of high artistic quality have survived fro the Magdalenian period. Made by chiselling or sculpting stone or bone, they mainly depict animals, and are thought to have been used to bring good fortune in hunting.

Rock engravings

A type of art made by chiselling or by painting on rocks is to be found in all parts of the world. The age of the representation is deduced from the kind of extinct animal portrayed and from the different techniques and styles. The figures below depict the ostrich and other animals of the savannah; found in the Algerian Sahara, these show that the area underwent climatic changes long ago.

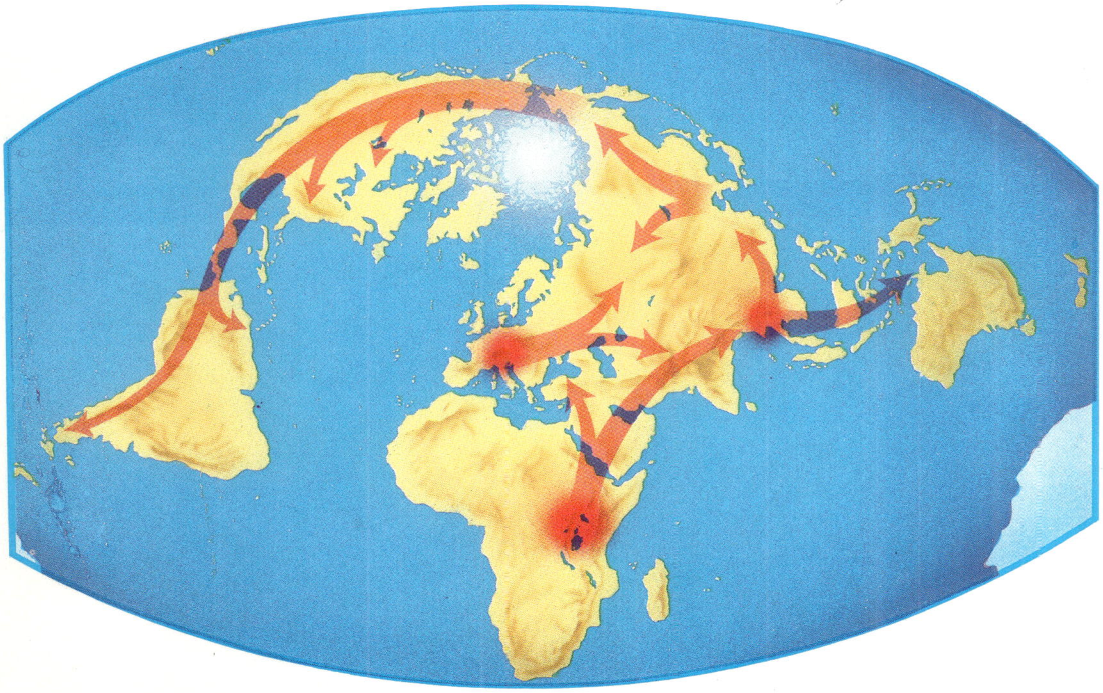

Man populates the world

The ability to hunt in groups and the freedom of movement possessed by *Homo erectus* allowed man to migrate from Central Africa (probably via the Nile valley) to the tropical areas of India and South-east Asia, and also to Europe. During a time of warm climate, about one hundred and fifty thousand to two hundred thousand years ago, a sub-species of *Homo sapiens, Homo sapiens steinheimensis*, peopled the plains of Northern Europe. After a period of glaciation, this population was replaced by another ethnic group with different skull characteristics, that is known today as Neanderthal. These new peoples occupied Western Europe up until the last glaciation of the Pleistocene Age, when they were succeeded by modern man, about thirty-five thousand to forty thousand years ago. The New World, however, was not populated by *Homo sapiens* until much later: the first remains of human beings found in America are ten thousand years old. It is probable that groups of hunters moved from Siberia to Alaska during the last glaciation, when the two continents were linked by an ice bridge. Each successive population movement was the result of the alternation of warm and cold periods—changes which prompted the movement of hunters who followed the migration of animals. This was essential since the animals were a vital source of food and clothing.

Prehistoric man

Prehistory is the term normally applied to the long period stretching from the time when man began to produce weapons and tools in stone, to the Bronze and Iron Ages (fourth millennium BC) when writing was evolved. Prehistoric man, lacking the means of writing, expressed himself by drawing and painting — animals, people, objects, weapons and even ideas — on the walls of caves.

His daily existence was strictly dependent on the environment, as he did not have at his disposal the technical means — apart from an early knowledge of fire — of contending with changes in climate: these changes affected the availability of animals and vegetables on which he depended for survival.

However, the existence of stone tools confirms that prehistoric man was able to make clothing from animal skins, using primitive methods to clean and cure the skins and then either join them together or secure them around his body for warmth and protection.

Social organization was based on clans or tribes: these were most probably nomadic, wandering from region to region in pursuit of the herds of wild animals, at times dictated by the changes of season.

Only in the Neolithic Era did the first settlements appear, the result of a growing ability to cultivate the soil, to breed domestic animals, to drain swamps and to make increasingly sophisticated tools.

A decisive step forward, affecting social structures, was the development of food surpluses, resulting from increased crop production. This enabled the tribes to support both an elite of warriors (from whose ranks the tribal leader was chosen), and also a select group of priests. A priesthood helped to satisfy a basic urge of man: the need to have something supernatural in which to believe, to explain what he either feared (the natural phenomena) or was unable to understand (the creation — the existence of a world full of uncontrollable and conflicting forces).

In consequence, various types of religious observance emerged, such as the cult of the dead, the diffusion of myths, the special importance attached to human and animal skulls, and the rites connected with fertility and the seasons.

These were all an attempt to allay natural fears and explain unpredictable and sometimes disastrous events.

The invention of agriculture
The map (*right*) shows the different and changing patterns of agricultural and farming activities in various parts of the world, together with the regions of origin of the main crops. Cultivation of cereals and raising of sheep developed in temperate and tropical areas, while in other latitudes, economies based on hunting, fishing and gathering persisted. All evidence, such as this prehistoric rock painting at Tassili of women working crops (*left*), points to the fact that, where climatic conditions were favourable — with sufficient and not excessive amounts of rainfall as well as enough warmth and sunlight to enable plants to flourish — the practice of agriculture encouraged the development of the first settlements. Apart from his agricultural skills, Neolithic man was a talented craftsman: he knew how to work terracotta and to make different objects, such as vases. *Above*, a vase found in northern France near Amiens. Previously, leather bottles had been made in the same shape. At this stage of his development, man was able to adapt and evolve designs to suit new requirements and newly discovered materials.

Dwellings and sacred buildings

The first villages of prehistoric man were built on piles, but recent discoveries, such as those at Ledro and Fiavé in northern Italy, have shown that the piles were rarely set up in water, such as in this reconstruction (*left*) at Unteruhldingen on Lake Constance in Switzerland. More often they were sunk in low-lying or swampy areas. Another type of building was the *dolmen* (*below*, at Sartene in Corsica), made of two or more big stone slabs, vertically sunk into the soil and surmounted by a horizontally laid stone. These *dolmen*, which had a sacred function and sometimes incorporated important tombs, can be found from the British Isles to the Mediterranean. The name may come from the Breton words *tol*, meaning table, and *men*, meaning stone.

The wheel, a vital discovery

In the fourth millennium BC, perhaps in Western Asia, man developed the wheel, perfecting the transportation of heavy objects by rolling them on tree trunks. From the first solid wheel, lighter wheels were developed, such as this one (*left*) found at Mercurago in Novara, northern Italy. The spread of wheeled transport nevertheless depended on the availability and domestication of such animals as horses, donkeys, oxen and llamas to do the work of pulling.

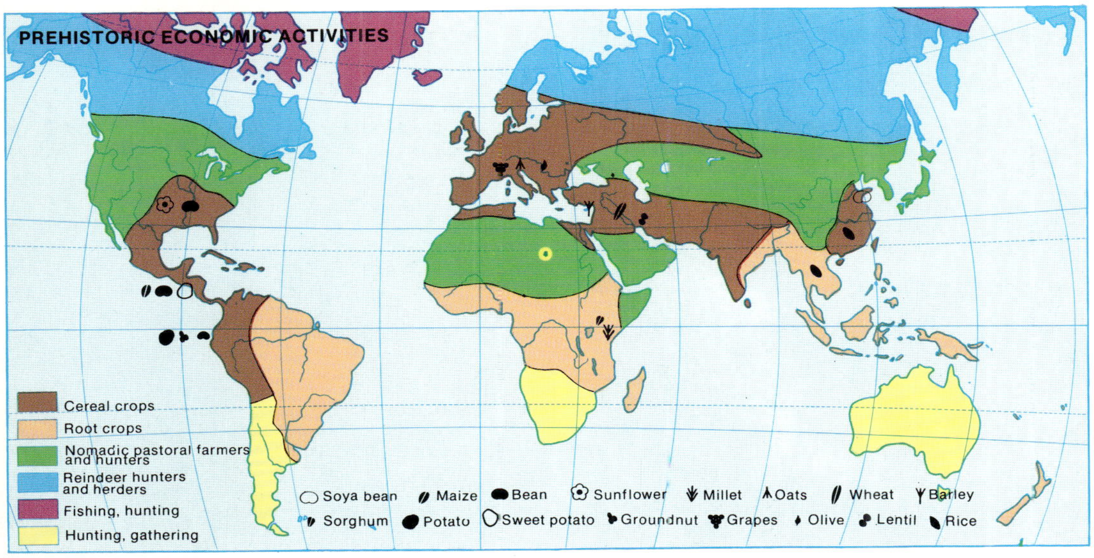

Extraordinary monuments made of rough stone

The megalithic temple (*above*) on Gozo, a small island near Malta, is a huge complex known as the *Gigantija*, a Maltese word meaning "giants' work". Stone was normally only used in building dwellings for divinities or the dead. Apart from the *dolmen* and the big Megalithic constructions, other stone buildings survive, but their purpose is not always known. These monuments, typical of prehistoric civilization, are called the *cromlechs*: round in shape and made of huge rough stones sunk vertically into the soil, they are evidence of the existence of an organized society capable of transporting such materials for vast distances. How the huge and enormously heavy pieces of stone were in fact transported and put into their present positions is not clear. These *cromlech* also show a remarkable level of technological achievement: the big vertical slabs were roughly squared off and worked so that the horizontal slabs would slot into them. Besides the *cromlech* at Stonehenge and Avebury in southern England, other famous examples are the Ménec System and the Kerlescan Lines at Carnac in north-western France. These latter consist of several long avenues of *menhirs*, or standing stones, as well as some *dolmens*.

Urnfields

Much evidence of the activity of the early Europeans during the Bronze and Iron Ages has been found in the huge cemeteries of the period, the so-called urnfields. The buckle and the pendant (*right*) are burial jewellery from urnfields in north-west Switzerland. From the type of metal used in such objects and from the sophistication of the workmanship employed, it is possible to form some idea of the daily life and standard of living of the various communities.

The cult of the Sun

This bronze Sun chariot (*above*), found at Trundholm on the island of Zealand in Denmark, is probably an offering for a divinity: the solar disc and the horse are covered with a layer of gold, evidence of the remarkable skill of artists in the Baltic region at this time.

Small Sardinian bronzes

Apart from the *nuraghi* (prehistoric buildings), a series of bronze and iron objects and small statues of great originality were produced by the civilizations of Sardinia from the beginning of the second millennium BC. The small statue (*below*), found near the proto-Sardinian sanctuary of Albini and probably dating back to the seventh century BC, represents a man with four eyes, four arms and two shields. These features may indicate that this statue had religious significance.

The treasure of Hallstatt

In 1846, a cemetery containing a thousand graves was found in Hallstatt in Austria, which has given its name to the Early Iron Age in Western Europe. Scholars have distinguished two Hallstatt periods.

Hallstatt I (1000–700 BC), characterized by long bronze and iron swords, and Hallstatt II (700–500 BC), distinguished by a whole variety of ornamental objects — jewels in bronze and copper, razors, vases engraved with geometrical designs, and war or votive chariots. *Left*, a chariot found at Strettweg, near Judenburg in Styria. The tallest figure, 24 centimetres (9½ inches) high, is probably a fertility goddess. The other figures include warriors mounted on horseback and armed with weapons and shields complete in all detail.

The Bronze and Iron Ages

The peoples of the Near East seem to have been the first to discover and master the technique of using metal — well in advance of the populations of Asia and particularly of Europe.
The possibility of working metal was first realized by those who had already adapted stone for use. Initially, locally-mined copper (a metal which can be worked cold) was used as well as stone.
Experience in the working of copper greatly assisted human progress: mixing the heated metal with arsenic increased its resistance, while the addition of tin led to the production of bronze.
In the Near East bronze was used to produce weapons and agricultural tools from the fourth millennium BC. However, knowledge of metallurgy, which gave almost priestly power to those who possessed it, spread slowly: the evidence points to the fact that the Bronze Age developed in Asia in the third millenium, in the Aegean Islands during the second half of the second millenium and then developed last of all in Western Europe at the end of this period.

The discovery and exploitation of the properties of iron also occurred in the Near East. This knowledge was probably one of the reasons for the splendour of the Hittite Kingdom in the eighteenth century BC.
In the Bronze and Iron Ages, tribal structures developed greater organization, with growing specialization and division of labour, and changing practices.
Burials were replaced by cremations, and the ashes of the dead were interred in huge cemeteries or urnfields. Villages were no longer composed of pile-dwellings erected over water, but were built on land, surrounded by palisades and thickets to defend the huts from wild animals.
Signs of improving living conditions survive, including fine ornaments and elaborate offerings to divinities. The existence of Baltic amber in the tombs of Mycenae and of the majolica products which originated in contemporary Egypt in the British Isles also demonstrates that there were some lively trading contacts between the various peoples whose civilization was gradually developing in Europe and the Near East.

The great Asiatic civilizations
In the vast Asiatic continent there are traces of important prehistoric civilizations. In Japan there was the Jomon culture, characterized by ceramics decorated with rope-pattern impressions or reliefs; in the area of the Aral Sea there was Kelteminar culture, and near the Rivers Ob and Yenisey the Afanasyevskaya appeared (third millennium). Most important of all were the civilizations of India and China. In northern India, an urbanized civilization developed during the second half of the third millennium BC: its main centres were Mohenjo-Daro and Chanhu-Daro in Sind, and Harappa, in the Punjab. Here, many finds have been made — seals in steatite and metal, small bronze statues and the remains of dwellings. These proto-historical cultures developed various autonomous artistic styles which flourished particularly under the Maurya Dynasty (313-185 BC), and were especially concerned with sculptures, sometimes exhibiting Western influence (*above*, a young male dancer). In China, the cultures of painted ceramics (*Yang-shao*) and black ceramics (*Lung-shan*) which developed from the third millenium BC, were followed by the splendid Shang period, when working in bronze reached remarkable levels of achievement, which is seen in superbly decorated vases of different shapes (*below*, a rectangular cooking vessel of the *Feng-ting* type).

The rich furnishings of Neolithic tombs
A collection of prehistoric objects found in various parts of Europe. *Above left*, a bronze situla of the eighth century from the Villanova civilization which flourished in the region of modern Bologna during the Iron Age in Italy. No fewer than 14,841 objects of all types survive from the cremation grounds of this period found in a number of locations. *Left*, a Villanova urn. *Above*, a dagger and a throat ornament, made from a series of rings fused together, found near Stuttgart in southern Germany in the huge "princely tombs" which probably date from the Early Bronze Age, before 1500 BC.

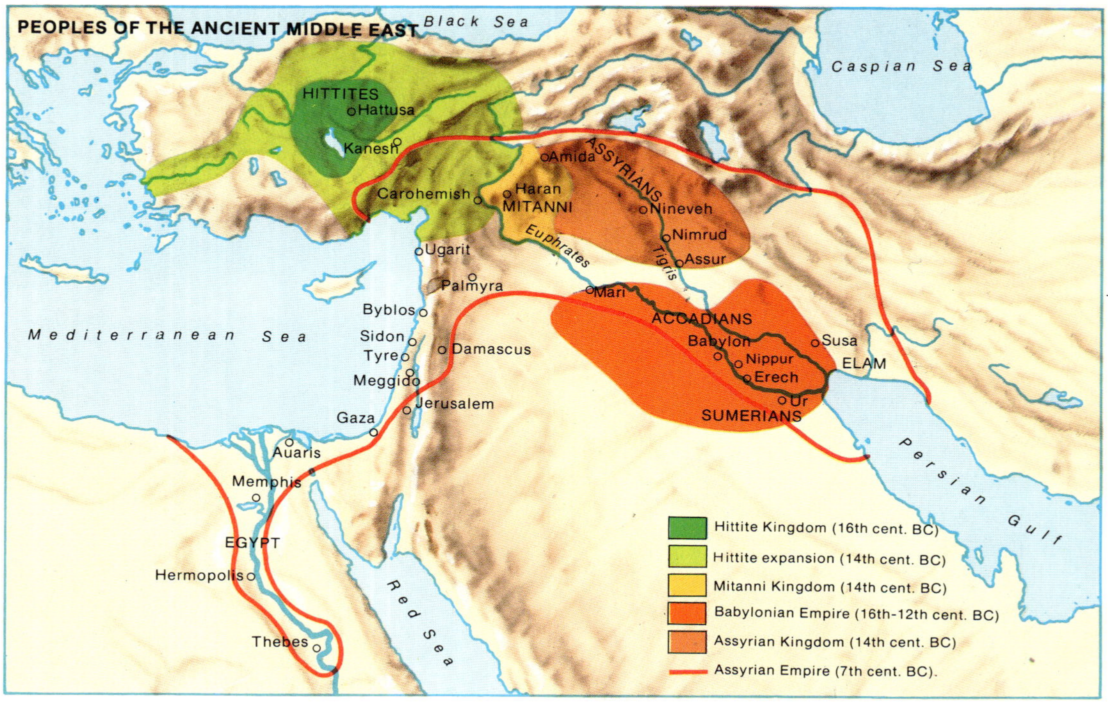

The Sumerian princes
Statue of a Sumerian prince. Statues like this one, typical of the cities of Lagash (uninhabited after the time of Hammurabi) and Mari, are characteristic of Sumerian sculptures: exact symmetry, staring and bulging eyes encrusted with shells and lapis lazuli, the head completely shaved in contrast with the full beard, the arms folded in prayer, the clothing carefully detailed. (The ever-present flounced skirt may have been made of roughly woven wool sewn on to a length of cloth, or of combed sheepskin, on which strands of wool were twisted into triangular shapes.) As is clear from the posture, this is a votive statue, in stone, of the type which the Sumerians used to place in front of altars in honour of the gods.

The civilization of the Sumerians
One of the rectangular panels (47 centimetres by 22 centimetres, 6 inches by 8½ inches) which, together with two trapezoid-shaped side panels decorated with pictures of animals, form the so-called "standard of Ur" — one of the most important artistic survivals of Sumerian civilization. The panels, in wood, decorated with shells and pieces of red limestone on a background of lapis lazuli, and held in position with bitumen, show scenes of war and peace. In the panel dedicated to war (*right*), the *ensi*, governor of the city state of Ur and the tallest of the figures in the top row, receives the vanquished. This panel also shows his army, composed of infantry and charioteers. In the panel dedicated to peace, the *ensi* gives a toast to victory and receives booty and tribute from the subject peoples. The standard, which dates back to the first half of the third millenium BC, was found in the royal necropolis at Ur (the modern Al-Muqayyar, in Iraq), the city which the Bible states to be the birthplace of Abraham. The significance and purpose of this remarkable and very ancient work of art is still unknown.

The Hittites: from Anatolia to fertile Mesopotamia
Coming from the region of Hattusa in Anatolia, the Hittites were of leading importance in the historical period after 1650 BC, under their Kings Hattusilis I and Mursilis I. Aided by their accomplishments in working iron, in about 1200 they established a vast kingdom which included Anatolia, Upper Syria and part of Mesopotamia. This brought them into conflict with Egypt under the Ramses. Hattusa was surrounded with strong walls whose huge gates were decorated with sculptures (*left*, the Lion Gate). The standard (*above*), in bronze, is associated with the Hittites' forms of worship.

The peoples of Mesopotamia

Cradle of the most advanced ancient civilization of the West, Mesopotamia, the land between the Rivers Tigris and Euphrates, occupied the northern part of the Fertile Crescent. Favoured in that period by a mild climate, a rich vegetation and plenty of water, the Fertile Crescent stretched from the Nile, across Palestine, Phoenicia and Syria, to the Tigris and Euphrates. From the fourth millennium BC, Mesopotamia was inhabited by the Sumerians who were capable farmers and skilled canal builders. Organized in city states governed by priest-kings, the Sumerians dominated Mesopotamia from the beginning of the third millennium BC, creating important cultural centres in the major towns of Ur (which has been identified as the birthplace of Abraham), Erech, Larsa, Lagash, Umma and Kish.

However, the city states of Sumeria were to be convulsed by a migration of Semitic peoples from Syria — the Accadians. Their warrior-king, Sargon, defeated the Sumerians and, according to tradition, founded a monarchy that extended from the Persian Gulf to the Toros Mountains and the coast of Lebanon.

But the power of the Accadians collapsed in about 2150 BC, unable to withstand the restlessness of the Sumerians and the arrival of new migrants, the Gutians, from Armenia and the Zagros Mountains. Consequently, a century later, the Sumerian towns of Lagash, Erech and Ur regained their power.

In about 1850 BC, new upheavals brought a Semitic dynasty to prominence in Mari, while in Babylon, the Amorites, the dynasty of the famous monarch Hammurabi, came to power. The era of Babylonian domination, despite being interrupted by periodic crises caused by uprisings of subject populations such as the Kassites and the Hurrians, lasted until about 1531 BC, when Mesopotamia was invaded by the Hittites from central Anatolia, led by Mursilis I. Although Babylon declined, the Hittites and the Hurrians saw their aspirations to control Mesopotamia threatened by the growing strength of the Assyrian Kingdom: this was eventually to dominate the whole region from the Persian Gulf to Palestine until 612 BC.

The long ascendancy of the Assyrians supported by the power of their armies, produced a reshuffling of ethnic groups in Mesopotamia — caused by the Assyrian policy of deporting entire populations, among them the Jews.

Later, two new powers emerged from the turbulence of the Assyrian Kingdom: the Medes of Cyaxares and a Chaldean dynasty in Babylon, whose leading figure was Nabopolassar. It was these two powers who destroyed Nineveh and inherited its culture and authority. Yet in spite of its competent monarchs, the New Babylonian Empire lasted only about eight decades: in 539 BC Cyrus, King of the Persians, conquered Babylon.

God's Chosen People
Originating in Lower Mesopotamia which they left for Canaan (the Promised Land) in about 1850 BC under the leadership of Abraham, the Jews were the first people to adopt monotheism. The Covenant between Jehovah and the Jews, entered into by Moses in the thirteenth century BC, marked the beginning of their most glorious period which culminated in the reigns of Saul, David and Solomon. *Above*, the caves at Qumran, near the Dead Sea, where the most ancient manuscripts of the Old Testament (*below*) were found in 1947.

Hammurabi, the great legislator
The basalt *stele* of Hammurabi, 2.25 metres (7.38 feet) high, is decorated in the upper part with the figures of the monarch (standing) and the God Samas, who dictated the laws to him. It contains 282 articles of law, written in cuneiform.

The invincible Assyrian monarchs
The Assyrians dominated Mesopotamia (the land between the two rivers) for about seven centuries. They were sustained by a permanent army in which military service was compulsory at all social levels (although this obligation could be discharged by substitutes). The Assyrian system of government was so oppressive towards the subject populations that frequent revolts broke out in all parts of the kingdom, compelling the ruler to mount a military campaign almost every year (Shalmanesser III led 32 expeditions in his 34-year reign) in order to bolster up his power and to conquer new lands.
The last great Assyrian King, Assurbanapal (*right*, characteristically portrayed in his chariot in a seventh-century relief found in Nineveh), tried to conquer Egypt, carrying on the campaign of his predecessor Esarhaddon, and succeeded in taking the Egyptian cities of Memphis and Thebes in 663.

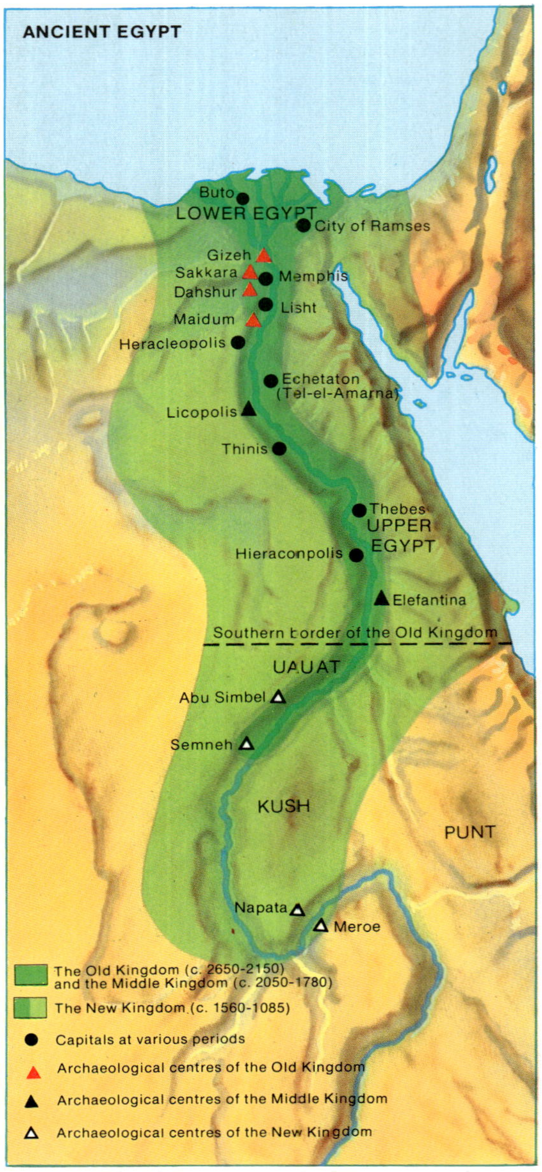

The Egypt of the Pharaohs

In the valley of the Nile, a narrow stretch of fertile land surrounded by desert, settlements were established very early: traces of the presence of hunters and gatherers in the area of the Nile delta date back to the Palaeolithic Era. It is certain that, in the Neolithic and the pre-dynastic period (from 8000 to 3100 BC), progress in controlling flooding and in agricultural methods, such as the introduction of systematic breeding of animals, brought increased wealth to the area. In consequence, Egypt became economically prosperous and developed specialized social groupings, such as priests and warriors, and was able to spare workers from agriculture to labour on the construction of ever bigger and more monumental buildings.

Around 3100 BC, the balance existing between the population groups in Lower Egypt (the Nile delta area) and Upper Egypt (the south of the country), which had led to the formation of two distinct kingdoms, was altered as a result of the conquest of the delta region by Menes, monarch of Upper Egypt. Under Menes, a period of great progress began: population growth, improvements in the quality of life, developments in the manufacture of ceramic and metal ware, the systematization of hieroglyphic writing, the practice of embalming and the cult of the dead. The first great period of Egyptian civilization (c.2650–2150 BC) is known as the Old Kingdom: the capital was first at Thinis, then at Memphis, in Lower Egypt. The pharaohs, at the head of an efficient administration, were in a position to implement huge architectural schemes, such as the building of the Pyramids. In the course of the First Intermediary Period, a series of domestic struggles led to the fragmentation of the state.

However, the unity of Egypt was restored during the Middle Kingdom (c.2050–1780 BC) when the irrigation schemes in the Fayum were completed, and the pharaohs extended their power to the south, in Nubia, and to the east, beyond Sinai. A new institutional crisis afflicted the Second Intermediate Period when Asiatic immigrants, the Hyksos, occupied most of Egypt. The recovery began under the monarchs of the Seventeenth Dynasty who led Egypt back to power and influence in the period known as the New Kingdom (c.1560–1085 BC): a new era of splendour began, epitomized by monuments such as those at Karnak, Abu Simbel and Luxor, the jewels of Tutankhamen, and the writings on papyrus. Under Amenophis IV, who took the name Akhenaton, an attempt was made to introduce monotheistic worship of the Sun, Aton, but at his death in 1362, the priests of the old cults regained control. After the Twentieth Dynasty, Egypt was once more weakened by internal disorders and external assaults, particularly those of the mysterious "Sea Peoples", probably Asiatic or Aegean navigators. Eventually, the throne of the pharaohs was occupied by Libyan and Ethiopian Dynasties (respectively, the Twenty-second and the Twenty-fifth), the country suffered invasions by Assyrians and Babylonians, and in 525 BC was finally conquered by the Persian, Cambyses.

The Pyramids and the Sphinx
The Pyramid of Mycerinus (*right*) is the smallest of the three at Gizeh, a short way from the left bank of the Nile, in the outskirts of Cairo. It is almost 62 metres (203 feet) high, less than half the height of the other two which today rise to about 137 metres (449 feet). Originally, before deterioration caused by the weather, the Pyramid of Cheops was 146.59 metres (481 feet) high and 230 metres (754 feet) wide at the base, while the Pyramid of Chephren was 143.65 metres (471 feet) high and 215.86 metres (708 feet) wide. A short distance from the Pyramids is the Sphinx (*above*), carved from a huge block of stone. It is 73.50 metres (241 feet) long and 20 metres (66 feet) high and has the body of a lion, symbolizing the power of the pharaohs, huge legs for crushing enemies, and a face which, according to well-established tradition, is that of the Pharaoh Chephren of the Fourth Dynasty.

The cult of the dead
Detail from a painting on a wooden box (*right*) of the Twenty-first Dynasty, showing the weighing of the heart of a dead person. Three Egyptian divinities can be identified: Horus the falcon, god of the sky, Anubis, who has a jackal's head and who is in charge of the weighing, and Thoth, the god of the moon, who has the head of an ibis. In tombs there have been many discoveries of small statues in painted wood (*ushabti*), such as the infantrymen (*above*) who were found in the tomb of Masathi, Governor of Asyut under the Middle Kingdom.

The Nile, source of life
The life of Egypt depended in ancient times almost entirely upon the periodic flooding of the Nile which fertilized the land, making agriculture more productive, as many paintings (*right*) and sculptures show. The main harvest was wheat, but barley and flax were also grown. River boats had trapezoid-shaped sails, such as those shown (*left*) in a fresco from the tomb of Sennefer of the Eighteenth Dynasty.

The glory of the pharaohs
The rock temple of Abu Simbel (*left*), built to the glory of Ramses II. From 1964 to 1966, it was dismantled and rebuilt to save it from the waters of Lake Nasser. *Right*, the face of Nefertiti, the bride of Amenophis IV (fourteenth century BC). *Below*, the gold mask of Tutankhamen, found in 1922 in a tomb in the Valley of the Kings.

The Persians

Among the various ethnic groups and the diverse cultures of the Iranian highlands, the Persians, initially settled in the area around Persepolis, rose to prominence in the course of the seventh century BC. This was roughly the period when the Medes (who originated from the region of Ecbatana) overthrew the Assyrian Empire, destroying Nineveh in 612 BC. Early in the next century, Cyrus, a Persian prince of the Achaemenid Dynasty, led his people against Astyages, the last King of the Medes. In a number of victorious wars, he took the whole of Iran, Chaldaea, Babylon, part of Syria, Cilicia and Lydia on the coast of Asia Minor. On his death in 529 BC, Cyrus, who had taken the title of "King of Kings" and was known as the Great, left behind him a vast Empire, well governed, rich and powerful. His successors, Cambyses (528–522) and Darius I (522–485), further extended the borders of their Empire: the former overran Egypt, the latter completed the conquest of Anatolia, coming into contact with Greek civilization. This contact with the colonies on the coasts of Asia Minor created tension, and was the chief cause of the Persian Wars.

Darius was also responsible for organizing his Empire into provinces (*satrapies*), ruled by governors (*satraps*) with complete powers locally, but subject to periodical controls by central government officials. These structural complexities are revealed in the detail of the reliefs still to be seen at Persepolis which, together with Ecbatana, Susa, Babylon and Pasargadae, was one of the five royal residences. These reliefs show dignitaries from every corner of the Empire in the act of paying tribute and homage to the King of Kings.

After the culmination of its power under Xerxes (485–465), the Persian Empire started a steady decline under the last Achaemenid monarchs: Artaxerxes I (465–424), Darius II (424–404), Artaxerxes II (404–358) and Artaxerxes III (358–338). At the head of an Empire already in crisis, the successor, Darius III, was not in a position to resist the assault of the Macedonians of Alexander the Great: defeated at the River Granicus (334), at Issus (333) and two years later at Arbela, he was betrayed and assassinated by a satrap, Bessus. After the death of Alexander the Great in 323, Persia was incorporated into the Kingdom of one of his *Diadochi*, Seleucus I Nicator, founder of the Seleucid Dynasty.

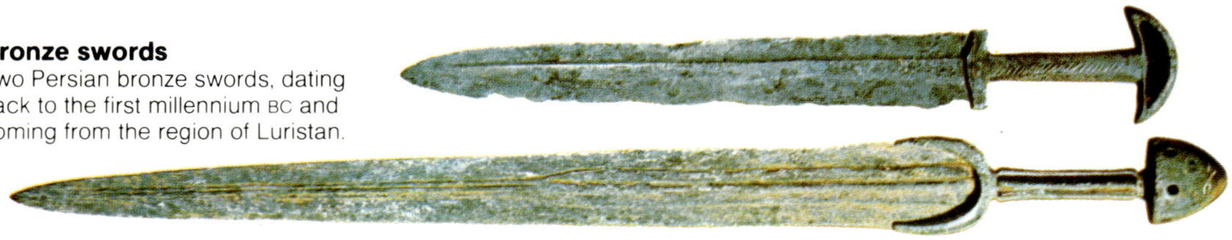

Bronze swords
Two Persian bronze swords, dating back to the first millennium BC and coming from the region of Luristan.

Cyrus the Great
Persian power was founded by Cyrus II the Great, the monarch who, within a few years, was able to rid his lands of the domination of the Medes. He conquered the dominions of the Lydians and the Babylonians, and created an empire that stretched from the eastern borders of Persia (the country which is now known to us as Iran) to the coasts of Asia Minor. Cyrus was renowned for being tolerant and enlightened: in every area, he permitted conquered populations to retain their religions and customs. He was also a great legislator: the Laws of the Medes and the Persians were respected throughout the empire. The rectangular building (*above*), at Pasargadae, is known as his tomb and stands near other monuments which have survived as evidence of Persian greatness, including the royal palace. Pasargadae is also known for a cuneiform inscription in which Cyrus proclaims himself King of Kings. He died in 529 BC.

The reliefs of Persepolis
Beautifully carved figures of Persian and Median warriors (*left*) shown in a relief at the royal palace, which stands on an elevated rectangular terrace, 450 metres (1471 feet) by 300 metres (984 feet), at Persepolis. *Right*, a sculpture in the great audience hall of the palace, showing a dignitary paying homage to Darius. The bas-reliefs in Persepolis show the wealth and power of the Persian Empire: the crowds of courtiers, the ranks of the guards of honour, the rich offerings being made by the people, all testify to the great work of unification and pacification carried out throughout the empire by the Achaemenid monarchs.

Alexander the Great
Portrait of Alexander the Great (*right*), son of Philip II of Macedon, taken from a mosaic recording the Battle of Issus. According to tradition, the young conqueror, having reached Persepolis (*below*, the palace of Darius I), changed his practice of sparing Persian cities and decided to burn it down in revenge for the burning of Athens by Xerxes in 480 BC. From Persepolis, Alexander proceeded with the conquest of the eastern provinces of Persia and, after a campaign lasting three years, he reached the borders of India, the limits of the known world. He fought and defeated the Indian monarch Poros at the River Hydaspes, so opening the route to India and the mysteries of China. A revolt in his army prevented him from going on, and he had to return to Babylon where he died in 323. He was only 33, and had reigned for thirteen years.

The masterpieces of jewellers
Very skilled in working gold, the craftsmen of the Achaemenid court (who were mainly Medes and Egyptians) brought together the artistic traditions of both the subject peoples and their Persian masters. The result was a style which became typical of the Achaemenid Dynasty and which lasted until the fall of the empire. Some of the objects which survive are true masterpieces, such as the small gold chariot (*above*), 10 centimetres (4 inches) long, found in 1877 among the ruins of a temple near the River Oxus (Amu Dar'ya) in Turkmenistan, and perhaps a present from Xerxes to his son. Another masterpiece is the *Rhyton*, a drinking cup with a lion's head, finely worked in gold (*below*).

The first maritime civilizations

At the beginning of the third millennium BC, on the islands in the Aegean Sea, a flourishing mercantile civilization grew up, contemporary with the increasing use of copper and bronze. To start with, the main centre of this culture was the Cyclades; later it was Crete, which particularly influenced the region of the Eastern Mediterranean.

The evolution of ship-building and navigation, based on observation of the stars, allowed ships from the Aegean and Crete to voyage into the open sea, and to trade with Cyprus, Rhodes and the coasts of Asia, Africa and southern Italy.

The strength of Minoan Cretan civilization, named after the legendary King Minos, gave rise to the concept of "sea-power": evidence of this is provided by the layout of Cretan towns — Knossos, Phaistos and Mallia — which had no need of defensive walls, because their sea defences were sufficient.

Minoan civilization was hit by crisis for reasons still unknown — perhaps an earthquake or an invasion — in around 1700 BC. Then it enjoyed another period of splendour, the age of the "younger" palaces, but declined irreversibly from the fifteenth century BC onwards.

Nevertheless, in some Greek cities of the Peloponnese, such as Mycenae, Argos, Pylus and Tiryns, the Mycenaean civilization developed in the same epoch; this was linked with the Minoan civilization in its art, language and customs, and it came to influence the whole of Greece up to the eleventh century.

In Asia Minor, the Phoenicians managed to carve out a maritime civilization for themselves in the strip of land roughly corresponding to modern Lebanon, despite being hemmed in by mountain chains and squeezed between the great civilizations of Mesopotamia and Egypt. Here, they organized themselves into towns, such as Byblos, Sidon and Tyre, which, although bound together by ties of friendship and commerce, were at the same time autonomous.

Compilers of the first alpabet, the Phoenicians were also highly skilled navigators: one legend credits them with having circumnavigated Africa, and they certainly reached Sardinia, Spain where they founded Cadiz, and the African coast where the King of Tyre's daughter, Elissa (Virgil's Dido), is reputed to have founded the North African city of Carthage in 814.

The throne of Minos
The throne room in the royal palace at Knossos in Crete, residence of the legendary King Minos. The oldest parts of this palace date back to the earliest years of Minoan civilization, around 2200 BC; other parts, such as this room and the frescoes, post-date the upheavals which damaged the palace in the course of the eighteenth century BC, and are evidence of the splendour of the period of the so-called "younger" palaces (1600–1400 BC).

Masterpieces in stone
Typical of the artefacts of the period, this vase in chlorite, decorated with goats and dating from the sixteenth century BC was found among the ruins of the palace at Zakros in the island of Crete. Other notable remains of Minoan civilization include small statues in bronze, such as that of the famous Serpent Goddess, the double-headed axes which had a mysterious ritual meaning, and a number of seals and small jewels worked from the hard stone of the island.

A labyrinth of splendid rooms
The northern entrance (*left*) to the royal palace at Knossos is one of the most characteristic features of the complex building excavated by Sir Arthur Evans from 1900 onwards. The whole site, built on more than one level on a hill-side, occupied an area of about 150 square metres (5790 square feet) and consisted of hundreds of rooms, corridors, staircases and courtyards. The largest rooms were decorated with wonderful frescoes of animals, especially sacred bulls, servants (*below*) and acrobats. Some of the frescoes now on the site are modern copies, whose originals are kept in the Herakleion Museum.

The great city, enemy of the Achaens
Part of the archaeological finds at Troy in Asia Minor, showing the *buleuterion* or meeting-place of the council, a building of late date. The oldest traces of urban settlement at Troy (which have been given the name Troy I by archaeologists) date back to 3000 BC. Studies springing from Schliemann's original hypotheses have ascertained that the town made famous by Homer was Troy VII A, and that this was destroyed by fire in about 1260 BC. Following this, the town was rebuilt around 1100 (Troy VII B1 and B2), again in about 700 (Troy VIII) and finally in the Roman period (Troy IX).

The "mask of Agamemnon"
This mask, in beaten gold, was found by Schliemann during excavations of a tomb at Mycenae in 1874. He believed it to be the death mask of Agamemnon, King of Mycenae and Argos, and legendary leader of the Greek expedition against the city of Troy. In reality, the tombs and their furnishings are of the sixteenth century BC and therefore date from well before the deeds recounted by Homer.

Golden Mycenae
The Lion Gate which led to the *acropolis* of Mycenae. According to legend the town was founded by Perseus, famed as the killer of Medusa and the saviour of Andromeda, and its strong city walls are said to have been erected by the Cyclops. Mycenae rose to great prominence in the period from about 1400 to 1150 BC, under the leadership of the dynasty, usually identified with Atreus, whose most famous member was Agamemnon. Although at the height of its power it was an influential cultural centre, Mycenae declined after 1000 BC because of the Dorian invasions and the rise of other cities.

The manoeuvrable ships of the Phoenicians
Relief of a Phoenician ship, from a second century BC sarcophagus, found in Sidon. Compelled to earn their livings from the sea because they were limited to a narrow strip of territory (roughly equivalent to the coasts of modern Syria and Lebanon) the Phoenicians formed commercial links with all the major ports of the Mediterranean as early as the third millennium BC. This fact is also reflected in the Bible.

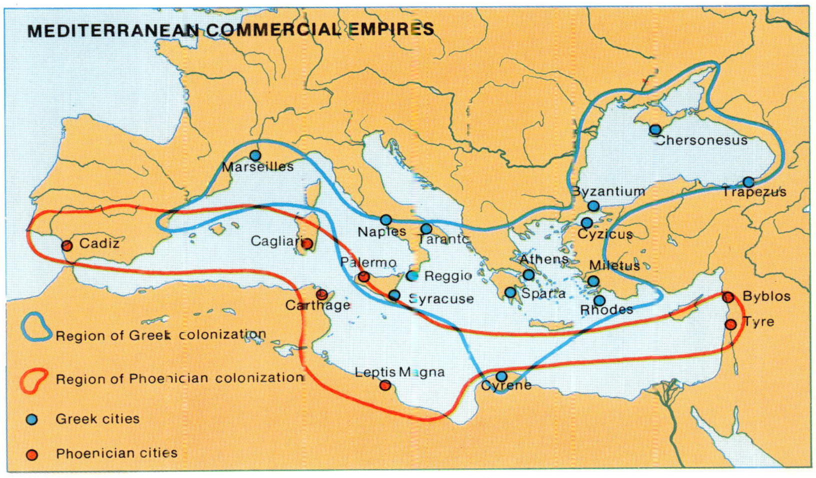

A busy commercial port
Part of the remains of ancient Byblos (the Gebal of the Bible), one of the busiest ports of Phoenicia. Others were Tyre, well-known from the Old Testament, and Sidon. This region was famous both for its trade in copper, which was brought overland from the Caucasus, and especially for the valuable wood grown in the mountains of Lebanon. (The cedars of Lebanon were proverbial at this time.) This wood was much sought after in the ancient world for use in all types of building work, civilian (it was used for Solomon's temple in Jerusalem) and naval, and one of the commodities exchanged for it was papyrus from Egypt. Phoenicia was also famous for the so-called Tyrian purple, a widely-used dye made from shellfish.

The golden age of Pericles
During the period when he ruled Athens — c.495–429 BC — Pericles (*above*) encouraged literature and the arts, and beautified Athens with marvellous buildings: the most notable is the Parthenon (*left*), a huge temple in Pentelic marble, built on the Acropolis by Ictinus and Calicrates. It stands near the remains of another temple which was dedicated to Athena Parthenos, protector of the city, and which contained a huge statue of her by Pheidias.

Ancient Greece

Successors to the Bronze Age and the flourishing civilization of Mycenae, and influenced by great migrations such as the Dorian, the Greeks emerged from the monarchical forms of government, recorded by Homer, to develop (from the eighth century BC onwards) their characteristic feature of the *polis*, or city state. Greek cities, with their public buildings and temples, frequently stood on hills, which were usually fortified (*acropolis*). Political structures varied from city to city: some were ruled by monarchs, some by oligarchies, some by democratic governments whose decisions were made by the active members of the population. A similar variety of social structures was also evident: some, such as Sparta, were rigidly divided by class while others were more egalitarian.

The Greek city states, despite their appearance of unity and harmony, were divided from each other by rivalries and jealousies. The first city to establish its dominance was Sparta, which was already reigning supreme in the Peloponnese by about the eighth or seventh century. After the interruption caused by the Persian Wars, when the Greeks were united against the common enemy (fighting at Marathon, Thermopilae, Salamis and Plataea), Athens took the leadership, especially as a cultural centre, reaching its zenith in the age of Pericles (461–429).

However, the ruinous rivalry between Sparta and Athens, which culminated in the Peloponnesian Wars (431–421, 418–413, 413–404), began the decline of Greece, which proved irreversible despite a brief period of Theban dominance. The competition between the Greek cities increased, and this divisiveness was soon used to advantage by Philip II of Macedon: defeating a Greek coalition at Chaeronea in 338 BC, he established his power over the whole of Greece.

Socrates and Plato, geniuses of philosophy
Athens, the major cultural centre of ancient Greece, was the home of Socrates (*above*) and his most famous pupil, Plato (*left*). The former, enemy to all dogmatic teaching, was accused of impiety during the decline that followed the defeat of Athens in the Peloponnesian War, and was compelled to commit suicide by taking hemlock (399). The latter, Plato (427–347), made his teacher the protagonist in his *Dialogues*.

The Persian Wars
When Darius, King of Persia, decided to attack Greece, he had to face the combined forces of Athens and Sparta. After landing in Attica, he was unexpectedly defeated at Marathon by the Athenians. In 480, his successor, Xerxes, reached Athens which he took and sacked. However, the Athenian victory at Salamis, where the Persian fleet was destroyed, turned the tide of the war. The subsequent successes at Plataea and the Mycale Mountains put an end to the Persian danger. *Left*, a detail from the François Vase showing Ajax carrying the corpse of Achilles on his shoulders.

Delphi, the oracle of Apollo
The *tholos* in the sanctuary of Athena Pronaia at Delphi (*left*), the site of a famous temple dedicated to Apollo, where the God delivered prophecies. Rich offerings were made to him: *above*, the famous statue of the charioteer (fifth century), given by the Tyrant of Gela.

Seaman and merchants
The shallow drinking cup of Exekias, dating from about 540 BC (*right*), showing the God Dionysus in a boat surrounded by dolphins. Because of the geography of their homeland the Greeks were skilled and successful seafarers. They colonized the whole Mediterranean region as a means of relieving long-standing problems of over-population and scarcity of resources; the most successful of their ships, which used both sails and oars, was the trireme, a manoeuvrable vessel with three decks, capable of carrying 170 people

The golden world of the gods of Olympus
A detail from one of the friezes of the Parthenon, showing (*from the left*) Poseidon, God of the sea, Apollo, God of light, beauty, arts and divination, and Artemis, Apollo's sister and the virgin Goddess of the hunt. As early as the time of Homer, gods had fundamental importance for the Greeke, who loved to give them human feelings and passions. Living on top of mountains, in particular on Olympus, the Greek gods resembled a large family: at the head was Zeus, master of the sky and lord of thunderbolts, and beside him was his wife Hera, Goddess of marriage and protectress of women. And, like an ordinary family, the gods and goddesses have their disagreements and their conflicts.

The Peloponnesian Wars
The fundamental role played by Athens in the Persian Wars gave it the leadership of other Greek cities, a supremacy it exercised through the Delian League which it used to subdue its allies. This led inevitably to war with Sparta, which lasted from 431 to 404 BC, and ended in the defeat of Athens which, deprived of its fleet and maritime empire, was forced to recognize the supremacy of Sparta. The Spartans were famed for their courage and tenacity in battle, and for their simple lifestyle.

Romans and Etruscans
The *Lupa Capitolina (far left)*, the symbol of Rome, recalls the legend of Romulus and Remus (the twins aree a Renaissance addition): it is an Etruscan bronze from the fifth century BC, and shows the influence of the Etruscans on Rome at the start of the monarchical period. *Left*, a small statue of an Etruscan warrior of the sixth or fifth century BC. The decline of Etruscan civilization, which reached its lowest point in 395 with the conquest of Veii by the Romans, was caused by divisions among its towns.

The Punic Wars
A small statue of one of the elephants which Hannibal (247–183) took with him to Italy at the start of the Second Punic War. Although Rome was defeated on the Rivers Ticinus and Trebia (218), at Lake Trasimene (217) and at Cannae (216), it recovered and, led by Scipio Africanus, crushed the Carthaginians at Zama (202).

Gladiatorial games
introduced to Rome by the Etruscans in 529 BC, gladiatorial contests (*bottom left*) were one of the favourite spectacles of the Romans.

Rome and its Empire

Founded — according to tradition — on the Palatine Hill on 21 April 753 BC, Rome was, to begin with, merely a small monarchy. The last of its seven legendary kings, Tarquin the Proud, was overthrown in 509: this event freed the town from Etruscan influence and inaugurated a Republic, ruled by two consuls each holding office for one year. In the first centuries of the republic, Rome extended its power over Italy, cleverly alternating wars and treaties, and subduing Latini, Volsci, Aequi, Etruscans, Samnites and the towns of Magna Grecia. The wars with Carthage (264–146) gave Rome predominance in the Mediterranean, a power further consolidated by its conquest of Macedonia (168), Greece (146) and part of Asia Minor (133). However, torn apart by civil wars (Marius against Sulla, Caesar against Pompey), the Republic — despite new conquests in Gaul and parts of Asia — was gradually replaced by the Empire: on 16 January, 27 BC, Octavian received from the Senate the title of Augustus.
Reorganized by Augustus, the Empire enjoyed two centuries of peace and prosperity, and was further extended under Trajan (98–117). However, at the beginning of the third century, pressure from Barbarian tribes and the difficulties of ruling such a vast territory, brought about the decline of the Empire. In 285, Diocletian began the division of its territories into East and West: this arrangement, confirmed by Theodosius in 395, was the origin of the Western Roman Empire which lasted until 476, and the Eastern Roman Empire, which survived until 1453.

Augustus, the first Emperor
Octavian, adopted son and heir of Julius Caesar, defeated Mark Antony at the battle of Actium (31 BC), and established himself in many of the key positions in the Republic. As the Emperor Augustus, he introduced far-reaching reforms in taxation and social conditions, eliminated corruption, and shared the work of administration with the Senate and business classes of Rome.

The rival of Caesar
Pompey, victor of many campaigns in Asia and conqueror of Spain and Africa, quarrelled with Caesar who defeated him at the Battle of Pharsalia (48 BC).

The conqueror of Gaul
Julius Caesar, having won many victories and then glory with the conquest of Gaul (58–51 BC), became Dictator for life in 44 BC, dominating the Republic.

The Emperor Hadrian
Hadrian, Emperor from 117 to 138, is remembered less for his military expeditions than for his building activities. (Hadrian's Wall, the Castel Sant' Angelo and the Villa Adriana at Tivoli).

Outstanding architecture, even in the provinces
Skilful builders, the Romans have left behind them splendid remains in many parts of their Empire. Leptis Magna, a Phoenician colony on the Libyan coast, was extended and embellished with major constructions such as the theatre (*below*), by Augustus, Hadrian and Septimus Severus. At Jerash in modern Jordan, there was considerable development during the Antonine period: the ruins of the *Forum*, the baths, two theatres, a temple dedicated to Artemis, a huge *nymphaeum* and wide roads, such as the main street (*above*) still survive.

The fortunes of the early Christians
Spread in the Empire by the first disciples of Christ (the preaching of Peter and Paul is a matter of historical fact), Christianity — despite the tradition of religious tolerance of the Romans — was persecuted because of its denial of other religions and its refusal to recognize the divinity of the Emperor. Compelled to meet in underground cemeteries, the catacombs (*below*, the papal crypt in the Catacombs of St Calixtus in Rome), the early Christians managed not only to survive but also to spread their beliefs throughout the Roman Empire, despite attempts (by Nero, Domitian, Trajan, Diocletian and others) to exterminate them. Later, Christians were permitted freedom of worship by Constantine in the Edict of Milan, 313, and became an important unifying force when the Empire was threatened by Barbarian invasions in its final years. *Above*, an illumination in characteristic style in an old Bible found at Reichenau, in Germany, showing Christ and the apostles.

The lions of Asoka
The capital of a column erected by the great Maurya monarch, Asoka, who introduced Buddhism into India. The four lions are standing on the "wheel of life", one of the most common Buddhist symbols.

The famous caves of Ajanta
A fresco from the Ajanta caves, in the hills of the Deccan in western India, showing Avalokitesvara, a *bodhisattva* (this is the name given in Buddhism to one who has achieved "enlightenment").

Ancient Oriental civilizations

In the Indian subcontinent, the ancient civilization of the Indus, whose principal centres were at Mohenjo-Daro and Harappa, was inherited yans. From the first millenium to the sixth century BC, these peoples — masters by the Arof the chariot — were dominant in northern India: they introduced divisions by caste and their deeds were recorded in the *Rigveda*, one of the sacred books of Hinduism. In the fourth century BC, the Maurya Dynasty began to expand, under the leading figure of Emperor Asoka: having embrached Buddhism, he reorganized the state on humanitarian principles. Later, in the fourth century AD, the Gupta Dynasty rose to power. Founding a vast empire in northern India, it kept power for more than a century. During these centuries, a process began in China which was to repeat itself frequently: a dynasty would first take power and then lose it, followed by a long or short period of unrest often leading to open civil wars, until finally a new dynasty would gain control. First, the Shang superseded the Hsia in the second half of the second millenium BC, to be followed in the eleventh century BC by the Chou, who ruled until 256 BC. Then, after the "Epoch of the Warring States", the Ch'in Dynasty established a centralized government for the first time in China. The Ch'in were followed by the Han (206 BC–AD 220) who greatly extended their territories. After another period of instability, the Tang Dynasty took control and ruled until 907, giving China a period of splendour and prosperity, as evidenced by the porcelain it produced.

The spread of Buddhism in India
A gigantic statue (*left*) of the recumbent Buddha, at Polonnaruwa, an island off Sri Lanka (Ceylon). Buddhism was probably introduced to Sri Lanka in the third century BC by Mahendra, a relative of Asoka. *Top of page*, a *stupa* (a Buddhist mound, containing sacred relics) at Sanchi in Madhya Pradesh. It is surmounted by an umbrella-shaped *tee* and a relic-casket, both in stone. The casket carries sculptures of the faithful at prayer, of animals, of flowers and of *bodhisattvas*. Today, *stupas* can be seen in many countries of the Far East where Buddhism is, or has been, widespread. Some of them are very ancient.

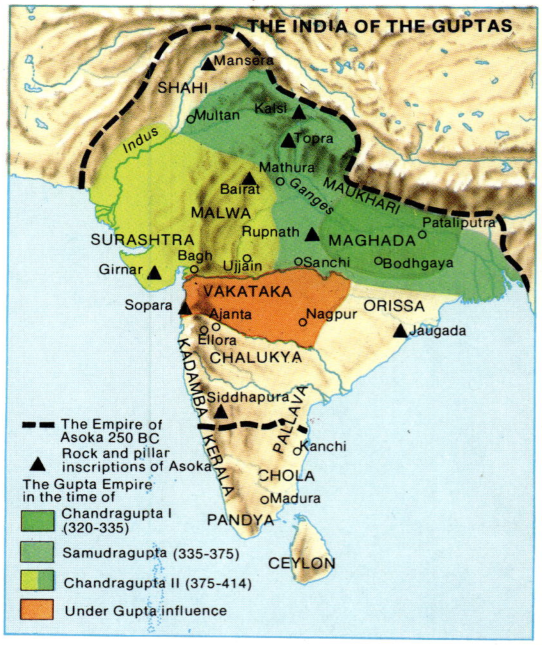

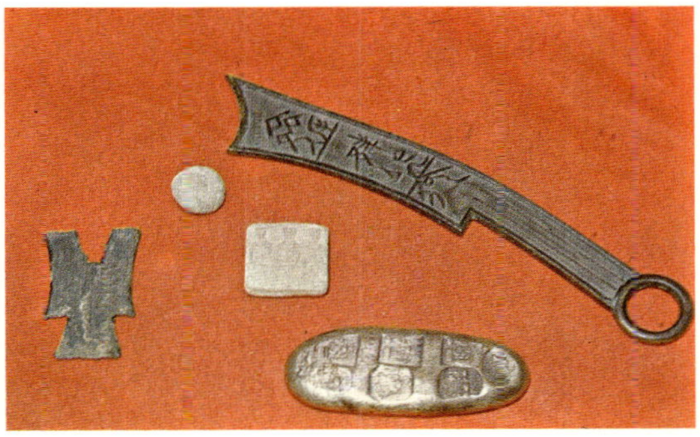

The Great Wall

The Great Wall (*left*), even today more than 2400 kilometres (1500 miles) long, was begun in the third century BC by order of the Emperor Shih Huang-ti of the Ch'in Dynasty, to protect the northern frontiers of China. Emperor Shih also introduced extensive administrative and legal reforms. *Above*, coins of various shapes (one even in the form of a knife) used in China under the Chou, the dynasty founded by the legendary army leader and Emperor, Wu, in the eleventh century BC.

Confucius and Lao-tze, spiritual fathers of China

In its attempts to build a just and harmonious society, Chinese culture has been deeply influenced by the teaching of Confucius (c.552–479 BC), who preached the virtues of moral precepts such as self-discipline, loyalty and respect for parents. Elaborate celebrations in memory of the ancestors are a distinctive feature of Confucianist ritual. Another very important figure in the history of Chinese philosophy is Lao-tze (sixth century BC) (*left*), who laid down the principles of Taoism, a route to salvation based on the balance of light (*yang*, male) and darkness (*ying*, female) in every individual and in the universe. *Below*, two bronze leopards encrusted with gold and silver, dating from the period of the Western Han Dynasty (206 BC–AD 8). *Right*, a small ceramic statue of a dignitary of the Tang Dynasty which ruled from 618 until 907.

The arrival of Buddhism in Japan

The belltower (*shoro*) of the Buddhist temple complex Yakushi-ji at Nara, the oldest in Japan. Buddhism, based on the teaching of Gautama Buddha, preached salvation through renunciation of desires. A disciple who has mastered all his passions can attain a state of *Nirvana*. This religion was introduced into Japan by Prince Shotoku Taishi who was Regent from 600 to 621. The same Prince built the temple to accommodate the statue of Yakushi, the Healing Buddha, whom the Emperor Yomei (the Prince's father) had held in high honour. In 794, Kyoto succeeded Nara as the imperial capital of Japan.

The great Barbarian invasions

Even though the Roman Empire had been reunified by Theodosius the Great, it nevertheless looked extremely vulnerable, at least in the west, at the end of the fourth century. The Mauri were threatening its African frontiers; several warlike Germanic tribes were raiding the borders along the Rhine and the Danube; the Parthians were menacing its Asian possessions; the Picts and Scots were assaulting its positions in the British Isles. The Empire — ungovernable in size, encumbered by a rotting administration, largely dependent for its protection on some of the very tribes which were threatening its frontiers, and with a population varying between 60 and 70 million — was in no condition to put up a lengthy resistance.

The first great migration of Visigoths into Moesia (376) (caused by the pressure from Huns and other populations of the Central Asian steppes) had been halted by Theodosius, who had made a settlement with their chief, Alaric, conceding to them the status of *foederati* of the Empire. Later, raids by the Visigoths in the Balkans, Dalmatia and Italy had fully stretched the resources of the Roman army, led by a Vandal general, Stilicho. He had also to face renewed attacks in 405 from Vandals, Alans and Ostrogoths. Moreover, whole tribes of Vandals, Suevi and Alans, having crossed and devastated Gaul, despite the resistance of the Franks allied to Rome, settled in Spain and from there moved to Africa. In 407 the Romans left Britain, which was soon afterwards settled by various Nordic peoples — Caledones, Jutes, Saxons and Angles. Worse was to follow. Taking advantage of the death of Stilicho and of the weakness of the Emperor Honorius's armies, Alaric and his Visigoths succeeded in conquering and pillaging Rome on 24 August 410: so ended the glory of Rome.

After this disaster, disintegration and change continued almost inevitably. While the Burgundians and the Alamanni were flooding into the regions beyond the Rhine, a new advance by the Huns (now unified by their King Attila) was devastating the areas of the Danube and southern Gaul. However, they were defeated by a coalition of Roman and Barbarian forces (on the Catalaunian plains in Champagne, 451) and retired to their Danubian lands after — according to a legend — the intervention of Pope Leo the Great, though not before they had sacked Aquileia, Milan and Pavia. Following the death of Attila in 453, the unity of the Huns disintegrated. New populations and new kings appeared on the scene: the Heruls and the Sciri of Odoacer, the monarch who in 476 deposed Romulus Augustulus, marking the official end of the Western Roman Empire; the Ostrogoths of Theodoric, the ruler who was fascinated by Roman civilization, and who was the first to consider the possibility of Romans and Barbarians living peacefully and profitably together to mutual advantage: the Lombards of Alboin and Cleph who, after wreaking havoc in northern Italy, moderated their ferocity as they came into contact with Christianity and the civilization of Rome.

Ferocious, despite their Christianity
Pouring in hordes across the Danube in 376, the Visigoths carried out extensive raids in Italy, Gaul and Spain for over a century. Despite having become Christian (as the numerous crosses found at Jaen in Spain indicate), the Visigoths — as Arian Christians — persecuted all the romanized Catholic populations.

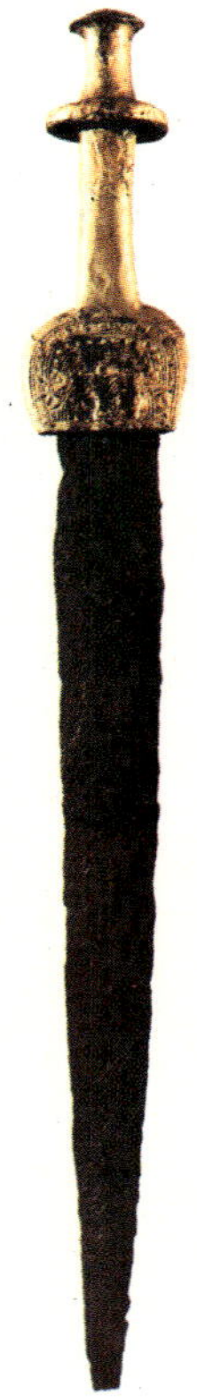

A kingdom conquered by an entire people
Above, a Visigothic sword of the seventh century. Having founded a kingdom in 407 with its capital at Toulouse, the Visigoths, allied with the Roman general Aetius, fought the Huns on the Catalaunian plains in 451, and took possession of Spain. However, defeated at Vouillé in 507 by the Franks led by Clovis, they gave up all their French possessions, only keeping their lands in Spain until the Arab invasions in 711.

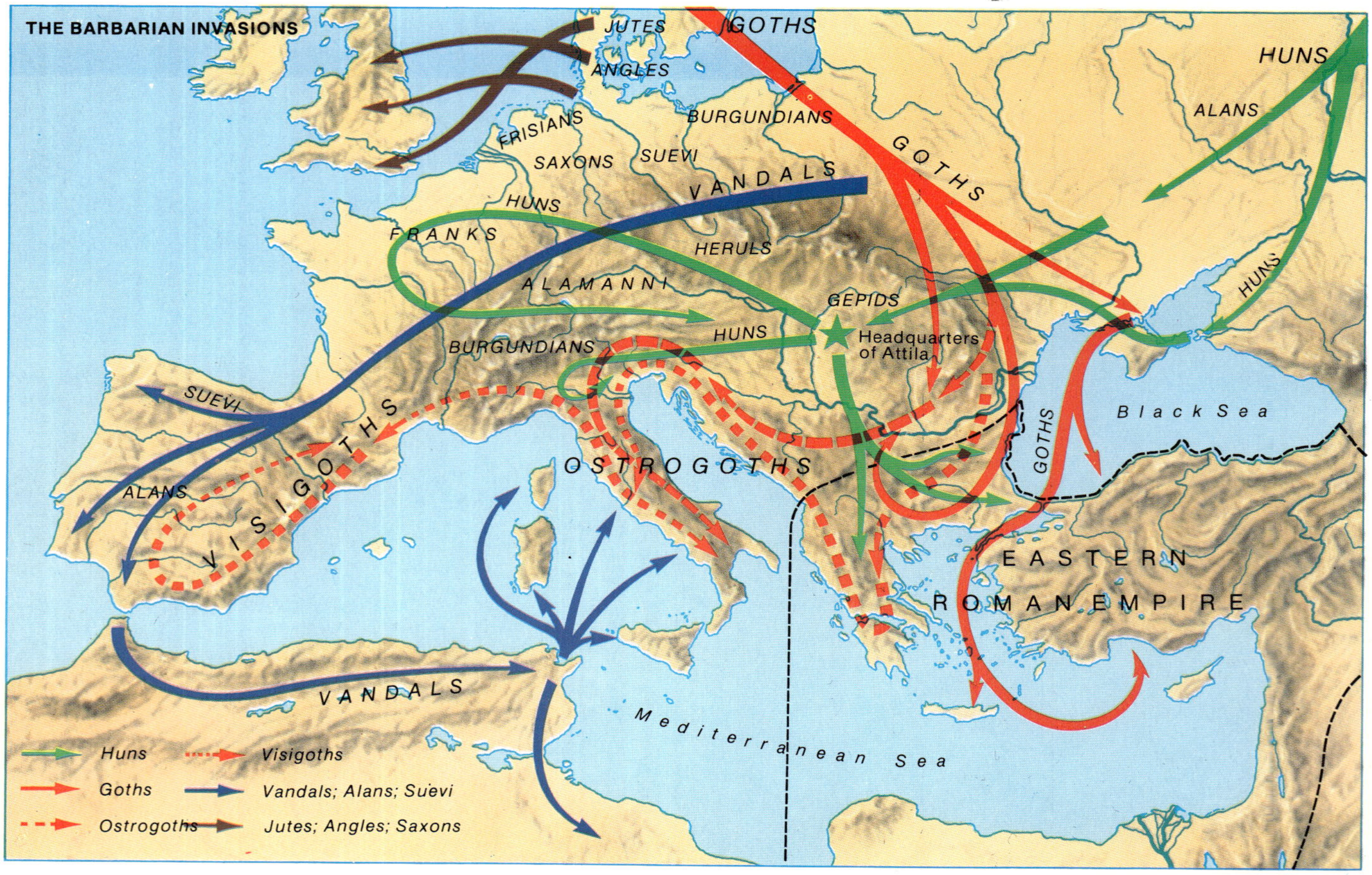

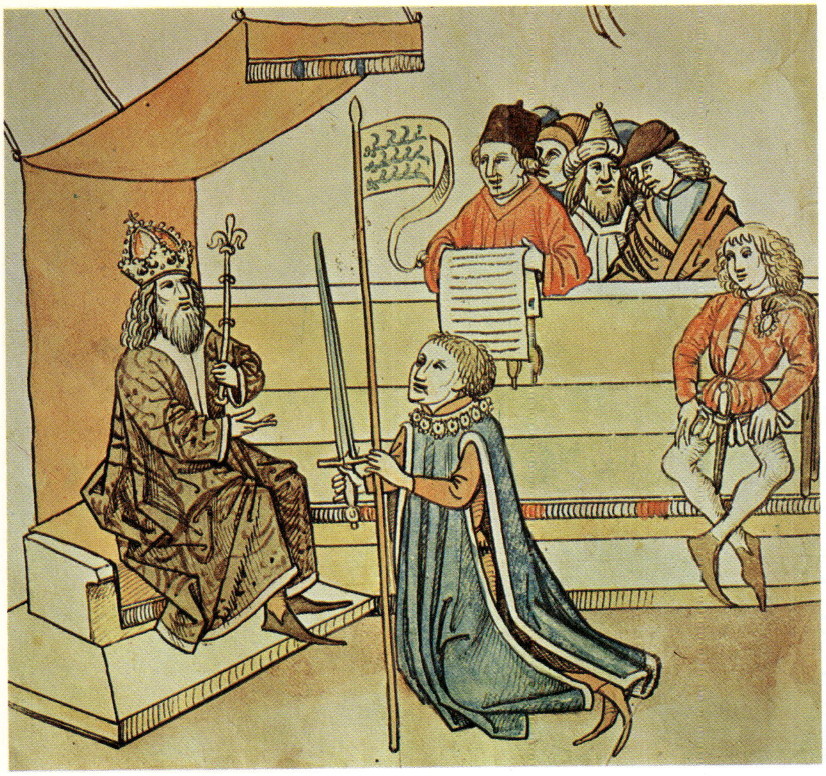

Gold and jewels for the Barbarian kings

Buckle of the sixth century (*right*) attributed to an Ostrogothic artist, and decoration from the front of a helm (*below*) showing the coronation of the Lombard King Agilulf the monarch who was persuaded by his wife Theudelinde to have their son baptized, thus starting the conversion of his people to Christianity. The two jewels indicate the level of creativity and technical perfection attained by Barbarian artists, both in working metals and in cutting and setting gems. Images of animals were the favourite decoration: for example, the Germanic tribes normally chose the eagle as their symbol. This is the historical origin of the use of the eagle as a symbol of national identity and pride in later years and particularly in twentieth-century Germany.

The Lombards

With the promulgation of the Edict of Rothhari, the Lombards had a code of law for the first time. Consisting of 388 chapters, it was issued on 22 November 643 in Pavia: although the illustration (*above*) from the *Codex Legum Longobardorum* suggests that it emanated solely from the will of the ruler, it was in fact issued by an assembly of the whole army (*gairethinx*) where the soldiers shook their lances to indicate agreement (*wapnatak*). *Below*, detail of a bas-relief at Cividale del Friuli, showing Ratchis, King of the Lombards from 744 to 749. He was persuaded by Pope Zacharias to give up the throne and retire with his wife and sons to Monte Cassino to enter the religious life, leaving his kingdom to his brother Aistulf. After the death of Aistulf in 756, Ratchis attempted to regain the throne in order to prevent it from passing to Desiderius, but was dissuaded from doing so by Pope Stephen II.

The great Theodoric

The mausoleum of Theodoric at Ravenna, where the Ostrogothic ruler was buried in 526. Son of Theodemir, Theodoric succeeded him on his death in 474. Sent to Italy by the Byzantine Emperor Zeno, Theodoric defeated Odoacer and made Ravenna his capital, where he surrounded himself with Roman advisers, such as Cassiodorus and Severinus Boethius. He was the first of the Barbarian kings to give civilian office to Romans, reserving military positions for his Ostrogothic warriors. In the final years of his reign he quarrelled with the Eastern Roman Emperor Justinian, and the Pope because of their persecution of Arian Christians. As Arians themselves, Theodoric and the Ostrogoths reacted by putting to death many of their Roman advisers, including Boethius.

The Byzantine Empire

The marvellous mosaics of Byzantium
In 726, the Emperor Leo III forbade the reproduction of holy images and consequently many masterpieces of Byzantine art were destroyed. When this prohibition was lifted, the enthroned Christ from Santa Sophia (*above*) was one of the many fine mosaics to be produced.

Heir to the Roman Empire in the East, the Byzantines perpetuated its traditions for many centuries after the collapse in the West. Contributing to this was their success in escaping the threat of Barbarian invasions: in doing so, they were helped by the position of their capital, Constantinople (or Byzantium), and by their diplomatic skill in devising all sorts of means to buy the friendship of tribal leaders such as the Visigoth Alaric, the Hun Attila, and the Ostrogoth Theodoric.

In the first phase of the history of this Empire, from the accession of the Emperor Arcadius in 395 to its culmination in the reign of Justinian (527–565), the concept of universal dominion was still alive. Inherited from Rome, this idea was given renewed prestige by the publication of the *Corpus Iuris Civilis*, a codification of Roman law.

Later, after the Empire had already been influenced by Greek and oriental culture and habits, it was strengthened by Heraclius (610–641) who made Greek the official language and introduced a new constitution. However, soon after his death, Byzantium had to face both external and internal dangers. From abroad, its enemies included the Arabs who, emboldened by their rapid conquests of Syria, Palestine and Egypt, besieged Constantinople between 673 and 678. At home, religious controversy caused a series of crises: Emperor Leo III, the Isaurian (717–740), adopted a policy of iconoclasm, prohibiting the worship of images, and Photius, the Patriarch of Constantinople, led the schism from the Roman Papacy between 863 and 867.

The emperors of the Macedonian Dynasty, particularly Basil II (963–1025), freed the Empire from the threat of the Bulgars. A few years later, a new and final split from Rome (1054), during the patriarchate of Michael Cerularius, aggravated the tension with the Western world, which burst out in 1204 when the Latins besieged and took Constantinople in the course of the Fourth Crusade. In 1261, the Emperor Michael VIII Palaeologus regained the capital, and the Byzantine Empire survived for two more centuries. However, it was under constant threat from the Ottoman Turks and finally, in 1453, they occupied Constantinople and made it their capital, thereafter called Istanbul.

Justinian the legislator
An illuminated page from a manuscript of the *Corpus Iuris Civilis*. This work, written between 528 and 533 by a group of jurists headed by Tribonian, contains 4500 regulations and includes the *Pandectae* or *Digesta*, which were written by lawyers of the previous centuries, and the *Institutiones*.

Ravenna, meeting point of two cultures
Under Justinian, the Byzantine Empire renewed its expansion seizing lands from the Barbarian tribes. The generals of Justinian reconquered the coasts of northern Africa (534), Dalmatia (535), Italy (536–553) and southern Spain (554). Ravenna, which had been made the capital of the Western Roman Empire by Honorius in 402 became the residence of Theodoric the Great from 493. His thirty-three year rule was a period of unprecedented peace and prosperity for Italy. Ravenna was conquered by Belisarius, general of Justinian, in 540, and in 584 became the capital of the Exarchate, the territories in Italy ruled by Byzantium. One of the monuments in Ravenna which shows the fusion of several different cultures is the tomb of Galla Placidia (*left*), daughter of Theodoric: built in the fifth century, its interior is entirely covered with mosaics of sacred subjects. Among the Byzantine buildings of Ravenna are the superb churches of San Vitale and Sant' Apollinare in Classe. *Right*, a solid gold image of the Byzantine Emperor Anastasius I (491–518), who in 498 recognized Theodoric as ruler of Italy and Dalmatia.

Dedicated to divine wisdom
Santa Sophia, the great basilica built for Justinian at Constantinople between 532 and 537, by the architects Anthemius of Tralles and Isodorus of Miletus. The building, with an almost square plan, is surmounted by a huge central dome, 31 metres (102 feet) round and 16 metres (52 feet) high, which is flanked by two semi-domes. Turned into a mosque by the Turks who added four minarets to the outside, the basilica was restored for the first time in 1847 by the Swiss architects Gaspare and Giuseppe Fossati, and then made into a museum by the president of the new Turkish republic Kemal Atatürk in 1935. It was at this time that the Byzantine mosaics, previously covered with plaster, were again brought to light.

Justinian and his court
One of the mosaics (*above*) in the church of San Vitale at Ravenna, showing the Emperor Justinian (distinguished by his crown and halo), surrounded by dignitaries of his court, making an offering to the church. This mosaic, dating from between 446 and 548, is similar to another in the same church, dedicated to the Empress Theodora wife of Justinian.

The last emperors
An illumination (*below*) from a Byzantine codex showing the sovereigns of the Palaeologus Dynasty which ruled the Empire from 1261 until the Turkish conquest in 1453. This dynasty was founded by Michael VIII who, from a base at Nicaea and helped by Genoa, recaptured Constantinople during the temporary absence of the Emperor Baldwin II. Successive monarchs of this dynasty then had to come to terms with the increasing menace from the Turks, partly because they had insufficient money to hire mercenaries, but also because their territories were no longer extensive enough to yield adequate number of soldiers. The days of the Empire were numbered. Any help from Western Europe was contingent on the union of the Roman and Byzantine churches, which was unacceptable to the Byzantine people and clergy despite the signing of the Decree of Union by the Emperor John VIII in 1439. Already encircled since the conquest of the Balkans by the Turks (Battles of Kosovo, 1389, and Nicopolis, 1396), the Empire was forced to capitulate on 29 May 1453. The last Emperor, Constantine XI, died during the final Turkish assault.

A history of Byzantium
The illustrated *Chronicle of John Scylitzes* recounts the history of the Byzantine Empire from 811 to 1057. The picture above shows the siege of Messina by the Arabs who took the town in 843, ending three centuries of Byzantine rule. It clearly indicates that the Arabs were both well armed and numerically strong.

The Emperor John VIII
John VIII Palaeologus, penultimate Byzantine Emperor (1428–1448) (here portrayed in a medal by Pisanello), tried in vain to get help from the West in saving Constantinople from the Turks, even to the extent of proposing to the Councils of Ferrara and, later, Florence (1439) the end of the schism and the reunification of the Orthodox Church and Papacy.

Muhammad the Conqueror
Muhammad II, seventh Ottoman Sultan, who ruled from 1444 to 1446 and then again from 1451 to 1481, besieged Constantinople in April 1453 with an army of skilled artillerymen (some recruited from the West) and over 160,000 soldiers. This victory, much praised by Muslim historians, earned Muhammad the title *Fatih*, or Conqueror.

The expansion of Islam

Islam arose in the seventh century AD in Arabia, as a religious movement founded on the teachings of Muhammad, the Prophet who propagated the word and commands of Allah. The new religion — Islam is an Arabic term which means submission and dedication to the will of God — immediately became a movement of irresistible vitality after the death of Muhammad in 632. Under the first four Caliphs — Abu Bakr (632–634), Omar (634–644), Othman (644–656) and Ali (656–661) — it spread from Arabia with prodigious speed: Syria, Palestine, Persia and Egypt all fell into the hands of the Muslims. The expansion of Islam was not even slowed down by the conflict between Ali, the son-in-law of Muhammad and fourth Caliph, and Mo'awiya, secretary to Muhammad and successor to Ali in 661. This was a conflict based on religious and ideological divisions whose consequences are even today to be found in the split between the Sunnis and the Shi'is: the former recognize as legitimate all the first four Caliphs, while the latter acknowledge only Ali and his descendants.
Mo'awiya founded the Omayyad Dynasty which directed its followers from Damascus towards new conquests: in 698, the invasion of northern Africa was completed; in 711, a great army leader, Tariq, began the conquest of the Iberian Peninsula; and in 732, the Muslim army reached the gates of Poitiers, where it was stopped by Charles Martel.
However, even if Muslim expansion continued — the invasion of Sicily in 827, the advance towards Central Asia, the conquest of Kilwa in eastern Africa in 980, and the foundation of Timbuktu in 1107 — the increasingly frequent internal quarrels divided and weakened the Islamic world. In 750, the Abbasid Dynasty, founded by Abu'l-Abbas, succeeded the Omayyads who, nevertheless, retained power in Spain. In 909, the Muslim dominions in Egypt and other parts of Africa succumbed to the Fatimids. Later, in 1171, Saladin, the great Muslim leader, founded the Ayyubid Dynasty, while at the same time other rulers, such as the Almoravids and then the Almohades in Spain and Africa, the Mamelukes in Egypt and the Nasrids, the last Islamic rulers in Spain, governed in their own right. Even if they retained religious unity, the territories ruled by the Muslims had ceased to be politically unified as early as the tenth century.

There is no God but Allah
A Turkish illustration of an episode from before the birth of Muhammad. The Prophet's grandfather, Abd al-Muttalib, is shown praying in front of the Kaaba (*above*) in Mecca. This shrine was already being venerated before the preaching of the Islamic religion, as it contains the Black Stone, believed to have been given to Abraham by the Archangel Gabriel.

Muhammad, Prophet of God
Two more Turkish illustrations (although Islamic orthodoxy prohibits the representation of the human image). The first shows a moment in Muhammad's life: the Prophet is welcoming guests from the four corners of the earth (*above*). The second (*below*) draws its inspiration from Muhammad's ascent into heaven.

The Islamic calendar
An illumination from a Turkish manuscript of 1237 showing the announcement of the end of Ramadan, the Islamic holy month during which it is compulsory to fast from dawn to sunset in commemoration of the revelations of Allah to Muhammad. The Islamic calendar has twelve months, of either 29 or 30 days each, in a year of 354 or 355 days. In consequence, from one year to another, dates of festivals and the beginnings of months vary by ten, eleven or twelve days.

Mosques and minarets

The minaret of the great mosque Al-Mutawakkil at Samarra in Iraq (*left*), where the Abbasid caliphs once lived, is well-known as al-Malwiyah, "the spiral", because of its shape. From the summits of minarets, the *muezzin* summons the faithful to prayer (*salat*) five times daily — this is one of the obligations of Islam. Apart from prayer (said at dawn, immediately after midday, in the afternoon, at dusk and at nightfall, not necessarily in a mosque), the faithful are required to profess their faith (*shahada*), to give alms (*zakat*), to make the pilgrimage to Mecca (the *Hajj*) and to fast during daylight in the month of Ramadan (*sawm*).

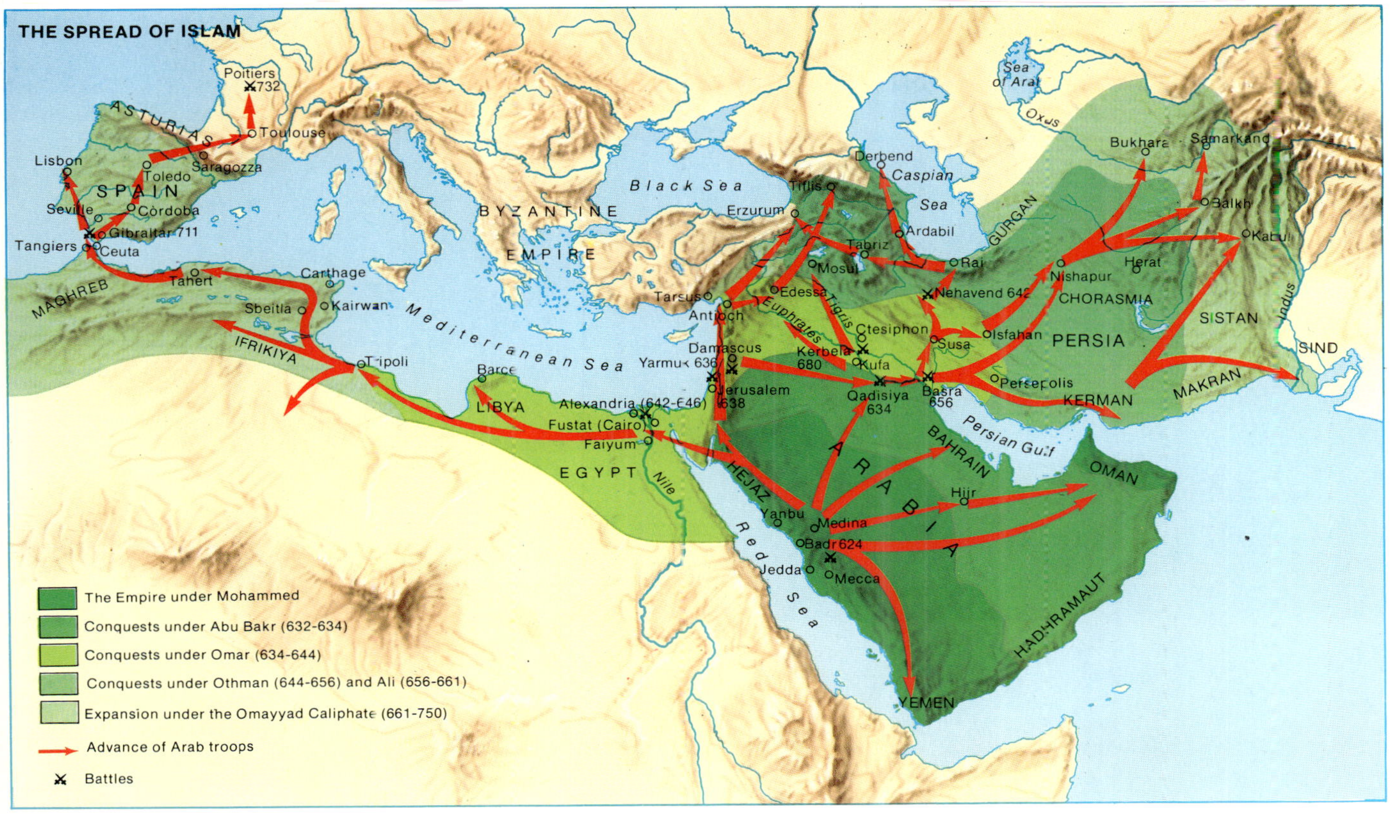

A masterpiece of Islamic art

The dome of the great Royal Mosque at Isfahan, the capital of the Persian monarch Abbas I the Great, the most famous member of the Shia Safavid Dynasty which ruled from the beginning of the sixteenth century to 1736. The dome, which is 54 metres (177 feet) high and 21.5 metres (70 feet) round, is completely covered with multi-coloured ceramic tiles, depicting the "tree of life", one of the most typical of Islamic artistic designs. (It is against the tenets of Islam to portray figures — hence the use of geometric, floral and calligraphic decoration on Muslim buildings.) The blue tiles on the drum which supports the dome carry writing from the Quran. The mosque was built between 1612 and 1630 by Ali Akbar, architect to Abbas the Great.

The Holy Book

The Quran is the word of God to the Muslim faithful who believe that it was transmitted to Muhammad by the Archangel Gabriel. Written in Arabic, it consists of 114 chapters (*suras*) containing dogma and moral precepts. *Below*, a page from a sixteenth-century Quran, decorated in red and gold.

The last stronghold

A view of the Alhambra, the fortress-palace called after the colour of its red stone. Built in the course of the thirteenth and fourteenth centuries, the Alhambra is in fact a complex of military buildings, palaces and gardens which dominates Granada from a hill. The favourite headquarters of the Nasrids, the last Islamic rulers in Spain, the Alhambra was also the residence of Muhammad XII Boabdil, the Muslim prince who in 1492 surrendered to the Catholic monarchs, Ferdinand of Aragon and Isabella of Castile (the patrons of the explorer Christopher Columbus.)

Scandinavian gods
Runic inscriptions on stones at Jelling in Denmark (*above*), dating back to 983 and showing Christ and a dragon. They commemorate the conversion of the populations of Northern Europe to Christianity in the ninth century. According to oral tradition and the evidence of sagas, such as *Edda*, the main Scandinavian divinity was Odin (or Wotan), God of war and death. He lived in the mythical Valhalla with his son, Thor, and a number of other gods and goddesses, as well as his assistants, the *valkyries*.

Viking ships
Discoveries of sacred ships in various burial grounds, and of designs on stone and coins have permitted several different types of Viking ship to be identified: the *kvar*, which was a coastal ship; the *knar*, a tall boat; and the *langskip* and *skoeid*, which were 30 metres (98 feet) long by 5 metres (16 feet) wide and able to cross the oceans.

Helmets and swords
A finely-worked sword and a helmet of the seventh century AD, pre-dating the Viking period. The Vikings themselves were much-feared warriors who terrorized the coasts of Europe, sometimes penetrating along the rivers into the interior.

William the Conqueror
The Bayeux Tapestry (*right*), commissioned by Archbishop Odo who fought with William the Conqueror, tells the story of the rivalry between the Anglo-Saxon Harold, King of England after the death of Edward the Confessor, and William of Normandy. Having crossed the Channel with 3,000 foot-soldiers and 2,000 cavalry, William defeated and killed his enemy at Hastings, on 14 October 1066.

The peoples of the North: Vikings and Normans

From the beginning of the eighth century AD, Scandinavia witnessed the consolidation in power of a warrior people, known as the Vikings (perhaps from *Vikingr*, or people of the fjords). Skilful and adventurous seamen as well as colonizers and merchants, they set off from Scandinavia in many directions, seeking conquest and pillage wherever they landed.

To begin with, they sailed out into the North Sea, settling in the Orkneys, Shetland and Faeroe Islands, and along the British and Irish coasts (capturing Dublin in 841).

In the same period, other groups of Vikings established themselves on the French coast near Rouen, in Normandy, and at the mouth of the Rhine at Doorstad.

Further north, Viking ships colonized Iceland. From here, according to legend, in 982, Erik the Red sailed westwards and reached the southern tip of Greenland. Later, in about the year 1000, his son, Leif Eriksson, may have reached the American coast and founded a colony in Markland, the modern Newfoundland.

At much the same time, the Danish King Canute (Cnut) the Great (995–1035) unified Denmark, Norway and most of England under his rule; while yet another Viking, Rollo, embraced Christianity and founded a duchy in Normandy, the territory from which William the Conqueror set out to invade England and to win the Battle of Hastings in 1066.

Before this, in around 1040, seven brothers from Hauteville in Normandy landed on the coast of southern Italy to begin the Norman connection with the Mediterranean. One of them, Robert Guiscard, drove the Byzantines out of Italy and was rewarded by the Pope with the title of Duke of Puglia and Calabria; while between 1061 and 1091 a second brother, Roger, freed Sicily from Arab control. In 1130 the latter's son, Roger II, became King of Sicily.

Elsewhere, in the vast and sparsely populated territory of Eastern Europe, other Vikings (known as Varangians) established themselves through conquest, travelling by river as far as Kiev and Constantinople. One of their leaders, Rurik, was among the founders of the Principality of Novgorod (862), later incorporated in the Principality of Kiev, the first united Russian state.

The Normans in Sicily
The Norman, Robert Guiscard, was crowned Duke of Puglia by Pope Gregory VII at Ceprano in 1080 (*above*). Having driven the Byzantines and Arabs from southern Italy, the Normans played a decisive role in the conflict between Pope Gregory VII and the Emperor Henry IV during the Investiture Struggle. In 1084, Robert Guiscard freed the Pope who was besieged in Castel Sant' Angelo by the Emperor's army, although he proved unable to prevent his own troops from sacking Rome. *Right*, the cloister of the Benedictine Monastery of Monreale was built, together with the adjacent church and royal palace, by the Norman King William II (the Good) between 1172 and 1185.

Lords of southern Italy
The Normans, apart from exercising their royal prerogatives such as the right to mint money (*above*, a coin from the time of Robert Guiscard), had considerable influence on the history of the twelfth and thirteenth centuries. Constance, daughter of Roger II, married Henry VI in 1186 and became Empress on his coronation in 1191. She was the mother of Frederick II, the Emperor who built Castel del Monte (*right*).

Empire and feudalism
Charlemagne organized Western European society on feudal principles, establishing a rigid, pyramidical structure in which the monarch assigned land to a trusted noble, who, in turn, divided it among a number of his own vassals. *Left*, a precious bust of Charlemagne.

Charlemagne and the Holy Roman Empire

On Christmas Day in the year 800, the people of Rome acclaimed Charlemagne who had just been crowned Emperor by Pope Leo III. With the inauguration of the Holy Roman Empire, the monarchy of the Franks reached the zenith of its power, ruling over most of Western Europe. Of Germanic origin, the Franks had settled along the Rhine during the third century AD but later moved into Gaul. Then, after the collapse of the Roman Empire (476), they extended their dominions from the Pyrenees to the Rhine under their King, Clovis I (481–511). Following Clovis's death, his kingdom was divided among his sons, in accordance with Barbarian custom. Gradually, three distinct powers emerged — Neustria, Austrasia and Burgundy — and, where monarchs were weak, power was assumed by senior officials, the so-called mayors of the palace. At the end of the seventh century, one of these, Pepin of Heristal, managed to restore the unity of the empire as it had existed under Clovis. His dominions were maintained and strengthened by his successors: Charles Martel (715–741), Pepin the Short (741–768) and his sons, Carloman and Charles, who became the sole ruler and was the future Charlemagne. He embarked on a series of conquests: in 773–774 he took the kingdom of Lombardy; in 778 he incorporated Bavaria into his dominions after overthrowing Duke Thassilo; in 806, at the end of a campaign begun in 772, he subdued the Saxons. By his death in 814, the Carolingian, or Frankish, Empire stretched from the Pyrenees to Central Europe. Charlemagne gave this huge area a new type of political organization, which provided the basis for the development of feudal society. The Empire was divided into districts, or counties, each presided over by a count. These counties were then subdivided into smaller units, controlled by *vice-comes* and *centenarii* (or vicars), but around the frontiers of the Empire, the counties were grouped into marches, governed by margraves. A series of relationships, grounded on personal loyalty, linked the emperor with his margraves and counts, right down to the lowest of his vassals. These bonds of fealty were sanctioned by a ceremony of investiture, during which the lord confirmed his vassal in possession of a fee — normally a piece of land — in exchange for an oath of loyalty.

Apart from this reorganization of his Empire, Charlemagne also wished to be recognized as a patron of culture and scholarship. During his reign he encouraged what amounted to a cultural rebirth, and a well-known symbol of this activity was the *schola palatina* at Aix-la-Chapelle, which flourished under the direction of Alcuin.

The Emperor Charlemagne
Charles, King of the Franks, was crowned Emperor by Pope Leo III on 25 December 800 (*below*) in St Peter's Cathedral, Rome, in a church on the site of the present one. The Holy Roman Empire was destined to last, at least formally, until 1806 when the Emperor Francis II was compelled to give up his title by Napoleon. The first of the Holy Roman Emperors to wear the jewelled crown (*above*), which incorporated — according to tradition — one of the nails from the Cross, was Otto I of Saxony in 951. Previously, it had been used by Berengar I, King of Italy from 888. This crown is now preserved in Monza Cathedral.

Bartering
In the commercial crises of the early Middle Ages, bartering was often the only means of payment.

The knights
Within the feudal system, which normally denied a landed inheritance to all but the eldest son, the younger sons of noble families had only two careers open to them — to become clerics or knights. If they chose the latter, they could offer their martial courage and skill in the use of the sword, but it was wars or heroic deeds in the service of a king or powerful lord which were the most likely means to a fortune. Warfare therefore became a common occupation of these men, while tournaments and military practice (*left*) (in which, as in battle, feudal knights wore heavy armour) were, together with hunting, among their favourite pastimes. As time went by, the knights developed certain conventions of behaviour: these came to be idealized in the image of the knight in shining armour, whose mission was to defend the weak and rectify injustices perpetrated upon the humble. Eventually, crusading to free Jerusalem and the Holy Sepulchre from the infidel became the major objective of knights.

Agriculture and the serfs
During the feudal age, peasants were tied to the land as serfs. They were not permitted to leave or change their work, and harsh penalties were imposed on fugitives. Indeed, since serfdom was their only source of food and shelter they rarely tried to escape. If their lord was benevolent they often found that serfdom brought protection with it. They also had to hand over a part of their crops to their lord and render him service by way of free labour on the land, in his castle or in his army.

Culture and urban development
Charlemagne was not only a great monarch and military leader but also a patron of culture (*above* Archbishop Turpin and his chaplain Egmeaux working on the biography of the Emperor). Moreover, he encouraged commerce and economic expansion, and thriving trading centres such as St Denis (*below*), Beaucaire, Champagne, Lyons, Frankfurt, Bruges, Piacenza and Pavia all held regular fairs.

The castle, centre of power
All feudal society revolved around the castle, home of the great lord and secure defence against the threats of possible enemies. Surrounded by a crenellated wall, the castle had comfortable apartments for the lord, his family and advisers, together with other rooms for servants and guards. When the lord went off to war — or the Crusades — he was confident his family would be safe inside the fortifications. *Right*, a well-preserved castle in Val d'Aosta, dating back in part to the eleventh century.

"God wills it"
At the Council of Clermont-Ferrand of 1095 (*left*), Pope Urban II summoned the faithful to the Crusade, promising plenary indulgence to those swearing to take the Cross and go to Palestine to fight against the Muslims.
From the beginning, the First Crusade split into two quite separate sections. The first, made up of about 20,000 of the faithful who had been galvanized by the preachings of Peter the Hermit, joined a group of adventurers led by Walter the Penniless; but, decimated by illness and ambushes near Constantinople in August 1096, the survivors were massacred by the Turks near Civitot a few weeks later. The second group, consisting of heavily armed knights (*below*, two knights of the twelfth century), was led by Count Raymond IV of Toulouse, Godfrey of Bouillon (Duke of Lower Lorraine), Baldwin of Flanders, and Bohemond of Taranto and his nephew Tancred. It reached Jerusalem on 7 June 1099 and took it on 14–15 July.

The Crusades

The conquest of Jerusalem
Fourteenth-century picture showing the crusaders at the gates of Jerusalem (*below*). After scaling the walls on 14 July, the crusaders occupied the city on the following day and, fighting from house to house, massacred thousands of infidels, not only Muslims but also Jews. Godfrey of Bouillon (rather than Raymond of Toulouse) was chosen as leader of the new state created by the crusaders, but he refused the title of King, preferring that of Protector of the Holy Sepulchre. On his death (1100), his brother Baldwin founded the Latin Kingdom of Jerusalem.

The beginning of the era of the Crusades coincided with the rebirth of Europe after the year 1000. The preachings of Peter the Hermit and the actions of Pope Urban II provided the inspiration which persuaded people to listen to the words of St Matthew (X.38) and to take the Cross in order to free Jerusalem and the Holy Sepulchre. The Crusades were, in origin, a violent reaction to the denial to Christian pilgrims of access to the holy places — a prohibition introduced by the Seljuk Turks who had been masters of Jerusalem from 1076. This overthrew a tradition of open access, inaugurated by the Caliph Omar in 638, when Jerusalem had been conquered by the Arabs who, like the Christians, considered it to be a holy city and centre of pilgrimage.
However, apart from this grave provocation to the religious views of medieval Europe, there were also political, social and economic motives for the Crusades. Politically, there was the need to shore up the Byzantine Empire which was menaced by Islam. This combined with the rather remote possibility of the reunification of the Eastern and Western Churches, with the Papacy hoping for an end to the schism (1054) of Michael Cerularius, Patriarch of Constantinople, and the return of the Orthodox Church to the Catholic tradition. The social and economic causes included the need to find new territory for the surplus population which had greatly increased in the West since the year 1000; the desire of the emerging European nations (France and England) and of the Italian maritime cities (Genoa, Pisa and Venice) to establish and expand their commercial connections with the Orient; the ambition of thousands of young nobles of low rank to seek their fortunes abroad and to escape the rigidities of the feudal dynastic system which restricted privileges to the first-born; and, of course, the lure of the fabulous wealth which was supposed to exist in the East.
After the Fourth Crusade (1204), the motivation became increasingly non-religious. By then, the faith in God and the will to embark on the long and difficult task of reconquering the holy places, which had sustained Godfrey of Bouillon and his companions in 1099, no longer provided the major impulse behind the crusading movement.

The Knights Templar

Seal of the religious and military Order of Knights Templar, founded at Jerusalem in 1119 by Hugo de Payens, with the task of protecting pilgrims in the Holy Land from attack by Muslims and brigands.

The Latin kingdoms in the East

Seeking adventure in the Holy Land (*left*), the crusader knights hoped to gain personal advantage from their endeavours. In the conquered regions they founded kingdoms, principalities and duchies, and built fortresses like the famous Crak des Chevaliers (*above*) in Syria, which resisted Muslim assaults from 1142 until 1271. After Saladin had reconquered Jerusalem in 1187, the Holy Sepulchre remained in the hands of the Muslims who later threatened the great city of Constantinople (*right*).

CHRONOLOGY

First Crusade. 1095 At the Council of Clermond-Ferrand, Pope Urban II summoned the Christian princes to the Crusade. 1096 Following the preaching of Peter the Hermit, a Crusade of adventurers and so-called beggars was formed, but was annihilated on 21 October near Civitot. 1097 The crusaders under Godfrey of Bouillon took Nicaea and besieged Antioch. 1098 The crusaders took Antioch (3 June) and defeated a Turkish army (28 June). 1099 The crusaders reached Jerusalem and took it (14 July).

Second Crusade. The conquest of Edessa by the Turks (1144) induced Pope Eugene III to preach another Crusade. 1148 Failure of attempt to take Damascus.

Third Crusade. The news that the Sultan Saladin had taken Jerusalem (1187) led to a new Crusade. 1191 Philip II Augustus and Richard I took Acre in July and Richard defeated Saladin, making peace with him in the following year.

Fourth Crusade. 1202 The crusaders conquered Zara for Venice. 1204 The crusaders pillaged Constantinople and founded the Latin Empire in the east, ruled by Baldwin IX.

Fifth Crusade. Determined upon by the Lateran Council of 1215, it began with the landing of Andrew II of Hungary at Acre (1217). 1219 John of Brienne, King of Jerusalem, took Damietta.

Sixth Crusade. Organized under pressure from Pope Honorius III, it was led by Frederick II (1228) who obtained Jerusalem from the Sultan Elkamil without fighting.

Seventh Crusade. Entrusted to the leadership of Louis IX of France who (1250) conquered Damietta but was defeated at Mansura.

Eighth Crusade. Louis IX died during the siege of Tunis (1270).

The metamorphosis of medieval society

The Hanse and their monopoly of northern commerce
Granted the status of a free city in 1226 by the Emperor Frederick II, Lübeck (*above*, the Holstentor, built between 1466 and 1478) was an active commercial centre, one of the most flourishing of the Hanseatic League. The Hanse, which was a trading corporation, grouped together many North European cities. Each town had its own seal (*below*, the seal of Wismar showing a Hanse ship).

In the eleventh and twelfth centuries, the self-contained economy of European medieval society entered upon major changes. The availability of additional labour, consequent upon the increase in population, permitted new land to be brought into cultivation, resulting in a greater abundance of agricultural produce. This led to an expanding trade in goods between country and town, where at the same time, new social groups, such as artisans and merchants, were emerging. The artisans — metalsmiths, gunsmiths, jewellers, drapers and shoemakers — formed themselves into guilds or corporations in the towns; the merchants maintained trade between town and town, nation and nation, travelling along hazardous routes often infested with brigands.
In the course of the thirteenth century great commercial activity spread throughout Europe, from the Mediterranean to the Baltic, from the Atlantic to Russia. From the main centres of origin — the Netherlands in the north and Italy in the south — trade spread first along the coasts and then gradually into the interior of the Continent. All this activity gave rise to the growth of money-changing, letters of credit and exchange, and the use of gold as a means of international payment. Linked with commerce were the fortunes and rivalries of the maritime cities of the Mediterranean. Here, Pisa, Marseilles and, most of all, Genoa and Venice, fought each other for the monopoly in the trading of silk, brocades and spices — the spice trade being especially vital because, at that time, it provided the only means of preserving food and, sometimes, of curing certain diseases.
In the heart of the Continent, especially in Burgundy and Champagne, the growth of trade made the fortunes of several towns, such as Troyes, Provins, Bar-sur-Aube and Langy which were the sites of international fairs. Further to the north, the towns of Flanders, such as Ghent, Tournai and Saint-Bertin, flourished due to their manufacture of fine cloth; while in Germany, Scandinavia and the Baltic, the merchants — dominating the life of cities such as Lübeck and Hamburg — made an agreement in 1241 setting up the Hanse trading corporation. To begin with, this included Bremen and Brunswick but later, many other cities joined in so that eventually, from Russia and Sweden to the British Isles, 164 towns were engaged in the monopoly of northern commerce.
Politically, however, the Europe of the flourishing merchant cities faced a crisis in the fortunes of the Empire and the Papacy, the two powers which had dominated the scene at the time of the Investiture Struggle. Now, the popes were compelled to leave Rome for Avignon, where they resided from 1309 to 1377; while the emperors were no longer able to control either the German princes or the increasingly powerful free cities, and lost much of their prestige.

Rebirth in the year 1000
Between the year 1000 and the fourteenth century, there was a significant increase in the population of Europe. Many cities — Milan, Florence, Palermo, Rome, London, Cologne, Ghent and Paris — had more than 50,000 inhabitants each. At the same time, the commercial routes of Europe were becoming clearly defined. Spices and other precious goods from the Orient were transported by caravan as far as the ports of Asia Minor, Palestine and Egypt, and then shipped to the European coastal cities of Venice, Genoa, Pisa and Marseilles. From there, they were conveyed northwards along two main established trading routes: one across France to the ports of the Channel and Flanders; the other, via the Brenner Pass, to Augsburg and the Rhine, and on to link up with the Hanse trading network. In its turn, the Hanse sent southwards the products of Northern Europe, including amber, furs, salt and wood.

The first Habsburg Emperor

Seal of Rudolph I, King of the Romans and of Germany from 1273 to 1291. His election ended the interregnum, the period of crisis which followed the deaths of the Emperor Frederick II (1250) and his heirs. Habsburgs ruled most of Central Europe until 1914

The Papacy at Avignon

The coronation of Pope Clement V (*right*), Pope from 1305 to 1314. It was in 1309, during his pontificate, that the Holy See was transferred from Rome to Avignon. His successors at Avignon were John XXII (1316-1334), Benedict XII (1334-1342), Clement VI (1342-1352), Innocent VI (1352-1362), Urban V (1362-1370) and Gregory XI (1370-1378) who, in 1377, restored the Papacy to Rome. The disputed election of Urban VI, successor to Gregory XI, gave rise to the Great Schism, a division which lasted until 1417 and during which one or more anti-popes were elected as rivals for each pope.

Genoa and Venice, perpetual rivals

Towards the end of the eleventh century, Genoa gave itself autonomy within the Empire — officially recognized later on by the Emperor Frederick I Barbarossa — and in 1139 acquired the right to mint its own coinage. Its period of greatest power came after the fall in 1261 of the Latin Empire in Constantinople when the new Byzantine monarch, Michael VIII Palaeologus, granted the Genoans the trading advantages previously monopolized by the Venetians, as a reward for their assistance in helping him to the throne. However, it was Venice which was the undisputed mistress of the Adriatic from the eleventh to the fourteenth centuries: although the hundred-year war between the two cities weakened both, it confirmed the supremacy of Venice. *Below,* the departure of Marco Polo from Venice for the East. This illustration shows the magnificence of the city and the use of the canals to replace roads — much as they are used today. *Left,* a thirteenth-century picture of Genoa, illustrating the conflict between the Guelphs, supporters of the Papacy, and the Ghibellines, who supported the Empire.

The reconquest of Spain and Portugal

The King of Castile, Alfonso X, dictating to his clerk. He has been called the Wise because of his scholarly interests and the support he gave to the famous University of Salamanca, founded in about 1230. It was a major academic centre, attracting scholars from all over Europe, and earning the city a large revenue. He claimed the imperial throne during the interregnum (1250-1273), by virtue of his family connections with Frederick II of Hohenstaufen. Within Spain, Alfonso allied with the monarchs of Aragon and Portugal to continue the reconquest—the liberation of the Iberian Peninsula from Muslim domination. Previously, another coalition of Iberian forces had been responsible for the defeat of the Moors in the decisive Battle of Las Navas de Tolosa on 16 July 1212.

At the court of the Great Khan
Kublai, grandson of Genghis Khan and Emperor of China, where he founded the Mongol Dynasty of Yuan, is the powerful monarch who features in Marco Polo's *Il Milione*. In this illustration (*above*) from an old edition of this book, the Mongol Khan is portrayed at his dinner table, in one of the fabulous palaces of Chanbalik. The legendary splendour of Kublai's court created a continuous demand for money which, in turn, caused several revolts. Kublai was a patron of Chinese culture and literature. His army (*left*, Mongol cavalry) succeeded in conquering Korea, but failed to complete the invasion of Japan.

The Mongols

The Mongols — one of the many nomad groups which inhabited the vast expanses of the Central Asian steppes — rose to prominence suddenly in the twelfth century when their leader, Yesügei, began unifying the various tribes living on the northern borders of China. Turning them into a nation of invincible warriors, capable of winning an empire, was the work of Yesügei's son, Temujin. Known as Genghis Khan, he succeeded in subduing the whole of Asia, from the northern frontiers of China to the Caspian Sea, between 1206 and 1227, the year of his death. The expansion continued under his descendants: Ugudei (1229–1241) introduced an administrative structure modelled on that of China into his empire and embarked on the conquest of both China and Korea; Batu Khan and his military leader, Subutai, established themselves in Russia, and conducted a long expedition (1236–1241) into Poland, Hungary and the Balkans, reaching as far as the Adriatic; Kublai (1260–1294), the great Khan mentioned by Marco Polo in his book, *Il Milione*, attempted to subdue Japan and also completed the conquest of China where he founded a dynasty, the Yuan, which was to rule until 1368; and Hulagu (1251–1265) conquered Persia and inflicted heavy defeats on the Seljuk Turks and on the caliphs of Baghdad and Damascus. These successes were followed by a troubled period in which the unity of the Mongol territories was threatened by domestic rivalries. Yet this was not quite the end of their power. Under another great military leader, Tamerlane, the Mongols experienced a further historical moment of glory seizing the land around Samarcand, but after his death in 1405, no one else was able to prevent the decline of his kingdoms.

The great generals
Genghis Khan (*left*) whose name, adapted from the Chinese, means "perfect warrior", was the monarch who unified the Mongol tribes, leading them to the conquest of a vast empire. His rise to power began in about 1184 when, scarcely seventeen, he took the title which his father had held and which had been in dispute since the latter's death nine years previously. His power reached its peak in 1206, when the assembly of the Mongol people, the *Kurultai*, proclaimed him supreme ruler. At the head of a huge army of 700,000 men, entirely composed of cavalry and highly skilled archers whose advances in Asia and Europe were marked by massacres of the populations of whole cities, he conquered the whole of Asia from Peking to the Caspian Sea, within the space of only fifteen years. One and a half centuries later, his legendary achievements were emulated by Tamerlane (*right*, enthroned with the symbols of power). Between 1369 and 1405, he conducted a series of campaigns in many parts of Asia, from Corasmia to Persia and from India to Syria, defeating Bayazid I at Angora in 1401.

Beyond the mountains of Afghanistan
Lying across the only caravan route from the steppes of Asia to Persia, Afghanistan was one of the first territories invaded by the Mongol hordes of Genghis Khan. Bamian (*above*), with its red towers, and Herat, an important commercial centre, were conquered and destroyed in 1221. But while Bamian failed to recover its ancient splendour (still evident today in its fine Buddhist monuments), Herat became one of the favourite seats of Tamerlane, and was a centre of culture, arts and science in his kingdom.

The felt-walled tent, home of the nomads
Even today, the nomads of Mongolia migrate into the vast steppes of Central Asia in search of new pastures for their horses and sheep, taking with them all their possessions including their tents. These are cylindrical in shape and made of interwoven slats of wood. The roof is conical, covered with a layer of felt or skins, and pierced to provide an opening for letting out smoke from the fire. The interior is furnished with rugs and carpets, and the fire is always positioned in the centre of the tent to emphasize its sacred, purifying function. Traditionally, it was the women who wove the richly patterned rugs from the wool dyed with plant extracts. Parents encouraged their daughters to master the skill, which commanded a high bride-price: a wife who wove attractive rugs could earn a great deal of money for her husband. The customs and achievements, both legendary and factual, of these old nomadic tribes and their leaders have come down to us in poems, such as the *Secret History of the Mongols*. This dates back to 1241, and tells of Genghis Khan and his successors. Another important source is the *White History*, attributed at least in part to Kublai himself.

Outstanding horsemen
Accustomed to the saddle from an early age, the Mongols made extremely fast horsemen, often taking their enemies completely by surprise. Highly skilled at using bows and arrows even when at the gallop, their warriors also invariably carried a sword and the typical round shield. They wore armour made from tanned hide, consisting of overlapping plates which were lacquered to keep out the rain. The rider and his horse were so closely identified that in many cases when the man was killed in battle, they were both buried together, so that the horse could carry him into the afterlife.

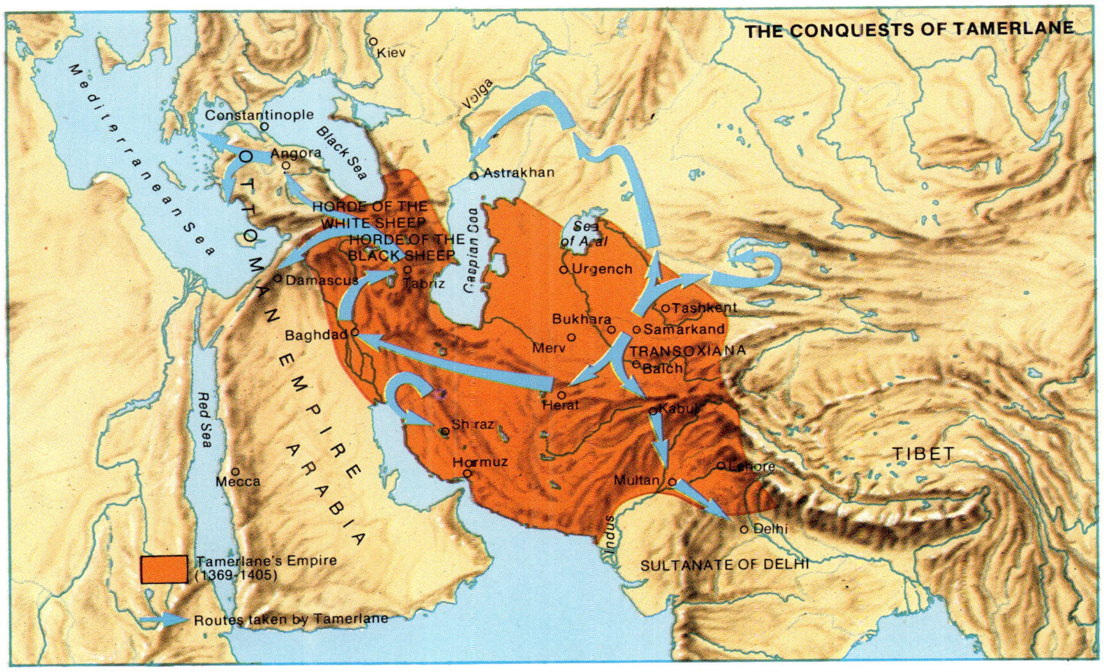

Europe at the time of the Hundred Years' War

Europe in the thirteenth and fourteenth centuries experienced both crisis and change. Internationally, the Imperial idea was in slow and irreversible decline and national monarchies were beginning to take its place. At the same time, the Papacy was in crisis because of the transfer of the Holy See to Avignon, and the bitter struggle between popes and anti-popes. Complicated by years of cold weather, there were also important changes in agriculture at this time: production was increasingly geared to satisfying the needs of urban life with its demands for grain, meat, milk and cheese. Moreover, growth in population was leading to a greater need for food at a time when famines and shortages were common: the consequent malnutrition produced epidemics and illnesses of all types. On the social level, there were frequent peasant revolts against the aristocracy, merchants and urban communities. Two were particularly serious: the *jacquerie* in France (1358) and the Peasants' Revolt in Kent and Essex under Richard II (1381).

Politically, Europe was devastated by the conflict between France and England known as the Hundred Years' War. It began in 1328 as a dynastic dispute, when Philip of Valois (nephew of Philip IV the Fair (1285–1314)) ascended the French throne on the death without direct heirs of the last Capetian King, Charles VI. The throne was also claimed by another nephew of Philip IV, the English King Edward III, who was moreover a vassal of the French monarchy in respect of his continental lands. The War saw two different cultures opposing each other. Not ony did the two sides pursue contrasting methods of warfare — the French employing heavy cavalry, the English using quick-footed infantry and skilful archers; but they had also evolved different political structures — the French still tied to a feudal system with its requirements for the king to ask his barons for the feudal aid in order to collect money, whilst the English were already at a stage where the king had to consult Parliament if he needed to impose new taxes.

The kingdom of the tzars

Dmitri Donskoy began the process of freeing Russia from Mongol domination by winning the Battle of Kulikovo in 1380. Then, Ivan III (1462–1505), Grand Duke of Moscow, refused to continue paying tribute to the Khanate of the Golden Horde and started the process — continued by his successor, Vassili III (1505–1533) — of unifying central and northern Russia. To commemorate the conquest of the old Mongol capitals of Kazan and Astrakhan, Ivan IV the Terrible built the Cathedral of St Basil (1555–1560) (near the Kremlin walls), with its characteristic domes (*above left*). It was the same Ivan IV (1533–1584) who, in 1547, made himself the first "tzar", concentrating absolute power in his hands and consolidating the administrative structure of Russia. *Above*, an allegorical illustration from the *Chronica* of Sercambi showing the effects of the epidemics of bubonic plague which devastated Europe from 1348 onwards. It was probably the most serious pestilence ever recorded: spreading from Asia Minor into the Mediterranean and then as far as England, it caused more than 25,000,000 deaths in Europe and 23,000,000 in Asia.

The Charter of English liberties
Magna Carta, the Great Charter of Liberties (*left*), granted by King John on 15 June 1215 under pressure from the barons, is considered to be the fundamental document in the history of English liberties. Issued at Runnymead, *Magna Carta* subjected the monarch to the control of twenty-five barons, providing remedies if its terms were ignored. It also contained clauses of benefit to the non-baronial and peasant population. Original copies of the 1215 charter can be seen at the cathedrals of Lincoln and Salisbury, as well as in the British Museum.

The heroism of Joan of Arc
Summoned, according to tradition, by heavenly voices to fight to free France from English domination during the Hundred Years' War, Joan of Arc (*right*, a tapestry showing her meeting King Charles VII at Chinon) defeated the English at Patay and forced them to lift the siege of Orleans. However, falling into the hands of the Burgundians, she was handed over to the English, condemned by an ecclesiastical tribunal as a witch and heretic, and burnt alive at Rouen on 30 May 1431. She was later canonized and is still regarded as a national heroine in France.

The beginning of the Hundred Years' War
The accession to the throne of Philip of Valois, King of France as Philip VI from 1328 to 1350 (*above*, presiding at a meeting at court), was one of the causes of the Hundred Years' War. Edward III of England, son of a daughter of Philip IV the Fair, considered himself to have a better claim to the French throne than the chosen king, who was a nephew of Philip IV the Fair and therefore not a direct heir. In the first stages of the conflict, the French were defeated at Crécy (1346) and had to hand over the important port of Calais (1347) which they did not regain for over a hundred years. John II the Good (1350–1364), the successor of Philip VI, was defeated by the English under the Black Prince (Battle of Poitiers, 1356), and was taken as a prisoner to London. He was only permitted to return to France after signing the Treaties of Brétigny and Calais (1360).

Hus at the stake
The Bohemian reformer, Jan Hus, Rector of the University of Prague, was an advocate of the necessity of overhauling the hierarchy of the Church, and a follower of Wycliffe, whose ideas had been condemned as heretical. He was arrested in 1415 during the Council of Constance, despite having a safe conduct from the Emperor Sigismund. Accused of advancing the doctrine of predestination, he was found guilty of heresy and burnt alive at the stake on 6 July 1415. The same Council put an end to the Great Schism in the Catholic Church, which had started in 1378 with the serious friction between popes and anti-popes: the unity of the Church was restored by the election of Pope Martin V in 1417 in place of John XXIII, Gregory XII and Benedict XIII.

Agincourt, a triumph for English archers
The Battle of Agincourt (*right*), on 25 October 1415, again swung the balance of war in favour of the English. (Henry V's archers were particularly effective on this occasion.) Previously, Charles V of France (1364–1380), supported by the brave military leader, Bertrand du Guesclin, had succeeded in regaining some of the initiative despite the domestic upheavals caused by the *jacquerie*, the peasant rebellion led by Jacques Bonhomme, and the revolt in Paris under Etienne Marcel. The Treaty of Troyes (1420) established Henry V of England as Regent of France during the incapacity of Charles VI, and as heir to the throne. However, Charles VII (1422–1461) began the French recovery and the English, defeated at Formigny (1450) and Castillon (1453), were forced to abandon all their continental possessions with the exception of Calais.

The age of geographical discoveries

The Renaissance belief that men were not created to live as savages but to pursue virtue and knowledge was at the foundation of the great explorations of the fifteenth and sixteenth centuries. However, the quest for knowledge was not the only cause. The discoveries of Copernicus and Kepler had discredited the traditional Ptolemaic theory about the shape of the Earth; there had been progress in the art of deep-sea navigation, with the introduction of faster ships, higher and stronger masts, new sails, and better use of compasses and sextants; there was the need to look for new routes to India and the Orient in order to avoid the exhausting and dangerous journeys along caravan tracks by then controlled by the Ottomans; there was the mission to spread Christianity; and, last but not least, there was the greed for gold and silver, the illusion of easy riches to be found in the mythical land of El Dorado, which the *conquistadores* thought they had found when they first saw the riches of the Inca Empire in Peru.

The consequences of the great explorations —where the Portuguese, sailing along the African coasts, and the Spaniards, retracing the voyages of Columbus and Magellan, were in the forefront, followed by the Dutch, English and French — were of major importance since they transformed every aspect of human life in Europe. At the political level, the cities of the Mediterranean lost ground, while England and France became more powerful; the Iberian Peninsula underwent deep social changes; the first colonial empires were born; and the first big trading companies, such as the famous East India Companies, were established. At the social and economic level, the introduction of new produce into Europe (such as the potato, maize, cocoa and indigo) and the influx of massive quantities of precious metals, especially gold and silver, contributed to a huge rise in prices, a decline of certain social groups (such as aristocratic landowners), a shortage of manual labour in some areas (particularly in the Iberian Peninsula, in part as a consequence of the emigration of thousands of would-be *conquistadores*) and the rise to power of the mercantile bourgeoisie.

The *Reconquista* is completed
Ferdinand of Aragon (1479–1516) and Isabella of Castile (1474–1504), the "Catholic monarchs" whose marriage in 1469 had unified Spain, entering Granada (1492) after defeating Boabdil XII, King of the last Moorish monarchy in Spain.

Henry the Navigator
Son of John I, King of Portugal from 1385 to 1433, Prince Henry (1394–1460) organized a number of expeditions which explored the African coast as far as the Gulf of Guinea, and began a profitable trade in ivory, gold, pepper and black slaves.

The first guns
Late fifteenth century cannon and cannonball; the cannon could fire stone or iron cannonballs over a distance of 300 metres (984 feet). The gunpowder which it used was made of a highly explosive mixture of saltpetre, sulphur and charcoal.

Maps and instruments for sailing the oceans
Improved maps and nautical instruments contributed to the success of the explorations. *Above*, an astrolabe of the sixteenth century. *Left*, a map of part of the American coast, drawn by Juan de la Cosa. He was one of the seamen who took part in Columbus's first voyage, when three caravels, *Niña*, *Pinta* and *Santa Maria* landed on a small island of the Bahamas, renamed San Salvador. Columbus led three more voyages to the New World. On the second, 1493–1496, he explored the islands of the Caribbean; during the third, 1498–1500, he reached the coast of the American Continent for the first time (near the delta of the Orinoco); finally, on the fourth voyage, 1502–1504, he followed the coast of modern Honduras and Panama, looking for a passage to India. (This was the origin of the name West Indies which was given to the Caribbean islands.)

Spanish explorations
- Christopher Columbus (1492-93)
- Ferdinand Magellan (1519-22)
- Spanish possessions

Portuguese explorations
- Bartholomew Dias (1487)
- Vasco da Gama (1497)
- Amerigo Vespucci (1501-02)
- Portuguese possessions

French explorations
- Jacques Cartier (1534)
- French possessions

English explorations
- John Cabot (1497)
- John and Sebastian Cabot (1498)
- English possessions

Dutch explorations
- Willem Barents (1596-97)

Across the Atlantic
Christopher Columbus (1451–1506), almost certainly born in Genoa, sailed westwards from the Spanish port of Cadiz to discover the new lands of America.

A passage to India
The Portuguese Vasco da Gama (1469–1524) was the first man to reach India by sailing round the Cape of Good Hope (1497). This route enabled traders to avoid the long and dangerous land journeys.

Sailing round the world
Ferdinand Magellan (1480–1521), a Portuguese navigator in the service of Spain, began the circumnavigation of the world in 1519.

The courageous ships of the Portuguese
Left, Portuguese carracks of the sixteenth century. It was in ships such as these that Pedro Alvarez Cabral (1460–1526), probably by chance, reached the coasts of Brazil on 22 April 1500 (*above*), and took possession of the land in the name of King Manuel the Fortunate. Brazil was to remain a Portuguese possession, in accordance with the partition of the New World already established by the Treaty of Tordesillas (1494) which drew a vertical line on the map 370 leagues west of Cape Verde. Portuguese is the language of Brazil to this day.

The conqueror of Mexico
Hernán Cortés (1485–1547), the Spanish adventurer in the service of Charles V, who led an expedition which landed in Mexico in 1519, and crushed the powerful Aztec Empire.

The conqueror of Peru
Francisco Pizarro (1471–1541), the Spanish adventurer who (leading about three hundred men) conquered Peru after taking the Inca, Atahualpa, prisoner on 16 November 1532.

Chichen Itzá, jewel of the Toltecs
Founded in the middle of the sixth century AD by the Maya, Chichen Itzá became the main centre of Toltec civilization in the second half of the tenth century. As testimony to its magnificence, some huge monuments survive, for the most part dedicated to the plumed serpent deity, Kukulkan. The most notable is the so-called *Castillo (left)*. Towards the middle of the fifteenth century, the town was suddenly abandoned, for reasons which remain unknown. *Below*, a detail from the *Codex Vindobonensis*, a pre-Columbian manuscript of the Mixtecs, a people settled around Mitla, in the modern Mexican state of Oaxaca.

Huge sculptures
Among the great pre-Columbian civilizations of Central America was that of the Olmecs which developed from the end of the first millennium BC. They have left behind them some colossal basalt heads (*left*, 3 metres (10 feet) high and weighing several tonnes. *Below*, the so-called "stele C", one of the statues of Copan, today in Honduras. These examples of Maya culture date from the third to the ninth century AD.

The kingdoms of Central America

The populations that spread throughout the American Continent many centuries before Columbus's arrival most probably descended from Asian tribal hunters who had crossed the Bering Straits during the last glaciation, when Asia and America were still linked because the ocean levels were lower.

There are many other interesting theories about the origin of the American populations, but what is certain is that by 1492, the Continent was inhabited by very different groups. In the north there were the Red Indians, divided into several tribes according to their habitat (mountains, forests, plains). Fairly advanced cultures, such as the Olmecs, Toltecs, Zapotecs, Huaxtecs and Totonacs developed in Central America; while on the neighbouring islands there were relatively primitive Caribbean peoples.

The first major settlement in the Mexican valley was the ceremonial centre of Teotihuacán, which had its heyday between the third and sixth centuries AD, and deeply influenced other Meso-American civilizations. However, it was the Maya who in two main periods, between the fourth and the fifteenth centuries, developed the most advanced culture. In many places in Mexico and Guatemala, they have left behind spectacular evidence of their remarkable achievements in a whole range of activities, from astronomy to architecture.

Between the twelfth and sixteenth centuries AD, another civilization grew considerably: that of the Aztecs. They were chiefly warriors and established themselves around Tenochtitlán, their capital, which is the site of today's Mexico City.

The Aztec calendar
The Maya and the Aztecs devoted themselves to astronomy, carefully studying the movement of the planets. At the centre of this Aztec stone (*above*), surrounded by data relating to the calendar and other symbols not yet explained, is the face of the Sun God, Tonatiuh.

Palaces, temples and human sacrifices
An arrow-shaped doorway of the Palace (*below*), the finest building in Uxmal, an important Maya centre in Yucatan. A *Chac-Mool* (*above*), from Chichen Itzá, is one of the typical reclining stones on which prisoners were sacrificed to the gods. All pre-Columbian cultures used to offer human victims to the deity.

The Inca Empire

In the millennia before the arrival of the Europeans, the northern regions of South America were populated by a variety of different peoples, with their own diverse cultures. Among those who have left behind evidence of their civilization are the Chibcha, settled many centuries BC in a large territory represented by the modern Costa Rica, Panama and Colombia. They were so skilful in working gold that the *conquistadores* thought of them as the inhabitants of the mythical Kingdom of El Dorado. In the region of the present-day Ecuador and Peru, along the coast and on the slopes of the Andes, the cultures of the Chimú, Nazca and Mochica developed. From the beginning of the thirteenth century these were absorbed into the Inca Empire, the most powerful state of South America.

Under the leadership of the legendary Manco Capac, descendant of the Sun God, the Incas subjugated the several peoples of the Andes, gradually extending their rule (at first exercised only around Cuzco) both northwards towards modern Ecuador, and southwards as far as the Rio Maule, which bordered the territory of the Araucans. The achievements of the Incas were remarkable: an efficient system of administration and communications, a strong economy based on farming and handicrafts, and a balanced social and political structure of family clans who shared land and other possessions. Their Empire reached its zenith at the end of the fifteenth and the beginning of the sixteenth centuries, before being bloodily subdued by the Spanish *conquistadores*, led by Francisco Pizarro, in 1532.

Archaeological research and excavations have revealed the remains of buildings, roads, irrigation systems and bridges all constructed by the Quechua people of the Inca Empire.

Machu Picchu, a fortress town
Machu Picchu (*above*), built at a height of over 2,500 metres (8,200 feet) above sea level and discovered by Bingham in 1911, was probably the refuge of the last Incas. Before the Inca Empire, the main cultural centres in the region were at Nazca and Moche, whose artisans became famous for their ceramics.

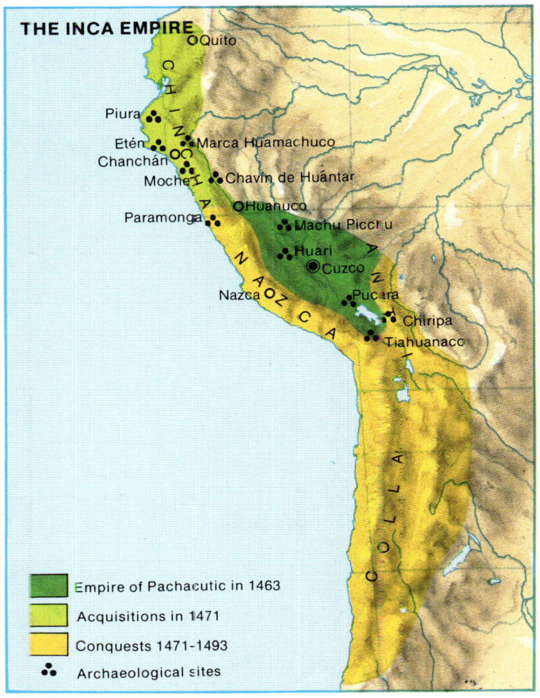

The Birth of Venus
A masterpiece of 1482 by Sandro Botticelli. He was one of the best-known painters of the Renaissance, a period of profound artistic achievement encouraged by kings, popes and princes. Botticelli worked in the Florence of Lorenzo de Medici, a true cradle of culture, with architects such as Brunelleschi and Michelozzo, the sculptor Donatello, and painters of the stature of Paolo Uccello, Ghirlandaio, Verrocchio and Pollaiuolo. Outside Italy, the outstanding painter was Titian, who worked at the court of Charles V in Madrid, while Francis I of France patronized a group of artists and architects (Serlio, Rosso Fiorentino, Niccolò dell' Abate), as well as the astonishing goldsmith, engraver and sculptor Benvenuto Cellini, who was born in Florence in 1500.

The Renaissance

During the second half of the fifteenth century, the new geographical discoveries represented perhaps the most obvious sign of the many sweeping changes that were occurring throughout the world.
At the political level, the first national monarchies — France, Spain, England, Russia, Portugal — were progressively asserting their authority, replacing the medieval conception of a "universal" power for which the Papacy and the Empire had struggled fiercely in the past. At the same time, the remnants of the feudal system were disappearing. The nobility found its power more and more limited by a central authority that extended its control over matters such as justice and taxation. In the field of warfare, the cult of chivalry was in decline while methods of fighting were being altered by the introduction of firearms. Moreover, the rapid growth of towns marked the rise of bourgeois merchants and craftsmen, as well as a new group of entrepreneurs — the bankers — who were sometimes even in a position to influence the rise and fall of kings, as did the Fuggers of Augsburg, supporters of Charles V.
As these political and social changes were shaping a new world in Europe, a cultural renewal was also developing. The Renaissance, backed by the intellectual movement known as Humanism, affected all fields of human knowledge, from science to philosophy, from poetry to architecture, from the arts to people's habits. While the Humanist challenged the theologically-influenced medieval conceptions as outmoded and promoted the values of classical antiquity and an interest in the individual, the Renaissance man rediscovered the outer world and championed the need for the individual to shape it and study its realities. The resulting Renaissance culture flowered above all in the courts of kings and princes: in Italy, it was fostered by the Medici in Florence, the Gonzaga in Mantua, the Sforza in Milan, the Papacy in Rome, the Estensi in Ferrara, the Aragonese in Naples; and elsewhere, by the national monarchies of France, Spain and England, including Francis I of France who distinguished himself by his great patronage of literature, music, painting and architecture.

An age of geniuses
Panorama of Florence (*left*) with the Church of Santa Maria del Fiore: its famous dome was built by Brunelleschi and its bell-tower by Giotto. Florence was also the city where the many-faceted Leonardo da Vinci worked as a young man, as did Michelangelo, the superb sculptor and painter. Other prominent figures of the Renaissance were the architects Bramante and Amadeo, and the painters Raphael, Cosimo Tura, Francesco del Cossa, Piero della Francesca, Mantegna, Corregio, and Carpaccio. *Right*, a drawing of the human body by da Vinci, together with an example of his famous mirror writing, read from right to left.

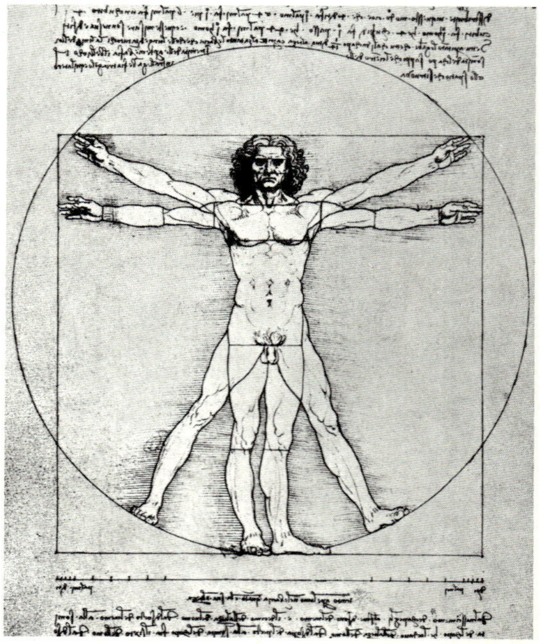

A great humanist
Erasmus of Rotterdam (c.1469–1536), eminent scholar, philosopher of tolerance and rationalism. Among other books, he wrote *The Praise of Folly* (1511), the *Colloquia* (1518), and *De libero Arbitrio* (1524), a polemic against Luther.

The richest town of the Low Countries
A section of a contemporary illustrated map of Antwerp (*right*), showing the docks and busy river traffic. During the sixteenth century, Antwerp, a port on the estuary of the River Scheldt, became the most important commercial centre of Europe, primarily because it controlled the north-south trade (in English wool, Flemish cloths, alum, amber, spices and salt); until 1585, it was also the site of an important fair. However, in the second half of the sixteenth century, a rebellion broke out against Spanish domination of both Antwerp and other Low Countries towns. Caused by rigid fiscal policies and an attack on urban privileges, as well as by an attempt to impose Catholicism on a largely Protestant population, it led to wars, devastation and a severe economic crisis.

Royal advisers
Thomas More (*left*, with his family), author of *Utopia*, Chancellor and adviser of Henry VIII of England, was beheaded in 1535, after his refusal to recognize the king as Supreme Head of the Church in England. Jacob Fugger the Rich (*right*, with his chief accountant, Mattheus Schwarz) was one of the most famous members of the well-known family of Augsburg bankers, who supported and financed Charles V. Elected Holy Roman Emperor in 1519, Charles V abdicated in 1556, having ruled over the largest empire since that of Charlemagne.

The father of printing
Known to the Chinese for a long time, printing was introduced to Europe by Johann Gutenberg of Mainz (c.1400–1468), a German who studied the possibility of printing with moveable type. In 1453, together with Johann Fust, he printed (*below*) the famous 42-line or Mazarine Bible by this method. The development of printing techniques was to revolutionize the western world and its culture.

The sun and its planets
Planetarium constructed according to the system of Nicholas Copernicus, the Polish astronomer (1473–1543) who propounded the theory that the planets, while rotating on their own axes, move in circular orbits round the sun, not the earth, as the traditional Ptolemaic geocentric system had maintained.

The new scientific conception of the world
Lens (*below*) by Galileo Galilei (1564–1642), the scientist who, with his findings in astronomy and physics, confirmed Copernicus's theory. Condemned by the Church for this, he was forced to disown his work under threat of torture.

The age of the Reformation

Traditionally, the Church was the community of all the faithful, united in the profession of the same faith and by participation in the same sacraments, under the authority of the Roman pontiff. However, the Church had not always dedicated itself solely to the proclamation of the Gospel and the saving of souls. Many times in the course of its history, voices had been raised calling for a return to its early purity, some from the safety of orthodoxy like St Francis and St Dominic, others from a more exposed position, such as the Cathar preachers, Peter Valdes (c.1140–1217), John Wycliffe (c.1320–1384) and Jan Hus (1369–1415).

At the beginning of the sixteenth century the corruption of the papal court and the sale of indulgences damaged the standing of the pope and the Church to such an extent that the defiance of a German Augustinian monk, Martin Luther (1483–1546), provoked an irreparable split. On 31 October 1517, Luther nailed to the door of Wittenberg Church his ninety-five theses attacking the sale of indulgences and the excessive riches of the Church. This act is considered to be the start of the Reformation.

Almost at once, the reform movement split into various groups: the Lutheran, which followed the principles laid down by the Confession of Augsburg of 1530 — the overriding authority of the Scriptures and the belief that faith alone provided the means to salvation; the Calvinist, inspired by the ideas of John Calvin (1509–1564) and distinguished by moral rigour and a belief in the doctrine of predestination; and the Zwinglian, also based on rigid adherence to the Bible and inspired by the outstanding Zurich preacher, Huldreyth

The Council of Trent
The Council was summoned by Pope Paul III in 1542 and finally closed in 1563, after many sessions during the pontificates of Julius III and Pius IV. It rejected the doctrine of salvation by faith alone, denied that the Holy Scriptures should be open to free interpretation or that they were the sole basis of faith, confirmed papal supremacy, and defined Roman Catholic doctrine.

Luther expounds his theses
When summoned to defend himself before Cardinal Cajetan in 1518, Luther (*left*) refused to abandon his position and two years later was excommunicated. Outlawed by the Emperor Charles V in 1521, he sought refuge in the Castle of Wartburg under the protection of the Elector of Saxony, Frederick III, and worked on his translation of the Bible into German.

John Calvin
Working mainly in Geneva where, in 1541, he established a theocracy, Calvin (*right*) preached the need for a return to primitive Christianity. His doctrines, stressing the sinfulness of man and expounded in the *Institutes of a Christian Religion* (1536), were the basis of Puritanism in the English-speaking world.

Henry VIII
Pope Clement VII's refusal to annul Henry's marriage to Catherine of Aragon was the immediate cause of the Reformation in England. The Act of Supremacy, 1534, made the King Supreme Head of the Church, while the doctrines of the new religion were further defined under Edward VI and Elizabeth I.

Zwingli (1484–1531). In England, what was eventually to be called Anglicanism was established, a movement which owed its rise to Henry VIII's decision to break with the Church of Rome in the 1530s.

The Papacy reacted to these various reform movements by calling the Council of Trent (1545–1563), which resulted in many initiatives for internal reform of the Catholic Church.

In parallel with the disintegration of its religious unity, Europe also witnessed the crumbling of the unity of the Empire and the growth of national monarchies. Charles V, elected Holy Roman Emperor in 1519, ruled over the largest empire since the time of Charlemagne. However, his attempt to create a centralized government soon failed, due to the opposition of the large towns and the unwillingness of the German princes to submit to the authority of the Habsburgs. Moreover, outside the Empire, he became involved in a series of wars with Francis I of France for the mastery of Europe.

Even though these wars, fought mainly in Italy, ended in the defeat of the French and the Peace of Cateau-Cambrésis (1559), the days of the imperial idea were clearly drawing to a close: such a concept could hardly flourish faced with the claims of the single autonomous state and the centrifugal power of the Reformation. In 1556, Charles V abdicated, dividing his empire between his brother, Ferdinand, and his son, Philip II. The latter inherited Spain and its possessions, including Italy, and thus found himself in the front line of defence against the new power now asserting itself in the Mediterranean, the Ottoman Turks.

The Turkish peril
Having conquered the Balkans, the Turks under Suleiman I defeated the army of Louis Jagiello at Mohacs in 1526 (*left*), seizing Hungary and opening the way to Vienna. However, the Ottoman expansion suffered a serious setback on 17 October 1571, when at the Battle of Lepanto (*above*) a Christian fleet commanded by Don John of Austria and composed of ships from Venice, Genoa, Malta, Spain, the Papal States and Savoy, defeated the Turkish navy. It was the last great battle in which both sides used oar-propelled ships.

The "invincible" Armada
Elizabeth I of England (1558–1603) (*near right*) and Philip II of Spain (1556–1598) (*far right*) became strong enemies because of the political and religious rivalry between their two kingdoms. Philip's attempt to invade England in 1588 with a seemingly invincible Armada ended in its destruction (*below*).

Charles V
Ruler of an Empire "on which the sun never set" (including Spain and its overseas colonies, Flanders, and the imperial lands in Austria and Germany), Charles V (*left*) was elected emperor in 1519, at the age of nineteen. He was in charge of a world disrupted by enormous problems — from his rivalry with Francis I of France to his quarrels with Pope Clement VII (which in 1527 led to the sacking of Rome), and from the threatening presence of the Turks, to the Reformation and the wars of religion. Tired of so much conflict, he abdicated in 1556 and spent the last two years of his life in the monastery of Yuste, in Estremadura, visited only by his family, his historians and his couriers.

The Thirty Years' War

Begun in 1618 as a result of the rivalry between the Empire and some of the German princes, and complicated by religious divisions, the Thirty Years' War eventually involved most European powers. In Germany, the princes aimed at political and religious autonomy, based on the principle *cuius regio, eius religio* which had been recognized by the Peace of Augsburg, 1555. Catholic Spain was involved first against the Protestant United Provinces, and later — because of the deep rivalry between the Habsburgs and the Bourbons — against France. For its part, France was intent on weakening the Habsburgs. Denmark under Christian IV and Sweden under Gustavus Adolphus intervened to help the Protestant princes. It was not until 1648 (Treaty of Westphalia) that peace was restored to a devastated Europe.

The Battle of the White Mountain
Fought near Prague on 8 November 1620, this Battle was won by the combined armies of the Catholic League and Spain, commanded by Tilly, who defeated the Protestant forces of Bohemia and the Palatinate, led by Prince Christian I of Anhalt. King Frederick of Bohemia had to abandon Prague, where the remaining Protestants were either persecuted or compelled to convert immediately to Catholicism.

Ferdinand II
Crowned Emperor in 1619, he was a firm supporter of the Counter-Reformation. He died in 1648, shortly before the Peace of Westphalia.

Gustavus Adolphus
King of Sweden from 1611, Gustavus II Adolphus defeated the imperial armies at Lützen (1632), where he was killed in combat.

Wallenstein
One of Ferdinand II's best commanders, Albrecht von Wallenstein (1583–1634) fell under suspicion of treason and was assassinated.

The Peace of Westphalia
With the Peace of Westphalia (*above*, signatures of some of the negotiators), the Empire was broken up into a federation of states and the autonomy of the German princes from imperial control was recognized. France and Sweden were given some territories in Germany, while Switzerland and the United Provinces were recognized as independent.

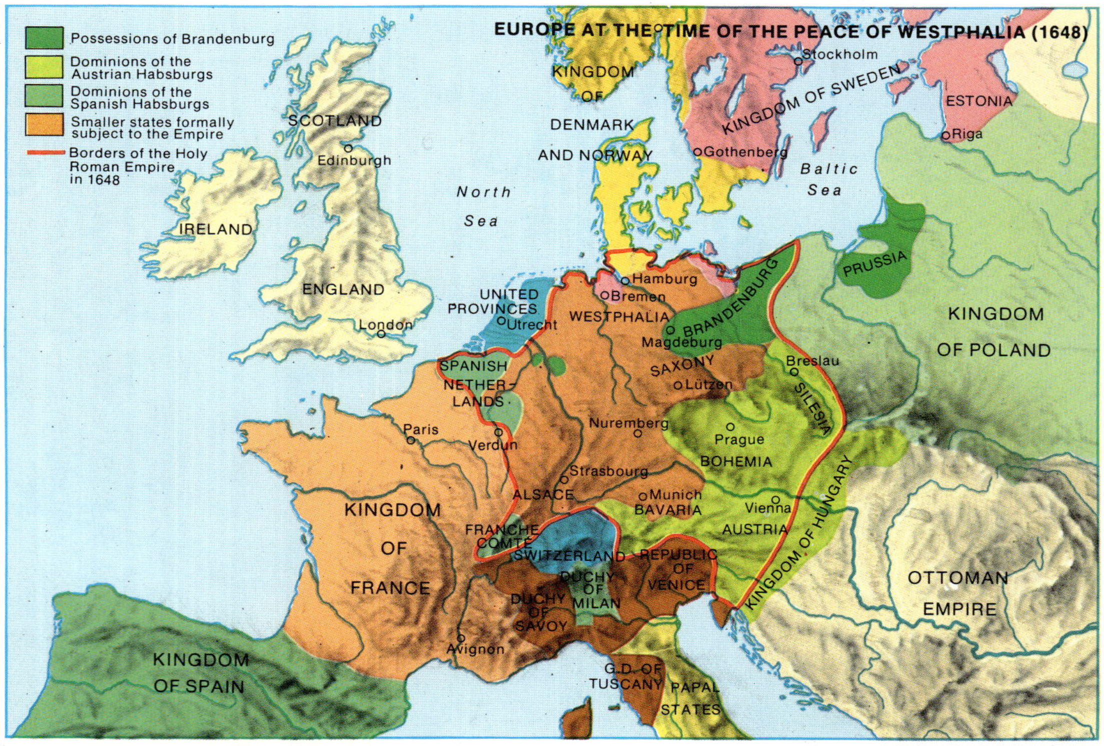

The English in North America
This Dutch map of 1623 (*right*) shows Central and part of North America. Spain had firm control in the areas of Mexico and Florida, while English colonists were settled in Virginia and, further north, in New England (now Massachusetts). Many of the English colonists who landed in America (*far right*) were Puritans and Quakers, who had been persecuted in England for their religious beliefs.

The cradle of democracy
The Palace of Westminster, London, was rebuilt in 1834 on the site of a previous palace which had been given to the House of Lords and House of Commons by King Edward VI in 1547. In the conflicts of English history, especially in the seventeenth century, Parliament has had a role of the greatest importance, whether in the civil wars which ended with the death (on the scaffold) of King Charles I (1649) or, by contrast, in the transfer of the English throne to William III (of Orange) and his wife, Mary (1689).

Charles I
Ascending the throne in 1625, his policies eventually provoked violent opposition. Defeated by Cromwell at Naseby (1645), he was later brought to trial and executed on 30 January 1649.

The seventeenth century

This was a century which saw enormous changes — demographic, economic and scientific. Its populations and economies were faced by epidemics of plague and cholera, while the devastation of the Thirty Years' War and the resulting severe famines led to millions of deaths. At the same time, the agricultural products of America such as maize, potatoes and tobacco were becoming more and more important, while in the field of science, outstanding men such as Kepler, Galileo, Harvey, Newton, Francis Bacon and Descartes were discovering and establishing some of the most fundamental principles.
The Thirty Years' War (1618–1648) dominated the politics of the first half of the century. It saw the Holy Roman Empire and Spain struggling with the German Protestant princes supported by Sweden and France. The Peace of Westphalia, which followed the defeat of the Empire, confirmed the religious settlement made at Augsburg (1555), and put an end to the threat of Habsburg political domination of Europe. Spain had to abandon its claim to the United Provinces, whose independence was recognized. France emerged strengthened from the conflict and, in the second half of the century, entered the splendid age of *le Roi Soleil*, Louis XIV.
In the earlier years, Great Britain was also divided by conflict. The Stuart King James I (1603–1625) and more particularly his son Charles I (1625–1649) embarked upon policies which seemed designed to reduce the prerogatives of Parliament and to eradicate religious minorities, whether Catholic or Puritan. As a result, many such people left for North America: groups of Puritans founded colonies in Massachusetts (1620), and in Connecticut and New Hampshire (1630), while Catholics established themselves in Maryland (1634). Nor did the flow of emigration stop with the outbreak of the English Civil War and the military victories of the Puritan commander, Oliver Cromwell, in and after 1645. Other Puritans inspired by egalitarian ideals, together with members of radical Protestant sects such as the Quakers, continued to leave for the New World where they colonized Rhode Island, New Jersey and Pennsylvania.

Oliver Cromwell
A Member of Parliament and leader of the opposition to the king, he governed as Lord Protector after the king's death until his own death in 1658.

The deserted city
The Diwan-i-Khas, or hall of private audience (*left*), is one of the most famous monuments of Fatehpur Sikri, the city founded in 1569 by Akbar the Great, nephew of Babar as an offering to the gods for the birth of his son. Fatehpur Sikri was the capital of the Mogul Empire until 1584, when Akbar himself decided to move the capital to Lahore. Characteristic of Mogul architecture is the use of red stone, which can also be found at Agra, Delhi and other places.

Asia from the sixteenth to the nineteenth century

From the beginning of the sixteenth century, the ancient civilizations of Asia entered into contact with the great colonial powers. At first, European penetration was confined to the coasts, where a number of flourishing towns were founded: on the shores of India, for instance, after a short-lived Portuguese presence, both the French and the British established themselves, though the latter emerged supreme after the Battle of Plassey (1757). Well before this, the Mogul Dynasty, founded by Babar, a successor of Tamerlane, had taken firm root in the Indian subcontinent. Babar defeated the Sultan of Delhi, Ibrahim Lodi, at the Battle of Panipat (1526) and, despite an interlude in the troubled reign of Humayun, the fortunes of the Moguls were consolidated by a number of great monarchs — Akbar, Jahangir, Shah Jahan and Aurangzeb — who developed a flourishing civilization at their courts. The decline of the dynasty, which after the Treaty of Allahabad (1765) could no longer withstand the power of the British, reached its nadir in 1858, when Bahadur Shah II was deposed.

In 1644, China (where the Ming Dynasty had been in power from 1368) fell into the hands of a new dynasty originating in Manchuria and called the Manchu — or Ch'ing. The dynasty was responsible for redistribution of land and the reconstruction of Peking. However, at the beginning of the nineteenth century it began to decline due to the opposition of various secret societies within China and the penetration of its coasts by Europeans.

The Portuguese in Macao and the British in Canton and Hong Kong pushed for the opening of China to the West: the Opium

Dances and music at court
The Mogul sovereigns, when they were not at war, loved the pleasures of the court where they lived in a festive atmosphere, surrounded by artists.

Ming horseman
After vases, horses and horsemen are among the favourite subjects of artists of the Ming Dynasty.

The splendid capital of the North
Peking, already the capital of China at the time of the Sung, was confirmed in its position as City of the Khans during the Mongol domination. At the beginning of the Ming Dynasty, it passed through a critical period when the court moved to Nanking. Later, in 1409, it became the capital again and it retained this position when the Ch'ing Dynasty rose to power in 1644. In the centre of the oldest zone of Peking lies the Forbidden City (*above*), reserved for the emperor, his family and courtiers.

Ceramics
Highly skilled for many centuries in the manufacture of ceramics, the Chinese perfected its production during the Ming Dynasty (1368–1644), when an imperial factory was founded in Kiangsi. During the subsequent Ch'ing period, ceramics of great artistic value (*below*) were produced: very vivid colours were applied over a layer of enamel and then fired.

Wars, which were more than merely a dispute about this drug, were primarily a test of strength. They showed the superior power of the Europeans who, in 1860, compelled the government in Peking to open several of its ports to foreign ships. The Ch'ing Dynasty was further weakened by the Taiping Rebellion against foreigners (1850–1864), the war against Japan for Korea (1894), and the Boxer Rising, which was harshly repressed by the Europeans. The death knell of the dynasty came in 1911, when a revolution led by Sun Yat-sen led to the foundation of the republic.
In Japan, as well, the main problem in this period was how to resist Western penetration. After 1603 when Ieyasu Tokugawa obtained from the Emperor the title *shogun* for his family, and established his government at Edo (Tokyo), Japan chose a policy of isolation. In 1624, all foreigners were expelled and their ships were only allowed to call at the island of Tsushima.
The extermination of the remaining Catholic communities in 1637 also isolated Japanese thought and culture from external influences and particularly from the West. It was not until 1853, when an American fleet commanded by Admiral Matthew Perry entered the Bay of Edo, that the country reopened its frontiers to the West. Then, from the beginning of 1868, the reforms of the Meiji period initiated the modernization of Japan.

Japan under Tokugawa
After its unification by Hideyoshi Toyotomi at the end of the sixteenth century, Japan was ruled for more than 250 years by *shoguns* of the Tokugawa family (*above*, a *shogun* with some *samurai*, warriors recruited from the noble class). In this period began the persecution of Portuguese missionaries who had originally arrived in Japan in 1542 and worked diligently to spread the Catholic faith in the Orient.

Le Roi Soleil and his splendid palace

Louis XIV came to the throne in 1643 at the age of seven. To begin with, his mother, Anne of Austria, acted as Regent, while Cardinal Mazarin was the dominant statesman of the period. Later, Louis himself took firm control and retained it until his death in 1715. He reorganized the finances, remoulded the army as the instrument of a strong foreign policy, and centralized the administration. In 1661, he began the building of the Palace of Versailles (*left*), sited in a magnificent park.

New industries and economic reform

Under the leadership of the statesman Colbert and the influence of mercantilist ideas, the France of Louis XIV witnessed major industrial development, such as the manufacture of the famous Gobelin tapestries, and the growth of colonial trade. *Left*, making playing cards. This was also a time when better communications began to make trade easier between Europe and the colonies.

ENCYCLOPÉDIE,
OU
DICTIONNAIRE RAISONNÉ
DES SCIENCES,
DES ARTS ET DES MÉTIERS,
PAR UNE SOCIÉTÉ DE GENS DE LETTRES.

Mis en ordre & publié par M. *DIDEROT*, de l'Académie Royale des Sciences & des Belles-Lettres de Prusse; & quant à la PARTIE MATHÉMATIQUE, par M. *D'ALEMBERT*, de l'Académie Royale des Sciences de Paris, de celle de Prusse, & de la Société Royale de Londres.

Tantum series juncturaque pollet,
Tantum de medio sumptis accedit honoris! HORAT.

The Enlightenment

François Marie Arouet, known as Voltaire (1694-1778) (*above*) and Jean-Jacques Rousseau (1712-1778) (*right*) are probably the most important figures of the Enlightenment, the European cultural movement of the eighteenth century that sprang from a belief in human progress and in man's emancipation through reason. The Enlightenment influenced the reformist ideas and policies of many European monarchs, from Frederick II of Prussia to Maria Theresa and Joseph II of Austria.

The *Encyclopaedia*, a major contribution to knowledge

Published between 1751 and 1772 by Denis Diderot and Jean d'Alembert, the *Encyclopaedia* dealt with science, arts and crafts. In accordance with the ideals of the Enlightenment, it sought to bring man's achievements in science and thought to the attention of a wider public. Among the contributors were Montesquieu, Voltaire, Rousseau, Condillac, Condorcet and Buffon.

The Age of Absolutism

The final establishment of the national state during the seventeenth century coincided with the emergence of the ideology of absolutism. According to this theory of kingship, the subject had to render total obedience to the monarch as if he were a god, because the sovereign was seen by man to be the embodiment of divine power. In consequence, the monarch possessed unlimited authority, personified the nation, and could make use of all its resources and wealth — which were, in the final analysis, his own property — and had the complete right to repossess these by means of taxation. In the light of such concepts, a king faced by opposition had not only the right but also the duty to stamp it out.

France was the leading country of Europe at this time, as a result of the shrewd policies of Cardinals Richelieu and Mazarin, and the achievements of Louis XIV. The age of *le Roi Soleil*, seen by some as the embodiment of absolutism, was also remarkable for its advances in the arts and sciences (La Fontaine, Corneille, Racine, Molière, Pascal, Vauban and Descartes). This climate of achievement persisted into the eighteenth century as the Enlightenment.

In England, absolutism reached a crisis with the revolutions that removed Charles I (1649) and James II (1688) from the throne, and led to the eclipse of the Stuarts. Spain, under the last Habsburg Kings, Philip IV and Charles II, continued its decline, but Central and Eastern Europe saw the consolidation of three great powers.

First, Austria succeeded in crushing the Ottoman menace, particularly serious in 1683 when the Turks had reached the gates of Vienna. It then gained the Low Countries and the Milanese from Spain by the Treaties of Utrecht and Rastatt (1713 and 1714), and subsequently enjoyed a period of prosperity under the wise administration of Maria Theresa (1740–1780). Secondly, Prussia under Frederick II greatly increased its territories. Thirdly, Russia was given a modern administrative structure by its Tzar, Peter the Great. By contrast, the Ottoman Empire entered upon an irreversible crisis. The military defeats inflicted upon it by Prince Eugene of Savoy at Buda, Mohacs, Zenta and Peterwardein drew attention to the deep malaise of this heterogeneous state — the incapacity of its despotic sultans, the corruption of its vizirs and court, and the obvious incompetence of its administrators.

Peter the Great and his capital
Peter the Great, Tzar of Russia from 1682 to 1725, supervising (*above*) the building of St Petersburg, the new city founded in 1703. A clever and energetic reformer, Peter tried to give a modern structure to his country, opening government posts to people who were not of noble rank, and forging links between Russia and Europe.

The Turks at the gates of Vienna
After a siege of two months by a Turkish army of more than 200,000 men, commanded by the Grand Vizir Kara Mustapha, Vienna was relieved on 12 September 1683.

The final battle at the Kahlenberg was won by a coalition of Saxon, Austrian, Bavarian and Polish forces commanded by Charles V of Lorraine and John III Sobieski.

Maria Theresa and her enemy, Frederick II
Maria Theresa, the great Empress who, as ruler of Austria, Hungary and Bohemia from 1740 to 1780, introduced important reforms. She frequently found herself confronted by Frederick II King of Prussia from 1740 to 1786 (*below*, on horseback in heroic pose as a military leader). The two monarchs were enemies in both the War of the Austrian Succession and in the Seven Years' War, conflicts in which Frederick demonstrated his military genius to the full, especially in winning the historic battles of Rossbach and Leuthen

The American Revolution

After the restoration of the monarchy (1660), England had progressively reduced the autonomy of its twelve colonies (thirteen from 1733) on the Atlantic coast of North America. Following this, many other factors contributed to an increasingly tense relationship: the imposition of higher taxes, the English monopoly on maritime trade, the rules designed to force the colonies to exchange their raw materials only with England's manufactured goods.

In 1765 the levying of a new tax, the Stamp Duty, was the final straw: popular discontent erupted in a welter of violent riots which were ruthlessly put down by British troops.

Spurred on by these events, in 1774, the representatives of the colonies met at Philadelphia and set up a Continental Congress that claimed a series of rights and liberties, among which was the principle of no taxation without representation — the demand that taxes should not be imposed without the consent of representatives of the American colonists. In the following year hostilities broke out between British forces and the American army commanded by General George Washington who succeeded in maintaining a strong army and in preserving its morale throughout the Revolution. In 1776, while the conflict was raging, the Congress proclaimed the establishment of the United States of America and approved the Declaration of Independence. After various indecisive battles when the British seemed to be winning, the Americans gained an important victory at Saratoga (1777); and in the following year the United States formed alliances with France, which wanted to take revenge on Britain for the humiliation suffered during the Seven Years' War, and with Spain, which was bound to France by an agreement. After fierce fighting in which the British often took the offensive, the conflict finally ended with the American victory at Yorktown (1781). In 1783, the Treaty of Paris ratified the independence of the United States of America.

The birth of the United States
Events and protagonists in the struggle for American independence: the massacre at Boston (*above*) on 5 March 1770, during the first violent clashes between colonists and British troops, when the latter opened fire on the rebels; Franklin, Adams and Jefferson (*left*) drafting the Declaration of Independence, later signed by representatives of the thirteen colonies who gathered in the Congress on 4 July 1776 (this is the event which is still commemorated by Americans each year on 4 July — Independence Day); the first lines of the Declaration (*right*); the Battle of Princeton (*below right*) which ended in a British defeat (1777).

IN CONGRESS. July 4. 1776.
The unanimous Declaration of the thirteen united States of America

The first President of the United States
George Washington (*below*), the commander of the American forces against the British. Unanimously elected President of the United States on 4 March 1789, he led his country until 1796, when Thomas Jefferson was chosen to succeed him.

The Industrial Revolution

Coal, looms, self-propelled vehicles, trains
Coal mining in Great Britain (*above*), at the beginning of the eighteenth century: coal was fundamental to early industrialization since it fuelled the steam engines and provided power for the factories. The textile industry (*below left*, an eighteenth-century power loom) was the first to feel the effects of the introduction of machinery. At the same time, work on self-propelled vehicles (*below right*, Cougnot's steam engine) and locomotives led to the building of the first railway lines (*at the foot*, a train used on the Liverpool–Manchester line in 1832).

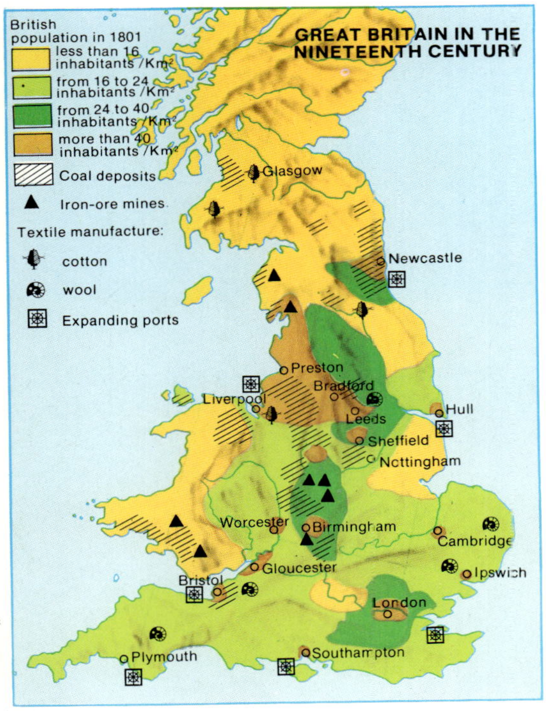

Originating in Great Britain as a consequence of a series of technological innovations and improvements and the substitution of machines in place of human labour, the transformation of industry was so great that it has frequently been called a revolution. Its traditional starting date is 1770, the year in which the spinning jenny (pioneered by James Hargreaves six years earlier and perfected by Richard Arkwright) came into use. Further advances were made with Samuel Crompton's spinning mule (1779), Edmund Cartwright's power loom (1785), the discoveries of Abraham Darby in the production of cast iron, and James Watt's radical improvements to the steam engine. Parallel with the introduction of new machinery came a reorganization of working methods, with the rise of the factory and the first steps towards division of labour. As a result, a new class of wage worker emerged, recruited from farm labourers and domestic servants, as well as a new group of capitalists who relentlessly expanded both international and home trade.

The storming of the Bastille
The dismissal of the Minister Necker, and the concentration of troops in the suburbs of Paris — seemingly designed to intimidate the Third Estate which had met (despite the king's prohibition) in the Jeu de Paume and formed the National Assembly — heightened discontent in the capital. On 14 July 1789, Parisians took to the streets and converged on the Bastille but, when they asked for weapons, the governor of the fortress gave orders to fire on them. Despite losses, the crowds assaulted the Bastille and destroyed it (*left*).

The *Assignats*
On 2 November 1789, to ease the financial position, the Constituent Assembly confiscated the property of the Church in exchange for *assignats (above)*, notes issued as paper currency which circulated until 1796.

The French Revolution

The French Revolution was to mark the end of absolutism and feudal rights, and the rise to power of the new bourgeosie. Despite these momentous consequences, the Revolution began quietly with the meeting of the Estates General on 5 May, and then erupted violently on 14 July, when the populace of Paris stormed the Bastille.

The first phase started with the establishment of the National Constitutent Assembly, the *Constituante*, which on 26 August issued the Declaration of the Rights of Man. This Assembly ruled France for the next two years, introducing reforms in every field, from the administration of justice to the abolition of aristocratic privileges, and from reform of the machinery of state to reorganization of the army. On 1 October 1791, it was succeeded by the Legislative Assembly, in which there was significant representation of the bourgeoisie. This new body was the scene of constant feuding between the Girondists, the Cordeliers and the Jacobins; while the Parisians further complicated the situation by storming the Tuileries on 10 August 1792 and imprisoning the royal family. By this time, France was at war with a coalition of her neighbours and on 20 September gained a decisive victory over the Prussians at Valmy.

This began the second phase of the Revolution when the Legislative Assembly was replaced by the Convention, dominated by Robespierre, Danton and Marat: on 22 September, it abolished the monarchy and proclaimed a republic. The final phase, when France was surrounded and threatened by its enemies, was marked by the "Reign of Terror" which lasted from 5 September 1793 until Robespierre's arrest on 9 Thermidor (27 July 1794): during this period thousands of people, among them the King, Louis XVI, and his wife, Marie Antoinette, were guillotined.

The King and Queen
Louis XVI (*left*), born in 1754, ascended the throne in 1774. He has been characterized by historians as a weak and hesitant man, dominated by his wife, Marie Antoinette of Austria (*right*), who married him in 1770, and whose arrogance and extravagance made her unpopular in France. As a consequence of the King's attempt to escape on 20-21 June 1791, when he was stopped at Varennes, he came to be regarded as a traitor and in August 1792, after the storming of the Tuileries, the Royal Family was imprisoned. The King was guillotined on 21 January 1793, and the Queen on 16 October, despite attempts to save their lives.

The Incorruptible
Maximilien de Robespierre (*above*), born in Arras in 1758, became one of the most prominent revolutionary figures during the Convention. He was a lawyer, a leading Jacobin — a member of the group which advocated the most radical changes — and a member of the Committee of Public Safety. Originator of the Terror, he and ten colleagues ruled France from July 1793 until 9 Thermidor (corresponding to 27 July in the old calendar) 1794, when he was arrested at the Hotel de Ville in Paris, together with his brother, Augustine, and his friends Saint-Just, Couthon and Le Bas. He was guillotined on the following day.

The days of the Terror

An execution in the Place de la Révolution in Paris during the Terror, when about 50,000 people were guillotined. The Jacobins' rule of terror was made possible by their excellent organization, compensating for relatively low membership.
The revolutionaries also brutally repressed peasant risings in the Vendée in support of the monarchy (*right*), although the region was only finally pacified in 1796.

The Declaration of the Rights of Man

The inspiring principles of the Declaration of the Rights of Man and of the Citizen, proclaimed on 26 August 1789 by the National Constituent Assembly, were confirmed by the Convention in 1793. Despite the division of the latter's 749 members into three rival factions — the Girondists who were enlightened bourgeoisie, the ultra-revolutionary "mountain" or Jacobins, and the "plain" or "morass" who had no clear policy — the Convention enacted a remarkable and wide-ranging programme. Among its achievements were the introduction of the decimal system, and the promulgation of the first regulations controlling education which was made compulsory and free at primary and secondary level.

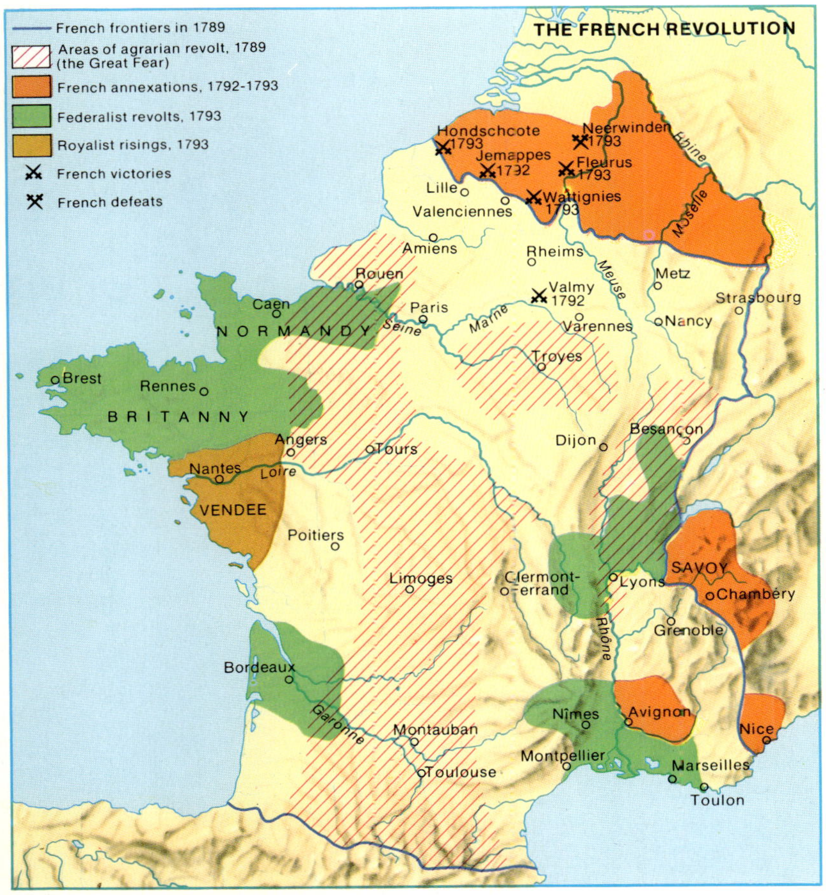

CHRONOLOGY

1789 5 May Convocation of Estates General. 17–20 June The Third Estate announced the establishment of the National Assembly and swore "not to separate until a constitution has been devised". 9 July Proclamation of National Constituent Assembly. 14 July Storming of the Bastille. 4 Aug Abolition of feudal privileges. 26 Aug Declaration of the Rights of Man.
1790 12 July Civil constitution of the clergy.
1791 17 March Abolition of guilds and monopolies. 20 June King stopped at Varennes. 27 Aug Declaration of Pillnitz by European monarchs to ally against France. 4 Sept Proclamation of new constitution. 1 Oct The Legislative Asembly succeeded the Constituent.
1792 20 April France declared war on Austria and Prussia. 20 June First storming of Tuileries. 10 Aug Second storming of Tuileries; Royal Family imprisoned. 2–7 Sept September Massacres ordered by revolutionary tribunal. Formation of the Convention. 20 Sept Abolition of monarchy. 22 Sept Proclamation of republic. 6 Nov Battle of Jemappes.
1793 21 Jan Execution of Louis XVI. 1 Feb First coalition against France. 10 March Beginning of risings in the Vendée. 2 June Parisians besieged the Convention. 24 June The "mountain" had the Constitution of Year 1 approved. 13 July Assassination of Marat. 5 Sept Beginning of Terror. 5 Oct Introduction of revolutionary calendar. 16 Oct Execution of Marie Antoinette.
1794 5 April Danton and Desmoulins guillotined. 26 June Battle of Fleurus. 27 July Robespierre arrested.

France victorious

The Battle of Fleurus on 26 June 1794 (*below*), when the French, under Jourdain, defeated the Austrians, was yet another glorious victory for the national army of volunteers, following its successes at Valmy and Jemappes (20 September and 6 November 1792).

Napoleon, First Consul
After the fall of the Directory through the *coup d'état* of 18–19 Brumaire (9–10 November) 1799, in which Napoleon's brother Lucien played an important role, three provisional consuls were appointed — Napoleon, Siéyès and Ducos. A new constitution, approved in February 1800, gave Napoleon the title of First Consul for ten years. *Left*, the imperial eagle which was mounted on the banners of Napoleon's army and carried in all his campaigns.

Napoleon

"I have always been alone among people ... the world on one side and I on the other," Napoleon Bonaparte wrote in his *Memoirs*.
The rise to power of the future Emperor of the French was as dazzling as his victories on the battlefield, and his political and military achievements supported each other. His successful campaign in Italy in 1796–1797, and in Egypt in 1798, consolidated the reputation that the young general had gained saving the Directory from the Parisian rising of 13 Vendémiaire (5 October) 1795. Then, four years later, when the Directory was overthrown by the *coup d'état* of 18–19 Brumaire (9–10 November) 1799, Napoleon took part in the triumvirate of consuls who came to rule France. In the following year, further military success in Italy, especially at Marengo, secured for him the dominant position in French politics and, in 1802, he was appointed consul for life. Recognizing the need for reconstruction in a state still far from stable after the turmoil of the Revolution, he introduced a new legal code, signed a concordat with Pope Pius VII making peace with the Church, established an efficient bureaucracy, and reorganized taxation and finance. Finally, he made himself Emperor.
However, he wanted to dominate Europe as well as France, and to compel his neighbours to become his vassals. He therefore embarked upon a whole series of wars: against Austria and Prussia in 1805, the year of Austerlitz (but also of the British naval victory under Nelson at Trafalgar); against Russia and Prussia in 1806–1807, with his victories at Jena, Auerstedt and Friedland; against Britain in Spain, in the long and weary campaign that lasted from 1808 to 1813 and established the reputations of the Duke of Wellington and his soldiers; against Austria again in 1809, the year of Wagram; and against Russia in 1812, in the expedition that turned to tragedy and humiliation for him. This disaster in the snows of Russia, together with the crushing defeats at Leipzig (1813) and Waterloo (18 June 1815), exploded the myth of his invincibility and provoked the question: "Was it real glory?"

CHRONOLOGY

1795 5 October (13 Vendémiaire) Napoleon took part in the repression of a rising in Paris.

1796 7 March He married Josephine de Beauharnais. April He started the first campaign in Italy.

1798 21 July Battle of the Pyramids. 1 Aug Naval Battle of the Nile

1799 *Coup d'état* of 18–19 Brumaire (9–10 Nov).

1800 Second campaign in Italy and victory at Marengo (14 June).

1801 15 July Concordat with Pius VII.

1804 2 Dec Coronation in Notre-Dame.

1805 Battles of Ulm (20 Oct). Trafalgar (21 Oct) and Austerlitz (2 Dec).

1806 14 Oct Battles of Jena and Auerstedt.

1807 8 Feb Battle of Eylau. 14 June Battle of Friedland. 25 June Meeting at Tilsit.

1808 30 Aug Battle of Sintra. 27 Sept to 14 Oct Meeting at Erfurt.

1809 22 May Battles of Aspern and Essling. 5 July Battle of Wagram.

1810 1 April Marriage with Marie Louise of Austria.

1811 20 March Birth of his son, the King of Rome.

1812 24 June Invasion of Russia. 7 Sept Battle of Borodino. 14 Sept The French in Moscow. 19 Oct Beginning of the retreat. 25 Dec Battle of Berezina.

1813 2 May Battle of Lützen. 20 May Battle of Bautzen. 21 June Battle of Vitoria. 16 Oct Battle of Leipzig.

1814 4 April Abdication in favour of his son.

1815 1 March Landing at Golfe-Juan. 16 June Battle of Ligny. 18 June Battle of Waterloo. 21 June Second Abdication

"Forty centuries look down upon you"
It is with these words that Napoleon is said to have inspired his soldiers before the Battle of the Pyramids, 21 July 1798 (*left*). However, the campaign in Egypt, which was intended to cut Britain's communications with India and to obtain its recognition of the French territorial gains, did not succeed, because the French fleet was destroyed by Nelson in the Battle of the Nile on 1 August. Napoleon handed over command of the expedition to Kléber, and returned to France.

The solemn coronation
The official coronation of Napoleon Bonaparte as Emperor of the French took place in Paris on 2 December 1804, in Notre-Dame, in the presence of Pope Pius VII (*right*). After a plebiscite, and by a unanimous decision of the Senate, the consulate was to become a hereditary monarchy. In May 1804 the Empire was officially proclaimed: Napoleon preferred the idea of an empire to that of a kingdom, popularly connected with the fallen Bourbon Dynasty. Napoleon I crowned himself, to show that he had gained the title solely through his own merit, although formally it was the Senate of the French Republic who had appointed him.

The Fourth Coalition
From 1805 onwards Napoleon was engaged in a long series of wars, with the result that from time to time various of the European states formed coalitions against France. After crushing the Third Coalition at Austerlitz (2 December 1805), Napoleon defeated Prussia at Jena and Auerstedt (14 October 1806) and its ally Russia, which fought back strongly at Eylau on 8 February 1807 (*above*), but was finally defeated at Friedland on 14 June. Tzar Alexander I and the French Emperor met at Tilsit on 25 June. The "Emperor of the East" and the "Emperor of the West", having first discussed partition of Turkey, signed a pact of friendship.

The Battle of Borodino, the last illusion
The victory of Borodino on 7 September 1812, opened to Napoleon the route to Moscow which the French army then occupied a week later. The inhabitants fled to the countryside, leaving the Russian capital to be plundered and burned. However, the shortage of food and the onset of winter compelled Napoloen to give orders on 19 October for the retreat which was to result in tragedy for his veterans.

Waterloo, the end
Defeated at Leipzig (16 October 1813) and forced to abdicate, Napoleon retired to Elba. But he played his last card in the spring of 1815, when he resumed power for a hundred days. After the decisive defeat at Waterloo (*right*), he was deported (*below*) to the Atlantic island of St Helena, where he died on 21 March 1821, as a prisoner of war.

The July Revolution in France

The authoritarianism of Charles X led to an insurrection in Paris on 27–29 July 1830. The king abdicated and Louis Philippe, Duke of Orleans (*left*), was proclaimed "King of the French".

The independence of Greece

The Battle of Navarino (20 October 1827), during which the combined naval forces of Russia, Britain and France defeated the Turkish fleet (*right*), was a decisive event in the long struggle, begun in 1822, for Greek independence.

Paris in revolt

In 1848, the wind of of revolution blew in many capitals. In Paris (*above*, soldiers near the Seine), the serious disorders of 21 February, combined with economic discontent, led to further demonstrations. These prompted King Louis Philippe, a weak and unpopular monarch who had come to the throne in 1530, to leave France and, soon afterwards, a government on radical lines was set up, followed by the proclamation of the Second Republic.

The "Five Days" of Milan

On 18 March 1848, sparked off by news of the revolution in Vienna, Milan rebelled against Austrian rule (*left*). After fierce fighting in many parts of the city, the Austrian troops, commanded by Josef Radetzky, veteran of the Turkish and Napoleonic wars, were forced to retreat. Even Prussia was affected by the revolutions: in Berlin (*right*, the rising of 18–19 March) Frederick William IV promised to support the cause of German unification, while a Parliament was elected and opened in Frankfurt on 18 May.

The Liberal Revolutions

In Europe, while rationalism, liberalism and romanticism were shaping a new world, and the impact of the Industrial Revolution was causing sweeping changes in society, the Congress of Vienna (1815) had attempted, on a more narrowly political level and with considerable success, to put the clock back and restore the old order. Prussia, Austria and Russia had combined to help one another in the repression of liberal movements, while in France Louis XVIII promulgated laws against liberals and radicals, even if he kept within the constitution which he himself had consented to in 1814. Often, demands for reform could only be halted by means of fierce repression (as in Spain and Naples in 1820), but in Greece the revolutionaries were successful and the country finally gained independence in 1829.

In 1830, another wave of uprisings shattered Europe: in France, the July Revolution brought Louis Philippe to the throne; in Poland and the Duchies of Modena and Parma, the governments were challenged; and in Belgium, independence was achieved.

In Britain, the 1830s saw the implementation of major reforms by the Whig governments; but in many other parts of Europe there was a renewal of strong repression. However, 1848 — "the year of revolutions" — brought political turmoil.

The spark which lit the fuse went off in Italy, where the election of Pope Pius IX, known for his mildly liberal views, kindled the hopes of the patriotic movement. A number of risings prompted Ferdinand II of Naples, Charles Albert of Savoy and the Pope himself, to grant constitutions to their states.

In France, an insurrection in Paris induced Louis Philippe to go into exile, and led to the installation of a radical republican government, soon to be supplanted by Napoleon III.

Vienna also felt the wind of revolutions: Metternich had to flee to London, and the Emperor Ferdinand escaped to Innsbruck. In Berlin, Frederick William IV was almost dethroned. At the same time, the Italian cities of Milan and Venice rebelled against their Austrian masters, while in April 1849, even the Hungary of Kossuth began fighting for independence.

Napoleon III
In 1870, Napoleon III, Emperor of France (*right*), declared war on the Prussia of Bismarck (*below*), but capitulated after the defeat at Sedan and the siege of Paris (*above*). The Prussian victory was a decisive event in the unification of Germany. At the palace of Versailles, on 18 January 1871 William I was crowned Emperor of Germany.

The unification of Italy
The expedition of Garibaldi and the Thousand sailed from Quarto, near Genoa, on 5 May 1860 (*below*), and led to the freeing of the Kingdom of The Sicilies from Bourbon rule. Following plebiscites there, in the Marches and in Umbria, the Kingdom of Italy was proclaimed on 17 March 1861, and Victor Emmanuel became King. Later, the annexation of Venice (1866) and Rome (1870) virtually completed the unification.

The Crimean War
Russian policies in the Balkans triggered off the Crimean War (1854–1856). Turkey received support from Britain, France and Piedmont, whose Prime Minister, Cavour (*left*), used the war to focus attention on the Italian question. *Below*, Italian troops.

The expansion of the United States

The legendary Alamo
The Franciscan mission of Alamo where (on 6 March 1836) 187 Americans including the famous Davy Crockett lost their lives fighting against a more numerous Mexican force. After Texas's independence and Mexico's refusal to acknowledge the River Grande as the southern frontier of this state, a war broke out between the USA and Mexico (1846–1848). Mexico lost and had to give up New Mexico and Arizona.

The thirteen colonies, which had declared their independence on 4 July 1776 and won the war against Britain, formed the nucleus of the United States of America, which soon grew in both size and strength: Vermont (1791), Kentucky (1792), Tennessee (1796) and Ohio (1803) all joined the Union, while Louisiana was purchased from Napoleon. In 1812, the USA's independence was again at risk because of a new, two-year war with the British, but another phase of expansion began soon afterwards. Thousands of migrants, more than a quarter of a million a year, flooded in from Europe: first came Anglo-Saxons and Scandinavians, then Germans and Irish — the latter driven abroad by the terrible famine of 1846 — and finally Italians and Slavs. For all these people there were various reasons for individual and collective decisions to emigrate: poverty at home combined with tales of abundance and opportunity available in America, the example of relatives and, in many instances, religious persecution. Initially, they settled along the Atlantic coast; later, they followed the pioneers westwards in search of land and fortune. This period was marked by long and violent wars with the Indians, who were gradually torn from their land. In the meantime, Florida was purchased from Spain in 1819, and Texas, which had unilaterally declared its independence from Mexico, was admitted to the Union in 1845. This, and the pioneers' advance, led to a war with Mexico which brought further territorial gains to the Union. With the admission of California in 1850, where the Gold Rush had started in the previous year, the USA now stretched from the Atlantic to the Pacific.

However, this huge expansion, the increasing industrialization of the Atlantic coast states, and the development in the west of agriculture (previously a monopoly of the "Old South"), were shattering the old political balances. The crisis erupted over the problem of slavery, aggravated by the election of the abolitionist Lincoln as President. South Carolina's example in breaking away from the Union on 20 December 1860 was followed by six other southern states (Texas, Georgia, Louisiana, Florida, Mississippi and Alabama), later joined by Tennessee, Arkansas, North Carolina and Virginia. The resulting Civil War was between two unequal forces: the population of the South, the Confederates, was only 8,700,000 (including 3,500,000 slaves) as against 22,700,000 in the North, the Federal side. The Northern armies' victory at Vicksburg and Gettysburg in 1863 proved a decisive turning-point. After four years of fierce fighting, the Confederates had to surrender and, with the abolition of slavery, a new period of expansion began.

The conquest of the West
As early as 13 July 1787, the Union had declared that the rich, virgin lands of the West were its own property, and slavery was forbidden there. Each piece of land was to belong to the colonists who, having settled on it, were to register their title to it and pay the Treasury a modest sum (usually a dollar for each acre). The pioneers carried all their possessions with them when they set out to start a new life in the West. The journey was long and hard and many of them suffered bitter disappointment as well as extreme poverty on arrival. They travelled in large wagons (*left*), and had to face the resistance of the Indian tribes of the plains (among others, the Sioux, Choctaw, Cherokee, Cheyenne), who led a nomadic life hunting bison (*right*, a bison's skin painted with figures of Indian warriors). As the colonists advanced westwards, so did the railways: on 10 May 1869, at Promontory Point, Utah, the railway lines of the Union Pacific and Central Pacific met (*left*), allowing trains to cross the continent from one ocean to the other.

Auction sale of slaves
Bought and sold as objects, often to be used as agricultural tools, the black slaves (*above*) were exploited as free labour in the big farms of the South: their white masters had the power of life and death over them. *Below*, Ulysses S. Grant, commander of the Northern army and President of the USA from 1869 to 1877.

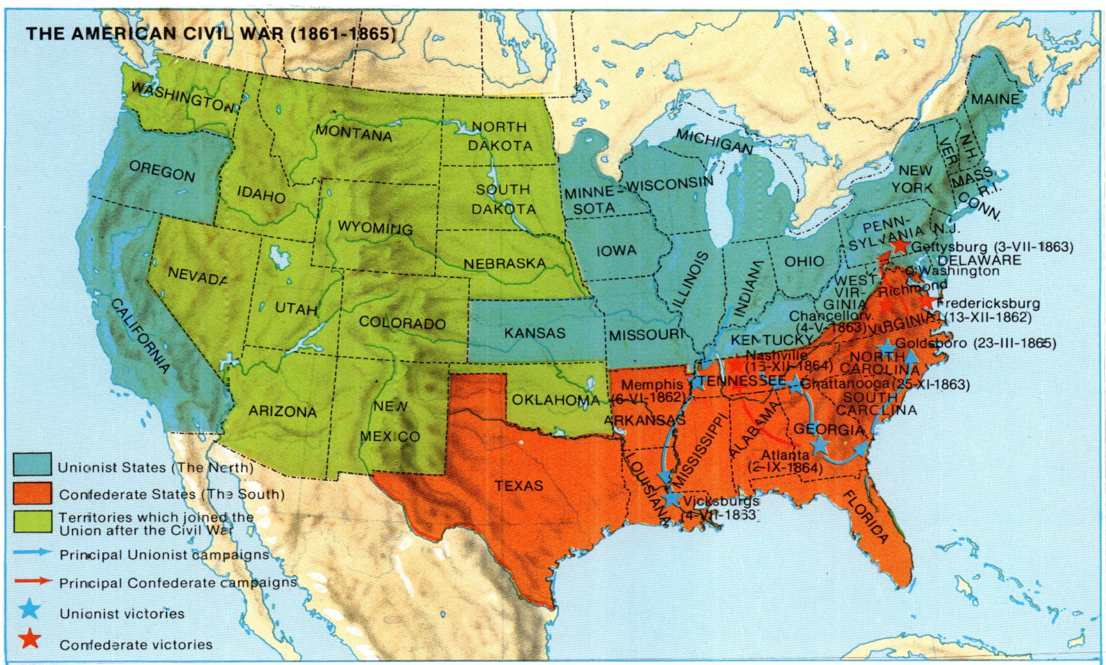

CHRONOLOGY

1860 20 Dec South Carolina seceded from the Union.
1861 4 Feb Formation in Montgomery of the Confederate States of America and (9 April) election of its President, Jefferson Davis. 12–13 April Confederate victory at Fort Sumter. 15 April Lincoln's proclamation against the insurrection of the Southern states. 19 April Naval blockade of the Confederate coast. 21 April Confederate victory at Bull Run, Virginia.
1862 7 April Costly Northern victory at Shiloh, Tennessee. 26 June to 1 July Battle for Richmond, Virginia. 29 Aug Second Battle of Bull Run. 17 Sept Battle of Antietam Creek. 13 Dec Southern victory at Fredericksburg.
1863 4 May Confederate victory at Chancellorsville. 3 July Northern victory at Gettysburg. 4 July Northern victory at Vicksburg.
1864 5 Aug Northern naval victory at Mobile. 2 Sept Northern occupation of Atlanta, Georgia. 19 Oct victory of the North at Cedar Creek. 21 Dec Northern forces entered Savannah, Georgia.
1865 31 Jan The Thirteenth Amendment to the Constitution was passed, abolishing slavery. 1 April Northern victory at Five Forks. 3 April Northern forces occupied Richmond. 9 April Lee surrendered at Appomattox.

Lincoln, the abolitionist
Campaign poster for the presidential election of 1864 (*above*), in which Lincoln was re-elected by a large majority. On 16 April, a few days after the victory of the North, he was assassinated by a fanatical Southerner. *Below*, Jefferson Davis, President of the Confederation.

A fratricidal war
The Battle of Franklin in Tennessee (*below*) was fought on 30 November 1864. The total death toll for both sides in the Civil War was over 600,000.

The surrender of the Old South
General Robert E. Lee (*below*), commander of the Confederate army, signing the surrender at Grant, Virginia, on 9 April 1865.

The shortest route to the East
The opening of the Suez Canal on 17 November 1867, in the presence of the Empress Eugénie (wife of Napoleon III) greatly shortened the journey to the East by sea. At that time, the voyage through the Canal, from Port Said to Suez, a distance of just over 160 kilometres (100 miles) took approximately forty-nine hours, but this was nothing compared with the journey round the Cape.

Imperialism and colonialism

After the first stage of colonization, which had followed the geographical discoveries in the fifteenth and sixteenth centuries, the European colonial powers developed a new imperialistic thirst in the course of the nineteenth century. They became particularly attracted to the new territories that were being explored in the heart of Africa. Great Britain took the lion's share and succeeded, through shrewd expansionism, in building an empire "from Cairo to the Cape". France pushed its territories southwards, from its possessions in Algeria, Tunisia and Morocco, and overran most of equatorial Africa, but had to give way to Britain's supremacy (Fashoda Crisis, September 1898) and abandon its ambition of securing a whole strip of land from the Atlantic to Djibouti. Other European powers were left with merely the crumbs: Germany occupied South West Africa, Togo and Cameroon; Italy took Eritrea and Libya, but had to give up its attempt to subjugate Ethiopia (then known to Europeans by the name of Abyssinia) after its crushing defeat at Aduwa in 1896; Portugal obtained Angola and Mozambique.

Elsewhere, Spain and Portugal had lost their colonies in Latin America, where a number of independent states had emerged. In Asia, Britain was predominant, having possession of India, Burma and Malaya, while France had to be content with Indo-China, and the Netherlands preserved its supremacy in Indonesia.

While the European powers adopted different methods to rule their various territories in this period, they nevertheless had a common purpose — the constant, even ruthless, exploitation of the resources of their colonies, without giving the local populations any real advantages in return.

The colonization of Africa
During Queen Victoria's long reign (1837–1901), Great Britain became the most powerful of the colonial powers. In Africa, it faced strong resistance from the indigenous populations, especially the Ashanti (who lived in the region of modern Ghana) the Zulus (of Natal), as well as from Boer colonists. *Right*, an episode in the Boer War (1899–1902), showing the colonists attacking an armoured train. The French were also colonizing Africa. *Left*, French troops under Colonel Bonnier entering Timbukto on 10 January 1895.

The Japanese defeat of Russia

An episode in the war between Russia and Japan (1904–1905), showing a naval battle off the Korean coast. The war, starting with the surprise Japanese attack on the Russian naval base at Port Arthur, ended in defeat for Russia after the already weakened fleet of the Tzar was completely destroyed in the Battle of Tsushima (27–28 May 1905).

The Boxer Rising

At the beginning of the twentieth century China was shaken by an anti-Western revolt, organized by the followers of the xenophobic Boxer movement. In Tientsin, Shanghai and especially in Peking, European legations and residential districts were attacked. Only the presence of large contingents of Western troops prevented a massacre of all these foreigners. In Peking, the diplomatic quarter withstood continuous assaults by the Boxers for fifty-five days, from 20 June to 14 August 1900, while the Empress Tsuki and the Chinese government watched helplessly. An international expeditionary force was then sent in, the Europeans were freed, and the revolt was bloodily suppressed.

The Mexican Revolution

Between 1876 and 1910, Mexico underwent rapid economic development, supported by foreign investment. However, this brought wealth to only one part of the population and, in 1910, the peasants revolted under the leadership of Emiliano Zapata and Pancho Villa (*right*), who demanded (among other reforms) the distribution of land among the peasants. There were many fierce clashes with the conservatives until, in 1917, under Carranza's government, a more progressive constitution was introduced, granting agricultural reforms and limiting the power of the Church.

The First World War

The First World War was largely the product of the long-existing tension between Russia and Austria-Hungary, both impatient to extend their control over the Balkans.

It started on 28 July 1914, when Austria-Hungary declared war on Serbia and, within only a few days, the conflict had spread to Germany, the ally of Austria, and on the other side, to Russia, France and Britain, who supported Serbia.

After the Germans' attempt to outflank the French in order to reach the Channel and Paris, an attempt which failed with their defeat near the Marne, the conflict became one fought in the trenches — a stalemate that caused massive bloodshed (by the end of the war the estimated number of deaths was 8,209,000 in the armed forces and 5,522,000 among the civilian populations, not counting over twenty-one million soldiers wounded. In 1914, the Russians attacked in Galicia, but suffered severe losses against the Germans at Tannenberg and near the Masurian Lakes; Turkey joined in on Austria and Germany's side, while Japan allied itself with France and Britain. In the following year, both Bulgaria and Italy entered the war: the former with Austria, the latter against. In May 1915, the British liner *Lusitania* was torpedoed by a German submarine: 1,200 people, 140 of them American, drowned, leading to angry protests from the USA.

In 1916, both sides launched massive attacks, but none proved to be decisive: the Germans struck at Verdun; the Austrians in northern Italy *(Strafexpedition)*; the French counter-attacked near the Somme; the Russian Brusilov tried to break through the German line in Poland; the Italians gained a short-lived victory capturing Gorizia.

In 1917, on 7 April, the entry of the USA into the war marked the turn of the tide. Since February of that year, the Eastern front had been seriously weakened as a consequence of the Revolution in Russia; Germany and Austria had therefore been able to move many troops to the Western front, where Germany attacked again near the Somme and Verdun, and troops of both countries inflicted great losses on the Italians at Caporetto in October, crushing their defences, and pushing them back as far as the River Piave.

In 1918, after Russia's withdrawal from the war was counter-balanced by the USA's decisive intervention, Germany and Austria-Hungary, shattered by deep crises at home and unable to withstand renewed attacks by the Allies that autumn, asked for an armistice.

The assassination at Sarajevo
On 28 June 1914, in Sarajevo, the capital of Bosnia-Herzegovina,a Bosnian nationalist, Gavrilo Princip, shot the Archduke Francis Ferdinand, heir to the throne of Austria-Hungary (*above*). In consequence, Austria sent Serbia an ultimatum which plunged Europe into the First World War which was to continue until 1918.

Francis Joseph
The old Emperor of Austria-Hungary (*above*) died in November 1916, after a reign of sixty-eight years. He was succeeded by his grand-nephew Charles, who abdicated in November 1918, after the defeat of his empire and its allies.

The Kaiser
William II, Emperor of Germany from 1888 to 1918 (*above*), declared war on Russia and France in August 1914. After the defeat and the proclamation of the Weimar Republic, he abdicated and went into exile in the Netherlands.

The Allies
George V (*left*), King of England from 1910 to 1936. Victor Emmanuel III (*above*), King of Italy from 1900 to 1946. General Joffre (*right*), Commander of the French army in 1914. Russia also formed part of this alliance.

The Russian offensive
Wartime painting (*above*) showing the successful Russian offensive in Galicia against the Austrians in the early months of the war, in September 1914. This led on to the victory at Lemberg.

The US President
In 1918, Woodrow Wilson (*above*) enunciated his peace proposals, the Fourteen Points.

The Piave: resist or die
Painting of the fighting at the River Piave (*below*), where the Italian army, led by General Diaz, held the line in November and December 1917, halting the Austrian advance begun at the Battle of Caporetto.

CHRONOLOGY

1914 28 June Assassination of Archduke Francis Ferdinand at Sarajevo. 28 July Austria declared war on Serbia. 1 Aug Germany declared war on Russia, France (3 Aug) and Britain (4 Aug). 5 Aug German invasion of Belgium and France. 26-29 Aug German victories over the Russians at Tannenberg and at the Masurian Lakes. 6-13 Sept French victory on the Marne. 29 Oct Turkey entered the conflict on Germany's side.

1915 4-22 Feb German victory at the Masurian Lakes. 25 April The Allies landed at Gallipoli. 26 April Italy signed the Treaty of London. 7 May Sinking of the British merchant liner *Lusitania*. 24 May Italy entered the War against Austria. 5 Oct The Allies landed at Salonika in southern Greece. 14 Oct Bulgaria sided with Germany.

1916 21 Feb Beginning of the Battle of Verdun. 31 May Naval Battle of Jutland. 1 July Beginning of Battle of the Somme. 9 Aug The Italians took Gorizia. 26 Aug Italy declared war on Germany. 27 Aug Romania declared war on Austria. 5 Nov Proclamation of the restored Kingdom of Poland.

1917 8 Feb Kaiser William II's declaration of unlimited submarine warfare. 11 March The British entered Baghdad. 15 March Abdication of Tzar Nicholas II. 7 April The USA entered the war. 16 April French offensive on the Chemin-des-Dames. 27 June Greece joined the Allies. 24 Oct Beginning of the Central Powers' offensive at Caporetto. 7 Nov October Revolution in Russia. 15 Dec Beginning of peace negotiations between Russia and Germany at Brest-Litovsk. 18 Dec The British entered Jerusalem then under Turkish rule.

1918 8 Jan Wilson's proclamation of the Fourteen Points. 21 March German offensive in Picardy. 15-18 Aug German and French offensives in Champagne. 24 Oct Austrian defeat at Vittorio Veneto. 3 Nov Villa Giusti Armistice between Italy and Austria. 11 Nov Armistice at Rethondes between Germany and the Allies.

The Russian Revolution

Vladimir Lenin (Vladimir Ilyich Ulyanov) portrayed, flanked by the red flag of the revolution, while making a rousing speech (*right*). He returned to Russia after the Revolution of February 1917 had led to the abdication of Tzar Nicholas II, and the formation of a socialist government under Kerensky. Lenin led the Bolshevik Revolution on 25 October (7 November according to the Gregorian calandar), establishing a new government of soviets under his leadership.

Destructive new weapons

The war effort speeded up the development of aviation (*above*), begun in 1903 with the Wright brothers' first flight. In 1918, 8,500 fighting and reconnaissance aircraft were in use on the various fronts. On the ground, a typical weapon of trench warfare was the machine gun (*below*), like this Austrian 8 millimetre *Schwarzlose* model.

Bloody Sunday

The name given to a tragic day, 22 January 1905, when Cossack guards at the Winter Palace (Tzar Nicholas II's residence in St Petersburg), fired on an unarmed crowd of demonstrators who had gathered to hand in a petition to the Tzar. It was one of the most dramatic incidents of the 1905 Revolution, which made the Tzar promise to establish a Parliament, the *Duma*, and to introduce a wide range of social and economic reforms in an attempt to calm the widespread unrest.

The rise of the dictators

Meeting of the victors
Lloyd George (British Prime Minister), Victor Emmanuel Orlando (Italian Prime Minister), Georges Clemenceau (French Prime Minister and Chairman of the Versailles Conference), and Woodrow Wilson (President of the USA), photographed in Paris in the spring of 1919.

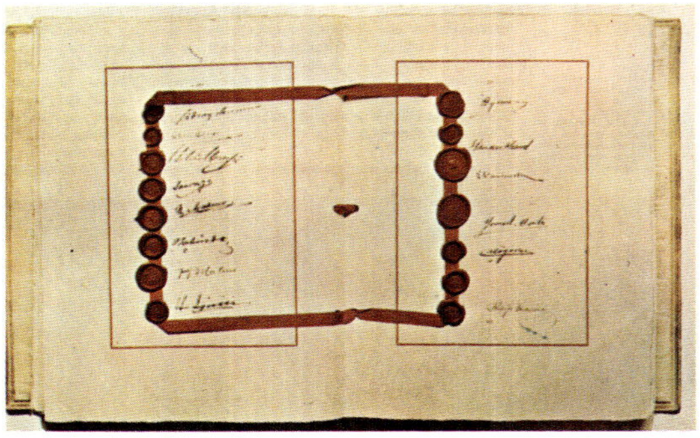

The peace treaties
A page of the Treaty of Versailles, signed on 28 June 1919 by the victors and Germany. Later, the Treaties of St Germain, Neuilly and Trianon were signed with Austria, Bulgaria and Hungary.

In many countries, between the First and Second World Wars, totalitarian regimes established themselves. Some rose to power in the chaotic months immediately after the First War: one such was the dictatorship of Admiral Miklós Horthy in Hungary, which took over after a brief period of Communist government under Béla Kun. Others followed: in Italy, Benito Mussolini, taking advantage of political unrest deliberately exacerbated by the violence of his Fascist squads, compelled the king to appoint him Prime Minister in 1922; in Portugal, Salazar became effective dictator in 1932 after a period of economic crisis; in Germany, Adolf Hitler became Chancellor in 1933 through an open vote, though against a similar background of political and economic turmoil, further stirred up by his uniformed private army, the SA or Brownshirts. Once in power, both Mussolini and Hitler extended their dictatorship everywhere, emasculating parliaments and other bodies of the democratic state.

Other dictators gained complete control gradually: in Brazil, President Getulio Vargas established his regime in 1934; in the USSR, Joseph Stalin, using his position as First Secretary of the Communist Party, steadily increased his authority after Lenin's death in 1924 and eliminated all opposition during the great purges of 1936-1938. In countries like Poland and Argentina, it was the army that provided the basis of the dictatorship. In Spain, too, it played an important role, enabling General Francisco Franco, leader of the Fascist forces, to defeat the left-wing government after three years of violent civil war (1936-1939), and set up a dictatorship which was to last for over thirty years. In China, another general, Chiang Kai-shek, used the army as a means of enormously increasing his personal power.

Many of these political developments were taking place against a background of huge economic and technical change. Following on from the upheavals produced by the First World War, the Great Depression of the 1930s — beginning in the USA — soon severly dislocated the economies of Europe. But this period also saw astonishing progress: recent inventions such as radio and television were perfected; sound was introduced into films; photography and aircraft were improved; and penicillin was discovered; while the scientists who were working at this time were men of all nationalities of outstanding stature — including Einstein, Bohr, Planck, Fermi and Oppenheimer.

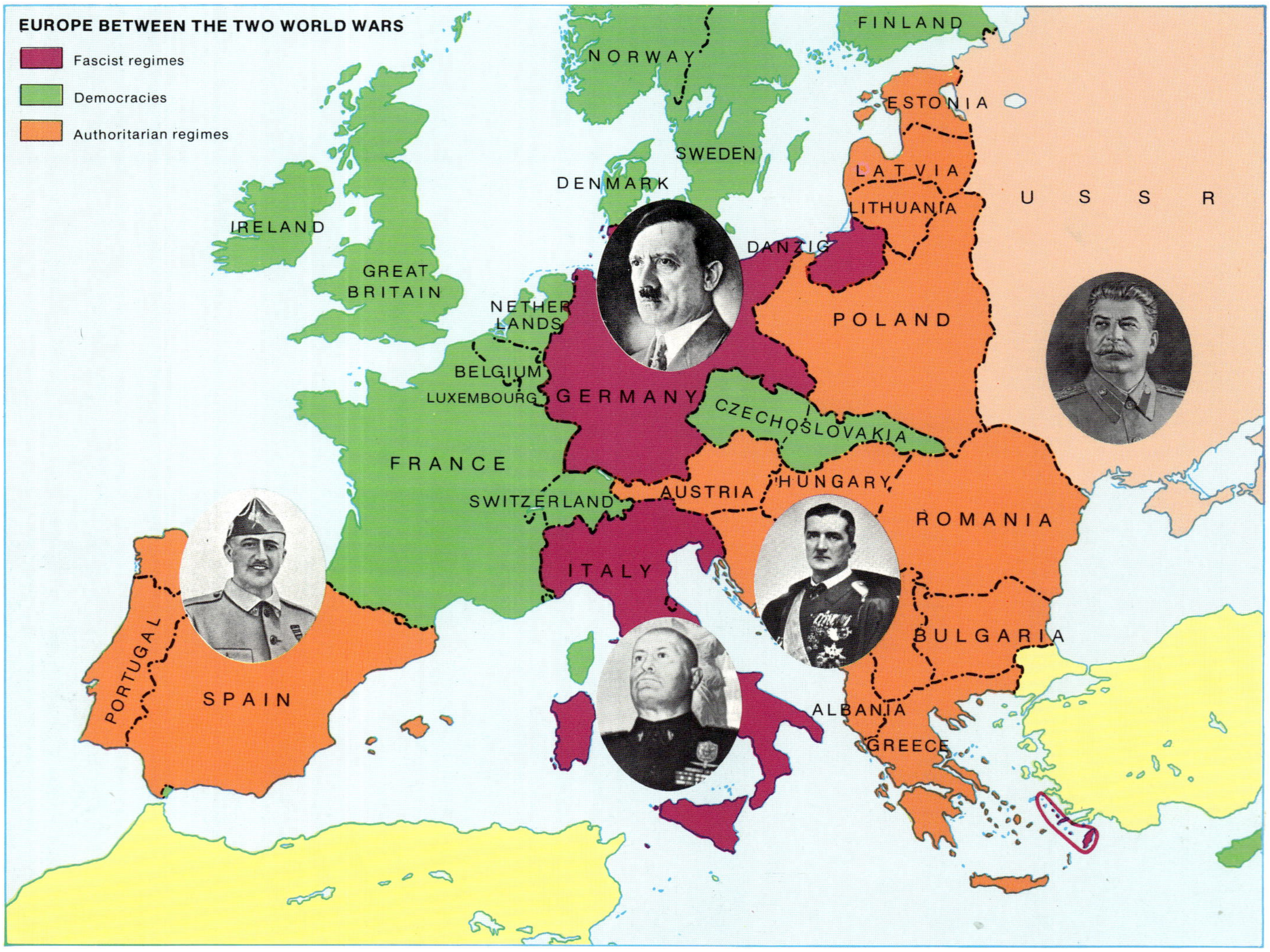

On the eve of a new war
The growth of nationalism and the rise of dictators in most European countries became a serious threat to political stability, especially in the late 1930s. It was in this period that Hitler, having stamped out domestic opposition, embarked upon the aggressive foreign policy which was to plunge the world into war. In Europe only France and Britain opposed Hitler's policies: Spain and Portugal were ruled by Franco and Salazar; Italy, under Mussolini, allied with Germany; Stalin signed a non-aggression pact with Hitler in August 1939, creating the pre-conditions for an attack on Poland and its partition; the small Balkan states tended to support Germany; and Switzerland and the Benelux countries had declared their neutrality. In the event, this declaration of neutrality did nothing to protect either Belgium or the Netherlands. Both were invaded and occupied by the German army in May 1940.

Depression and the New Deal

Black Thursday, 24 October 1929, on the New York Stock Exchange, marked the start of a huge crisis which was to lead into the Great Depression. Many shares lost all value and within three years five thousand banks failed (*left*, a crowd in front of the Chelsea Bank, New York, in December 1930). In 1933, to tackle the Depression, President Franklin Roosevelt introduced the New Deal, a programme of massive public works which included school building, drainage schemes and road improvements.

The genius of the theory of relativity

Albert Einstein (1879-1955), the scientist who opened new horizons in twentieth-century physics. Persecuted by the Nazis, he left Germany in 1933 and moved to the USA where he taught at Princeton University.

Italy gains an "empire"

On 3 October 1935, Italian troops, under orders from Mussolini, invaded Ethiopia. Despite protests and sanctions by the League of Nations, the campaign (seen below in an Ethiopian picture) was soon over. Addis Ababa was taken on 5 May 1936 and four days later Mussolini proclaimed the foundation of an "empire".

Across the Atlantic

The *Spirit of St Louis*, the aircraft used by Charles Lindbergh in the first uninterrupted flight across the Atlantic, from New York to Paris, on 20 May 1927. His time for the flight was 33 hours 29 minutes.

The great dam

The Hoover Dam, on the Colorado River, was one of the major successes of the New Deal.

The Left in power in France

After a violent period of fighting from 6 February 1934, the Popular Front (*left*, a poster of the period) established itself in power in France. Backed by left-wing parties, it was presided over by Léon Blum, who held office from May 1936 to June 1937.

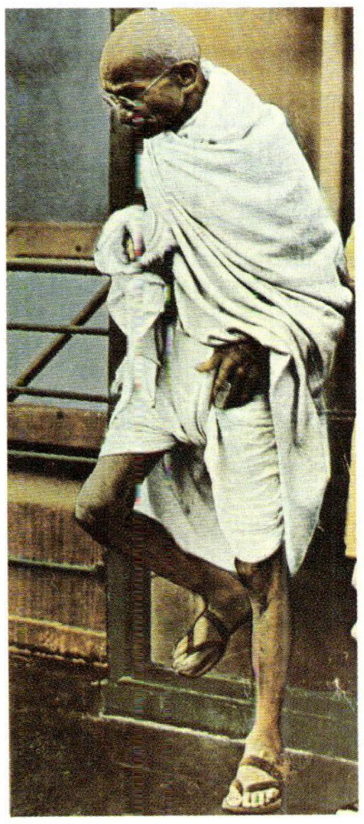

The apostle of non-violence

Mohandas Karamchand Gandhi, the Mahatma ("the noble-hearted"), who struggled for Indian independence advocating non-violence and civil disobedience.

The Spanish Civil War

This lasted from July 1936 to March 1939 and started with military uprisings in Spain and Spanish Morocco, led by Franco. He received the support of Germany and Italy, while the Socialist government was assisted, vainly, by volunteers of the International Brigades.

Mao, leader of the Communists

After the Chinese Communists had been massacred in Shanghai in April 1927 and a peasant uprising had failed in Hunan, Mao Tse-tung escaped in September to the mountains in Ching-kang with a few men, leading them in guerilla warfare (*right*).

Munich

The agreement signed in Munich by Hitler, Mussolini, Daladier and Chamberlain (*left*) on 30 September 1938 to bring "peace in our time" actually meant giving in to Hitler's demands for the Sudetenland. Already, in March, Hitler had taken over Austria (the *Anschluss*) without any opposition from European governments. On 15 March 1939 the Nazis occupied Prague (*right*); it was then clear that the agreement had been worthless.

The Second World War

Hitler's generals
Above, Hitler (*third from left*) with his supreme commander, General Keitel (*second from left*). *Left,* General Erwin Rommel.

The Supreme Allied Commander
The American General Dwight "Ike" Eisenhower (*right*), from 1943 Commander-in-Chief of the Allied forces. *Below,* a German *Panzer* unit.

Rooted in the expansionist madness of Hitler and the German Nazis and planned through shrewd alliances, the Second World War might well have broken out earlier but for the tacit acceptance by France and Great Britain of Hitler's annexation of Austria (March 1938) and Czechoslovakia (March 1939). It was triggered off by the invasion of Poland by Hitler's armoured columns on 1 September 1939. On 3 September, France and Britain declared war on Germany, while Italy declared itself non-belligerent. After a period of twilight war, Hitler ended the delay on 10 May 1940. Avoiding the powerful Maginot defensive line, his armies invaded northern France across Belgium and the Netherlands. On 14 June, the Germans entered Paris; four days earlier, Mussolini had joined the war on Hitler's side. The war fronts expanded: in the Balkans there was fighting in Greece and then in Yugoslavia; in North Africa the forces of the Axis, commanded by Romel, confronted the British in a continuing series of offensives and counter-offensives; in the skies above England, fierce aerial combat — the Battle of Britain — compelled Hitler to postpone his plans for invasion across the Channel.

On 22 June 1941, Hitler attacked Russia, advancing in three directions: on Leningrad in the north, on Moscow in the centre, and on Stalingrad in the south. At first, it was a triumph for him, but then the difficulty of maintaining supplies and the hostile climate held up the Germans (as it had held up Napoleon and his army so many years before) only a short distance from their objectives. However, the decisive event of 1941 was the United States' entry into the war, following Japan's surprise attack on the American naval base at Pearl Harbor, Hawaii (7 December). In the same period, the Japanese took possession of the greater part of Asia: Indochina, Malaya, part of China, Burma, the Philippines and Indonesia.

The crucial year of the conflict was 1942: the Germans were held up at Stalingrad and Leningrad; in North Africa, the Axis forces lost the battle of El Alamein and Anglo-American troops landed in Algeria and Morocco; the Japanese navy was defeated in two decisive battles (the Coral Sea and Midway Islands). In 1943, the Axis armies were forced out of Africa; on 9–10 July, the Allies invaded Sicily, contributing to the fall of Mussolini's government and an armistice with Italy. On 6 June 1944, Allied troops landed in Normandy (D-Day). At the same time, the Germans were compelled to retreat into Poland and well to the north of Rome. In the spring of 1945, they found themselves fighting inside Germany on two fronts, Russian and Western. The Japanese, too, were in trouble. In Italy, the last German soldiers surrendered on 25 April; and on 7–8 May Germany itself signed an unconditional surrender. To compel the Japanese to surrender, the Americans made use of a new and terrible weapon, the atomic bomb. It was dropped on Hiroshima (6 August) and Nagasaki (9 August) and, shortly afterwards, Japan surrendered.

The indomitable British
Prime Minister Winston Churchill (*right*) making the "V" (for victory) salute, and (*above*) General Montgomery, victor at El Alamein.

The Japanese attack on Pearl Harbor
At 7.50 a.m. on 7 December 1941, Japanese aircraft, launched from carriers of a fleet commanded by Admiral Nagumo, attacked Pearl Harbor, Hawaii. *Left,* ships sunk around Ford Island during the bombing. Eight American battleships were destroyed or damaged, and thousands died. The Japanese lost only 29 aircraft out of the 384 which took part in the attack.

Yalta: dividing up the world
Churchill, Roosevelt and Stalin (*left*) meeting at Yalta, in February 1945, to make the post-war settlement of Europe. *Right,* Allied troops just after the D-Day landings in Normandy: 39 divisions (more than 2 million men), 11,000 aircraft and more than 4,500 ships took part in this amazing and successful operation which turned the tide of the war in Europe.

From the Sahara to the Russian steppes

Right, English soldiers attacking an Italian tank on the North African front, which the Axis had to abandon in 1943. *Below*, cavalry of the Italian expeditionary force in Russia, retreating near the Don in the winter of 1942. They found the weather more difficult than the enemy.

Hitler's first triumph of the war

After invading the Netherlands and Belgium (*above*, fighting near Malmédy), the German armies turned towards Amiens and then the English Channel, forcing the disastrous evacuation of the remainder of the British army from Dunkirk. On 14 June, the Germans entered Paris and eight days later. Hitler (*left*) was photographed in front of the Eiffel Tower.

CHRONOLOGY

1939 1 Sept Germany provoked the outbreak of war by invading Poland. 3 Sept Britain and France declared war on Germany; neutrality of the United States. 17 Sept Russian troops entered eastern Poland. Sept to Oct French operations in the Saar. 30 Nov Russia attacked Finland.

1940 9 April to 10 June Germany occupies Norway. 10 May to 25 June Battle for France. 15–28 May Capitulation of the Netherlands and Belgium. 28 May to 4 June Evacuation of Dunkirk. 10 June Italy declared war on Britain and France. 14 June The Germans reached Paris. 17 June Pétain asked for an armistice. 15–29 June Russia occupied the Baltic States, Bessarabia and Bukovina. 18 June De Gaulle's appeal from London. 22–24 June French armistice with Germany and Italy. 10 July Pétain took full powers. 27 Sept Three-power pact between Germany, Italy and Japan. Aug to Sept Romania lost North Transylvania to Hungary and South Dobruja to Bulgaria. 7 Oct Germans entered Romania. 24 Oct Meeting between Hitler and Pétain at Montoire.

1941 11 March Lend-Lease from the US to Britain. 6–18 April Battle of Yugoslavia. May Air and naval battle for Crete. 8 June to 14 July Battle for Syria. 22 June Start of Hitler's offensive against Russia. 14 Aug Atlantic Charter. 7 Dec Pearl Harbor: the USA entered the war.

1942 Jan to July Rommel's attacks in Libya. The Japanese took the Philippines (Jan), Singapore (15 Feb), Rangoon (8 March) and Indonesia, and attacked the Aleutians (June), New Guinea and Guadalcanal (Aug). 23 Oct Battle of El Alamein. 8–11 Nov Allied landings in Algeria and Morocco. 27 Nov Self-destruction of the French fleet at Toulon.

1943 14 Jan Casablanca Conference. 23 Jan The British took Tripoli in Libya. 2 Feb German armies at Stalingrad surrendered. 7 May The Allies entered Tunisia: collapse of the Axis power in Africa. 10 July The Allies landed in Sicily. 25 July Fall of Mussolini's government: succeeded by Badoglio. 2–3 Sept The Allies landed in Calabria. 8 Sept Italian surrender and armistice. 2 Dec Teheran Conference.

1944 22 Jan Allied landings at Anzio. Feb to May Battle of Monte Cassino. 4 June The Allies reached Rome. 6 June Normandy landings: establishment of bridgehead (9–18 July), breakout from Avranches (31 July). 15 July Landings in Provence. 25 Aug Liberation of Paris. 1 Oct The Allies reached the German frontier in Belgium and the Netherlands. 16 Dec to 16 Jan 45 Failure of von Rundstedt's attack in the Ardennes and Alsace.

1945 17 Jan The Russians entered Warsaw. 12 Feb Yalta Conference. Turkey and the Arab states joined in against Germany and Japan. 12 April Death of Roosevelt. Truman became the US President. The Russians entered Vienna. 25 April Inaugural conference of the United Nations opened in San Francisco. Partisan rising in Italy. 30 April Hitler committed suicide. 2 May The Russians entered Berlin. 7 May German surrender signed at Rheims and (8 May) Berlin. May British military intervention in Syria and evacuation of French forces there. 17 July to 2 Aug Potsdam Conference. 26 July Attlee became British Prime Minister. 6 Aug Atomic bomb dropped on Hiroshima. 8 Aug Russia declared war on Japan. 9 Aug Atomic bomb dropped on Nagasaki. 14 Aug Sino-Russian alliance. 2 Sept Confirmation of Japanese surrender.

A terrible new weapon

The decision of the American President Truman to use the atomic bomb to end Japanese resistance claimed thousands of victims. The bombs were dropped from a B29 "Flying Fortress" in August 1945. According to an American enquiry which was held in 1953, the bombs caused 80,000 dead and 80,000 wounded in Hiroshima, 35,000 dead and 60,000 wounded in Nagasaki.

The end of Nazi Germany

Allied propaganda poster (*left*) with the breaking of the swastika symbolizing the destruction of Nazi Germany. In the later stages of the war, Allied mastery of the skies led to heavy bombing of Germany: in the raids on Hamburg in July 1943 (*above*), approximately 50,000 people died. Aircraft flew on daily missions from airbases in the United Kingdom.

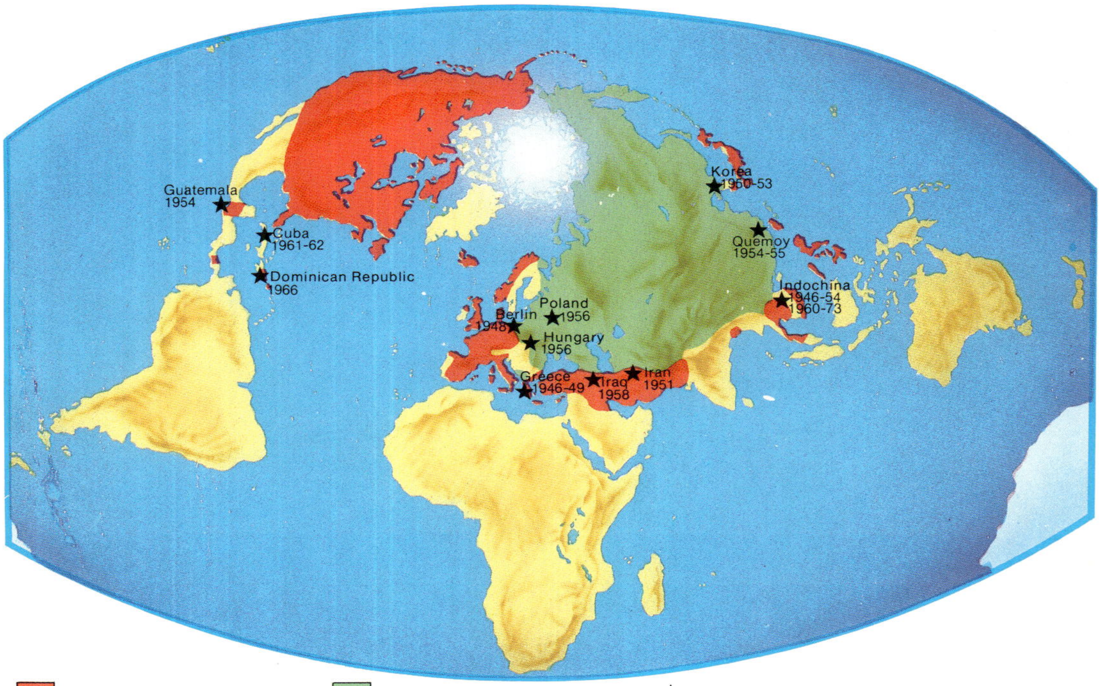

The Cold War

The world that emerged from the Second World War was polarized: the USSR (on one side) and the West, led by the USA (on the other) formed two conflicting blocs. A "Cold War" began between them, destined to last until the early 1970s. This period was marked by friction, tension and muscle-flexing; however, it never involved the two superpowers in a direct conflict. The first phase of the confrontation took place in Europe. Between 1947 and 1949, the USSR extended the power of Communism by imposing similar regimes in Bulgaria, Romania, Hungary, Poland, Czechoslovakia and East Germany. The USA introduced the Marshall Plan, offering economic assistance to Europe, but this was rejected by the USSR. There soon followed a crisis over the divided city of Berlin, which the Russians cut off from West Germany for almost a year: provisions for its Western sectors had to be supplied through an enormous American airlift. In 1949, the USA founded the North Atlantic Treaty Organisation (NATO). In the same year, the establishment of a Communist regime in China shifted the focus of Russian-American antagonism to Asia. This reached its climax with the Korean War (1950–1953). Events such as Stalin's

The infamous Wall
Berlin, partitioned into four zones by the victors at the end the Second World War (*below*), was cut off from the West by the Russians from June 1948 to May 1949; it was only through an airlift provided by the USA that West Berlin had the essential supplies to survive. In June 1953, there were violent anti-Soviet demonstrations in the Eastern zone, strongly suppressed by the Communist government. Eight years later, in August 1961, the Western part of the city was divided from the Communist zone by a wall (*above*), closely watched over by armed guards, the *Vopos*, and designed to stem the flood of East German refugees, attracted to the West by the apparent freedom and greater prosperity.

Aid for Reconstruction
Poster (*below*) advocating acceptance of the plan which General George Marshall put forward on 5 June 1947, to provide massive aid for European recovery. Of the total amount, eighty-six per cent was a gift, the remainder was a loan. The plan was known as the Marshall Plan, and the money was provided by the United States of America.

VIVA LA NUOVA ITALIA DEMOCRATICA

l'Unità

ORGANO DEL PARTITO COMUNISTA ITALIANO

VIVA LA REPUBBLICA DI TUTTI GLI ITALIANI

Il popolo italiano ha combattuto e vinto la più grande battaglia politica della sua storia

La Repubblica democratica sorge come il nuovo Stato di tutti gli italiani

Una festa nazionale per salutare la nascita della Repubblica

LA REPUBBLICA E L'UNITA' NAZIONALE

Risultati del Referendum istituzionale

Risultati delle elezioni alla Costituente

Democristiani · Socialisti · Comunisti · U. D. N. · U. Q. · Repubblicani · Blocco Libertà · Partito d'Azione

Quanti deputati avranno i grandi partiti alla Costituente

Italy decides to become a republic
In a referendum on 2 June 1946, Italians chose whether to retain the monarchy or set up a republic. On 10 June, the Republic was proclaimed after fifty-four per cent had voted in favour. Three days later, Umberto II, the last King of the House of Savoy, went into exile. Towards the end of June, a constituent assembly elected Enrico de Nicola provisional Head of State; and work began on drafting a new constitution, with the assistance of all the groups that had fought in the Resistance. The constitution, approved on 22 December 1947, guarantees freedom and equality to every citizen. *Above*, the newspaper *l'Unità*, organ of the Italian Communist Party.

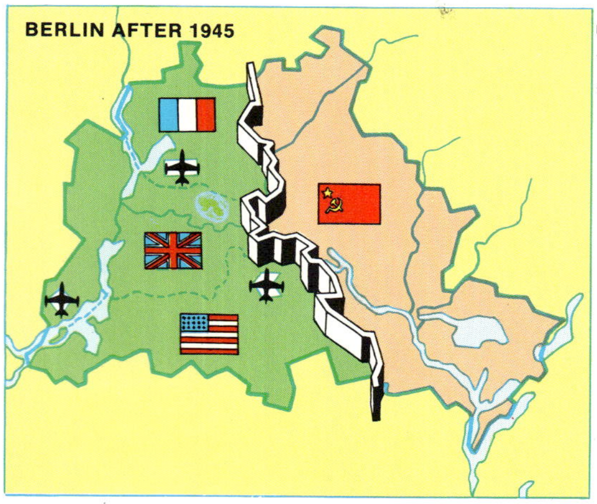

The United Nations, guarantor of peace
The Charter of the United Nations (UN), signed on 26 June 1945 by representatives of fifty nations who gathered in San Francisco, aims at the "safeguarding of world peace, protection of human rights, equal rights for all people ..." (Art. 1). The Organization has its headquarters in New York but has agencies and projects throughout the world.

death (1953), Khrushchev's rise to power, and his denunciation of Stalin's methods during the twentieth Party Congress resulted in some easing of tension and the growth of relatively peaceful coexistence. However, the logic of the Cold War was still behind the setting up, by the USA, of the SEATO alliance (1954) for Southeast Asia, and the Baghdad Pact (1955) (which developed into CENTO) for the Middle East, both modelled on NATO. The USSR reacted by establishing the Warsaw Pact (1955). Afterwards, periods of severe tension developed again between the two blocs: in 1956 the Suez Crisis, the Arab-Israeli War, and the uprising in Hungary which was harshly suppressed; in 1958 the American intervention in the Lebanese Civil War; in 1961 the erection of the Berlin Wall and, in 1962, the Cuban Missile Crisis. However, the Vietnam War, especially between 1964 and 1970, marked — at least for the time being —the final stages of the Cold War; in 1971, President Nixon's visits to Moscow and Peking, the four-power agreement over Berlin and the resulting improved relationship between the two parts of Germany, helped to lessen the tension between East and West divided by the so-called "Iron Curtain".

Red China
Parade in Peking in 1965 (*above*) to commemorate the proclamation of the Chinese People's Republic on 1 October 1949. Communist troops, having taken Peking on 31 January 1949, later occupied the whole country, while Chiang Kai-shek and the remnant of the Nationist forces fled to Taiwan.

Mao, the Great Helmsman
Mao Tse-tung (*right*), born at Shao-shan in Hunan in 1893, was among the revolutionaries who proclaimed the Chinese Republic in 1911; he was also one of the founders of the Chinese Communist Party. With Chou En-lai, Lin Piao, Chu Teh and others, in 1934–1935 he led the "Long March" of the Communists against the Nationalists and later against the Japanese who had invaded China.

The unending Arab–Israeli conflict
The confrontation between Palestinian Arabs and Jews under British mandate exploded immediately after the proclamation of Israel's independence under David Ben Gurion (*above left*) on 14 May 1948. Egypt, Iraq, Syria, Jordan and Lebanon joined in attacking Israel but were forced to make an armistice early in 1949. A second war broke out against Egypt in October 1956, a third against Egypt and Syria in June 1967: both were won by Israel. Then came another conflict — the Yom Kippur war in 1973, when Israel was taken by surprise and suffered severe losses. This was followed, in 1982, by an Israeli invasion of Lebanon. *Above*, Israeli armoured vehicles on the Golan Heights.

The Korean War
On 25 June 1950, Northern troops invaded South Korea, which was then supported by contingents of many countries, commanded by the American General MacArthur (*left*); China intervened on North Korea's side (*below*). The Armistice of Panmunjom ended the conflict on 27 July 1953.

The problem of illiteracy

An open-air school near Bissau (*above*), capital of Guinea-Bissau, the ex-Portuguese colony which became independent on 10 September 1974. The major problems for the new African states include illiteracy, the need to establish an efficient administration, relations among the various ethnic groups sometimes divided by long-standing tribal hatreds, and the struggle against famine and underdevelopment.

The struggle for independence

Many African countries reached independence only after intensive guerilla warfare, led by their national liberation movements, against the old colonial powers. Under the leadership of experienced revolutionaries, often backed by foreign countries, they faced all sorts of difficulties in a tragic escalation of assassinations and brutal repression from police and army, before being able to persuade the majority of their people to join their fight for independence. One typical example was Angola (*above*), where MPLA, the movement led by Agostinho Neto, had been fighting for years against the Portuguese before achieving independence on 11 November 1975. When independence had been won, many of these countries still faced bitter strife and tribal warfare.

The tormented independence of Zaire

Soldiers of Zaire (*right*), formerly the Belgian Congo: its independence represents one of the most troubled chapters in recent African history. Between 1960 and 1965, the country went through a disastrous period of unrest, with fighting between the various factions, the assassination of Patrice Lumumba, the leader of the left, and an attempt at secession by the rich mining province of Katanga. The coup of General Mobutu on 25 November 1965 seemed to put an end to the political turmoil.

The new Africa

President Lamizana of Upper Volta (now Burkina Faso), with the French President de Gaulle, during his visit to Paris on 14 July 1968. France, of all the ex-colonial powers, is the one that has kept the closest economic links and bonds of friendship with African states that have gained independence (Upper Volta on 5 August 1960). A major factor is, of course, the French language which is still used in these countries — known as "francophone". This means that they are influenced by French education and culture, that they import French books and other commodities and that their young people often study in French universities. For their own part, African countries have set up international associations like OCAM (the Joint African Mauritian Organization) at Nouakchott in 1965, and OAU (the Organization for African Unity) at a conference in Addis Ababa in May 1963. The latter, similar to the UN in structure, consists of a General Secretariat, an Assembly of Heads of State and Government which meets once a year, and a Council of Foreign Ministers who assemble every six months; but there is often disagreement within the Organization and, even if problems arising in Africa (like those in Chad) are dealt with, it is very rare for politically acceptable solutions to be found, and effective measures enforced.

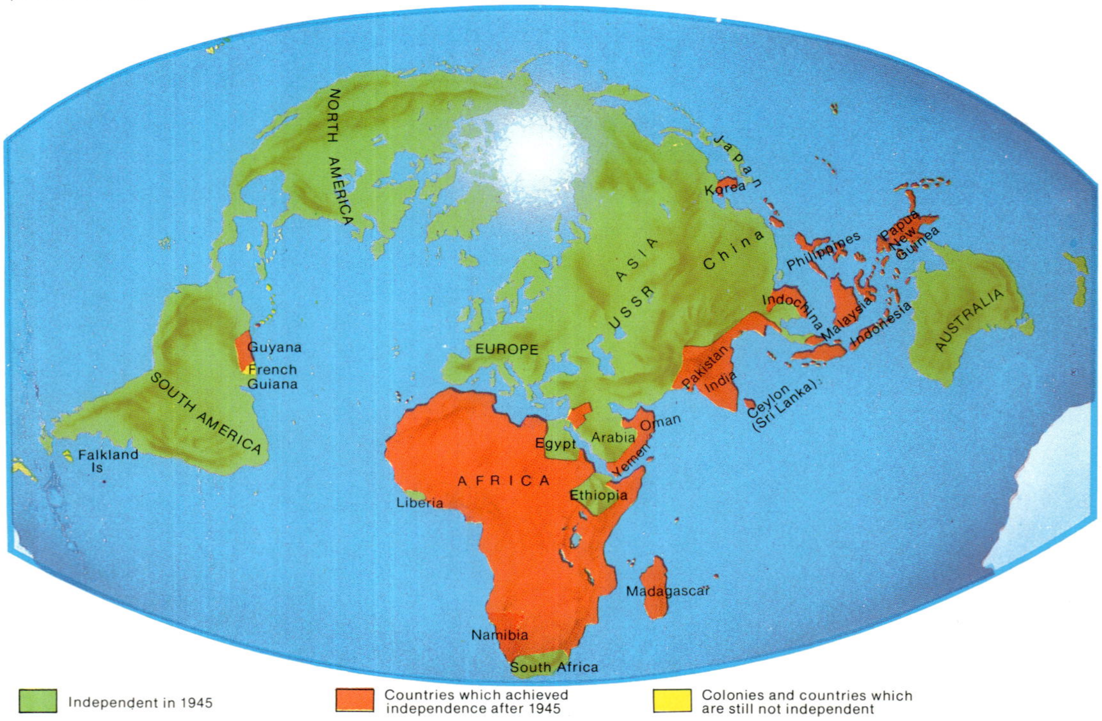

Decolonization

The Second World War speeded up the process by which countries subject to the colonial powers gained their independence. These colonies had frequently been directly involved in the conflict and, in some cases, they had changed hands during it, especially in Asia, where Japanese conquest had for a time replaced the European powers. Many colonies had contributed significant numbers of fighting men to the war effort of their mother countries, particularly Great Britain and France. Naturally, after the war, they expected a recognition of their sacrifice. Furthermore, the European colonial powers — severely weakened in world influence by the war — had claimed to be the defenders of liberty and democracy in the fierce struggle against the Axis forces. Now the colonies decided to claim the same liberty and democracy for themselves.

As a result, between 1946 and 1951, the first phase of decolonization began: Syria, Lebanon, Egypt, Eritrea, Libya, the Philippines, India, Pakistan, Burma and Indonesia all achieved independence. Then, after a brief pause in the early 1950s, the process of decolonization (sometimes controlled, but more often resisted by the colonial powers) gained new strength following the Bandung Conference (1955), where some thirty Afro-Asian countries joined together to fight colonialism in all its forms. Then, between 1955 and 1958, Cambodia, Sudan, Morocco, Tunisia, Ghana, Malaysia and Guinea all gained independence.

The year 1960 was actually called the "year of Africa", since as many as seventeen countries freed themselves from colonial control; while in the early 1960s, Sierra Leone, Uganda, Algeria (after a very hard struggle against France), Zambia and The Gambia achieved their independence.

By 1965, only Portugal still kept its colonies, but at a very high military and economic cost. Between 1973 and 1975, it was compelled to recognize the independence of Guinea-Bissau, Angola and Mozambique. In 1975, the war in Vietnam ended, a conflict that can in some ways be considered as a continuation of the colonial struggle against French rule in that region between 1946 and 1954.

The era of colonialism was virtually over.

The President of the "New Frontier"
In November 1960, the election of John Fitzgerald Kennedy (*right*) as President of the USA seemed to represent a turning-point in American politics: a deeper commitment to detente, measures to improve the living conditions of black people, the launching of an ambitious programme of aid for Latin America (the Alliance for Progress) and an overhaul of tariff regulations on imports from Europe. However, the assassination of the President in Dallas, on 22 November 1963, abruptly interrupted these policies and destroyed the mood of optimism.

After Stalin
Nikita Khrushchev (*left*), First Secretary of the Soviet Communist Party from September 1953 to 13 October 1964, started the process of de-Stalinization and introduced a period of detente with the USA; but his country's relations with China worsened and his Virgin Lands policy, aimed at increasing agricultural production, was a failure.

Cuba and Fidel Castro
Fidel Castro (*right*), the revolutionary leader who took power in Cuba in January 1959, initiated the transformation of the country on socialist lines. Since then, he has been the rallying point for all the revolutionary movements in Latin America and the Third World, giving them aid and military support. His policies are a constant source of concern to the USA, since they are considered dangerous to the existing political structures in Central and South America.

The "non-aligned" countries
The Yugoslav President Tito, the Indian Prime Minister Nehru and the Egyptian President Nasser (*from the left*) during a conference held in Belgrade in 1961 to discuss the problems of the "non-aligned" countries, that is, those states which do not adhere to either bloc (the Western one led by the USA and the Eastern one led by the USSR). These non-aligned states, often referred to as the "Third World", face serious problems connected with their economic underdevelopment, over-population, and lack of clear role — despite their size and number — in international politics.

The bloody war in Vietnam
Ho Chi Minh (*above*), the Vietnamese politician who directed the struggle against the French colonial power and then, after founding North Vietnam (March 1946), led his country in the long war against South Vietnam which was backed in vain by the USA. *Right*, an American position near Nam Dinh.

Towards the future

The opulent society
Las Vegas, centre of gambling and amusement in the Nevada Desert, symbolizes the wealth of the richest society in the world, the USA. The average American's income is twenty-five times greater than that in some parts of Africa or Asia: this means that the money (or its equivalent in food and other commodities) needed to live for two weeks in the USA would suffice for a whole year in some developing countries. However, even the "affluent society" of North America may not be all that it seems on the surface. It has many of the problems also evident in Western Europe.

The destitution of the Third World
In many areas of Asia, Africa and Latin America, survival is the main consideration for the majority of the population: shortages of food and basic necessities cause thousands of deaths every year. Official aid and private donations do not remove the roots of the problem, which can only be solved by the introduction of modern techniques, especially in agriculture, and by establishing new and lasting infrastructures (such as wells, roads and schools).

At the end of the 2nd World War the countries of the so-called western and eastern blocs entered a phase of fierce rivalry. At the head of each bloc were the two great world powers — the USA and the USSR. This state of affairs, known as the "Cold War", continued for many years, creating, with the threat of total destruction, a real "balance of terror".
The first step towards change came in 1987 with the election of Mikhail Gorbachev as Secretary of the Communist Party. Considerable modification of internal policy, with the initiation of Perestroika — restructuring — and Glasnost — openness, was accompanied by a radical change in foreign policy. As a result, thanks also to the receptivity of heads of state like Ronald Reagan and George Bush of USA, moves were taken towards the banning of nuclear weapons; moves obviously enthusiastically supported by other countries, particularly the members of the EEC. Inevitably the easing of tension had beneficial effects also within those European countries still under the influence of Soviet power. In 1989 most of the totalitarian regimes of Eastern Europe collapsed. In Romania a popular uprising brought about the downfall of Nicolae Ceausescu. In Poland and Hungary the first free elections took place, while in Germany the Berlin Wall was pulled down — the prelude to the re-unification of the two Germanies on 3rd October 1990. In 1991 all the Soviet republics declared independence. The one exception to these fairly pacific revolutions has been the dissolution of the ex-socialist federal republic of Yugoslavia. After the proclamation of independence of the republics of Slovenia and Croatia on 25th June 1991, the country descended into a bitter and bloody civil war. Concentrated mostly in Bosnia and originating from religious and political motives the conflict involves Serbo-Bosnian and Serbo-Croat forces against Muslim forces. Despite the intervention of the UN and the involvement of many European countries a peaceful solution to the problems with agreement about the sub-division of the country has not yet been found.

The Third World and Socio-Economic Development

Moving from Europe to more global considerations it needs to be remembered that economic imbalance and disparity between industrialised and developing or underdeveloped countries not only continue but worsen.
Inflation and the productive recession which have put a break on the growth of western economies since the 1970's have, among other things, highlighted the problem of "the limits of development" i.e. how best to exploit the limited resources of the planet in the face of the growth of the world's population, particularly in the less developed countries.
In this context there is the ever more urgent need to avoid waste and the senseless destruction of resources, to which pollution has also contributed. It is also necessary to find a solution to the enormous social problems resulting from underdevelopment and the lack of infrastructures in the Third World, where thousands of people are still starving.
In May 1991 the population of Bangladesh was decimated by an incredible succession of violent typhoons and Peru was overwhelmed by a terrible cholera epidemic.
World peace is furthermore a long way off, and the Middle East remains one of the most explosive areas on the map. It was in 1991 again that a coalition of international forces, headed by the USA and authorised by the UN, intervened to liberate Kuwait which had been invaded by Saddam Hussein of Iraq.
At the end of this brief but violent war the whole world became aware of the tragedy of the Kurds, who are still being persecuted by the Iraqis.
The conflict between Israel and Palestine, which has long provided one of the major obstacles to peace in the Middle East, reached a turning point on 10th September 1993 with the historic accord of mutual recognition between Israel and the Palestinian Liberation Organization (PLO).

Reagan

Bush

Gorbachev

ATLAS

EUROPE

EUROPE IN THE FIRST MILLENNIUM BC

In the prehistoric period, the continent of Europe exhibited much diversity. The influence of the civilization of the Near East was felt above all in the Mediterranean regions, and penetrated only marginally into the remainder of Europe. As a result, the Bronze and Iron Ages developed differently in the various areas and centuries. Around 1000 BC, however, a large part of Central and Western Europe entered upon the first Iron Age — what is called the Culture of Hallstatt. Then, in about 500 BC, the second Iron Age or Culture of La Tène began: this lasted in Central Europe until the Roman conquest, and was dominated by Celtic people from the area of the Rhine, who spread throughout most of Europe between the sixth and the second centuries BC.

ROMAN AND CHRISTIAN EUROPE

The fourth century AD was a crucial period in the history of Eurpe and the Mediterranean basin. Although the Roman Empire had declined in power and extent compared with two centuries previously, it had been the means for the spreading of Christianity, the revolutionary new ideology destined to influence the history of Europe and the wider world. Spreading among humble people at first, Christianity was suppressed and persecuted by those in power, but it gained acceptance in the Edict of Milan (AD 313) and, within a century, it had become the official and sole religion of the Empire. However, this freedom brought to the surface dissensions and heresies: those in power tried to deal with these problems by summoning Church councils to define dogma and impose discipline. Of particular importance in the fourth century were the ecumenical Councils of Nicaea (325) and Constantinople (381): these gave precise definition to the basic doctrines of Christianity.

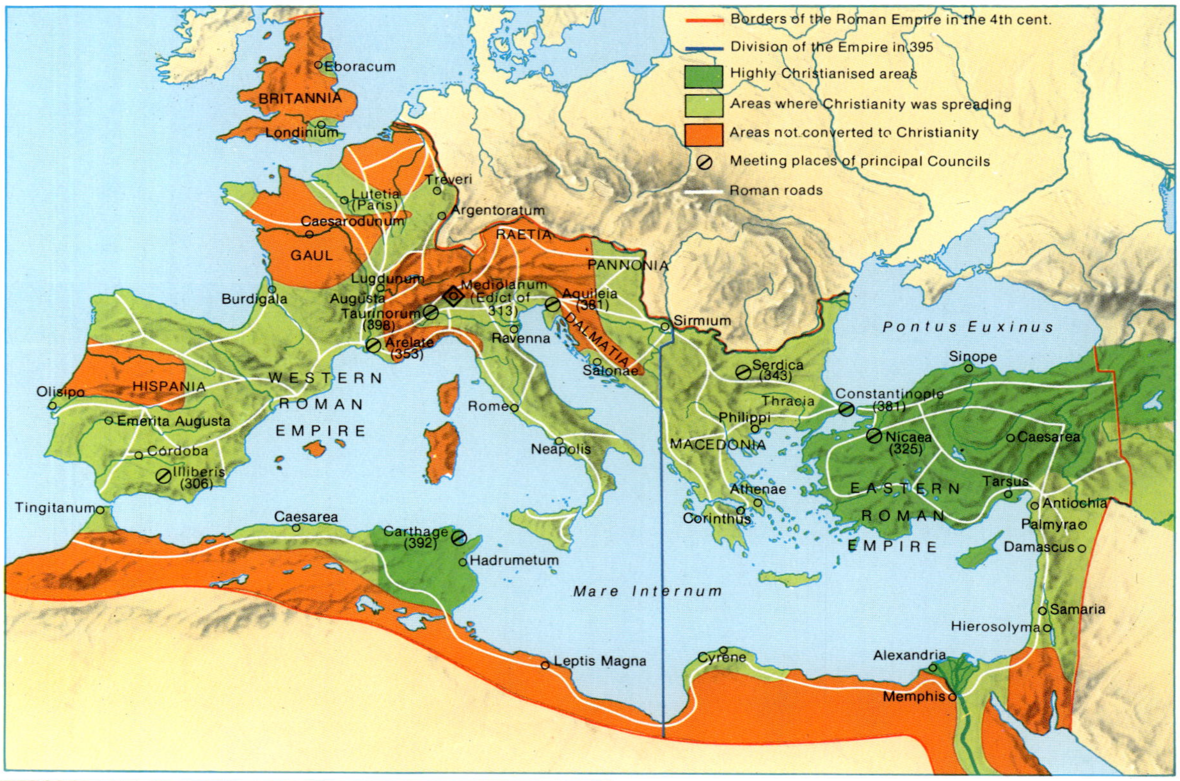

EUROPE AROUND AD 1000

No doubt to the superstitious European the approach of the year 1000 may have seemed to threaten the end of the world. In reality, there are many signs that the Europe of this time was bursting with vitality, so much so that it is possible to speak of AD 1000 as a year of rebirth. There is evidence of rapid population growth, a reawakening of economic and cultural activity, a reduction in the incidence of serfdom. At the more narrowly political level, however, many of the uncertainties and contradictions, the first signs of the future national state, began to appear: the reconquest of Spain, the consolidation of the Kingdom of France, the Norman Conquest of England, the establishment of the Kingdoms of Hungary and Poland; while in the East the Byzantine Empire was making a strong recovery under Basil II.

EUROPE IN 1559

For the whole of the first half of the sixteenth century, the history of Central and Western Europe was dominated by the rivalry between the Habsburg Empire and the Kingdom of France. The origin of the friction lay in the clever matrimonial policies of the House of Habsburg which led to the concentration in the hands of Charles V of an immense Empire "on which the sun never set". France felt very threatened by these policies and its King, Francis , reacted by forming many different alliances — even with the "infidel" Turks — to avoid encirclement. The tension only diminished when the two main protagonists left the scene; while the Peace of Cateau-Cambrésis, made in 1559 between Philip II of Spain and Henry II of France, established a new territorial settlement, more balanced than before but still advantageous to the Habsburgs and destined to last until the Thirty Years' War.

EUROPE AT THE CONGRESS OF VIENNA

After the changes caused by the Napoleonic hurricane, the Congress of Vienna, from October 1814 to June 1815, redrew the geographical map of Europe, attempting to restore the old order. In reality, while dismantling the Napoleonic structures, it did not completely succeed in re-introducing the *status quo*: its more important objective was to institute a political system designed to keep France under control. This explains the strengthening of states along the eastern frontiers of France, from the Netherlands to the Kingdom of Sardinia. Moreover, the Congress reduced the number of German states. In 1815, less than forty states survived out of the total of more than three hundred which had existed in the eighteenth century.

EUROPE AT VERSAILLES

By a turn of events which may now appear to be ironic, the First World War, triggered off by irreconcilable policies of nationalism, was ended on the basis of the Fourteen Points of the American President Wilson, underlining the importance of the principle of nationality. This principle was more easily declared than implemented, partly because the victors were not wholly prepared to accept it, but also due to the impossibility of fixing boundaries acceptable to all the various ethnic groups. At Versailles and the other conferences held in and around Paris, a solution was found: although not ideal, it did at the time reflect the balance of power among the treaty-makers.

Above, the British Prime Minister, Edward Heath, signing the treaty of accession to the European Economic Community.

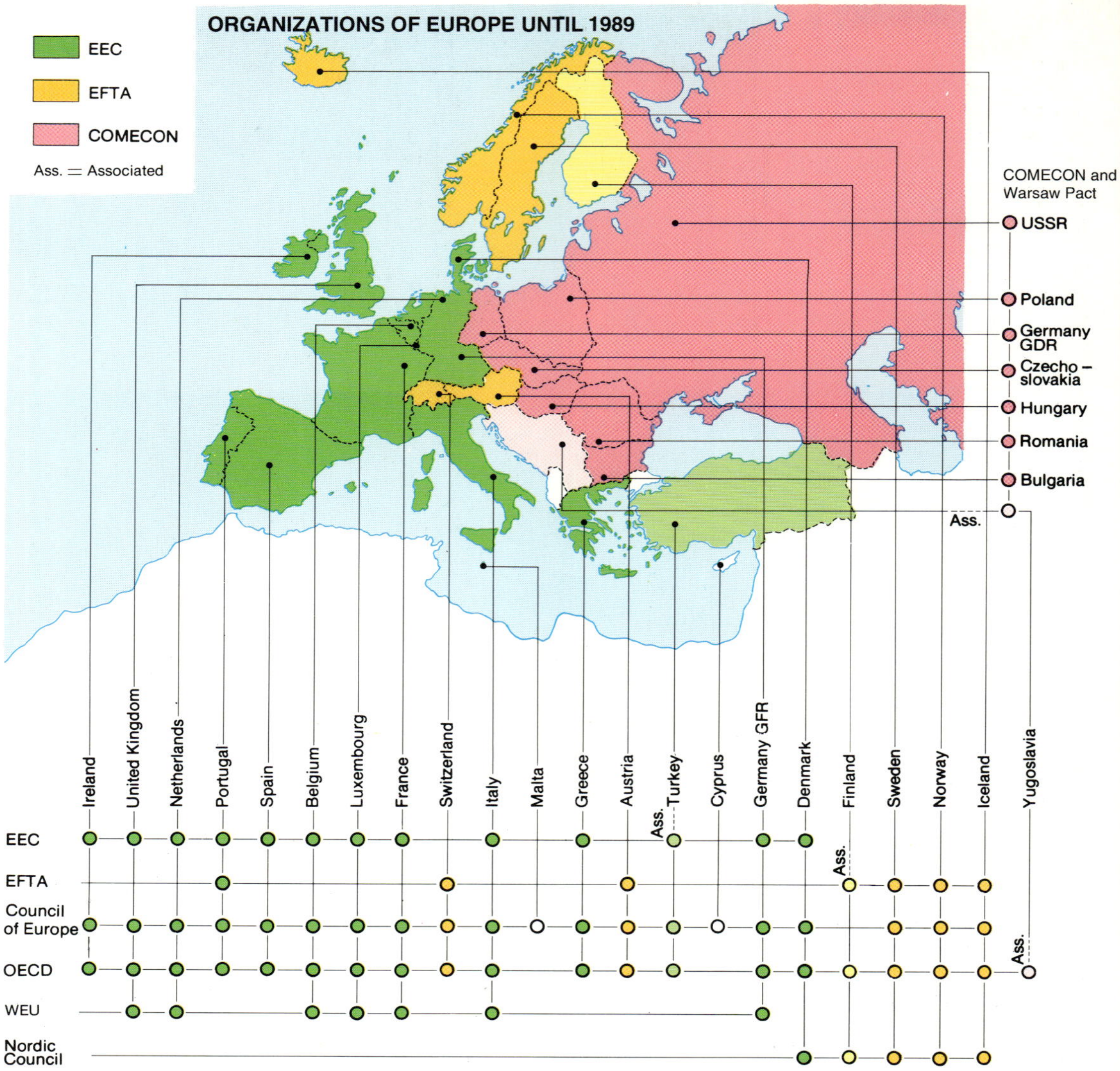

The European Communities

This title is normally understood to refer to three organizations set up to encourage economic collaboration: the European Coal and Steel Community (ECSC), established by the Treaty of Paris in 1951; the European Economic Community or Common Market (EEC); and the European Atomic Energy Community (EURATOM), set up by the Treaty of Rome of 1957. The founder members were France, the German Federal Republic (West Germany), Italy, Belgium, the Netherlands and Luxembourg, while Denmark, Ireland and the United Kingdom joined on 1 January 1973, Greece at the beginning of 1981, and Spain and Portugal in 1986. A basic aim of these organizations is the development and integration of the various national economic structures into a unified system designed to be the essential first step along the road towards federation among the states of Western Europe. The three communities share a common organization consisting of: the European Parliament which has 515 members elected by direct universal suffrage; the European Commission whose seventeen members have their headquarters in Brussels; the Council of Ministers, also based in Brussels and representing the governments of the member states; and the Court of Justice whose thirteen judges meet in Luxembourg.

ECSC – European Coal and Steel Community

This community was established on 18 April 1951 by the Treaty of Paris and came into force on 25 August 1952 after ratification of the Treaty (between 31 October 1951 and 16 June 1952) by the parliaments of the members states. The founder members were France, the German Federal Republic (West Germany), Italy, Belgium, the Netherlands and Luxembourg. Denmark, Ireland and the United Kingdom joined on 1 January 1973, Greece on 1 January 1981, and Spain and Portugal on 1 January 1986. The aim of the community is to encourage the economic development of the member states through the establishment of a common market in coal and steel, to ensure a progressively more rational distribution of production, to improve the working conditions of the industries' employees and to avoid economic crises in this field within the member states.

EEC – European Economic Community or Common Market

This community was founded by the Treaty of Rome of 25 March 1957 and came into force on 1 January 1958 after ratification of the Treaty (between 5 July and 4 December 1957) by the parliaments of the member states. It brought together six countries of Western Europe – France, the German Federal Republic (West Germany), Italy, Belgium, the Netherlands and Luxembourg – who previously, in 1952, had been responsible for the creation of the European Coal and Steel Community. The EEC was enlarged by the incorporation of Denmark, Ireland and the United Kingdom (1973), Greece (1981), and Spain and Portugal (1986). The EEC exists to promote the development and expansion of the economies of its member states, the institution of a common market through the progressive elimination of customs tariffs, the unrestricted circulation of capital and the free movement of workers within the community.

EURATOM – European Atomic Energy Authority

This community was established by the Treaty of Rome of 25 March 1957 and came into force on 1 January 1958. Its members are the twelve states of the EEC – France, Germany, Italy, Belgium, the Netherlands, Luxembourg, Denmark, Ireland, the United Kingdom, Greece, Spain and Portugal. It exists to coordinate research into nuclear energy, to promote a common market in materials and equipment, and to facilitate the free circulation of investment capital and the free interchange of technicians and technologists among the member states.

Benelux

This is an economic, not a political organization. It was set up on 3 February 1958 by the Treaty of the Hague and came into force on 1 November 1960. By means of a common commercial and social policy it aims at promoting economic union between Belgium, the Netherlands and Luxembourg.

COMECON
Council for Mutual Economic Assistance

This council was set up at Sofia on 14 December 1949 in accordance with the Treaty of Moscow of 25 January 1949, with the purpose of facilitating the economic and technical development and the commercial expansion of its member states: Bulgaria, Cuba, Czechoslovakia, the German Democratic Republic (East Germany), Hungary, Mongolia, Poland, Romania, the Soviet Union, Vietnam and Yugoslavia (the last two with special status). Albania was a member of COMECON until 1961. The council was dissolved on 28th June 1991.

Council of Europe

This council came into being on 5 May 1949 and today consists of Austria, Belgium, Denmark, France, Germany, Greece, Iceland, Ireland, Italy, Liechtenstein, Luxembourg, Malta, the Netherlands, Norway, Portugal, Spain, Sweden, San Marino, Finland, The Czech Republic, Slovakia, Hungary, Poland, Switzerland and the United Kingdom, together with two countries on the borders of Europe – Cyprus and Turkey. It aims at promoting closer cooperation among the member states in safeguarding their common cultural inheritance and in assisting their cultural, social and economic development. Its headquarters are at Strasbourg.

Nordic Council

This council was established on 16 March 1952 with the aim of promoting economic, social, cultural and judicial cooperation. Its founder members were Denmark, Iceland, Norway and Sweden, Finland joined on 28 October 1955.

EFTA – European Free Trade Association

The decision to establish this association was taken at conferences in Geneva (December 1958) and Stockholm (June 1959), and it came into force on 3 May 1960. Its surviving founder members are Austria, Iceland, Norway, Sweden and Switzerland; Finland joined on 27 March 1961 and Liechtenstein in 1960. Denmark, Ireland, Portugal and the United Kingdom left EFTA when they joined the EEC. By progressively eliminating customs tariffs and evolving a common commercial policy, EFTA aims at achieving expanding economic activity, full productivity, rational exploitation of resources, financial stability and rising standards of living in the member countries within the so-called European Free Trade Area. After the withdrawal of Denmark and especially of the United Kingdom (Which had promoted EFTA with the objective of safeguarding the economic interests of those European countries which were not members of the EEC), Austria, Iceland, Portugal, Sweden and Switzerland sought and obtained association with the EEC on 22 July 1972. Norway and Finland secured similar status on 14 May and 5 October 1973 respectively.

NATO – North Atlantic Treaty Organization

This is an international defensive alliance founded in Washington on 4 April 1949 between the United States of America, Canada and a number of European countries. It was established as a consequence of the North Atlantic

Treaty, also signed in Washington and commonly known as the Atlantic Pact. The objectives of NATO are to safeguard the liberties of the peoples of the member states, their common tradition and civilization, based on democracy and on individual rights and freedoms. NATO is essentially a military alliance but the Atlantic Pact included among its primary objectives the development of cultural, economic and social cooperation among its member states. Today, these states are Belgium, Canada, Denmark, France, Germany (since May 1955), Greece (since February 1952), Iceland, Italy, Luxembourg, the Netherlands, Norway, Portugal, Spain (since May 1982), the United Kingdom, the United States of America, Turkey (since February 1952). The supreme body is the North Atlantic Council, which is assisted by various civil and military groups. Among the former are the committees of the council and the International Secretariat, while the latter include the Military Committee, its executive and the various military commands – the Supreme Allied Commander, Europe (SACEUR); the Supreme Allied Commander, Atlantic (SACLANT); the Allied Commander-in-Chief, Channel (CINCHAN); and the Canada-US Regional Planning Group (CUSRPG). In 1966 and 1974 France and Greece respectively, withdrew from the Military Committee and terminated all their commitments to this side of NATO, although both remain members of the council.

OECD – Organization for Economic Cooperation and Development
This organization was established by the Convention of Paris, 14 December 1960, and came into operation on 30 September 1961 as successor to the Organization for European Economic Cooperation (OEEC). The OEEC had been created on 16 April 1948 to confront and resolve the problems of European reconstruction by sharing out Marshal Aid and promoting technical and economic collaboration in Europe. The objectives of OECD are to encourage the economic expansion of the member states, to abolish or reduce barriers to the international movement of capital, to develop world commerce on a multilateral, non-discriminatory basis, and to offer technical and financial aid to member states, especially the developing countries. OECD has its headquarters in Paris and its current membership is Australia, Austria, Belgium, Canada, Denmark, Finland, France, Germany, Greece, Iceland, New Zealand, Norway, Portugal, Spain, Sweden, Switzerland, Turkey, the United Kingdom and the United States of America, and – with special status – Yugoslavia.

Warsaw Pact
This pact was a defensive alliance, set up on 14 May 1955. It grew out of a treaty designed to promote friendship, political consultation and mutual military assistance, which was initialled by the member states at the end of a conference on safeguarding peace and security in europe, held at Warsaw in May 1955. The members of the Warsaw Pact were Bulgaria, Czechoslovakia, the German Democratic Republic (East Germany), Hungary, Poland, Romania and the Soviet Union. Albania left the alliance in 1968. It was dissolved on 1st July 1991.

WEU – Western European Union
This union was established by the Treaty of Paris of 23 October 1954, coming into force on 6 May 1955. It succeeded the European Defence Community (set up by the Treaty of Brussels of 17 March 1948), which had had the objective of promoting economic, social and cultural cooperation between Belgium, France, Luxembourg, the Netherlands and the United Kingdom, but which had also been designed to provide collective military security in the event of an eventual rebirth of German military power.
WEU's current membership is Belgium, France, Germany, Portugal, Spain, Italy, Luxembourg, the Netherlands and the United Kingdom. It exists to reinforce the security of its member states through coordination of their defences and it also promotes economic and social cooperation. Its headquarters are in London.

Europe and its political boundaries until 1989

ASIA

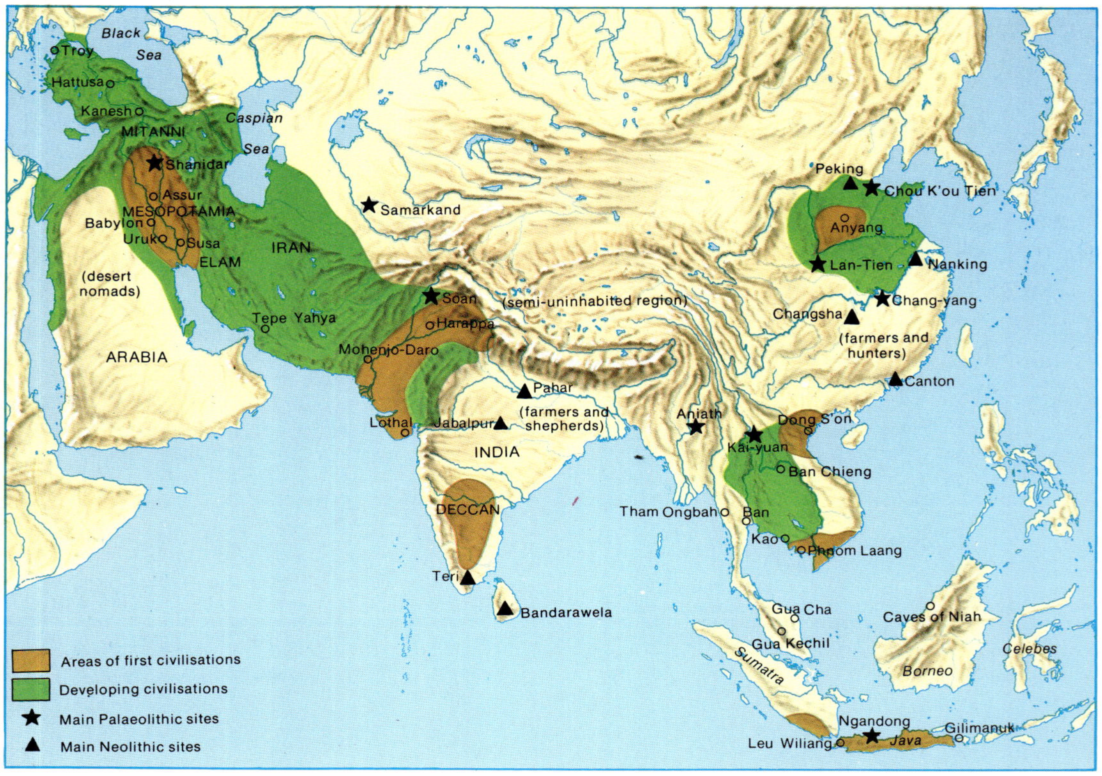

THE EARLIEST ASIAN CULTURES

Asia has traditionally been considered the cradle of civilization. While modern palaeontology considers Africa to have been the centre of the first human culture, it was Asia that developed the earliest communities which merit the name of civilization. However, to speak of Asia is to refer to such an enormous area that it can hardly be treated as one unit. In fact, it had three distinct centres of civilization, dating from the fourth and third millennia BC. These were far apart and isolated from each other — in the Near East with its focus in Mesopotamia, in the valley of the Indus, and in northern China. In addition to these, but of less significance, there were the civilizations of the Deccan in India, of the Indochinese Peninsula and of Java.

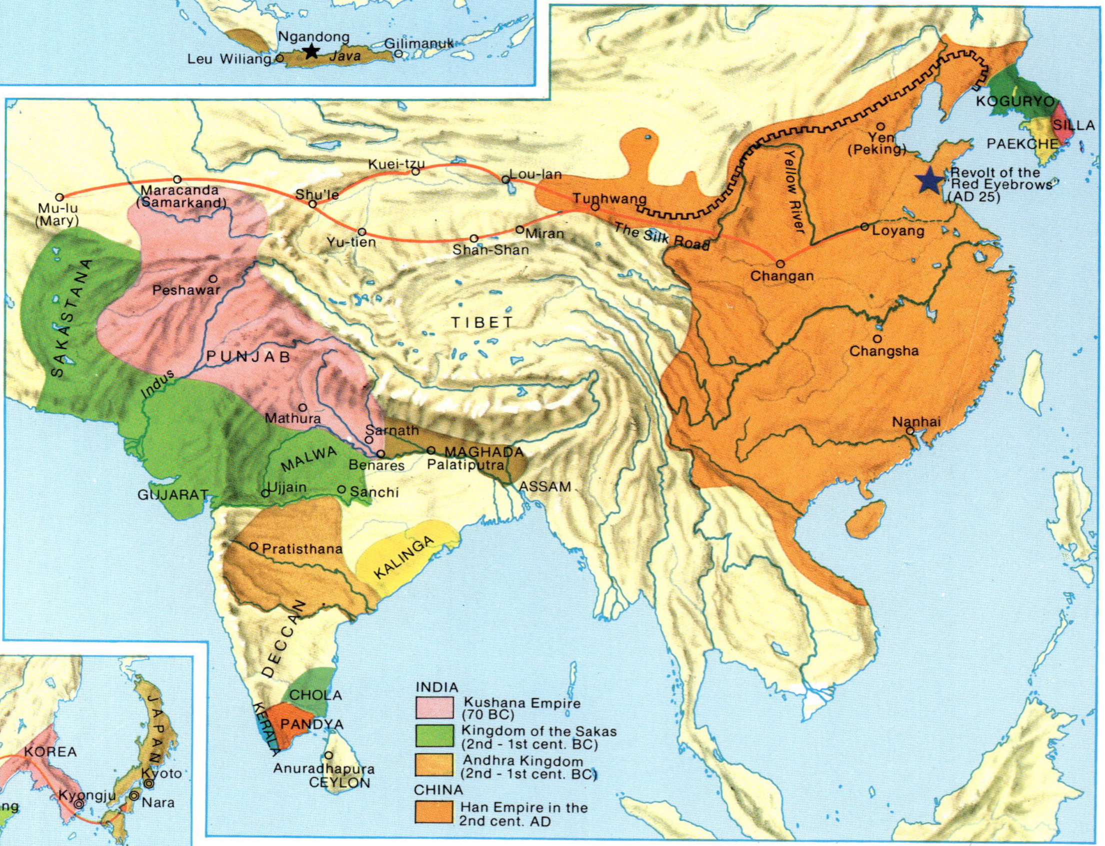

ASIA FROM THE FIRST CENTURY BC TO THE FIRST CENTURY AD

These centuries were a period of great change in Asia. The Indian subcontinent had seen the establishment of a flourishing empire under the Maurya Dynasty, which had taken in the whole area except for the extreme south. This was then replaced by small, rival kingdoms which came to be dominated by the Kingdom of Andhra, whose heyday was between the second and third centuries AD. In China, this period corresponded with the transfer of power from the Western Han to the Eastern Han Dynasty, an alteration which was marked by violent peasant uprisings such as the well-known revolt of the "Red Eyebrows" in AD 25.

THE RELIGIONS OF ASIA

Even though there is argument about the location of the first civilizations, there is no doubt that Asia was the centre of the first organized religions. Apart from Judaism, Christianity and Islam, which developed in the Mediterranean area after starting in Asia, all the other great religions were — and are — Asiatic, although some of them have now begun to make an impact in the West. Of these, Buddhism, Confucianism and Taoism originated more as philosophies than as religions centred on the concept of God; while Hinduism acknowledges many different deities and Shintoism venerates numerous *Kami*.

ASIATIC PEOPLES AND EMPIRES BETWEEN THE FOURTH AND THE SIXTH CENTURIES AD

The centuries which saw the crisis and fall of the Roman Empire in the West coincided with a period of great upheaval in the heart of Asia: for reasons still largely unknown, huge populations began moving from Central Asia towards the West, pushing before them the peoples they found settled on their routes. The groups which took part in these large-scale migrations are generally identified with the Mongolian peoples of Hsiung-nu and Juan-Juan, well known in the West as the Huns and the Avars. It was these people, and the populations that they absorbed en route, that descended upon the Roman Empire and demolished its already tottering structure.

ASIA BETWEEN THE TENTH AND THE TWELFTH CENTURIES

In this period, a number of remarkable developments occurred in Asia. In Central and Southern Asia, there emerged the expansionist Muslim Sultanate of the Ghaznevids, which was on the point of invading an India paralysed and weakened by internal conflicts. Further east lay China which, despite being divided between the Kingdom of Liao and the Empire of the Sung Dynasty, reached a high level of prosperity. In addition, other countries began to grow in importance: Japan in the Heian period, Indochina under the powerful Khmer, and Sumatra during the Srivijaya Empire.

NORTHERN ASIA AND THE EXPANSION OF RUSSIA

Today nearly half of Asia is incorporated in the Soviet Union, and the credit for this must go to two great Tzars, Ivan IV and Michael III. It was in fact Ivan the Terrible who, frustrated in his expansionistic aims towards the West, compensated for this by extending his power beyond the Urals. However, the colonization of the huge expanse of the steppes was the work of Michael, first Tzar of the Romanov Dynasty; in 1644, on the eve of his death, his Cossacks reached the Pacific coast for the first time.

ASIA IN THE FIFTEENTH AND SIXTEENTH CENTURIES

In the centuries preceding this period, the major phenomenon in Southwest Asia was the expansion of Islam. First of all it took strong root in India: here, the Empire of the Moguls, based in Fergana and founded in 1526 by Babar the Tiger, became the leading power in the north. Muslim power had also expanded elsewhere: by the fourteenth century it had reached as far as Indonesia. Other developments were also occurring in Asia: China under the Ming Dynasty reached magnificent levels of artistic achievement but, renouncing contact with the rest of the world, cut itself off from progress in other fields. By contrast, Japan under the Ashikaga Dynasty forged strong commercial links with other parts of the continent.

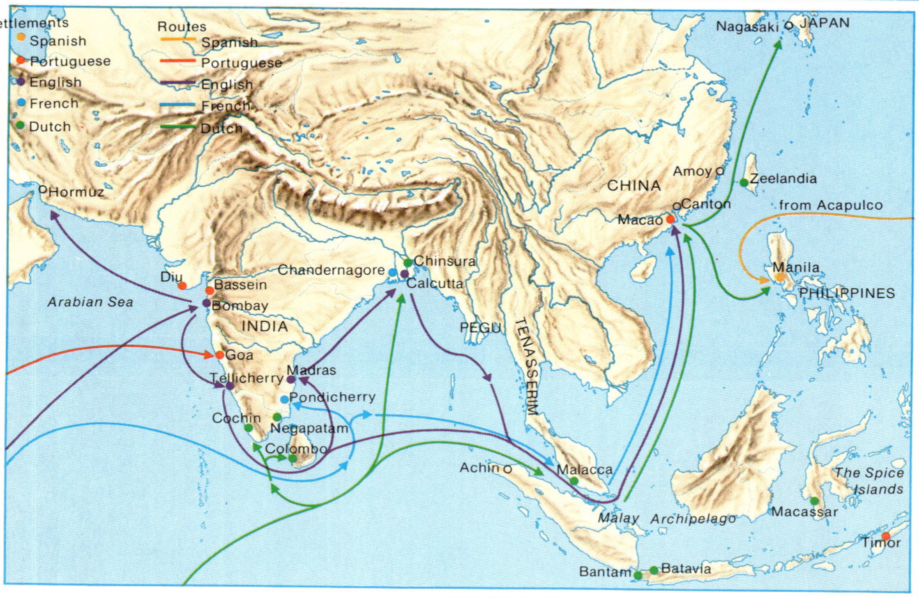

EUROPEAN PENETRATION INTO ASIA

Contacts between Europe and Asia go back many centuries but, for a long time, they were almost entirely limited to the nearest regions. Only in the late medieval and early modern period, with John of Plano Carpini and Marco Polo, followed by Vasco da Gama, did the Europeans discover the East Indies, Cathay (China) and Cipango (Japan). Thus began the process of European penetration into Asia, which was at first limited to the acquisition of trading-posts.

ASIA IN THE SEVENTEENTH AND EIGHTEENTH CENTURIES

Together with the intensification of European pressure, three major developments moulded the history of Asia in this period. In the Indian subcontinent, the Mogul Empire reached its climax, followed by rapid dissolution caused mainly by its lack of internal unity; in the Far East, the Manchu Dynasty, having overwhelmed China in 1644, progressively extended the frontiers of the Celestial Empire as far as Tibet and Mongolia; and in Japan, territorial unification was completed and the country then withdrew into splendid isolation for two centuries.

COLONIAL ASIA AT THE END OF THE NINETEENTH CENTURY

The main contestants in the race for colonial acquisitions in Asia were Britain, France and Russia, while the Netherlands remained secure in its possessions in Indonesia. The British took the lion's share, subjugating India, Ceylon (now Sri Lanka), Burma, Aden and Singapore.

MAO'S CHINA

The long history of China is full of extraordinary events but the most astonishing is the Long March between 1934 and 1935, when Mao Tse-tung and his comrades walked some 10,000 kilometres (nearly 6,500 miles) in 368 days, through thirteen provinces and sixty-three towns, while evading capture by the Nationalist forces.

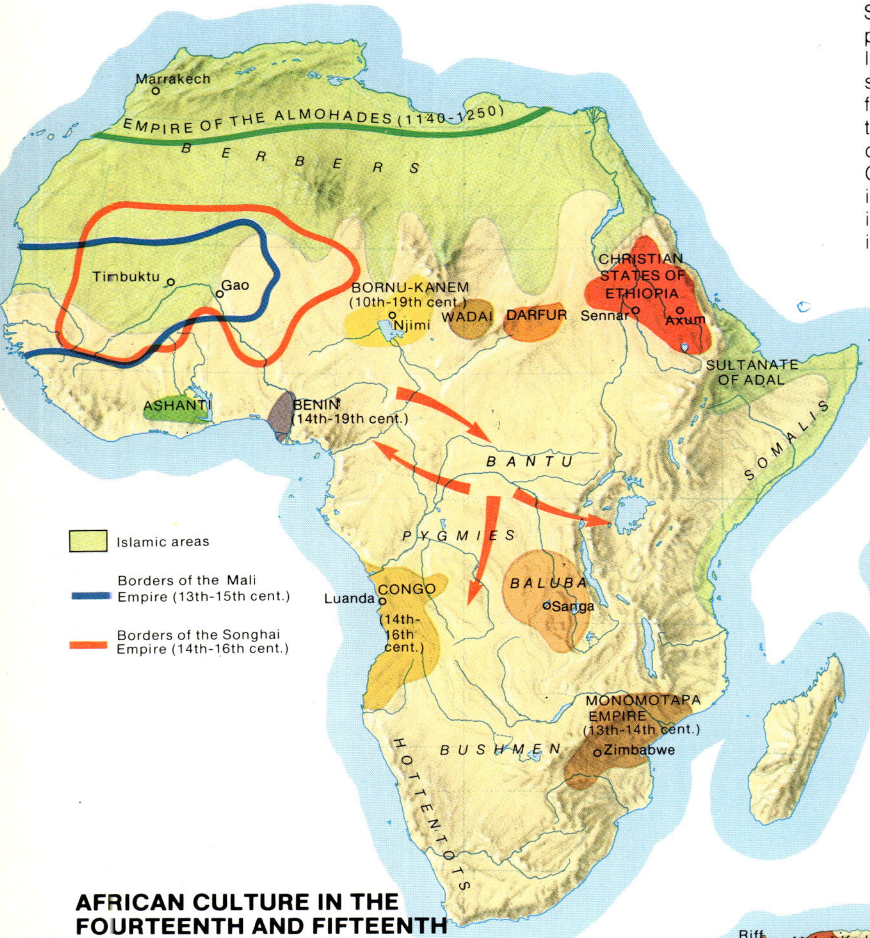

EUROPEAN PENETRATION IN AFRICA

Starting towards the end of the fifteenth century, as a partial consequence of the search for a route to the Indies, the European presence in Africa was limited for some centuries to coastal settlements designed chiefly for the trade in slaves. However, from the beginning of the eighteenth century, the Dutch (Boers) began limited colonization for agricultural purposes in the area of the Cape. In the following century there occurred massive intervention by the European powers, who penetrated into the interior of the continent to explore and partition it as though it were a prize of war.

AFRICAN CULTURE IN THE FOURTEENTH AND FIFTEENTH CENTURIES

The history of black Africa starts well before the arrival of white colonists. Unfortunately, African civilization before this did not make use of writing: it trusted entirely to oral tradition (except in Abyssinia, the mythical kingdom of Prester John, a Christian island surrounded by Islam). Elsewhere, north of the Equator, the Empires of Mali and Songhai, which emerged during the thirteenth and fourteenth centuries were also strongly Islamized: while south of the Equator and untouched by external influences were the typically African powers of Congo and Monomotapa.

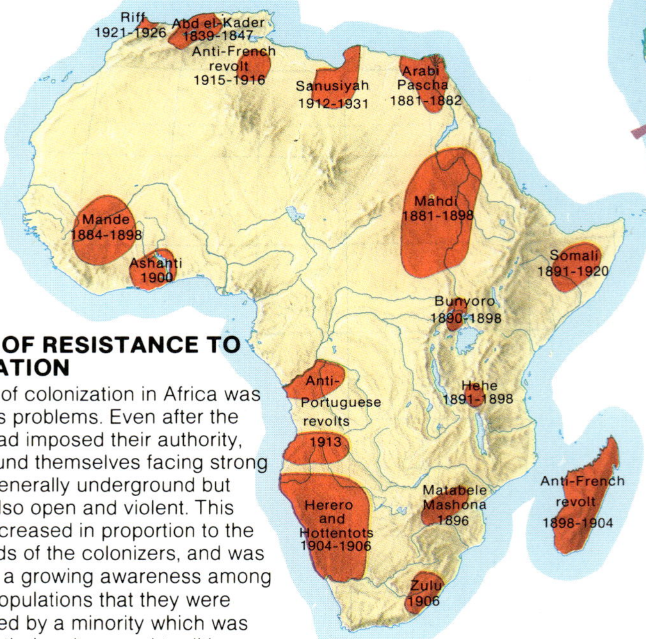

CENTRES OF RESISTANCE TO COLONIZATION

The process of colonization in Africa was not without its problems. Even after the Europeans had imposed their authority, they often found themselves facing strong resistance, generally underground but sometimes also open and violent. This resistance increased in proportion to the brutal methods of the colonizers, and was paralleled by a growing awareness among the African populations that they were being exploited by a minority which was quite alien to their culture and traditions.

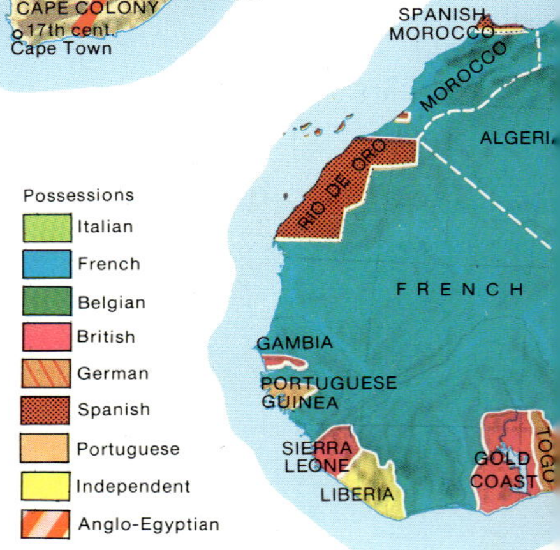

ETHNIC GROUPS

African ethnology has been and is still a real puzzle for researchers. The continent, which is so often called black, is in fact peopled by a mosaic of ethnic groups and subgroups, who range from the light-skinned (who live north of the Sahara) to the dark-skinned in the south. The exceptions are the inhabitants of the Sahara itself, and those of Ethiopia and Madagascar who have been subject to considerable metamorphosis.

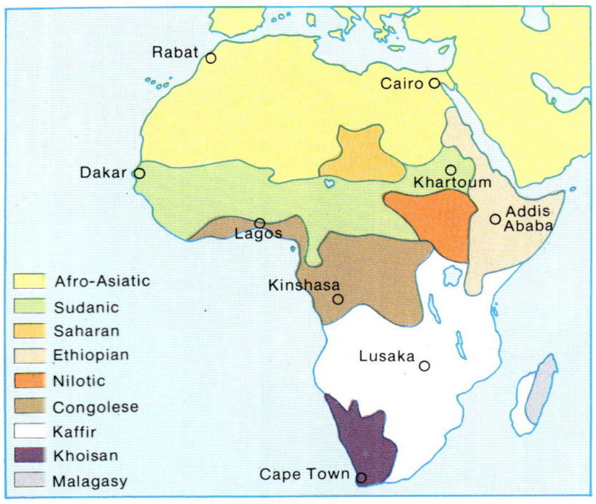

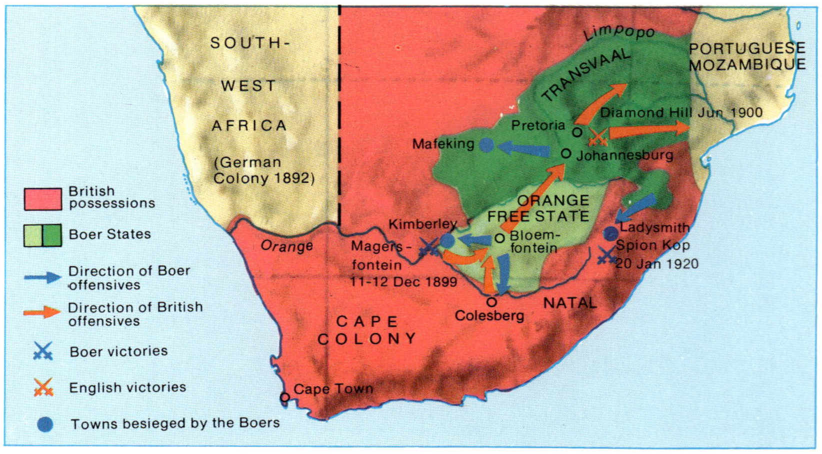

THE BOER WAR

This war, which was fought from 1899 to 1902, led to the defeat of the South African Boers by the dominant British power. It had an international significance out of all proportion to its military importance as the contest was so obviously not one between equals.

EUROPEAN EXPLORATIONS IN AFRICA

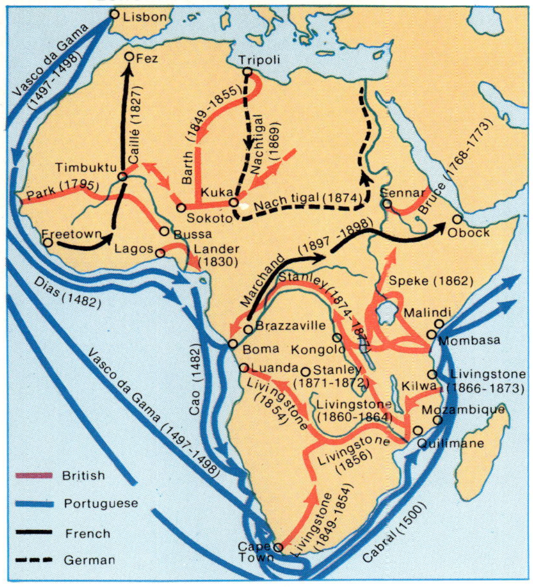

THE EXPLORATIONS OF AFRICA

Exclusively subject to the influence of Islam throughout the medieval period, Africa started to become a focus of interest for Europeans at the beginning of the modern era. From then onwards, exploration intensified: first, along the coasts and then later up the great rivers. It was only in the nineteenth century that European explorers dared to penetrate into the interior of the continent. Among the many — English, French, Germans and Italians — who contributed to the adventure of exploration, the Englishman Livingstone and the American Stanley stand out as legendary figures.

COLONIAL AFRICA

On the eve of the First World War there were only two regions of Africa independent of the colonial powers—Ethiopia to the east and Liberia to the west. The remainder of the continent was either directly or indirectly under European control. With the Italian conquest of Ethiopia in 1936, Liberia alone retained a degree of independence.

AFRICA

AFRICAN STATES WHICH HAVE REACHED INDEPENDENCE SINCE 1945

(The date of independence is given at the end of each entry)

ALGERIA French Colony. 3 July 1962.
ANGOLA Colony and later overseas Province of Portugal. 11 Nov 1975.
BENIN French Colony. Independent as Republic of Dahomey, 1 Aug 1960, as Benin from 30 Nov 1975.
BOTSWANA British Protectorate of Bechuanaland. 30 Sept 1966.
BURKINA FASO French Colony. Independent as Upper Volta, 5 Aug 1960, as Burkina Faso from 4 Aug 1984.
BURUNDI Part of Ruanda-Urundi, a Belgian Trusteeship. 1 July 1962.
CAMEROON French Trusteeship. 1 Jan 1960. The British Trust Territory of the Southern Cameroons joined on 1 Oct 1961.
CAPE VERDE Overseas Province of Portugal. 5 July 1975.
CENTRAL AFRICAN REPUBLIC French Colony of Ubanghi Shari. 13 Aug 1960.
CHAD French Colony. 11 Aug 1960.
COMOROS French Territory. 6 July 1975.
CONGO French Colony. 15 Aug 1960.
DJIBOUTI French Colony as French Somaliland until 1967; then the French Territory of the Afars and Issas. 27 June 1977.
EQUATORIAL GUINEA Spanish colony. 12 Oct 1968.
ERITREA Italian Colony, annexed to Ethiopia in 1962. 24 May 1993.
GABON French Colony. 17 Aug 1960.
GAMBIA British Colony. 18 Feb 1965.
GHANA British Colony of the Gold Coast. 6 Mar 1957.
GUINEA French Colony. 2 Oct 1958.
GUINEA-BISSAU Portuguese Colony. 10 Sept 1974.
IVORY COAST French Colony. 7 Aug 1960.
KENYA British Colony. 12 Dec 1963.
LESOTHO British Protectorate of Basutoland. 4 Oct 1966.
LIBYA Italian Colony, placed under British and French administration in 1943. 24 Dec 1951.
MADAGASCAR French Colony. 26 June 1960.
MALAWI British Protectorate of Nyasaland. 6 July 1964.
MALI French Colony. 22 Sept 1960.
MAURITANIA French Colony. 28 Nov 1960.
MAURITIUS British Colony. 12 March 1968.
MAROCCO French Colony and, in part, Spanish. 28 Mar 1956.
MOZAMBIQUE Colony and later overseas Province of Portugal. 25 June 1975.
NAMIBIA German and then South-African Colony. 21 March 1990.
NIGER French Colony. 3 Aug 1960.
NIGERIA British Colony and Protectorate. 1 Oct 1960.
RWANDA Part of Ruanda-Urundi, a Belgian trusteeship. 1 July 1962.
SAO TOMÉ E PRINCIPE Colony and overseas Province of Portugal. 12 July 1975.
SENEGAL French Colony. 11 Sept 1960.
SEYCHELLES British Colony. 28 June 1976.
SIERRA LEONE British Colony and Protectorate. 27 April 1961.
SOMALIA It resulted from the union of the Italian Trusteeship of Somalia and the British Protectorate of Somaliland. 1 July 1960.
SUDAN Anglo-Egyptian Condominium. 1 Jan 1956.
SWAZILAND British Protectorate. 6 Sept 1968.
TANZANIA It resulted from the union of Tanganyika, a British Colony (with Kenya and Uganda it formed East Africa) which became independent on 9 Dec 1961, and Zanzibar, a British Protectorate which gained independence on 10 Dec 1963.
TOGO German Colony, later a French Trusteeship. 27 April 1960.
TUNISIA French Protectorate. 20 Mar 1956.
UGANDA British Protectorate. 19 Oct 1962.
ZAIRE Belgian Colony as the Belgian Congo. 30 June 1960.
ZAMBIA British Protectorate of Northern Rhodesia. 24 Oct 1964.
ZIMBABWE British Colony. Independent as Republic of Rhodesia on 11 Nov 1965; then as Republic of Zimbabwe Rhodesia on 1 June 1979. Temporarily a British Colony from 11 Dec 1979. Final independence as Republic of Zimbabwe on 13 April 1980.

NORTH AMERICA

THE FIRST COLONIZERS

The origin of the peoples of the American continent is still a matter of debate. Nevertheless, ethnologists agree that the first immigration to America from North-east Asia occurred approximately 50,000–70,000 years ago. Further waves of Asiatic peoples came later, perhaps contemporary with the arrival by sea of migrants from Polynesia.

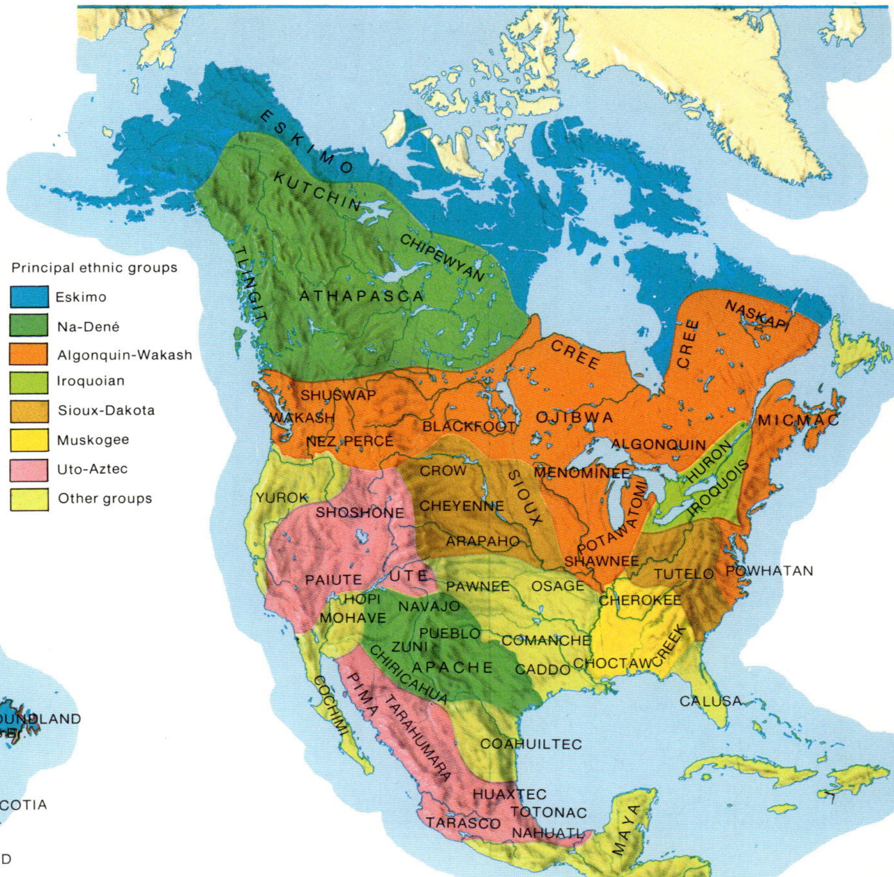

THE COLONIZATION OF AMERICA

North of the region of Mexico, conquered in the sixteenth century by the Spaniards and organized in the Viceroyalty of New Spain, European settlements developed gradually — and often in conflict with each other — during the seventeenth century. The race for colonies involved Sweden, the Netherlands, Russia, France and England. However, ultimately, France and England became the main competitors and the latter became dominant.

ETHNIC GROUPS

The Amerindians or American Indians were the original inhabitants of North America, now reduced in number to a few hundred thousand. The classification of the various ethnic groups is based on linguistic differences, of which there are six or eight major categories.

MEXICO 1836–1853

The period from 1824 to 1855 (the dates of the rise to power and subsequent overthrow of General Santa Ana) is one of the most troubled in Mexican history. In 1836, Texas declared itself independent before joining the United States in 1845, leading to a disastrous war which cost Mexico further losses to the USA — New Mexico and much of its Californian territory.

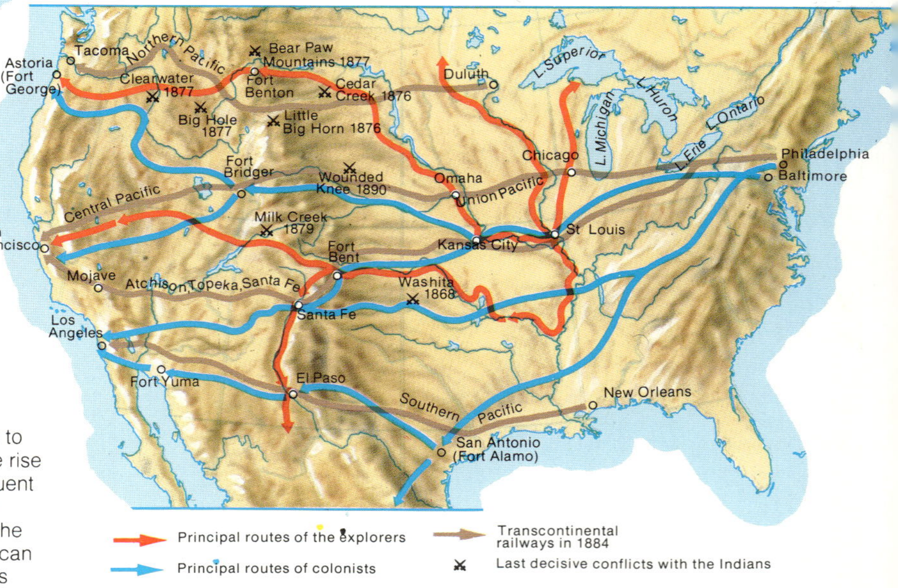

THE CONQUEST OF THE WEST

While it had required two centuries for the European immigrants to colonize the narrow strip of land along the Atlantic coast, it took less than a century — the nineteenth — for the American pioneers (explorers, fur trappers and farmers) to extend the frontier as far as the Pacific Ocean. The epic advance began along natural routes (the valley of the Ohio, the Great Plains, the Rocky Mountain passes) and was later facilitated by the building of roads and railways. The immense spaces were colonized at the expense of the Indians who were forced into special reservations established for this purpose.

NORTH AMERICA

THE ATLANTIC COAST

Up to the 1820s, North American life was confined to the areas of the Atlantic coast, from Florida to Labrador and extending no more than 300 kilometres (less than 200 miles) inland. The heart of the continent, although contested at the conference table between France and England, was in reality a stronghold of the American Indians. On the eastern seaboard, however, the English were gradually taking over French and Spanish possessions.

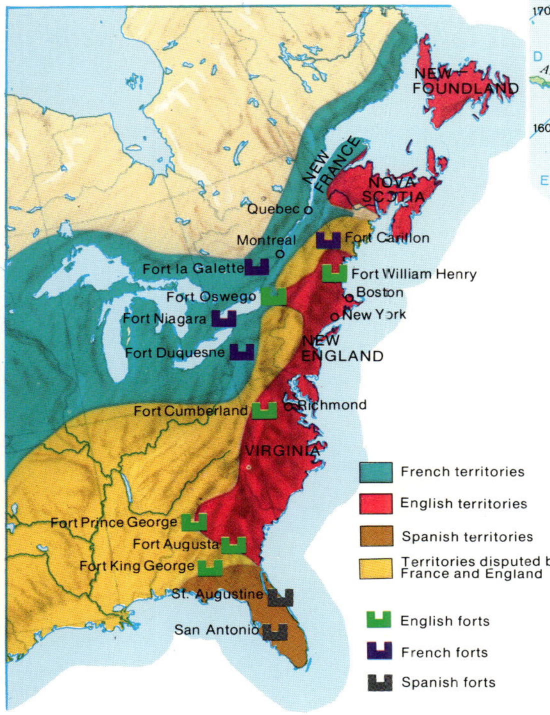

THE WAR OF INDEPENDENCE

After the elimination of the French presence in North America, England's oppressive policies towards its colonies caused great resentment. The incidents at Boston in 1773, the first Congress at Philadelphia in 1774, and the clashes at Lexington and Concord in 1775, marked the transition from political friction to open war. The victory of the colonists, supported by France and Spain, compelled the British to recognize the independence of the United States in the Treaty of Paris in 1783.

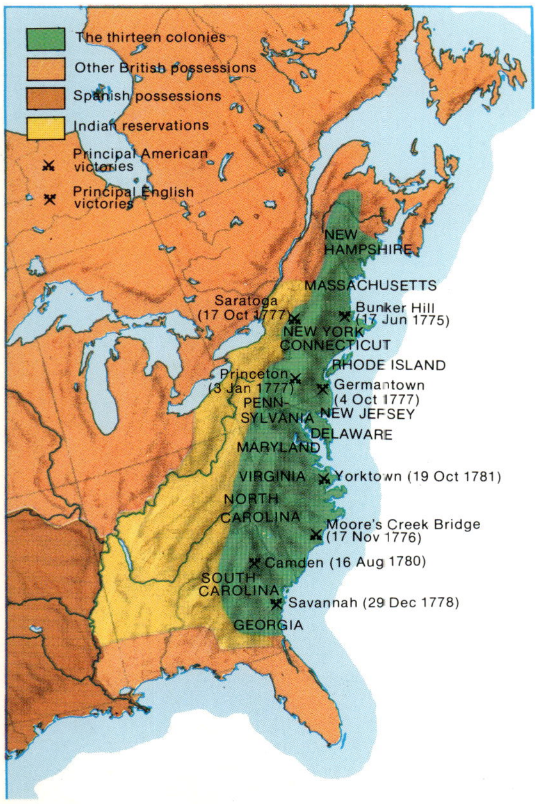

THE DEVELOPMENT OF THE UNITED STATES

The development of the United States took more than a century, and was the result of a variety of events. These included the War of Independence from Britain; the war with Mexico which ended in 1848; peaceful agreements with Britain in 1818 and 1846; and the purchases of Louisiana from France (for fifteen million dollars), Florida from Spain, Southern Arizona from Mexico and Alaska from Russia.

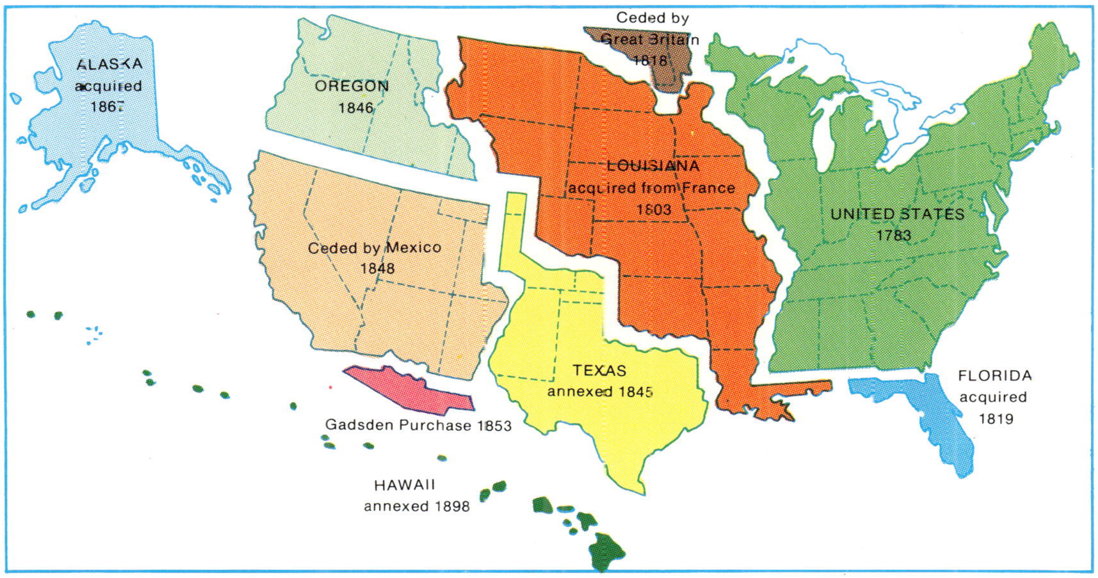

SOUTH AMERICA

ETHNIC GROUPS

South America, populated a long time ago by the same peoples as those that settled in the North, today presents a varied ethnic and linguistic picture. Nevertheless, except in the region of the Andes, the continent was thinly populated before the time of Columbus.

SOUTH AMERICA FROM THE CONQUEST TO THE TWENTIETH CENTURY

The Conquest (*below left*). The mirage of fabulous wealth, associated with the pre-Columbian civilizations of the Maya, Aztecs and Incas, was the great lure for the European conquerors. Once the Spaniards had crushed these great empires, they set up the four viceroyalties of New Spain, New Granada, Peru and Plata.

Independent America (*below centre*). The evolution of the Spanish colonies, combined with the increasing power of a Creole aristocracy and the example of the United States in gaining independence from the British, underlay the anti-Spanish movements which, between 1810 and 1826, led to the independence of Latin America.

The formation of the South American states (*below right*). The end of Spanish dominion left the problems of the territorial settlement of the continent unresolved. With the failure of Bolivar's scheme for unification, Latin America divided into a series of often rival states.

Region of Lapita pottery

Development of a Polynesian type of culture in about AD 300

First colonization of Eastern Polynesia by Lapita people around AD 300

First voyages of colonization from the primary dispersal centre

THE COLONIZATION OF OCEANIA

Melanesia was colonized between 1000 and 200 BC by seamen who spread the Lapita style of ceramics (so-called after a site in New Caledonia). Following this, the Marquesas Islands became the centre for the diffusion of Polynesian culture: it spread to the remotest islands, colonized between AD 400 and 850.

EYRE 1840

STUART 1861-1862

LEICHHARDT 1844-1845

STURT 1830

BURKE AND WILLS 1860-1861

THE EXPLORATION OF AUSTRALIA

The colonization of the Australian continent, discovered by Cook in 1769, was at first confined to the south-eastern coast. It was only around the middle of the nineteenth century that explorers started travelling into the interior in a vain search for fertile land. Further explorations in the deserts of the western and central areas continued into the early twentieth century.

The international organizations

After the Second World War, a number of international organizations were set up to facilitate economic, political and military cooperation. The United Nations Organization (UNO), to which almost all states belong, was founded in 1945 to secure world peace and to promote social, economic and cultural progress. Its two main directing bodies are the General Assembly and the Security Council. Special agencies, charged with handling particular problems, are the Food and Agriculture Organization (FAO), the United Nations Educational, Scientific and Cultural Organization (UNESCO), and the World Health Organization (WHO).

Europe

EUROPEAN ECONOMIC COMMUNITY (EEC). Its members are France, West Germany, Italy, the Netherlands, Belgium, Luxembourg, Great Britain, Ireland, Denmark, Greece, Spain and Portugal. Its main focus is on economic cooperation. Associated with it are.
European Coal and Steel Community (ECSC).
European Atomic Energy Community (EURATOM).

Other European organizations are:
BENELUX set up in 1958 to promote economic union between Belgium, the Netherlands and Luxembourg.
COUNCIL FOR MUTUAL ECONOMIC ASSISTANCE (COMECON) to coordinate the economic development of the states of Eastern Europe. Its headquarters were in Moscow. Dissolved on 28th June 1991.
COUNCIL OF EUROPE to encourage socio-economic development. It was set up in 1949 and includes, apart from the EEC countries, a number of other Western European states.
NORDIC COUNCIL for social and economic development and cooperation. Its members are Denmark, Iceland, Sweden, Norway and Finland.
NORTH ATLANTIC TREATY ORGANIZATION (NATO). It was set up in 1949 for military defence purposes. It includes many Western European states, together with its leading member, the United States.
WARSAW PACT. It brought together the countries of Eastern Europe, under the leadership of the Soviet Union, for purposes of cooperation and mutual assistance. These led to the formation of a unified military command. Dissolved on 1st July 1991.

Asia

COLOMBO PLAN. It was set up in 1950 to bring together a number of developing Asian and industrialized countries.
ARAB LEAGUE. A military and political organization, it includes Arab states in both Asia and Africa.

Africa

ORGANIZATION OF AFRICAN UNITY (OAU). It was founded in 1963 to promote unity and solidarity of African states.

Latin America

ORGANIZATION OF AMERICAN STATES (OAS). Its purpose is to guarantee the peace and progress of the continent. Its members include many countries of Central and South America as well as the United States.

Oceania

ANZUS PACT. Il promotes the mutual defence of Australia, New Zealand and the United States.

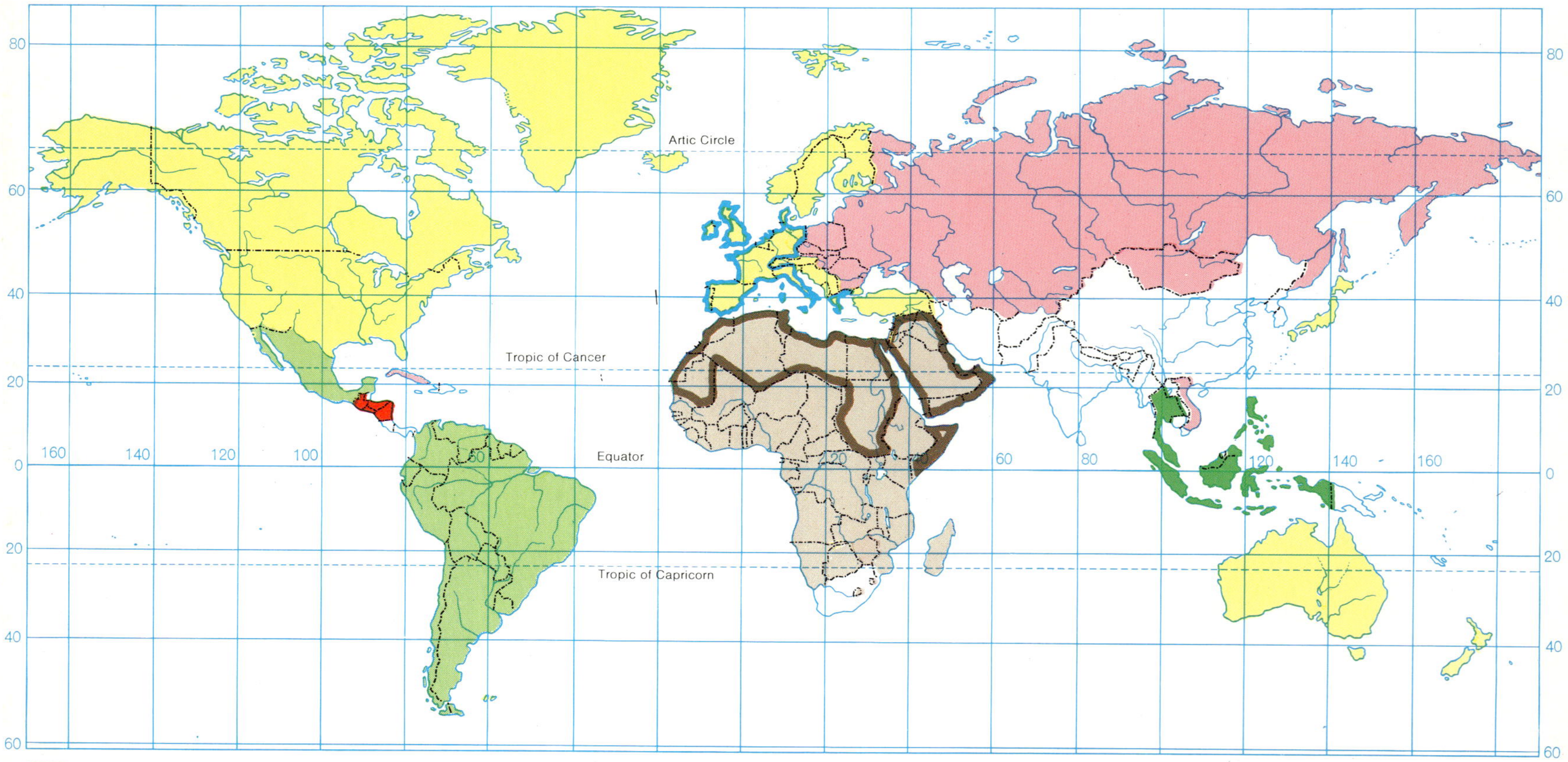

- OECD (Organisation for Economic Co-operation and Development)
- COMECON (Council for Mutual Economic Aid) - **Until 28/VI - 1991**
- EEC (European Economic Community)
- ALALC (Latin American Free Trade Association)
- OCAS (Organisation of Central American States)
- Arab League
- OAU (Organisation of African Unity)
- ASEAN (Association of South East Asian Nations)

CHRONOLOGIES

8000 BC

EUROPE

3000 Bronze culture in Crete.

2500 Start of Cretan Minoan civilization which then spread to other Mediterranean areas.

2000 Building of the great Minoan palaces in Crete.
Megalithic monument erected at Stonehenge in England.

1650 Zenith of Cretan civilization under the legendary King Minos.

1450 Cretan Minoan civilization destroyed by an unknown event, possibly an earthquake.

1320 Peak of Mycenaean civilization in Greece.

1280 Greek penetration of Asia Minor, perhaps as a consequence of Dorian invasions from the north. Period of the Trojan Wars.

1100 Phoenicians, colonizing the Mediterranean, founded settlements on the Sardinian coast.

1050 Culmination of the Villanova culture in Italy.

ASIA AND OCEANIA

2935 Period of the legendary Fu-hsi, first civilizer of China, who was married to Nü Kua.

2698 Reign of the legendary Yellow Emperor Huang Ti, traditionally credited with the invention of all sciences and arts and the introduction of silkworm farming.

2500 Yang-shao civilization developed in Honan, China. First traces of settlements in the Indus valley, India.

2300 Development of a flourishing civilization in the Indus valley, near Harappa and Mohenjo-Daro.

2000 First settlements in Melanesia by Indonesian peoples.

1760 Indus valley civilization destroyed by an Aryan invasion.

1600 Development of an urban civilization in China under the Shang Dynasty.

c.1300 Fiji and Western Polynesia populated.

1100 Start of the decline of the Shang Dynasty in China.

1027 The Chou Kingdom formed in China.

AFRICA AND THE MIDDLE EAST

3500 Development of a city state of farmers at Erech, principal centre of Sumerian civilization.

3400 In Upper and Lower Egypt, two distinct kingdoms formed from the diverse populations of the Nile valley. In Mesopotamia, cities such as Ur, Lagash, Umma and Kish developed.

3100 The semi-legendary Pharaoh Menes unified Egypt, establishing his capital at Memphis.

2750 Reign of the legendary Gilgamesh at Erech. Development of the Accadian Empire. Reign of Pharaoh Zoser in Egypt and beginning of the Third Dynasty which, together with the Fourth, Fifth and Sixth Dynasties, constituted the Old Kingdom which lasted until c.2150 BC.

2500 Conflict between the Sumerian cities of Ur, Kish and Lagash.

2350 Sargon the Great, King of the Accadians, conquered the Sumerian cities.

2180 Collapse of the Accadian Empire and rule by the Gutians. Kingdom of Gudea at Lagash.

2042 Revival, based on Ur, of Sumerian civilization under Shulgi, son of Urnammu.

1950 The Amorites, of Semitic stock, invaded Mesopotamia.

1792 The Amorite King Hammurabi of Babylon subjugated the peoples between the Tigris and the Euphrates.

1700 Apogee of Hittite civilization in Anatolia.

1575 In Egypt Kings Kamose and Amosis drove out the Hyksos invaders and founded the New Kingdom.

1500 Remarkable development of the Hittite Kingdom in Anatolia, the Mitanni Kingdom in northern Mesopotamia and of the Assyrians further south, along the Tigris.

1440 The Assyrians conquered by the Mitanni.

1360 The Hittites conquered the Mitanni.

1200 The "Sea Peoples" probably from the Caspian region, overthrew Hittite domination and reached Egypt, from where they were repulsed by Ramses III to settle on the coast of Palestine.

1124 Return of Babylon to prosperity and power under Nebuchadnezzar I.

1100 King Tiglathpileser I of Assyria defeated Babylon and conquered Mesopotamia.

1077 The Arameans defeated the Assyrians and seized Babylon.

AMERICA

3000 First production of ceramics in the region of modern Colombia and Ecuador.

2000 First manufactures in metal in the region of modern Peru.

1200 The Olmec civilization developed in Mexico, around the sacred city of La Venta.

SCIENCE AND TECHNOLOGY

3500 In Mesopotamia, the plough was invented, the first wheeled vehicles appeared, and working in copper and its alloys began.

3000 Invention of the potter's wheel.

2500 On the Asian steppes the horse was domesticated.

2000 Use of the sail in the Eastern Mediterranean.

1900 In Sardinia, the *nuraghi* were constructed. In Egypt, building began of the temples at Karnak. In China, large ritual bronze vases were made. The Hittites learned to work iron, although they did not succeed in melting it. The Egyptian method of raising river or canal water by bucket spread to Mesopotamia.

1760 The lost wax method was adopted in Mesopotamia.

1650 Introduction of ploughshares to Mesopotamia.

1520 First glass containers made in Egypt.

1500 Bronze urns and vases made in China.

1440 Developments in iron working in the Hittite region.

1400 The water clock was invented in the region of Egypt.

1360 The first copper coins were minted in Egypt.

1320 Copper and silver trumpets made in Egypt.

CULTURE AND ARTS

8000–4000 First agricultural settlements in Lower Mesopotamia (Tigris-Euphrates) and in the Nile valley.

3500 First cuneiform inscriptions in Mesopotamia.

3000 Beginning of hieroglyphic writing in Egypt.

2500 In Egypt, the age of the Pyramids, under Pharaohs Cheops, Chephren and Mycerinus.

2000 Pyramid texts, dealing with ritual and myth (found in Egyptian tombs).

1950 Evolution of cuneiform script in Mesopotamia.

1840 At Babylon, oral tradition took shape in the story of the Creation.

1760 Flowering of Hittite literature.

1680 The Phoenicians developed an alphabet of 22 phonetic symbols.

1520 Compilation of the *Rigveda* sacred books began in India.

1440 Akhenaton tried to enforce the monotheistic cult of the sun in Egypt.

1280 Ramses II built the rock temple of Abu Simbel and finished construction at Luxor.

AD 1000

EUROPE

950 Italic cultures developed side by side with the flowering of Etruscan civilization in Tuscany, Latium and Campania.

753 According to legend, Romulus founded Rome on 21 April.

750 Beginning of Greek colonization in the Mediterranean. Locri, Agrigentum and Syracuse founded.

683 Archons (the tyrants) took over government in Athens. Similar developments in other Greek cities, such as Corinth.

594 The laws of Solon in Athens.

509 Tarquin the Proud was driven from Rome and a Republic was set up.

490 The Athenians under Miltiades defeated the Persians at Marathon.

480 The invasion of Greece by the Persians under Xerxes was defeated after the heroic resistance of Leonidas at Thermopilae, and the Greek victories at Salamis and (479) Plataea.

478 Foundation of the Delian League in Greece. Greek victories against the Carthaginians (480) and the Etruscans (474).

431 The Peloponnesian War between Sparta and Athens lasted until 404 and led to the decline of both city states.

390 The Gauls reached Rome.

356 Philip II became King of Macedon.

338 The Battle of Chaeronea gave Philip II control of Greece.

ASIA AND OCEANIA

1000 Spread of the Aryans in India along the Ganges.

771 Nomadic invasion from the north pushed the Chou civilization into the Loyang region. It was followed by five and a half centuries of chaos.

700 Invasion of the Scythians into Western Europe from the steppes of Central Asia.

c.660 Reign of Jimmu, traditionally the first Emperor of Japan.

567 Supposed year of the birth of Buddha, who lived until 487.

551 Birth of Confucius. He died in 479.

539 The region of Kabul annexed to the Achaemenid Empire of Cyrus.

522 Darius I annexed the Indus basin to the Achaemenid Empire.

481 Beginning of the "Epoch of the Warring States" in China.

400 Start of the period of the Taoist classics.

AFRICA AND THE MIDDLE EAST

1000 David took over from Saul and led the Israelites against the Philistines.

961 Solomon, son of David, ruled the Jews.

922 On the death of Solomon, his kingdom was divided into two, Israel in the north and Judah in the south.

854 At Karkar a coalition of Arameans and Israelites defeated King Shalmaneser III of Assyria.

814 The Phoenicians founded Carthage.

c.750 Rise of the Kingdom of Kush in Nubia.

746 The Assyrian Empire revived under Tiglathpileser III, Shalmaneser V and Sargon II; Babylon reconquered.

704 Start of the reign of Sennacherib II, founder of Nineveh.

668 Start of the reign of Assurbanapal, last of the great Assyrian conquerors.

612 Chaldeans and Medes under Nabopolassar defeated the Assyrians: Nineveh destroyed.

605 Start of a new age of splendour in Babylon under Nebuchadnezzar II.

586 Nebuchadnezzar II entered Jerusalem, destroyed the Temple and deported the Jews to Babylon.

562 Death of Nebuchadnezzar II.

549 The Persian Cyrus conquered the Medes and founded the Achaemenid Empire. Two years later, he reached the coast of Asia Minor and subjugated the Greek cities there.

539 Cyrus conquered Babylon. The Jews returned to Palestine.

525 Cambyses, successor to Cyrus on the Achaemenid throne, conquered Egypt.

494 The Persians suppressed a revolt by the Greeks of Asia Minor.

456 Failure of an Egyptian revolt against the Persians.

343 Artaxerxes III dethroned the last Egyptian Pharaoh.

AMERICA

800 Flowering of the Chavin culture in Peru.

500 First examples of hieroglyphic writing at Monte Albán in Mexico.

400 The Mochica and Nazca cultures developed in the valleys of the Peruvian Andes.

SCIENCE AND TECHNOLOGY

1000 Iron ploughshares introduced in Mesopotamia.

750 The Assyrians built the first siege towers.

700 First Greek coins minted in silver.

580 Anaximander produced the first map of the known world.

520 Completion of the canal linking the River Nile and the Red Sea in Egypt.

CULTURE AND ARTS

969 Construction of the Temple of Soloman at Jerusalem.

850 The poems of Homer first written down.

800 Writing of the *Upanishad* in India.

776 First Olympic Games.

700 Development of the Hallstatt culture in Austria and Central Europe.

682 The Greek Terpander introduced the art of singing with a musical accompaniment.

650 Writing of *Deuteronomy*.

640 Birth of Thales of Miletus, the first great Greek philosopher.

588 Beginning of the preaching of Zoroaster.

530 Start of the teaching of Pythagoras.

528 Traditional date of death of Mahavira, founder of Jainism.

500 Arguments in China over the theories of Confucius.

487 Death of Siddharta Gautama, the Buddha.

479 Death of Confucius.

450 Development of the La Tène culture in Western-Central Europe.

438 Pheidias sculpted the statue of Athena Parthenos.

408 Meeting between Socrates and Plato.

384 Birth of Aristotle.

AD **334**

EUROPE

272 Rome completed the conquest of southern and central Italy.

264 Start of the First Punic War. Rome won (241) and took control of Sicily.

218 Second Punic War began with Hannibal's invasion of Italy. It ended after Scipio's victory at Zama in 202.

206 Roman conquest of Spain.

168 Following the victory of Lucius Aemilius Paullus at Pydna, Rome conquered Macedonia.

149 Beginning of the Third Punic War. It ended three years later with the destruction of Carthage.

146 Roman conquest and sack of Corinth. Domination of Greece by Rome.

133 Rome inherited the Kingdom of Pergamum from Attalos.

89 The Italic peoples were granted Roman citizenship.

58 Caesar began the conquest of Gaul.

49 War between Caesar and Pompey. Caesar became sole ruler of Rome (45).

44 Assassination of Caesar.

27 On 16 January, the Roman Senate gave the title of Augustus to Octavian who later became Emperor.

AD **14** Tiberius succeeded Augustus.

43 Roman invasion of Britain.

64 Persecution of Christians. The deaths of the apostles Peter and Paul probably occurred during this period.

96 Trajan became Emperor. Under him, Rome attained its greatest power.

135 Revolt of the Jews at Jerusalem during the reign of Hadrian (117-138)

166 During the reign of Marcus Aurelius (161-180), while Rome was at war with the Parthians, a plague spread westwards from Persia.

212 The Emperor Caracalla (211-217) granted Roman citizenship to all subjects of the Empire.

257 The Goths seized Dacia from the Roman Empire.

293 Diocletian (284-305) reorganized the Roman Empire.

ASIA AND OCEANIA

327 Alexander the Great reached the basin of the Indus.

323 Beginning of the Maurya Empire in India, which lasted until 185 BC.

273 The Empire of Asoka in India. It lasted until 232 BC. Asoka was converted to Buddism in 261.

221 Cheng, also named Shih Huang-ti, united China.

206 End of the Ch'in Dynasty in China.

202 The Emperor Liu P'ang took power in China: beginning of the Han Dynasty.

200 Invasion of India by Demetrius, Greek monarch from Bactria.

140 Accession of the Emperior Wu Ti in China: Confucianism became the official philosophy.

AD **25** After the usurpation of Wang Mang, the Han Dynasty regained power in China.

220 End of the Han Empire: China divided into three kingdoms.

224 The Kushan Empire, to the north-west of India, annexed by the Sassanid Empire.

AFRICA AND THE MIDDLE EAST

333 Alexander the Great won the Battle of Issus. In the next ten years, he conquered the whole of the Middle East as far as the frontiers of India.

323 Death of Alexander and the division of his empire among his generals (the *Diadochi*). Rise of new rulers, such as the Seleucids in Syria and the Ptolemies in Egypt.

146 End of the Third Punic War and destruction of Carthage by the Romans.

64 Syria became a Roman province.

30 Egypt became a Roman province.

AD **10** Decline of the Nubian Kingdom of Kush.

66 Jewish rebellion against Rome: Jerusalem and the Temple destroyed by the Emperor Titus after fours years of warfare.

135 Ruthless suppression of a revolt by Zealots in Palestine: beginning of the Jewish Diaspora (Dispersion).

224 Ardashir founded the Sassanid Empire in Persia.

AMERICA

250 Beginning of the decline of the Olmec civilization in Mexico.

117 Round pyramid at Cuicuilco in Mexico.

AD 200 Development of the culture of Teotihuacán in Central Mexico.

292 First datable inscription on a Maya monument (Stele 29, Tikal).

SCIENCE AND TECHNOLOGY

300 The mathematical school at Alexandria studied the lever, the siphon, the screw and the pulley. Euclid was its greatest scholar.

220 Archimedes established the general principles of hydrostatics.

c.200 The technique of blowing glass reached the Roman world from Syria. The making of parchment began at Pergamum.

140 Hipparchus measured the distance between the Earth and the Sun.

50 The Romans perfected watermills and aqueducts.

AD 60 Under the Han Dynasty, the Chinese discovered the *camera obscura*, concave and convex mirrors, and the use of paper. Their astronomers studied eclipses and the movement of the planets.

150 The astronomer Ptolemy collected his theories into his *Almagest*.

160 The Roman medical school reached its height with Galen's work.

CULTURE AND ARTS

312 Pyrrho founded scepticism.

300 Euclid wrote the *Elements*.

290 Foundation of the library at Alexandria in Egypt.

216 Writing of *Ecclesiastes*.

204 Completion of the Great Wall of China.

124 Foundation of the first university in China.

46 Julius Caesar reformed the calendar.

29 Virgil began writing the *Aeneid*.

AD 30 Jesus of Nazareth crucified at Jerusalem.

46 Beginning of the missionary activity of St Paul.

122 Construction of Hadrian's Wall in Britain.

186 In India, the final version of the *Ramayana* written.

242 Beginning of the preaching of Mani, founder of Manichaeism, who was crucified in 276.

300

EUROPE

313 After the victory over Maxentius at the Milvian Bridge, the Emperor Constantine issued the Edict of Milan granting Christians freedom of worship.

330 Constantine transferred the capital of the Roman Empire to Constantinople.

376 The Visigoths crossed the Danube.

395 Division of the Roman Empire between Honorius (Emperor in the East) and Arcadius (Emperor in the West).

402 Ravenna made the capital of the Western Roman Empire.

406 Beginning of the Vandal invasions.

410 Conquest and sack of Rome by the Visigoths under Alaric.

452 Major invasion of Huns under Attila, stopped – according to tradition – by the intervention of the Pope.

455 Rome conquered by the Vandals.

476 Deposition of the last Roman Emperor, Romulus Augustulus, by Odoacer, King of the Heruls. End of the Western Roman Empire.

486 Merovingian Dynasty founded by Clovis I, King of the Franks.

493 Theodoric, King of the Ostrogoths, took power in Italy and established his capital at Ravenna.

496 Conversion of the Franks to Christianity.

507 Clovis defeated the Visigoths at Vouillé, confirming the predominance of the Franks in Western Europe.

553 Reconquest of Italy and part of Spain (554) by the Byzantines under the Emperor Justinian (527–565).

568 Start of the invasion of Italy by the Lombards.

590 Beginning of the pontificate of Gregory the Great, during which the Lombards were converted to Christianity.

643 Edict of Rothari, the basis of Lombard legislation.

680 The Balkans invaded by the Bulgars.

711 Arab invasion of Spain across the Straits of Gibraltar.

ASIA AND OCEANIA

311 The Hsiung-nu, Hsien-pei and Tabgac, nomadic peoples from the Asian steppes, gradually devastated China.

320 The Gupta Dynasty rose to power in northern India.

c.360 Korea conquered by Japan.

455 Gurjara invasion of India from the north.

535 Fall of the Gupta Empire in northern India.

552 Buddhism introduced into Japan from Korea.

589 Reunification of China by the Sui Dynasty.

618 Tang Dynasty in China founded by Li Shih-min.

676 The Silla Kingdom formed in Korea.

710 Nara chosen as the capital of the Japanese Empire.

711 Arab conquest of the Sind region of India.

AFRICA AND THE MIDDLE EAST

309 Beginning of the long reign of Shapur II (to 379): culmination of the splendour of the Sassanid Empire.

330 Foundation of Constantinople.

350 The Kingdom of Kush was overthrown by the Emperor of Axum.

415 The Vandals in North Africa.

531 Chosroes I, Emperor of the Sassanids, started a long war against the Byzantine Empire of Justinian (527–565).

570 Birth of Muhammad.

576 Sassanid conquest of North Africa.

622 Flight of Muhammad from Mecca to Medina and the birth of Islam.

632 On the death of Muhammad, Abu Bakr and Omar, the first two Caliphs, began the expansion of Islam.

644 Othman succeeded Omar as leader of Islam.

656 Beginning of the caliphate of Ali.

670 The Arabs occupied Tunisia and founded Kairwan.

710 The Arabs in Morocco.

718 Constantinople withstood siege by the Arabs.

730 Settlement on Pemba, off the east coast of Africa.

AMERICA

300 Beginning of the classical period of the Maya. Foundation of the cities of Tikal and Uaxactun.

c.350 The Hopewell culture in North America.

383 The Toltecs built huge pyramids in Mexico.

400 Establishment of the Totonac civilization. The ceremonial centre of Tiahuanaco grew up near Lake Titicaca in South America.

455 The Maya founded Copán.

500 Zapotec civilization around Oaxaca. In the south-west of the modern United States, groups of Indians established settlements in Mesa Verde.

600 The ceremonial centre of Teotihuacán was sacked and burned.

SCIENCE AND TECHNOLOGY

c.310 Maya mathematicians invented zero.

c.500 Development of mathematics and astronomy in India. Aryabhata invented the decimal system and outlined the possibility that the Earth rotated.

570 Chen Luan described the first use of the abacus, ancestor of the calculator.

580 Attempts at Byzantium to make silk, previously a monopoly of the Chinese.

610 The Chinese doctor, Chao Yuan Fang, wrote a treatise in which he listed 1720 illnesses.

650 The first windmills built in Persia.

730 First evidence of the use of printing and of gunpowder in China.

CULTURE AND ARTS

303 Eusebius of Caesarea wrote his *Ecclesiastical History*.

325 Constantine opened the Council of Nicaea, called to combat the Arian heresy.

395 Bishop Ambrose died at Milan.

405 Translation of the Bible into Latin: the *Vulgate* Bible.

466 The game of chess, conceived as a war game, spread in India.

529 Spread of the Benedictine monastic Rule.

534 Justinian promulgated his legal code.

538 Consecration of the basilica of Santa Sophia at Constantinople.

688 Start of construction of the Dome of the Rock, Jerusalem (the Mosque of Omar), the first great Islamic monument.

EUROPE

732 The Arabs defeated by Charles Martel at the Battle of Poitiers.

751 Ravenna taken by the Lombards.

768 Charlemagne became King of the Franks.

773 The Lombards decisively defeated by Charlemagne.

800 Charlemagne crowned by Pope Leo III on Christmas Day, inaugurating the Holy Roman Empire.

843 Treaty of Verdun, dividing the Carolingian Empire into three parts.

860 Novgorod founded by Scandinavians.

871 Danish penetration into England stopped by Alfred, King of Wessex.

887 The deposition of Charles the Fat, last Carolingian monarch, led to a period of feudal anarchy.

955 The Magyars defeated at Lechfeld by Otto of Saxony.

962 Otto crowned Emperor at Rome; Holy Roman Empire reinvigorated by him.

987 Start of the Capetian Dynasty in France.

1014 Vikings defeated at Clontarf in Ireland and forced to leave the country.

1016 Canute (Cnut) the Great King of England, Denmark (1019) and Norway (1028). He died 1035.

1031 Fall of the Omayyad Dynasty in Spain.

1054 Beginning of the schism between the Greek and Latin Christian Churches.

1066 Battle of Hastings and Norman conquest of England.

1071 Byzantine power in southern Italy ended by Norman settlements.

1073 Gregory VII elected Pope. Beginning of the Investiture Struggle between the Papacy and the Empire.

1077 The Emperor Henry IV compelled to do penance at Canossa, forcing the Pope to lift his excommunication.

1095 At the Council of Clermont, Pope Urban II preached a Crusade to free the Holy Land from the infidel.

1096 Beginning of the First Crusade.

ASIA AND OCEANIA

794 Beginning of the Heian period in Japan: the capital transferred to Tokyo.

802 Foundation of the Kingdom of Angkor in Cambodia.

842 Buddhism and religions of foreign origin persecuted in China.

c.850 Migrants from Polynesia reached New Zealand and Easter Island.

907 End of the Tang Dynasty in China, followed by the confused period of the Five Dynasties.

960 Beginning of the Sung Dynasty in China.

962 The Ghaznevid monarchy, centred in modern Afghanistan, entered upon its most flourishing period.

1100 Zen Buddhism spread in Japan.

AFRICA AND THE MIDDLE EAST

750 Possible development in Zimbabwe of the legendary kingdom of gold.

762 Foundation of Baghdad by the Abbasid Dynasty who had succeeded the Omayyad Dynasty twelve years previously.

c.800 In Africa the Kingdom of Ghana flourished.

973 Cairo became the capital of the Fatimid Dynasty.

988 Foundation of the Islamic al-Azhar University at Cairo.

1055 The Almoravids conquered Sijilmasa, an important Saharan centre.

1062 The Almoravids founded Marrakesh.

1071 The Seljuk Turks inflicted the defeat of Manzikert on Byzantium.

1076 The Almoravids destroyed the Kingdom of Ghana.

1099 The Crusaders took Jerusalem and installed feudal kingdoms in Palestine and the Middle East.

1107 The Arabs founded Zanzibar.

AMERICA

889 Last inscriptions and stele datable to the classical Maya period.

900 The great Maya cities were struck by an unknown crisis and abandoned.

950 The Toltecs founded their capital at Tula.

987 Foundation of Chichen Itzá and of the League of Mayapan.

990 Inca expansion began in Perù.

1000 The Vikings reached Greenland and landed on the coast of North America (Vinland) but made no settlement.

SCIENCE AND TECHNOLOGY

760 The Arabs began the study of algebra and trigonometry.

853 First printed book produced in China.

900 Cotton and silk fabrics produced in Spain, according to techniques introduced by the Arabs.

940 In China, Than Chiao described four different types of optical lens.

1000 The first windmills built in Spain.

1045 Movable type in use in China.

1050 Adoption of the curved plough.

CULTURE AND ARTS

773 Spread of Arabic numbering.

788 Construction of the Great Mosque at Córdoba.

800 Construction of the Buddhist temple at Borobudur, Java.

863 Adoption of the Cyrillic alphabet in Slav regions.

883 *Cantilène de Sainte Eulalie*, the first literary work in French.

910 Abbey of Cluny founded.

935 Text of the Quran finalized.

1037 Death of the great philosopher of Islam, Avicenna.

1065 Earliest version of the *Chanson de Roland.*

c.1100 Foundation of the first universities in Europe: Bologna (1088), Paris (1150), Salerno (1173).

1114 First fairs in the Champagne region.

1122

EUROPE

1122 The Concordat of Worms proposed a solution to the Investiture Struggle.

1154 Invasion of Italy by the Emperor Frederick I Barbarossa.

1176 Frederick Barbarossa defeated at Legnano by the Lombard League.

1198 Innocent III elected Pope.

1212 Defeat of the Arabs at Las Navas de Tolosa in Spain.

1215 King John of England forced to grant *Magna Carta*, which set a legal limit to royal power for the first time.

1236 Beginning of the invasion of Russia by the Mongols who later reached Poland, Bohemia and the Balkans.

1242 Defeat of the Teutonic Order by Alexander Nevsky on Lake Peipus.

1261 Constantinople recaptured and again became the capital of the Byzantine Empire.

1291 Beginning of the Swiss Confederation.

1309 The Papacy transferred to Avignon, under the control of the King of France.

1325 The rise of Moscow started under Ivan I.

1337 Beginning of the Hundred Years'War between France and England.

1348 Spread of the Black Death throughout Europe.

1356 The Golden Bull of the Emperor Charles IV regulated the procedure for imperial elections.

1376 Return of the Papacy to Rome.

1378 Start of the Great Schism in the Western Christian Church.

1381 The Peasants' Revolt in England.

1389 The Battle of Kosovo gave the Turks control of the Balkans.

1397 Union of Kalmar among the Scandinavian states.

1410 Teutonic Knights defeated by the Poles at Tannenberg.

1415 The English defeated the French at Agincourt.

1453 End of the Hundred Years' War with the loss of almost all English lands in France. Loss of Constantinople to the Ottoman Turks and fall of the Byzantine Empire.

1478 Novgorod subdued by Ivan III who then freed himself from Mongol domination (1480).

1492 Fall of the Kingdom of Granada, the last Arab territory in Spain.

ASIA AND OCEANIA

1175 Muhammad of Ghur conquered northern India.

1185 Rise to power of Minamoto in Japan.

1206 Start of the Islamic Sultanate of Delhi.

1222 The Buddhist monk Nichiren started to preach in Japan.

1234 Beginning of the Mongol invasion of China.

1242 Batu Khan founded the Khanate of the Golden Horde in the lower Volga region.

1271 Meeting of Marco Polo and Kublai in China. Marco Polo's journey lasted until 1295.

1274 First Mongol attempt at invading Japan.

1279 Completion of the conquest of China by Kublai.

1281 Second Mongol attempt at invading Japan.

1335 Beginning of the Ashikaga Shogunate in Japan.

1368 The Emperor Chu Yuan-chang, who took the name Hung-wu, led a revolt against the Mongols and founded the Ming Dynasty in China.

1398 Tamerlane sacked Delhi.

1431 The Khmer city of Angkor was abandoned.

1469 Birth of Nanak, founder of the Sikh religion. He died in 1539.

1473 Birth of the Confucian philosopher, Wang Yang-ming (died 1529).

AFRICA AND THE MIDDLE EAST

1123 Ethiopia, an island of Christianity in Africa, sent an embassy to Rome.

1187 Saladin seized Jerusalem and destroyed the Crusader Kingdom.

1204 The Fourth Crusade assaulted and took Constantinople, founding the Latin Empire in the East.

1235 In Africa the Empire of Mali flourished.

1258 Baghdad sacked by the Mongols. Beginning of the decline of the Abbasid Dynasty.

1270 King Louis IX of France died during the Crusader siege of Tunisia.

c.1300 Rise of the Empire of Benin in Nigeria.

1307 Osman I founded the Ottoman Empire.

1361 The Ottoman Turks conquered Adrianople.

1380 Exceptional development of the Kingdom of Zimbabwe.

1382 David I of Ethiopia began a series of wars against the Muslims.

1402 The Ottomans were defeated by Tamerlane at Angora.

1415 The Portuguese occupied Ceuta in Morocco.

1435 The Tuareg conquered Timbukto.

1441 An Ethiopian ambassador was present at the Council of Florence.

1442 European adventurers began the slave trade.

1470 The Portuguese reached the coasts of Cameroon and Gabon.

1484 Diogo Cao explored the mouth of the Congo.

1487 Bartholomew Diaz reached the Cape of Good Hope.

AMERICA

1156 Tula, capital of the Toltecs, was abandoned.

1168 The Aztecs at Aztlán, Central Mexico.

1200 Reign of the legendary Inca monarch, Manco Capac.

1250 Mayapan, in Yucatan (Mexico), became the principal Maya city.

1300 The Chimú Kingdom formed in Peru, with its capital at Chanchán.

1325 Zenith of Aztec civilization and foundation of Tenochtitlán.

1441 The city of Mayapan destroyed. End of the Mexican period of Maya civilization.

1466 The Incas conquered the neighbouring Kingdom of Chimú.

1492 Columbus landed in America.

SCIENCE AND TECHNOLOGY

1150 The Arabs introduced paper making into Spain.

1161 In China, explosives were used for the first time in battle.

1175 Introduction in Styria of the first blast furnaces, allowing the production of cast iron.

1260 The Arabs in Spain began to use rudimentary cannons.

1286 The Englishman Roger Bacon made the first spectacles.

1306 Construction of a lock on the Thames.

1338 Illustration in the Luttrell Psalter of a spinning-wheel, which had, by this time, replaced the spindle and distaff.

1373 Development of locks on Dutch canals perfected.

1408 The Dutch perfected Archimedes' screw for removing water from the polder.

1416 Dutch fishermen adopted the trawl-net.

1445 Johann Gutenberg invented movable type. The Bible was the first book printed.

CULTURE AND ARTS

1150 Building of Angkor Wat in Cambodia.

1160 Writing of *Tristan and Isolde* and the epic of the *Nibelung*.

1163 Cathedral of Notre Dame, Paris, started.

1194 Building of Chartres Cathedral.

1226 Death of St Francis of Assisi.

1265 St Thomas Aquinas wrote the *Summa Theologica*.

1307 Dante began writing the *Divine Comedy* which he finished in 1314.

1339 Building of the Kremlin in Moscow.

1415 Jan Hus, Bohemian reformer, burnt at the stake as a heretic.

1421 Construction of the Temple of Heaven at Peking.

1447 Election of the first Dalai Lama in Tibet.

1493

EUROPE

1493 The Treaty of Tordesillas divided the New World between Spain and Portugal.

1517 Luther published his 95 Theses.

1519 Charles V became Holy Roman Emperor.

1526 The Battle of Mohacs gave the Turks mastery of Hungary.

1529 Vienna besieged by the Turks.

1534 Final rupture between King Henry VIII of England and the Papacy.

1541 Foundation by Calvin of his reformed Church in Geneva.

1545 Opening of the Council of Trent. It lasted until 1563 but failed to restore the unity of Western Christendom.

1556 Abdication of the Emperor Charles V. The Habsburg dominions were divided between the crowns of Spain and Austria.

1559 Treaty of Cateau-Cambrésis. Beginning of Spanish domination in Italy.

1571 Defeat of the Turkish fleet by the Christians at the Battle of Lepanto.

1581 The United Provinces proclaimed their independence from Spain.

1588 The "invincible" Armada of Philip II of Spain was defeated off the English coast by the navy of Elizabeth I.

1598 The Edict of Nantes followed the ending of the religious wars in France.

1618 Outbreak of the Thirty Years' War.

1630 Intervention of Gustavus Adolphus of Sweden in the Thirty Years' War.

1642 Start of the English Civil War.

ASIA AND OCEANIA

1498 Vasco da Gama discovered the sea route to India.

1514 First Portuguese landings in China.

1526 Battle of Panipat: Babar defeated the Sultan of Delhi and founded the Mogul Empire.

1542 Portuguese sailors and missionaries reached Japan.

1556 Start of the reign of Akbar the Great in India.

1557 Macao settled by the Portuguese.

1571 Conquest of the Philippines by Spain.

1582 Arrival of the Jesuit missionary Matteo Ricci in China.

1587 Start of prohibition and persecution of Christianity in Japan which also denied access to foreign shipping.

1590 Hideyoshi Toyotomi took power in Japan.

1592 Unsuccessful invasion of Korea by Japan.

1598 Tokugawa Ieyasu came to power in Japan.

1603 The Shogun Tokugawa moved the capital to Edo (Tokyo).

1619 The Dutch founded Batavia in Indonesia.

1638 The Russians reached the Pacific.

1640 The Dutch reached Ceylon and (1641) took Malacca.

1644 The Manchu or Ch'ing Dynasty replaced the Ming Dynasty in China.

AFRICA AND THE MIDDLE EAST

1500 Diogo Diaz landed in Madagascar.

1517 The Turks under Selim I occupied Egypt.

1518 Dom Henrique first bishop of the Congo.

1529 The Turks at Algiers.

c.1545 The Songhai destroyed the Empire of Mali.

1574 The Portuguese first settled in Angola.

1591 Start of the decline of the Songhai Empire.

1638 The Turks conquered Baghdad.

1641 The Dutch reached Luanda.

AMERICA

1493 First Spanish settlements on Hispaniola.

1497 Cabot reached Newfoundland.

1500 Cabral landed in Brazil.

1511 The Spaniards conquered Cuba.

1515 Foundation of Havana in Cuba. A Spanish expedition sailed up the River Plate.

1519 Cortés began the conquest of Mexico. Magellan rounded the straits named after him and reached the Pacific Ocean.

1520 On 30 June, the *Noche Triste*, Cortés was compelled to flee from Tenochtitlán.

1521 Cortés razed Tenochtitlán to the ground and began the construction of Mexico City.

1532 Pizarro began the conquest of Peru.

1533 Atahualpa assassinated by order of Pizarro.

1535 Lima, in Peru, founded. Cartier sailed up the River St Lawrence.

1540 Francisco de Orellana began the discovery of the course of the River Amazon.

1545 The Spaniards discovered the silver mines of Potosi (in modern Bolivia) and Zacatecas (Mexico).

1546 Maya uprising suppressed by the Spaniards.

1560 Sugar-cane introduced to Brazil by the Portuguese.

1607 First settlement by English colonists at Jameston in North America.

1608 French colonists founded Quebec.

1620 The Pilgrim Fathers, crossing the Atlantic in the *Mayflower*, landed in what became New England.

1625 Dutch colonists founded New Amsterdam.

SCIENCE AND TECHNOLOGY

1509 Peter Henle of Nuremberg invented the watch.

1518 Porcelain introduced into Europe from China.

1543 Copernicus published *Of the Revolution of Celestial Bodies*, revolutionizing astronomy.

1546 Existence of microbes suggested by Francastoro.

1556 Publication at Basle of Georg Bauer's *Bermannus; sive, de re metallica*, a fundamental work of chemistry and metallurgy.

1609 The telescope was invented in the Netherlands.

1610 Using a telescope, Galileo discovered the moons of Jupiter and the phases of Venus.

1612 Publication of *L'arte di fare il vetro* by Antonio Neri.

1620 The world's first weekly newspaper was published in Amsterdam.

1628 William Harvey published his discoveries about the circulation of the blood.

1632 Galileo wrote the *Dialogue on the Ptolemaic and Copernican Systems*, which was condemned by the Inquisition.

1642 Pascal invented the calculating machine.

CULTURE AND ARTS

1498 Girolamo Savonarola burnt at the stake in Florence.

1503 Leonardo da Vinci painted the *Mona Lisa*.

1508 Erasmus of Rotterdam argued in favour of a tax on the income of the rich.

1509 Birth of John Calvin.

1516 Machiavelli wrote *The Prince*.

1517 Luther published his 95 Theses at Wittenberg.

1530 The Collège de France founded under Francis I.

1534 Rabelais published *Gargantua and Pantagruel*.

1539 Mercator published his geographical map of the world.

1545 Ambroise Paré published *The Method of treating wounds made by Harquebuses and other Guns*. Interest taxed in France.

1547 Michelangelo took charge of the building of St Peter's, Rome.

1564 Birth of Shakespeare and Galileo.

1582 Reform of the Gregorian calendar.

1603 First performances by the Kabuki Theatre in Japan.

1605 Cervantes began writing *Don Quixote*.

1607 Monteverdi's *Orpheus*, the first opera.

1631 Rembrandt moved to Amsterdam and began painting his masterpieces.

1636 Foundation of Harvard College, the first university in North America.

1637 Descartes published *Discours sur la méthode*.

1648

EUROPE

1648 The Thirty Years' War ended by the Peace of Westphalia.

1649 Execution of Charles I of England and inauguration of a Republic.

1656 Turks defeated by the Venetians in the Dardanelles.

1660 Restoration of the English monarchy under Charles II.

1667 Beginning of the expansionist wars of Louis XIV, designed to impose French hegemony in Europe.

1683 Vienna besieged by the Turks.

1689 Bill of Rights agreed to by William of Orange, new King of England after the "Glorious Revolution" of 1688.

1699 Peace of Carlowitz by which the Austrian Habsburgs recovered Hungary from the Turks.

1703 St Petersburg founded by Peter the Great of Russia.

1709 Defeat of the Swedes at Poltava by Peter the Great.

1713 End of the War of the Spanish Succession by the Treaties of Utrecht and (1714) Rastatt.

1733 Start of the War of the Polish Succession which ended in 1738 with the Peace of Vienna.

1740 Outbreak of the War of the Austrian Succession. It was concluded in 1748 by the Peace of Aix-la-Chapelle.

1756 Beginning of the Seven Years' War: Prussia (under Frederick II) and Britain against Austria, France and Russia.

1772 First Partition of Poland.

1774 Treaty of Kuchuk Kainarji. Beginning of the decline of the Ottoman Empire.

1783 Crimea annexed by Russia. Independence of the United States recognized by Britain in the Treaty of Paris.

ASIA AND OCEANIA

1648 Tasman discovered Tasmania and New Zealand.

1653 Battle of Kumara between Russia and China.

1659 Beginning of the reign of the Mogul ruler Aurangzeb in India.

1661 Bombay acquired by England.

1689 Treaty of Nerchinsk between Russia and China.

1690 Calcutta founded by the English.

1707 Death of Aurangzeb. Beginning of the decline of the Moguls.

1717 Christianity prohibited in China.

1742 Beginning of the inland expansion of the British East India Company's power in India. It gained control of Bengal and Bihar.

1757 Battle of Plassey: the British destroyed French power in India.

1768 Start of Cook's voyages of exploration in the Pacific. Creation of the Colonial Office in London.

1788 First penal colony at Botany Bay in Australia.

AFRICA AND THE MIDDLE EAST

1652 The Dutch founded Cape Colony.

1659 The French founded St Louis in Senegal.

1660 Arabs from Oman drove the Portuguese from the Red Sea.

c.1700 Expansion of the Kingdom of Ashanti, on the Gold Coast.

1715 The French occupied Mauritius.

1775 First war between Boer colonists and black tribesmen in South Africa.

AMERICA

1655 The French established a settlement on Santo Domingo.

1664 The English took New Amsterdam from the Dutch, renaming it New York.

1684 The Frenchman La Salle explored the Mississippi basin and claimed possession of Lousiana for France.

1692 Last witchcraft trial at Salem in New England.

1718 Foundation of New Orleans.

1726 The cultivation of coffee introduced into the Antilles.

1728 Bering explored part of Alaska on behalf of the Tzar of Russia.

1756 Montcalm in Canada.

1759 During the course of the Seven Years'War, the British conquered Quebec. Montreal was taken in the following year.

1763 End of the Seven Years' War: Canada and Florida became British possessions by the Treaty of Paris.

1764 Louisiana ceded to Spain.

1770 The massacre at Boston: British troops fired on rebel colonists.

1775 Start of the American War of Independence.

1776 4 July: Declaration of Independence of the United States.

1783 Treaty of Paris; Britain recognized the independence of the United States.

SCIENCE AND TECHNOLOGY

1668 Issac Newton invented the reflecting telescope.

1675 Building of the Greenwich Observatory. Claus Römer calculated the speed of light.

1687 Newton's *Principia* was published.

1707 Denis Papin, an exile in Germany, built the first experimental steam boat.

1709 Abraham Darby discovered the coke-smelting method for producing pig-iron.

1714 Fahrenheit invented the mercury thermometer.

1718 Thomas Lombe invented a machine for weaving silk.

1733 John Kay invented the flying shuttle which made it possible to develop the mechanical loom.

1742 Celsius invented the centigrade scale.

1746 John Roebuck invented a method of producing sulphuric acid.

1752 Franklin invented the lightning conductor.

1758 Bird perfected the sextant.

1762 Harrison made the first chronometer.

1769 James Watt patented the steam engine. Richard Arkwright invented the water-powered spinning-frame.

1771 Galvani's research in electricity.

1774 Joseph Priestley discovered oxygen.

1782 Watt constructed a steam engine with rotary motion.

1783 Flight of the Montgolfier brothers.

1788 Meikle patented the threshing machine.

CULTURE AND ARTS

1653 Building of the Taj Mahal, India.

1661 Start of construction of the Palace of Versailles by Louis XIV.

1662 Foundation of the Royal Society, London.

1666 The Académie Française founded in Paris.

1670 Posthumous publication of the *Pensées* of Blaise Pascal.

1673 Molière wrote *Le malade imaginaire*, his last comedy.

1685 Bach and Handel born.

1690 John Locke published his *Essay concerning Human Understanding*.

1704 In England, Daniel Defoe published *The Review*, one of the first newspapers.

1714 Leibniz published *La Monadologie*.

1725 Vico began publishing the *Scienza Nuova*.

1730 The Wesley brothers founded Methodism.

1735 In Arabia, the Wahabite movement began preaching the need for a return to Islamic purity.

1738 Voltaire published his *Discours sur l'Homme*.

1751 Diderot and d'Alembert published the first volume of the *Encyclopaedia*: the work was completed in 1772.

1754 Building of the Winter Palace began in St Peterburg.

1759 Voltaire published *Candide*.

1762 Rousseau wrote *The Social Contract*.

1776 Adam Smith wrote *The Wealth of Nations*.

1781 Immanuel Kant published his *Critique of Pure Reason*.

1789

EUROPE

1789 Beginning of the French Revolution. Declaration of the Rights of Man.

1792 Proclamation of the French Republic.

1793 Second Partition of Poland.

1799 Napoleon made First Consul.

1804 Napoleon crowned Emperor.

1805 British defeat of Napoleon at the Battle of Trafalgar.

1807 Allied with Tzar Alexander I of Russia, Napoleon introduced the Continental System which lasted until 1810.

1808 The Peninsular War started by a French invasion of Spain.

1812 Napoleon invaded Russia. In the following year the remainder of his army was destroyed at Leipzig.

1814 Napoleon abdicated and was exiled to Elba.

1815 The Hundred Days: Napoleon escaped from Elba and marched on Paris. Defeated at Waterloo, he was exiled to St Helena where he died in 1821. The Congress of Vienna attempted to restore the old order of Europe.

1820 Revolutionary movements in Spain, Italy and Portugal.

1821 Greek War of Independence against Ottoman domination.

1825 Decembrist uprising in Russia against Tzar Nicholas I.

1829 Independence of Greece recognized by Turkey.

1830 Revolutionary uprisings in Paris, and in Prussia, Poland and Italy. Belgium became independent.

1833 Formation of the *Zollverein*, the customs union of the German states. Slavery abolished throughout the British Empire.

1834 Carlist Wars in Spain (until 1839).

1837 Accession of Queen Victoria in England.

1845 Great famine in Ireland caused massive emigration to the United States.

ASIA AND OCEANIA

1796 Conquest of Ceylon by the British who, three years later, took control of southern India.

1818 Marathas defeated by Britain which became effective ruler of the whole of India except Nepal, Sind and the Punjab.

1819 Singapore founded by the British.

1824 First Anglo-Burmese War.

1834 Birth of Ramakrishna, Hindu ascetic and preacher. He died in 1886.

1839 Outbreak of the Opium War between Britain and China, following Chinese confiscation of imported Indian opium.

1840 British annexation of New Zealand.

1842 Treaty of Nanking: the British obtained from the Chinese the cession of Hong Kong, trading privileges and extra-territorial rights for foreign legations in China.

1845 Outbreak of the Anglo-Sikh War.

AFRICA AND THE MIDDLE EAST

1795 The British took Cape Town from the Dutch.

1798 Napoleon's expedition to Egypt.

1806 First great migration of Dutch colonists in South Africa. They were searching for new land in the interior to escape pressure from the British colonial administration.

1808 Chaka the Great organized the struggle of the Zulus against the white settlers.

1811 Muhammad Ali assumed power in Egypt.

1822 First settlement of freed black slaves in Liberia.

1823 The explorers Clapperton and Denham reached Chad.

1830 The French conquered Algiers.

1835 A Turkish force occupied Tripoli.

1839 The British occupied Aden.

1842 Foundation of the Boer Republic of the Orange Free State following a further migration, the Great Trek, by Boer colonists.

1843 British annexation of Natal.

1847 Proclamation of the Republic of Liberia.

AMERICA

1789 George Washington elected President of the United States.

1791 Revolt of black slaves in Haiti.

1800 Toussaint Louverture became President of Haiti.

1803 Louisiana Purchase: the United States bought Louisiana from Napoleon.

1807 The Portuguese royal family, in flight from Napoleon, took refuge in Brazil.

1810 Beginning of a series of revolts in the Spanish colonies of South America. The Argentinians shot the Spanish Viceroy.

1811 Paraguay and Venezuela became independent.

1812 War between the United States and Great Britain.

1816 José de San Martín proclaimed the independence of the United States of the Rio de la Plata.

1819 Bolivar proclaimed Gran Colombia. The United States acquired Florida from Spain.

1821 John VI of Portugal returned home from Brazil.

1822 Pedro I, son of John VI, proclaimed Emperor of Brazil.

1823 Enunciation of the Monroe Doctrine.

1824 Independence of Bolivia.

1826 Proclamation of the Republic of Argentina.

1828 Independence of Uruguay.

1831 Pedro II succeeded his father as Emperor of Brazil.

1836 Attempted secession of Rio Grande do Sul from Brazil.

1840 The Canada Act united Upper and Lower (originally French) Canada.

1845 Texas joined the United States.

1846 War between the United States and Mexico; at its end (1848) New Mexico and California were ceded to the United States.

SCIENCE AND TECHNOLOGY

1795 The metric decimal system adopted in France and later elsewhere.

1796 Jenner discovered vaccination against smallpox.

1800 Volta invented the electric battery.

1806 Gas lighting in the streets of London.

1807 Fulton inaugurated a regular steam-ship service on the Hudson River.

1808 Dalton formulated atomic theory.

1819 Oersted discovered electro-magnetism.

1821 Faraday invented the generator and the electric motor.

1825 First passenger steam railway between Stockton and Darlington. Stephenson's *Rocket*.

1837 Wheatstone patented the electric telegraph.

1839 Theodor Schwann formulated cellular theory.

1840 In Britain, introduction of the first postage stamp.

1842 Long introduced ether anaesthesia into surgery.

1844 Morse sent the first telegraphic message.

1845 First Atlantic crossing of the *Great Britain*, the first propeller-driven iron ship.

CULTURE AND ARTS

1791 Death of Mozart.

1793 David painted *The Death of Marat*.

1798 Malthus published his *Essay on the Principle of Population*.

1799 Discovery of the Rosetta Stone in Egypt permitted the decipherment of Egyptian hieroglyphic.

1807 Hegel published *The Phenomenology of the Spirit*.

1810 Goya started painting *The Disasters of War*.

1824 Beethoven wrote the *Ninth Symphony*.

1830 Joseph Smith founded the Mormon Church in the United States. Stendhal published *Scarlet and Black*.

1832 Death of Goethe.

1833 Darwin began his voyage on the *Beagle*.

1840 Manzoni started publishing *I promessi sposi*.

1848

EUROPE

1848 Revolution in France and proclamation of Second Republic. Revolutions and uprisings in Italy, Austria, Hungary and Germany.

1852 Louis Napoleon crowned Emperor of France as Napoleon III.

1854 Outbreak of the Crimean War which ended (1856) with the Congress of Paris.

1861 Proclamation of the Kingdom of Italy. Abolition of serfdom in Russia.

1864 Prussia defeated Denmark and annexed Schleswig-Holstein.

1866 Prussia defeated Austria at Sadowa during the struggle for Italian independence.

1870 Franco-Prussian War. Italian unification completed with the conquest of Rome.

1871 Proclamation of the German *Reich* (Empire) under Kaiser William I. Establishment of the Third French Republic and suppression of the Paris Commune.

1878 Congress of Berlin dealt with the Eastern Question and colonial issues.

1882 Triple Alliance between Germany, Austria-Hungary and Italy.

1884 Partition of Africa among the European powers settled by the Treaty of Berlin.

1890 Dismissal of Bismarck.

1894 Dreyfus Affair in France.

ASIA AND OCEANIA

1850 Outbreak of the xenophobic Taiping Rebellion in China, which lasted until 1864.

1853 The American Commodore Perry sailed into the bay of Edo with a powerful naval squadron, forcing Japan to end its isolation.

1854 The Russians occupied the left bank of the River Amur.

1857 Indian Mutiny. Suppressed by the British in 1858, when India passed from the control of the East India Company to the British crown.

1858 Treaty of Tientsin: further Chinese ports opened to foreign commerce.

1868 Beginning of the Meiji period and of modern modernization in Japan.

1869 Birth of Gandhi.

1871 Abolition of feudalism in Japan.

1873 Hanoi conquered by Francis Garnier.

1886 Burma annexed to India, under British control.

1887 France established the Union of Indo-China, composed of Cochin China, Annam, Tonkin and Cambodia.

1893 Laos became a French Protectorate.

1894 Sino-Japanese War which ended in the following year with the victory of Japan and the establishment of its influence in Korea.

1895 Independence of Korea recognized by China.

AFRICA AND THE MIDDLE EAST

1857 Ranavalona II expelled Europeans from Madagascar.

1858 Speke and Burton explored the sources of the Nile.

1866 Livingstone left Zanzibar on his last journey.

1868 Discovery of diamond deposits at Kimberley.

1869 Opening of the Suez Canal.

1874 The British defeated the Ashanti and entered Kumasi.

1877 Stanley crossed Africa from Zanzibar to Boma (Congo).

1879 After lengthy wars, the Zulus under Cetewayo were forced to yield to British supremacy.

1881 The French occupied Tunisia.

1882 The British occupied Egypt.

1883 Menelik founded Addis Ababa.

1884 The Germans in South-West Africa.

1885 In the course of the Mahdi uprising, Khartoum was taken and General Gordon killed.

1886 Discovery of important gold-bearing deposits on the Witwatersrand.

1887 An Italian force was defeated at Dogali.

1889 Treaty of Uccialli between Menelik and Italy. Cecil Rhodes founded the British South Africa Company.

1895 Foundation of Rhodesia.

1896 Menelik's victory against the Italians at Aduwa.

1898 Fashoda Crisis in the Sudan between the British and the French.

1899 Beginning of the Boer War.

AMERICA

1848 Start of the Californian Gold Rush.

1861 Beginning of the American Civil War.

1864 Beginning of a war between Argentina and Paraguay.

1865 The American Civil War ended in the victory of the North (the Federal side) and the abolition of slavery. President Lincoln was assassinated.

1867 Russia sold Alaska to the United States. Canada became a British dominion.

1869 Trans-continental railway across the United States completed.

1876 Porfirio Diaz took power in Mexico.

1879 Start of the "Nitrate War" between Chile, Bolivia and Peru.

1885 Completion of the trans-Canadian railway.

1889 Pedro II compelled to give up the title of Emperor of Brazil and the monarchy abolished.

1891 Proclamation of the constitution of the Republic of Brazil.

1893 Protectorate over Hawaii established by the United States.

1898 War between the United States and Spain, leading to American annexation of Guam, Puerto Rico and the Philippines. Cuba became independent.

SCIENCE AND TECHNOLOGY

1850 Submarine telegraph cable laid across the English Channel.

1851 Singer perfected the sewing machine.

1856 Bessemer discovered the means of mass-producing steel.

1859 Sinking of the first oil well, in Pennsylvania, USA.

1861 Pasteur developed the theory that germs cause disease.

1863 First underground railway constructed in London.

1865 Foundation of the Massachusetts Institute of Technology.

1866 Nobel invented dynamite.

1874 The first electric tram entered service in New York.

1876 Bell patented the telephone, invented in 1854 by Meucci.

1877 Edison invented the phonograph.

1878 In London, the first streets to be lit by electricity.

1879 Edison patented the electric light bulb.

1882 First hydroelectric station, Wisconsin, USA.

1884 The Maxim gun perfected.

1885 Development of the internal combustion engine by Daimler and Benz.

1888 Dunlop invented the pneumatic tyre.

1895 Röntgen discovered X-rays. Marconi invented wireless telegraph. First public showing of a motion picture by the Lumière brothers.

1898 Marie and Pierre Curie discovered radium.

1899 Aspirin put on sale by the firm of Bayer.

CULTURE AND ARTS

1848 In London, Karl Marx and Friedrich Engels issued *The Communist Manifesto.*

1856 Flaubert wrote *Madame Bovary.*

1857 Baudelaire published *Les Fleurs du Mal.*

1859 Darwin published *The Origin of Species.*

1863 Impressionism launched at the Salon des Refusés in Paris; Manet, Pissarro and Cézanne were among those exhibiting.

1867 Marx published the first volume of *Das Kapital.*

1868 Dostoyevsky published *The Idiot.*

1874 The Impressionist movement held a further exhibition in Paris and won official acceptance.

1875 In New York, Blavatsky founded the Theosophical Society, aimed at spreading the knowledge of Eastern thought.

1880 Charles Russell founded the evangelical movement, the Jehovah's Witnesses.

1889 Eiffel Tower built in Paris in conjunction with the Centennial Exposition.

1891 Oscar Wilde published *The Picture of Dorian Gray.*

1896 Herzl published *The Jewish State*, a statement of the Zionist cause.

1897 In Austria, Klimt founded the Vienna *Sezession.*

1900

EUROPE

1904 Anglo-French *Entente Cordiale.*

1905 Revolution in Russia: a parliament conceded by the Tzar.

1908 Bosnia-Herzegovina annexed by Austria.

1912 The Balkan Wars (to 1913).

1914 Outbreak of the First World War following the assassination at Sarajevo.

1917 Russian Revolution.

1918 End of the First World War.

1919 Treaty of Versailles.

1920 Foundation of the League of the Nations.

1922 Mussolini became chief minister in Italy. Foundation of the Irish Free State (Eire).

1923 Deposition of the last Sultan and proclamation of the Turkish Republic.

1924 Death of Lenin.

1926 General Strike in Britain, the first of its type.

1928 Stalin introduced the First Five Year Plan for the industrialization of the Soviet Union.

1931 Inauguration of the Spanish Republic.

1933 Hitler took power in Germany. Burning of the Reichstag in Berlin.

1936 Outbreak of the Spanish Civil War.

1938 Occupation of Austria and Czechoslovakia by Hitler's Germany.

1939 German invasion of Poland: outbreak of the Second World War.

1941 German invasion of the Soviet Union.

1943 Defeat of the Germans at Stalingrad.

1944 Allied landings in Normandy.

1945 Surrender of Germany and Japan. The new European order settled by Churchill, Roosevelt and Stalin at the Yalta Conference. Formation of the United Nations Organization (UNO).

ASIA AND OCEANIA

1900 Xenophobic Boxer Rising in China, put down by a foreign expeditionary force.

1901 Creation of the Commonwealth of Australia.

1904 Russo-Japanese War: Japanese victory in 1905 following its seizure of Port Arthur and its destruction of the Russian fleet in Tsushima.

1907 New Zealand became a British Dominion.

1911 Revolution in the Chinese Empire. Chinese Republic established on 1 January 1912, under President Sun Yat-sen.

1925 Death of Sun Yat-sen.

1927 On 12 April Chiang Kai-shek ordered the liquidation in Shanghai of the Communists, who had previously been his allies in an attempt to reunify China and put an end to the chaos.

1931 On the pretext of an incident in Manchuria, the Japanese began a war against China which entrusted itself to Chiang Kai-shek. The war lasted until 1945, in spite of Japanese attempts to set up a puppet government in the areas under their control.

1934 Mao Tse-tung and his supporters began the Long March.

1937 Japan took Shanghai and Peking.

1941 Japan entered the Second World War with its attack on the American base at Pearl Harbor.

1945 The war ended with the defeat of Japan, made inevitable following the atomic bombing of Hiroshima (6 August) and Nagasaki (9 August).

AFRICA AND THE MIDDLE EAST

1901 Ashanti became a British colony. Victory by Britain in the Boer War.

1905 Extermination of Herero and Hottentots following uprisings in German South-West Africa.

1910 Creation of the Union of South Africa.

1914 Egypt became a British Protectorate.

1917 Inauguration of the railway line between Addis Ababa and Djibouti.

1923 Railway line between Dakar and Bamako.

1925 Jomo Kenyatta founded the Kikuyu Central Association, a movement for the independence of Kenya.

1935 Italian invasion of Ethiopia, annexed in the following year.

1940 Unsuccessful landings by British and Free French forces at Dakar in Senegal.

1941 South Africa entered the Second World War against Germany.

1942 Battle of El Alamein.

1944 Conference of French African countries at Brazzaville.

AMERICA

1903 Secession of Panama from Colombia. The United States made a treaty with the new government of Panama for control of the Canal Zone, where the Panama Canal was under construction.

1911 Peasant revolt, led by Emiliano Zapata, put an end to the dictatorship of Diaz in Mexico.

1914 Opening of the Panama Canal.

1917 The United States entered the First World War against the Central Powers.

1918 The Fourteen Points of President Wilson.

1920 The United States refused to ratify the Treaty of Versailles and withdrew into isolation. Beginning of Prohibition.

1929 The Wall Street Crash in New York and the start of the Great Depression.

1930 A military revolution brought Getulio Vargas to power in Brazil.

1932 Chaco War between Paraguay and Bolivia.

1933 President Franklin Roosevelt inaugurated the New Deal. End of prohibition.

1936 Pan-American Congress.

1938 Land redistribution in Mexico under President Cardenas.

1939 The United States proclaimed its neutrality on the outbreak of the Second World War.

1941 The United States entered the War against Germany and Japan.

1944 Peron came to power in Argentina.

1945 Atomic bomb dropped on Hiroshima (6 August) and Nagasaki (9 August). The United Nations Organization (UNO) founded at San Francisco.

SCIENCE AND TECHNOLOGY

1900 Max Planck enunciated quantum theory.

1903 First flight of a petrol-driven aircraft, by the Wright brothers.

1905 Einstein enunciated the theory of special relativity.

1908 Mass-production of cars began at Detroit with the Ford Model T.

1909 Production of bakelite, made of synthetic resin.

1912 Production of cellophane.

1920 Beginning of regular radio broadcasts in the USA.

1921 Development of the first teleprinter.

1922 Discovery of insulin.

1925 John Logie Baird invented television.

1928 Fleming made his first discoveries in the field of antibiotics.

1931 Wallace Hume Carothers invented nylon.

1932 Development of the first electronic microscope.

1935 First experiments with radar.

1939 Development of penicillin.

1941 In the USA, first flight of the jet-engined aircraft invented by Frank Whittle.

1942 Fermi built the world's first nuclear reactor at Chicago.

1944 The missile age began with the V-1 and V-2. DDT in use. IBM built the first large-scale automatic digital computer.

1945 The first atomic bombs made at Alamogordo, USA.

CULTURE AND ARTS

1900 Freud published his *Interpretation of Dreams* in Vienna.

1905 The Expressionist movement, *Die Brücke*, began in Germany. In Paris, Picasso entered upon his Rose Period in painting, leaving behind his Blue Period.

1907 Pope Pius X condemned modernism, because it looked upon dogma as a set of moral ideas and not as absolute truths.

1909 Publication of the "Manifesto of Futurism" in the Paris newspaper *Le Figaro*.

1910 Bertrand Russell began publishing his *Principia Mathematica*.

1911 The Expressionist group, *Blaue Reiter*, began work in Germany. Diaghilev presented the ballet *Petrushka* in Paris.

1913 Tatlin began the Russian artistic movement, Constructivism.

1915 Chaplin's film *The Tramp* and D.W. Griffith's film *The Birth of a Nation* were issued.

1919 Gropius founded the *Bauhaus* school of architecture in Germany.

1922 James Joyce published *Ulysses*.

1924 Schoenberg composed the first twelve-tone music.

1925 Watson announced his theory of behaviourism, seeking to explain human conduct in psychological terms.

1926 The film *Metropolis* issued.

1928 The publication of D.H. Lawrence's book *Lady Chatterley's Lover* provoked scandal.

1932 Trotsky began the publication of his *History of the Russian Revolution*. First performance of *The Threepenny Opera* by Berthold Brecht.

1937 Picasso painted *Guernica*

1940 Publication of *For whom the Bell Tolls* by Hemingway

1942 Camus published *The Stranger*.

1943 Sartre outlined the theory of existentialism in *Being and Nothingness*.

1946

EUROPE

1946 Opening of the Nuremberg war crimes trials.

1947 The Marshall Plan for European reconstruction.

1948 Communist governments took power in Czechoslovakia, Poland and Hungary. The Berlin Blockade.

1949 Formation of the North Atlantic Treaty Organization (NATO).

1951 Creation of the European Coal and Steel Community (ECSC).

1953 Death of Stalin.

1955 Creation of the Warsaw Pact.

1956 Revolts in Poland and Hungary.

1957 The European Economic Community (EEC) founded by the Treaty of Rome.

1958 Creation of the Fifth French Republic by De Gaulle.

1959 Foundation of the European Free Trade Association (EFTA).

1961 Building of the Berlin Wall.

1965 Death of Winston Churchill.

1967 Military coup in Greece.

1968 Student riots in Europe. The "Prague Spring" suppressed by Soviet tanks.

1973 Great Britain, Ireland and Denmark entered the EEC.

1974 End of the dictatorships in Portugal and Greece.

1975 Death of Franco: end of the dictatorship in Spain.

1979 The first elections for the European Parliament by universal suffrage. Salt Treaty II signed by Reagan and Breznev in Vienna. The Conservative Party, headed by Margaret Thatcher, the first British woman Prime Minister, comes to power in Britain. Suarez becomes Spain's first elected Prime Minister in 40 years. Murder of Lord Mountbatten by Irish nationalists. John Paul II makes first ever papal visit to Ireland.

ASIA AND OCEANIA

1947 Under pressure of popular movements led by Gandhi and others, Britain conceded independence to the Indian subcontinent, which was divided into India and Pakistan, and to Burma.

1949 The Communists, led by Mao Tse-tung, took Peking and proclaimed the Chinese People's Republic: Chiang Kai-shek fled to the island of Taiwan (Formosa). Independence of Indonesia.

1950 Outbreak of the Korean War which lasted until 1953: North Korea was supported by Communist China, South Korea by America and other Western nations.

1954 Following the military defeat at Dien Bien Phu, France withdrew from Indochina: the Geneva Conference recognized the independence of Laos, Cambodia and Vietnam. Vietnam was partitioned.

1957 War between North and South Vietnam.

1959 Border conflict between India and China.

1960 Beginning of Sino-Soviet dissension.

1963 American intervention in the conflict in Vietnam.

1965 Indo-Pakistan War over border issues.

1966 Beginning of the Cultural Revolution in China.

1972 Bangladesh broke away from Pakistan and proclaimed its independence.

1973 Paris Conference to end the fighting between the Vietcong and South Vietnam. American withdrawal from Vietnam.

1975 End of the war in South Vietnam and Cambodia with the victory of the National Liberation Front.

1976 Death of Mao Tse-tung.

1979 Russian invasion of Afghanistan.

AFRICA AND THE MIDDLE EAST

1946 Conference of Bamako.

1948 On 14 May, Ben Gurion proclaimed the State of Israel, producing an immediate Arab reaction and leading to the first Arab-Israeli War. In South Africa, the Nationalist Party announced the doctrine of apartheid.

1949 Foundation of the University of Makerere. Somalia was placed under Italian trusteeship for ten years.

1950 Kwame Nkrumah elected head of the new government in the Gold Coast.

1951 Independence of Libya.

1954 Beginning of the insurrection in Algeria.

1956 Nationalization of the Suez Canal by Egypt. Independence of Tunisia, Morocco and the Sudan.

1957 Independence of Ghana (Gold Coast).

1958 Independence of Guinea.

1960 Independence of Cameroon, French Congo, Belgian Congo (as Zaire), Gabon, Chad, Central African Republic, Ivory Coast, Togo, Dahomey, Upper Volta, Niger, Nigeria, Mali, Senegal, Madagascar, Mauritania and Somalia.

1961 Independence of Sierra Leone. The Union of South Africa left the Commonwealth and became the Republic of South Africa.

1962 Independence of Algeria (following the Armistice of Evian), Uganda, Rwanda and Burundi.

1963 Independence of Kenya. Failure of the Central African Federation: Zambia and Malawi left it (1964) to become independent; Rhodesia, remaining under white domination, declared itself independent (1965).

1964 Tanzania formed from the union of Tanganyika and Zanzibar.

1965 Independence of the Gambia.

1966 Independence of Botswana and Lesotho.

1967 Arab-Israeli War.

1968 Independence of Equatorial Guinea, Mauritius and Swaziland.

1973 Egypt and Syria fought the Yom Kippur War with Israel.

1974 Independence of Guinea-Bissau.

1979 Collapse of the Shah's government in Iran. An Islamic Republic founded by Ayatollah Khomeini.

AMERICA

1955 A military revolt in Argentina overthrew President Peron.

1959 Revolution in Cuba.

1960 John F. Kennedy became President of the United States.

1962 Cuban Missile Crisis.

1963 Assassination of Kennedy.

1964 Martin Luther King won the Nobel Peace Prize.

1968 Assassination of Martin Luther King.

1969 American military involvement in Vietnam.

1970 Salvador Allende elected President of Chile.

1971 The American President Nixon visited Peking.

1973 Coup in Chile: Allende was assassinated and Pinochet seized power.

1974 President Nixon was compelled to resign following the Watergate Affair.

1976 Election of President Carter.

1979 The Sandinistas came to power in Nicaragua.

SCIENCE AND TECHNOLOGY

1947 Rocket-propelled aircraft, designed by Bell, broke the sound barrier for the first time.

1948 Invention of the transistor.

1951 First nuclear power station.

1952 Development of the contraceptive pill.

1953 First experiments with the hydrogen bomb. Discovery of the first anti-polio vaccine. Watson, Crick and Wilkins discovered DNA.

1957 Sputnik I launched into space by the USSR.

1959 First experimental hovercraft flights.

1960 Invention of the laser.

1961 The Russian Yuri Gagarin became the first man in space.

1962 Telstar, the first communications satellite, launched into orbit by the USA.

1963 Discovery of quasars.

1965 First photographs of Mars sent back to Earth from Mariner IV.

1967 Christiaan Barnard performed the first heart transplant operation.

1969 The American astronaut Armstrong, on the Apollo II mission, became the first man to land on the Moon.

1976 Concorde becomes the first supersonic aeroplane to be used for commercial flights.

1977 Launch of Voyager I and Voyager II for exploration of the outer planets.

1978 First test-tube baby born in Britain.

1979 Barret's rocket-propelled car breaks the sound barrier.

CULTURE AND ARTS

1947 Le Corbusier built the first Unitées d'Habitation at Marseilles.

1948 First meeting of the World Council of Churches.

1949 George Orwell published *Nineteen Eighty-Four*.

1955 Pop-art started in London with the work of Hamilton, Blake and Paolozzi.

1958 Levi-Strauss published *Structural Anthropology*.

1959 Building of Brasilia by the architects Costa and Niemeyer.

1962 The Council Vatican II sought to eliminate divisions within the Roman Catholic Church.

1964 Herbert Marcuse published *One-Dimensional Man*. The *Thoughts* of Mao Tse-tung were also published.

1967 Publication of *One Hundred Years of Solitude* by Gabriel Garcia Marquez (Nobel Prizewinner 1982).

1974 The writer Solzhenitsyn was exiled from the Soviet Union.

1975 Declared International Women's Year by the United Nations, to assist the emancipation of the women of the world.

1978 "The Times" closes after 193 years. Nobel Peace Prize awarded to Sadat and Begin.

1980

EUROPE

1980 Death of Tito of Yugoslavia. Widespread strikes in Poland resulting in birth of Solidarity trade union organization.

1981 First peace demonstrations in Bonn. In Rome attempt on Pope John Paul's life. Greece become 10th member of ECU. Marriage of Prince Charles and Lady Diana Spencer.

1982 Martial law imposed in Poland. Breznev dies. Britain declares war on and defeats Argentina in Falklands War.

1983 Andropov elected President of USSR.

1984 IRA bomb Grand Hotel, Brighton, during Conservative Party political conference, killing 4 and injuring several Conservative MPs.

1985 Gorbachev elected General Secretary of Communist Party in USSR.

1986 Nuclear disaster at Chernobyl reactor. Emergency in Europe over resulting radioactive cloud. Terrorist attacks in France. Reagan-Gorbachev summit at Reykjavik. Spain and Portugal join EEC.

1987 188 die in Townsend Thoresen ferry disaster.

1988 Gorbachev elected President of USSR.

1989 Revolution in Romania and overthrow of Ceausescu, who is condemned to death and shot. Free elections in Poland and Hungary. Unrest in Czechoslovakia. Fall of Berlin Wall.

1990 Re-unification of the two Germanies. Lech Walesa elected President in Poland. Unrest in Yugoslavia and conflict between the various republics. Margaret Thatcher resigns and is replaced by John Major.

1991 Civil war in Yugoslavia. Independence of soviet Baltic states recognised. USSR dissolved and Community of Independent States (CIS) created.

1992 Croatia, Slovenia, Bosnia-Herzegovina and Macedonia leave the Yugoslav federation and declare their independence. The civil war in Bosnia-Herzegovina and Croatia continues.

1993 Peaceful and democratic division of Czechoslovakia into two independent republics – the Czech Republic and Slovakia.

ASIA AND OCEANIA

1980 Mrs Indira Ghandi wins absolute majority in Indian elections.

1983 Korean airliner shot down by USSR.

1984 Indira Ghandi assassinated. 2,700 killed by emission of toxic gas in Bophal in India.

1986 Cori Aquino wins presidential elections in Philippines and ends the Marcos dictatorship. Record low in the price of petrolium, which sells at 7 dollars a barrel. OPEC sets the price at 15 dollars. Australia given legal independence.

1987 Free elections in South Korea.

1988 Violent earthquake in Armenia. Benazir Bhutto elected Prime Minister of Pakistan. Russians begin withdrawal of troops from Afghanistan.

1989 Japanese emperor, Hirohito, dies after 62 years' reign. Popular movement in favour of democracy in Peking suppressed in bloody incident of Teinemann Square. End of war in Afghanistan. Vietnam withdraws from Cambodia.

1990 Bloody confrontations between Armenians and Azerians in Azerbaijan. Unification of North and South Yemen, and institution of Republic of Yemen, with San'a as capital.

1991 Rajiv Gandhi assassinated.

AFRICA AND THE MIDDLE EAST

1980 War between Iran and Iraq. Zimbabwe (ex-Rhodesia) becomes an independent republic.

1981 President Sadat of Egypt assassinated.

1982 Israeli invasion of Lebanon. Thousands killed in Palestinian refugee camps in Beirut.

1983 Limited representation given to Asians and Coloureds in South Africa.

1984 The worst famine in history hits central and eastern Africa.

1985 State of emergency and censorhip of the press in South Africa in reaction to black protests.

1986 Gulf of Sirte crisis between USA and Libya. Repression in South Africa. EEC and American embassies close in protest, and agree to sanctions.

1987 Bokassa, ex-emperor of Central Africa, condemned for embezzlement and murder, flees to Europe.

1988 Declaration of the state of Palestine. After 8 years the war between Iran and Iraq ends.

1989 Free elections in Namibia. Ayatollah Khomeni dies and is succeeded by Rafsanjani. De Klerk becames president of South Africa.

1990 After 27 years in prison Nelson Mandela, leader of the African National Congress, is freed. Namibia gains independence. Iraq invades Kuwait.

1991 De Klerk declares the end of apartheid in South Africa. Kuwait is liberated after 40 days by allied forces from USA, Britain, France, Italy, Saudi Arabia, Syria, Egypt and Kuwait, and headed by USA.

1992 The Algerian president Mohamed Budiaf is assassinated during a public ceremony.

1993 Eritrea declares independence from Ethiopia.

AMERICA

1980 Reagan elected President of USA.

1982 Falklands War between Britain and Argentina.

1983 Troops from USA and 5 Caribbean states invade the island of Granada.

1986 End of the Duvalier dictatorship in Haiti. Irangate explodes in USA. Reagan under accusation.

1987 Historic agreement between USA and USSR on nuclear disarmament.

1988 Democratic elections in Argentina. Alfonsin wins. Military coup in Haiti.

1989 George Bush elected President of USA. Democracy returns to Chile. USA invades Panama. Violent earthquake in San Francisco.

1990 Violetta Chamorra elected president of Nicaragua.

1993 Bill Clinton elected president of USA. Earthquake in Los Angeles causes widespread damage.

SCIENCE AND TECHNOLOGY

1980 First photographs of Saturn's rings and moons sent to Earth by Pioneer II and Voyager I.

1981 Flight of Columbia, the first space shuttle designed for more than one mission.

1982 First transplant of an artificial heart.

1986 First photographs of Uranus sent to Earth by Voyager II. In USA the space shuttle Challanger explodes 60 seconds after take-off. In Naples the first baby of predetermined sex is born.

1987 World population reaches 5,000,000,000. Work begins on construction of Channel Tunnel.

1988 German physicists exceed absolute zero by .15 degrees, touching –273.15 degrees. Death of Enzo Ferrari.

1989 Deaths of ethologist Konrad Lorenz and psychoanalist Cesare Musatti. American and then Italian scientists announce they have achieved "cold" nuclear fusion. Voyager sends pictures of Neptune. Europe launches Galileo space probe, destined for Jupiter.

1990 Launch of Ulysses, European space probe, whose mission is to send photographs of the polar areas of the sun.

CULTURE AND ARTS

1982 Death of Princess Grace of Monaco.

1983 Minting of first one pound sterling coin.

1984 Desmond Tutu, black Anglican bishop in South Africa, awarded Nobel Peace Prize.

1985 Italo Calvino dies.

1986 Deaths of Simone de Beauvoir, Jorge Louis Borges and Henry Moore. The famous "Caffè Greco" closes in Rome.

1987 Death of painter Renato Guttoso and Hollywood stars Rita Hayworth and Fred Astaire.

1989 Deaths of Laurence Olivier, Herbert von Karajan, and Salvador Dali. The Dalai Lama awarded Nobel Peace Prize.

1990 Deaths of actresses Greta Garbo and Ava Gardner and of writer Alberto Moravia. Gorbachev receives Nobel Peace Prize.

1992 The actress Marlene Dietrich dies.

1993 Deaths of William Golding, author of Lord of the Flies, and Italian film director, Federico Fellini.

BIOGRAPHIES

ABBAS THE GREAT (1571–1629). Shah of Persia, he ascended the throne in 1587. He was the most famous member of the Safavid Dynasty which ruled Persia from the beginning of the sixteenth century until 1736.

ADAMS, JOHN (1735–1826). One of the leading personalities of the American War of Independence, he became second President of the USA (1797–1801). In 1776, he contributed to the drawing up of the Declaration of Independence. At the end of the war, he played a major role in the peace negotiations with Britain, and became first Vice-President in 1789.

ADENAUER, KONRAD (1876–1967). German statesman. Mayor of Cologne from 1917 to 1933, he was dismissed and imprisoned by the Nazis. He was among the founders of the CDU (Christian Democratic Union) in 1945 and became President of the Parliament in Bonn in 1948. He was the first Chancellor of the German Federal Republic from 1949 to 1963. He worked vigorously for the post-war reconstruction of Germany and for European integration.

ADRIAN VI (1459–1523). Dutch Pope. He succeeded Leo X in 1522 after holding office as the Emperor Charles V's tutor, as Grand Inquisitor of Aragon and Navarre, and as Regent of Spain. He tried to stop the spread of Lutheranism, promoting a reformation of morals and an improvement in clerical discipline.

AGESILAUS (444–360 BC). King of Sparta. He ascended the throne in about 400 BC. He reopened the war against the Persians whom he defeated at Sardis (395), but had to return home to face an anti-Spartan league formed by Thebes and Athens, defeating it at Coronea in 394.

AISTULF (?–756). King of the Lombards from 749. He carried out an expansionist policy, occupying Ravenna and the Exarchate and putting an end to Byzantine rule (751). After being defeated at Pavia by Pepin the Short, King of the Franks (whom Pope Stephen II had called upon for help), he was compelled to return the occupied territories to the Papacy, and these became the nucleus of the Papal States.

ALARIC I (370–410). King of the Visigoths from 395, for a while he was leader of the Visigothic auxiliaries in the Roman army. In 402, he invaded northern Italy but was defeated by Stilicho at Pollentia. Having retired to Illyria, he later invaded Italy again, pillaging Rome in 410. He died near Reggio, on his way to Sicily.

ALBERONI, GIULIO (1664–1752). Italian cardinal. He was employed by Francesco Farnese, Duke of Parma, as his agent in Madrid, where he later became First Minister of Spain (1716), after negotiating the marriage of Philip V and Elizabeth Farnese.

ALBERT OF BRANDENBURG (1490–1568). Grand Master of the Teutonic Order and Duke of Prussia. Having embraced the Reformation, he secularized the possessions of the Order in 1525 and established the Duchy of Prussia, ruling it as his own property although declaring himself a vassal of Poland.

ALBIGENSIANS. Adherents of a religious sect based on the Manichaean heresy, which particularly flourished in the area of Albi in southern France, during the twelth century.

ALCIBIADES (c.450–404 BC). Athenian statesman, nephew of Pericles. During the Peloponnesian War, he organized and led the expedition against Syracuse (415); recalled home, accused of impiety, he went into exile in Sparta where he tried to mount a war against Athens with the support of Persia. After the political scene had changed, he returned to Athens in 407 as *strategos*, but after the defeats at Notium and Aegospotami (405), he retired to the Hellespont where he was assassinated.

ALEXANDER III (?–AD 1181). Originally Rolando Bandinelli, he was elected Pope in 1159. A vigorous exponent of papal authority against the Empire, he struggled with the Emperor Frederick Barbarossa, and was among the architects of the Lombard League which defeated the Emperor in the Battle of Legnano (29 May 1176).

ALEXANDER VI (1431–1503). Born Rodrigo Borgia, he was elected Pope in 1492 with the support of the Sforza. In 1497 he excommunicated Savonarola and, in the following year, had him burnt at the stake as a heretic.

ALEXANDER I (1777–1825). Tzar of Russia from 1801, he tried to implement a policy of reforms at home, while abroad he joined the Fourth Coalition against France in 1805. After his defeat, he signed the Treaty of Tilsit in 1807. In 1812, Napoleon's invasion of Russia ended in catastrophe. Alexander attended the Congress of Vienna and was one of the promoters of the Holy Alliance.

ALEXANDER II (1818–1881). Tzar of Russia from 1855, he signed the Treaty of Paris in 1856 at the end of the Crimean War. At home, he introduced a number of reforms: he abolished serfdom (1861), made military service compulsory and developed education. In 1887 he declared war on Turkey, winning in the following year. He was assassinated by a nihilist.

ALEXANDER III (1845–1894). Son of Alexander II, whom he succeeded in 1881. He repealed most of his father's reforms and started a ruthless persecution of the Jews. In foreign affairs, he cut his links with Germany and moved closer to France, signing a commercial treaty in 1893.

ALEXANDER THE GREAT (356–323 BC). Son of Philip II of Macedon, he was taught by Aristotle. While still very young, he distinguished himself in the Battle of Chaeronea against the Greeks (338). Having ascended the throne on his father's death in 336, he subdued Greece and carried on his father's project of a war against Persia. Crossing the Hellespont, he defeated Darius III at the River Granicus (334) and near Issus (333). Later, he conquered Tyre and Sidon, occupied Egypt and built Alexandria. In Asia, he defeated the Persians at Arbela (331), and took Babylon, Susa and Persepolis. He crossed the Indus and defeated King Poros. He died in Babylon at the age of 33, and is known as the greatest army leader of antiquity. As a consequence of his career, Greek culture spread far outside its original frontiers.

ALEXIUS COMNENUS (1048–1118). Eastern Roman Emperor from 1081, he attempted to recover the lost territories of the Empire. This led to wars first against the Normans, under Robert Guiscard (1081–1085), and then against the Pecheneg nomads and the Turks. He supported the First Crusade (1096–1099), obtaining sovereignty over Antioch.

ALFONSO V (1396–1458). King of Aragon and Naples, known as the Magnanimous, he succeed his father Ferdinand I as King of Aragon in 1416 and continued his policy of expansion.

ALFRED THE GREAT (849–899). King of

Wessex, he succeeded his father Ethelwulf in 871. He was involved in a long and victorious war against the Danes, who were defeated at Edington and compelled to sign the Treaty of Wedmore. Having retaken London (885), he obtained a new partition of territory along a line from London to Chester. To strengthen his kingdom against possible attack, he built fortresses and prepared a fleet. A great legislator, he brought order and efficient administration into Anglo-Saxon law. He also promoted and helped to popularize culture, having the most important Latin works translated into the vernacular.

ALLENDE, SALVADOR (1908–1973). Chilean politician, elected President in 1970 on the basis of a programme of social and economic reform. He led a coalition government, the *Unidad Popular*, which enacted extensive nationalization. He was overthrown and assassinated on 11 November 1973, during a coup backed by conservative groups.

AMBROSE (339–397). Church Father, born at Trier (Germany). His father, who was Prefect of Gaul, sent him to study in Rome. Governor of Liguria and Emilia from 370, he was acclaimed Bishop of Milan and consecrated in 374. A strong opponent of the Arian heresy, he fought for the independence and spiritual supremacy of the Church, and he introduced improvements into its liturgy.

ANGLO-SAXONS. Peoples of Germanic origin, the Angles, Saxons and other tribes invaded England at the beginning of the fifth century and dominated it until the eleventh century. The term became current in about the eighth century, to distinguish them from the Saxons of Continental Europe.

ANJOU. French feudal house, named after the province of Anjou, — the modern Maine and Loire. The founder was Charles, brother of Louis IX, King of France.

ANTIOCHUS III (242–187 BC). Called the Great, Seleucid King of Syria, he ascended the throne in 223 after his brother Seleucus III's death. He expanded and strengthened his kingdom: after conquering Armenia, he subjugated Bactria and Parthia; then he declared war on Egypt, from which he seized Coele Syria, Phoenicia and Palestine (204–194). Having formed an alliance with Philip V of Macedon, he was appointed *strategos*, with autocratic powers, by the Aetolian League and became an advocate of Greek freedom from Rome. In the subsequent, inevitable conflict with Rome, he was defeated at Thermopilae (191) and Magnesia (190), and forced to accept the harsh terms of the Peace of Apamea (188). He was killed in battle during the last expedition into the Orient.

ANTIOCHUS IV (215–163 BC). Son of Antiochus III, he was King of Syria from 175 after usurping the throne on the death of his brother Seleucus IV.

ANTONINUS PIUS (86–161). Roman Emperor from 138, he carried on the policy of his predecessor, Hadrian. He showed wisdom and a sense of justice in his dealings with the subjugated populations, and practised careful financial management of the provinces.

ANTONY, MARK (82–30 BC). Son of Marcus Antonius Creticus and nephew of Julius Caesar, he joined Caesar in the march beyond the Rubicon, and took part in the Battle of Pharsalia (48). Hoping to succeed Caesar, he fought Octavian but was defeated at Modena (43). A few months later, he allied with Lepidus and Octavian to form a second triumvirate, and together they defeated Brutus and Cassius, Caesar's assassins, at Philippi (42). In the subsequent partition of the Empire, Antony took the Orient, where, with Queen Cleopatra, he carried on a policy independent of Rome. This provoked Octavian's hostility and in the naval Battle of Actium (31), he defeated Antony who fled to Alexandria. When Alexandria fell into the hands of Rome, Antony committed suicide.

ARIANS. Followers of Arius (280–336) who originated the Christian doctrine that the Son was of a different order of existence from the Father. The Arian heresy began to spread first among various Germanic tribes in the fourth century and later more widely. It was condemned by the Council of Nicaea in 325.

ARISTIDES (535–462 BC). Athenian statesman and general, he took part in the Battle of Marathon, and was Archon in 489–488. Having been ostracized and exiled, he was granted amnesty in 480. He then returned to Athens and took part in the Battles of Salamis (480) and Plataea (479), as a leader of the Athenian forces. In the following years, he was the dominant political figure in Athens, known for his conservatism, honesty and patriotism.

ARTAXERXES II (?–358 BC). King of Persia, he succeeded his father, Darius II, in 404. At Cunaxa, near Babylon, in 401, he defeated his brother Cyrus the Younger, who had rebelled with the support of Greek mercenaries, among them Xenophon. Through interventions and alliances, exploiting the political scene in Greece, he initiated the Peace of Antalcidas with Athens and Sparta, subsequently gaining control of the Greek towns of Asia Minor.

ASSURBANAPAL (?–626 BC). King of Assyria from 668. Having completed the campaign in Egypt, which his father Esarhaddon had started, he moved against his brother Shamash-shum-ukin, who was leading a revolt of subject populations. He conquered Babylon in 648, and destroyed Susa in 639. He promoted arts and literature, and founded the great library at Nineveh. The splendour and magnificence of his court was famous.

ATAHUALPA (c.1502–1536). Last Inca King of Peru. On his father's death, he inherited the northern part of the empire, with Quito as capital; he fought against his brother Huascar, King of Cuzco, and usurped his throne after defeating and killing him in 1532. He was imprisoned by Pizarro, charged with his brother's assassination and, despite payment of a ransom, was executed.

ATATÜRK, MUSTAFA KEMAL (1881–1938). Founder and first President of the Republic of Turkey. A progressive, in 1919, he initiated resistance in Anatolia to the government in Istanbul. In 1920 he was elected President of Turkey by the Constituent Assembly in Ankara, and in 1922, at the end of the Greco–Turkish War, he finally freed Anatolia from Greek rule.

ATTALIDS. Dynasty of the kings of Pergamum in the third and second centuries BC, whose capital became one of the major centres of Hellenistic culture.

ATTILA (406–453). King of the Huns from 434, he unified their various tribes and subjugated the whole of Scythia. At war with Theodosius II, the Eastern Roman Emperor, from 441, he ended his devastations by gaining the territories on the right bank of the Danube. In 451 he invaded Gaul, but was defeated by the Roman general Aetius at Chalons. In the following year, he invaded Italy: after destroying Aquileia, he reached the Mincio where he was halted through the intervention of Pope Leo I. Returning to Pannonia, he died soon afterwards.

AUGUSTINE (354–430). Church father and philosopher, he was born at Tagaste in Numidia. Said to have led an intemperate life as a young man, during which period he embraced Manichaeism and Platonism, he returned to his Christian faith under the influence of his mother, Monica, and Bishop Ambrose of Milan who baptized him. In 396, he was elected Bishop of Hippo by acclamation. His most famous works are *De Civitate Deo* and *Confessiones*.

AUGUSTUS (63 BC–AD 14). First Roman Emperor. Known as Octavian until 27 BC, he was a nephew of Caesar who adopted him in 45 and made him his heir. On Caesar's death, he formed the second triumvirate with Antony and Lepidus (43) to give a new constitution to the Republic. In 42, he and Antony defeated Caesar's assassins, Brutus and Cassius, at Philippi but he later took up arms against Antony and defeated him at Actium (31), to become master of both the Roman and the Egyptian worlds.

AURELIANUS, LUCIUS DOMITIUS (212–275). Roman Emperor, elected as successor to Claudius II by the legions of Sirmium in 270. He put an end to a critical period for the Empire by mounting successful campaigns against the Goths, the Vandals and the Alamanni, and by re-establishing Roman authority over Palmyra, Egypt and Gaul (on the Catalaunian plains).

AVARS. People of Mongol origin, known as Yuan-Yuan, established in the steppes of Central Asia. In about the fifth century AD, they moved westwards and settled in southern Russia and Hungary from where they frequently attacked the Eastern Roman Empire.

AZEGLIO, MASSIMO D' (1796–1866). Italian writer and statesman. Advocate of Italian independence, he took to politics in 1844 as a representative of the moderate liberals. After the Austrian defeat of the Sardinians at Novara (1849), he was appointed Prime Minister by Victor Emmanuel II.

BABAR (1483–1530). Army leader of Turkish origin. Great-nephew of Tamerlane, he inherited (1495) the kingdom of Fergan in Central Asia from his father. Having been driven from his own dominions by the Uzbeks, he led his people in the conquest of northern India. After defeating the Sultan of Delhi at Panipat in 1526, he founded the Mogul Empire in India, choosing Agra as its capital.

BABEUF, FRANÇOIS NOEL (1760–1797). French revolutionary. Under the name of Gracchus, he published the newspaper *Le Tribun du Peuple*. After 9 Thermidor (27 July 1794), he sided with the radicals in the struggle against the Directory, and led the movement that aimed at putting advanced reforms into practice. With Philip Buonarroti and others, he organized the Conspiracy of Equals, but was arrested, sentenced to death and executed in 1797.

BADOGLIO, PIETRO (1871–1956). Marshal of Italy. Commander-in-Chief from the end of the First World War, he was Governor of Libya from 1929 to 1933, and later led the campaign in Ethiopia (1935–1936). In December 1940 he resigned the post of Commander-in-Chief, following the unsuccessful attack on Greece. After the arrest of Mussolini (July 1943), he was appointed head of a new government by King Victor Emmanuel III; he terminated Italy's alliance with Germany and, following the Armistice of Cassibile (3 September 1943), Italy joined the Allies.

BAFFIN, WILLIAM (1584–1622). English explorer and seaman. Between 1612 and 1616, he led numerous expeditions in search of the North-West Passage, and discovered the bay which bears his name. This bay, between Greenland and Canada, proved to be the entrance to the North-West Passage. However the Passage was not penetrated until Amundsen made the voyage in 1900.

BAKUNIN, MIKHAIL ALEKSANDROVICH (1814–1876). Russian revoluntionary and propagator of nineteenth-century anarchism. He was among the founders of the First International.

BALBOA, VASCO NUNEZ DE (c.1475–1519). Spanish *conquistador*, he was the first European to sight the Pacific Ocean. Leaving Panama in 1510 with 160 men, he crossed the Isthmus, one of the most difficult pieces of territory in the Americas, and reached the Pacific three years later.

BALFOUR, ARTHUR JAMES (1848–1930). English statesman and member of the Conservative Party. Prime Minister and Foreign Secretary. While holding office as Foreign Secretary, he wrote a letter to Lord Rothschild (2 November 1917) in which he promised that Great Britain would support the establishment of a Jewish national home in Palestine.

BARBAROSSA See Frederick I Barbarossa.

BARENTS, WILLEM (c.1560–1597). Dutch explorer and seaman, he led three expeditions searching for a North-East Passage (1594–1597). On the last voyage he discovered the Spitsbergen Islands and circumnavigated Novaya Zemlya, where his ship remained blocked in ice for the entire winter. He died on the voyage home.

BAR KOKHBA (?–AD 135). Leader of the Jewish revolt against the Romans, which ended with the conquest of Jerusalem by Hadrian in 135. Bar Kokhba, with a few followers, died on the battlefield at Bethar.

BASIL I (c.812–886). Byzantine Emperor, he ascended the throne in 867, after ordering the killing of Emperor Michael III; he was the founder of the so-called Macedonian Dynasty.

BASIL II (957–1025). Byzantine Emperor from 960. In 963, he embarked on a military programme to strengthen the Empire in three directions — in the Balkans (where he earned the nickname *Bulgaroctonus*, slayer of the Bulgars), in Asia Minor where he crushed the Arab menace, and in Georgia and Armenia, where he led victorious expeditions.

BAYAZID I (1354–1403). Ottoman Sultan who ascended the throne in 1389. He conquered vast territories from the Christian princes in Anatolia and the Balkans; he besieged Byzantium from 1391 to 1398, and defeated a European Crusader army at Nicopolis (1396). However, he was defeated at Angora by the Mongols of Tamerlane.

BAYAZID II (1447–1512). Ottoman Sultan, son of Muhammad I, he ascended the throne in 1481. He threatened Venetian possessions by victories at Lepanto and in the Peloponnese. On the Persian frontier, he had to face the growing power of the Safavid Dynasty. Shortly before his death, he abdicated in favour of his son, Selim.

BEN BELLA, AHMED (born 1916). Algerian statesman. One of the leaders of the revolts seeking independence from France, he was in prison from 1956 to 1962. After De Gaulle had agreed to Algerian independence in the Evian Agreements he was the first President of the Republic. He was overthrown in a coup in 1956.

BENEDICT OF NURSIA (c.480–547). One of the founders of monasticism in the West. Born into a wealthy noble family, he gave up everything to retreat into a hermitage at Vicovaro, near Subiaco. In 529, he founded a monastery on a hill near Cassino, giving it the famous rule *ora et labora*, (prayer and work) and he also established a nunnery, under his sister, Scholastica. The Benedictine Rule is the basis of Christian monastic organization.

BENEDICT XV (1854–1922). Born Giacomo della Chiesa, he was elected Pope in 1914. He led the Catholic Church during the First World War which he critized as useless slaughter, and was opposed by Italian nationalists who supported the War in the hope of winning extra territory in the north-east of Italy. He condemned modern ideas but opposed repression. In 1919, he approved the foundation of the *Partito Popolare*.

BERBERS. Nomadic peoples of North Africa, mainly inhabiting the Rif Mountains of Morocco, the Kabyles and Aurés. Converted to Islam during the Arab invasions in the seventh century AD they still maintain their traditional culture and language.

BERENGAR I (c.850–924). Marquis of Friuli and King of Italy from 888, he became Emperor in 915. Eight years later, he was defeated near Piacenza by Rudolf I of Burgundy. He was assassinated in Verona.

BERENGAR II (?–AD 966). Marquis of Ivrea and King of Italy from 950 to 961. He fought in vain against King Otto I of Germany, and died in prison at Bamberg.

BERING, VITUS (1680–1741). Danish explorer and seaman. He served Tzar Peter the Great and in 1728 discovered the straits between America and Asia which are named after him.

BISMARCK, OTTO VON (1815–1898). German statesman; principal architect of German unification. Having defeated Austria at Sadowa (1866), he assured Prussia's predominance in the new North German Confederation, of which he became Chancellor.

BOKASSA, JEAN BÉDEL (born 1921). Politician of the Central African Republic. Commander of the army from 1963, he rose to power in 1966 by means of a coup against President David Dacko.

BOLESLAW I (967–1025). First King of Poland, known as the Great. After co-operating with Otto III in his ambitious scheme to create a Christian Empire, in 1002 he embarked on a nationalistic policy in opposition to the Emperor Henry II, designed to secure his western frontiers which were eventually established in the Peace of Bautzen (1018). He expanded his eastern borders as far as Kiev and, on Henry II's death in 1024, he had himself crowned King of Poland.

BOLEYN, ANNE (c.1507–1536). Queen of England. She was a lady-in-waiting to Catherine of Aragon, first wife of Henry VIII, and became first his mistress and then his second wife (1533). Papal opposition to this new marriage of Henry VIII provoked the split between the English Church and the Catholic Church. Three years later, Anne was beheaded at the behest of Henry, accused of adultery and of incest with a brother. She was the mother of Elizabeth I.

BOLIVAR, SIMON (1783–1830). Patriot, hero of Latin American independence. He contributed to the liberation from Spanish rule of Venezuela (1813) and New Granada (1819). From 1817 onwards, he began the establishment of the Republic of Venezuela.

BONAPARTE. Corsican family. Its best-known member, Napoleon, distributed thrones and honours among his relatives. Lucien (1775–1840) took part in the coup of 18 Brumaire 1799 but, quarrelling with his brother, settled in Rome in 1804 and was only reconciled to Napoleon at the time of the Hundred Days.

BONIFACE VIII (1234–1303). Born Benedetto Gaetani, he was elected Pope in 1294 after the abdication of Celestine V.

BORGIA, CESARE (1475–1507). Ruler of the Romagna, he formed an alliance with King Louis XII of France who made him Duke of Valentinois. From 1499, he subjugated the small states of the Romagna and Central Italy, supported by his father, Pope Alexander VI.

BOURBON. Princely family of France dating back to the tenth century, with possessions in Spain and Italy as well. Louis I was the first to receive ducal rank (1327). The family occupied the throne of France from 1589 (Henry IV) to 1792 (proclamation of the Republic), and again from 1815 to 1830. In Spain, the Bourbon line ascended the throne in 1700 with Philip V, and ruled until 1931.

BOURGUIBA, HABIB IBN ALI (born 1903). Tunisian statesman. In 1934 he founded the Destour Socialist Party, which was often banned. He fought for Tunisia's independence from French rule, and carried on the negotiations which led to independence in 1956. In 1957, he was elected President and, in 1974, President for life.

BRANDT, WILLY (1914–1992). German statesman. Member of the German Social Democratic Party. He was Mayor of West Berlin from 1957 to 1966, when he became Foreign Minister and Vice-Chancellor in the coalition government of Kiesinger. From 1969 to 1974, he was German Chancellor and carried out a policy of dialogue with the Communist countries.

BREZHNEV, LEONID ILYICH (1906–1982). Soviet politician. Political commissar in the Red Army during the Second World War. In 1952, he became a member of the Central Committee of the Communist Party of the Soviet Union. He replaced Nikita Khrushchev as First Secretary of the CPSU in 1964.

BRUTUS, MARCUS JUNIUS (85–42 BC). Roman politician, he sided with Pompey against Caesar to defend the Republic. Reconciled with Caesar after the Battle of Pharsalia (48), he was appointed Governor of Cisalpine Gaul and Urban Praetor. Later he joined the conspiracy against Caesar and was among his assassins (44). Forced to flee from Rome, he was defeated at Philippi by Mark Antony and Octavian, and committed suicide.

BUDDHA (c.567–487 BC). Founder of Buddhism. Siddharta Gautama, called the Buddha (the enlightened one), was born into an aristocratic north Indian family from the Nepalese frontier. At the age of 29, against his father's wishes, he gave up his life of luxury to retreat into religious meditation.

BUONARROTI, PHILIP (1761–1837). Italian revolutionary, born in Pisa. He became a French citizen in 1793, but returned to Italy as a revolutionary agent in contact with Italian patriots. Returning to France, he came to know Babeuf, and together they organized the Conspiracy of Equals. He was arrested and imprisoned for three years (1796–1799). Then he moved to Geneva and Brussels.

BURGUNDIANS. Germanic peoples who settled on the left bank of the Rhine at the beginning of the fifth century. Defeated by Aetius in 436, they moved to the Rhône valley where they established a kingdom which was subjugated by the Franks in 534.

CABOT, SEBASTIAN (c.1480–1557). Explorer. He accompanied his father, John (c.1450–1500), on his second expedition which reached the coasts of North America. Entering the service first of England, then of Spain, and later of England again, he explored the estuary of the River Plata, searched for the North-West Passage, and may in 1509 have discovered Hudson Bay.

CAESAR, GAIUS JULIUS (100–44 BC). Roman general and statesman. Born of a noble family, he was *quaestor* in Spain in 68, and *curule aedile* in 65. In 60, he formed the first triumvirate with Crassus and Pompey; in the following year he became Consul and Governor of Cisalpine Gaul, and between 58 and 49, he extended the Roman conquests throughout Gaul and organized a victorious expedition to Britain. Declared a public enemy by the Roman Senate for refusing to give up his military command, he marched on Rome, crossing the Rubicon with his army in 49. Pompey fled from Rome, pursued by Caesar, and was defeated at Pharsalia (48). Later, Caesar went to Egypt where he imposed a protectorate, installing Cleopatra on the throne, and crushed the last resistance of Pompey's followers in Africa at Thapsus (46) and Munda (45). He returned to Rome in 45 as Emperor and Dictator for life, and began working on extensive reforms. He was murdered in a plot involving Brutus and Cassius.

CAETANO, MARCELO (1906–1980). Portuguese politician. Colonial Minister between 1944 and 1947, he was one of the closest collaborators of the Prime Minister Salazar, whom he succeeded in 1968. His reactionary regime was overthrown in a coup in 1974, and Caetano went into exile in Brazil.

CALIGULA, GAIUS CAESAR AUGUSTUS GERMANICUS (12–41). Roman Emperor from AD 37, successor to Tiberius. His despotism and attempt to turn the Empire into a divine monarchy of the oriental type led to conflict with the Senate. He was killed during a plot by Senators and Praetorians, led by Cassius Chaerea.

CALVIN JOHN (1509–1564). Religious reformer, born at Noyon in France. Founder of the doctrine and Church which bear his name. Collaborated with William Farel in the diffusion of Protestantism and made Geneva the centre of Calvinism, marked by rigid discipline and doctrinal orthodoxy.

CANUTE (Cnut) THE GREAT (c.995–1035). King of England, Denmark and Norway. He accompanied his father, King Sven of Denmark, on the invasion of England in 1013. He became sole King of England after defeating Edmund in 1016. On the death of his brother, Harold, he obtained the throne of Denmark and, with the support of the Pope and the Emperor, he attacked Norway, defeated King Olaf and became King (1028). Before his death, he divided his territories among his three sons; Sven (Norway), Harold (England) and Harthacnut (Denmark). He was a great legislator.

CARACALLA, MARCUS AURELIUS ANTONINUS (188–217). Roman Emperor, born at Lyon, son of Septimius Severus. In 211, he inherited his father's empire and reigned jointly with his brother Geta, whom he later murdered. In 212 he issued an edict, which gave Roman citizenship to almost all the inhabitants of the Empire.

CAROLINGIANS. Royal dynasty of the Franks, founded by Pepin the Elder (died AD 640), mayor of the palace of the Merovingian King Clothar II. The Carolingians gained the throne of the Franks under Pepin the Short who, in 751, was chosen as King after the last Merovingian, Childerich III, had been deposed. The Emperor Charlemagne was the most notable member of this dynasty, which reigned over the Franks until 987, and provided all the Holy Roman Emperors until 888.

CASIMIR III THE GREAT (1310–1370). King of Poland after the death of his father, Vladislav I, in 1333. He strengthened the kingdom, ending the war with the Teutonic Knights (Peace of Kalisz, 1343) and gaining the Principalities of Galicia and Wlodzimierz after long struggles with the Lithuanians and the Tartars. He improved the economy, favouring commerce with the Orient, protected the Jews, and founded Cracow University, the first in Poland (1364).

CASTRO, FIDEL (born 1926). Cuban statesman. In 1953 he led a revolt against the dictator Batista, as a result of which he was arrested and imprisoned. He then went into exile, first in the USA and later in Mexico. He returned to Cuba in 1956 and, with a few associates, started the guerilla movement which led to the fall of Batista's regime in 1959. As Prime Minister, he introduced radical socialist socio-economic reforms. Castro's Marxist ideology and his close collaboration with the USSR caused much concern in the USA, and led to the Bay of Pigs invasion in 1961 and the Missile Crisis of 1962.

CATHERINE II (1729–1796). Empress of Russia, she succeeded her husband, Peter III, in 1762. Learned, intelligent and open to progressive ideas, she introduced many administrative and fiscal reforms, although she embarked on more conservative policies following the peasant revolts led by Pugachev (1774–1775). She extended the borders of Russia by fighting two wars against the Turks (1771–1774, 1794), and by taking the Ukraine and Lithuania from Poland (1793, 1795).

CAVOUR, COUNT CAMILLO BENSO (1810–1861). Italian statesman. Minister of Agriculture (1850) and of Finance (1851) in the Piedmontese government of D'Azeglio, he became Prime Minister in 1852. Through his advice, Italy took part in the Crimean War, enabling him to bring the Italian question before the Congress of Paris in 1856. He secured the alliance of Napoleon III in the long struggle for independence from Austria (1859). Resigning after the Villafranca Armistice, he returned to power in 1860 and, through a series of plebiscites in areas freed by Garibaldi, he succeeded in carrying through much of the unification of Italy. On 17 March 1861, the Kingdom of Italy was proclaimed.

CEAUSESCU, NICOLAE (born 1918). Romanian politician. Secretary of the Communist Party from 1965, he became President of the State Council in 1967 and, after an amendment to the constitution, President of the Republic in 1974. Advocate of greater autonomy and independence from the Soviet Union for Communist countries, in 1968 he showed solidarity with Dubcek during the Russian invasion of Czechoslovakia. Together with Tito, he rejected the Soviet doctrine of limited sovereignty.

CELTS. Peoples of Indo-European language, present in Europe from the second millennium BC, in an area between the Rhine and the Danube. During the first millennium BC, they settled in Spain, the British Isles and northern Italy, spreading their knowledge of the use of iron. The Cultures of Hallstatt and La Tène indicate their level of development in this period. At one time, they had commercial links with the Greek world and were known to the Romans as Gauls. Rivalry among the tribes was a constant obstacle to the formation of a unitary state, although the greatest resistance to the Roman conquests of Britain and Gaul came from the Druid religious order — the most highly regarded social group. In Gaul, the occupation by Caesar merged the history of the Celts with that of the Romans.

CHAMBERLAIN, ARTHUR NEVILLE (1869–1940). British statesman. He entered politics in 1915, becoming Lord Mayor of Birmingham. In 1918 he was elected a Conservative Member of Parliament. He was respectively Minister of Health and Chancellor of the Exchequer on more than one occasion, and Prime Minister from 1937 to 1940. He was one of the authors of the Munich Conference of 1938, in the vain hope of saving the peace by giving in to German demands. Forced to declare war on Germany after its invasion of Poland (1939), he resigned office in the following year.

CHANDRAGUPTA (?–286 BC). Founder of the Maurya Dynasty in India. He took possession of the Maghada Kingdom, after defeating the last King of the Nanda Dynasty, and established a vast Empire stretching from Tibet to Afghanistan. Having halted the expansion of Seleucus I Nicator, he devoted himself to the strengthening of the Empire.

CHARLEMAGNE (742–814). King of the Franks, founder of the Holy Roman Empire. Eldest son of Pepin the Short, he inherited the Kingdom on his death and, for a while, ruled it jointly with his brother Carloman. Called to Italy by Pope Adrian I, he forced the Lombards to surrender and, in 774, he took the title of King of the Franks and the Lombards. From 778 he led a number of expeditions against the Muslims in Spain, and was defeated at Saragossa (779). He conquered the territories of the Saxons, the Bavarians and the Avars, extending his power over most of Europe. In 800, he was crowned Holy Roman Emperor by Pope Leo III.

CHARLES II THE BALD (823–877). Son of Louis the Pious. He became King of the Franks in 843; after the Treaty of Verdun partitioned the Carolingian Empire between himself and his half-brothers, Louis the German, Lothair and Pepin. He tried to consolidate monarchical power but, with the defeat of Kiersy (877), he had to acknowledge that qualified heirs were entitled to inherit the great fiefs. He was crowned Emperor in 875 by Pope John VIII.

CHARLES III THE FAT (839–888). King of Germany on the death of his father, Louis the German, in 876. He obtained the throne of Italy from his brother, Carloman, and was crowned King at Ravenna in 879. In 881, Pope John VIII crowned him Emperor at Rome and on the death of his cousin, Louis the Stammerer, he gained the Kingdom of the Franks and thus reunified the Carolingian Empire. However, at the Diet of Tribur (887), the great magnates of the Empire forced him to abdicate in favour of his nephew Arnulf, because of his cowardice in the face of Norman assaults.

CHARLES V (1500–1558). King of Spain as Charles I from 1516, and Holy Roman Emperor from 1519, when he inherited the Habsburg territories of his father Philip, Archduke of Austria. Charles V found himself the ruler of an Empire "on which the sun never set". This provoked the hostility of the European monarchs, in particular of Francis I, King of France, and between 1521 and 1544 the two monarchs fought a number of wars to establish supremacy over Italy. Crowned Emperor in Bologna by Pope Clement VII in 1530, Charles faced the resistance of the German princes in his attempts to unify the empire, and was also confronted by the Turkish threat. In religious affairs, he had to accept the Peace of Augsburg (1555), securing religious liberty for German princes and thus determining the religious division of the empire. Having failed in his attempt to create a centralized and unified empire, he abdicated in 1556 in favour of his brother, Ferdinand, who became Emperor, and of his son, Philip II, who obtained the Low Countries and Spain.

CHARLES VII (1403–1461). King of France on the death of his father, Charles VI the Mad, in 1422. He was induced to lead the counter-attack against the English, started by Joan of Arc, which resulted in the liberation of Orleans and Charles' coronation at Rheims (1429). After retaking Paris (1436), Charles remoulded the army and drove the English out of France (with the exception of Calais), bringing the Hundred Years' War to an end.

CHARLES VIII (1470–1498). King of France on the death of his father, Louis XI, in 1483. Taking advantage of the political unrest in Italy after the death of Lorenzo the Magnificent he went to Italy in 1494 to claim the Kingdom of Naples. Welcomed at Milan by Ludovico *il Moro*, he overcame the opposition of Florence and entered Rome unopposed. He took possession of Naples in 1495. However, the European monarchs and Italian princes, afraid of French domination united in a coalition against France, drove Charles out of Naples, and defeated him at Fornovo (1495). He died in France while preparing another expedition.

CHARLES I (1600–1649). King of England and Scotland, son of the Stuart King James I, whom he succeeded to the throne in 1625. Supporter of the High Church Arminian movement at home, he assisted the French Huguenots against Cardinal Richelieu, receiving subsidies from Parliament for the purpose. As relations between King and Parliament deteriorated, the latter presented the King with the Petition of Right (1628); in the following year, Charles dissolved Parliament and began eleven years of personal rule. However, he was compelled to recall Parliament in 1640, following an outbreak of rebellion in Scotland, although he failed to win the support of the majority of its members and, in 1642, civil war broke out. Defeated in battle, Charles was captured by the army of his opponents, led by Oliver Cromwell, put on trial and executed in 1649.

CHARLES II (1630–1685). King of England, son of Charles I. As a result of the Civil Wars, he took refuge in Scotland where he was crowned in 1651. Defeated in battle by Cromwell, he fled to France and only returned to England in 1660 when, on the restoration of the monarchy, he was proclaimed King. His apparent support for, and suspected sympathies with French absolutism, his tolerance of Roman Catholicism and the hostility of the Anglican Church towards Non-Conformity, led to friction with important groups in Parliament. In consequence, he obtained financial assistance from Louis XIV of France, and in return gave support to French policies.

CHARLES XII (1682–1718). King of Sweden from 1697, he was a great military leader and strong advocate of Lutheranism. Attacked by Russia, Denmark and Saxony-Poland, he defeated the Danes at Copenhagen and the Russians at Narva (1700), and compelled August II of Saxony to give up the Polish crown (1704). In 1708 he attacked Russia, aiming at Moscow, but the campaign ended with his total defeat at Poltava (1709). Having fled to Turkey, he tried unsuccessfully to persuade the Sultan to make war on Russia. In the meantime, his dominions in Germany had fallen into the hands of Prussia. He escaped from Turkey and, after a legendary ride across Europe, he met his army at Stralsund (1718). He died during the siege of Frederickshald, fighting against the Danes.

CHARLES ALBERT (1798–1849). King of Sardinia, son of Charles Emmanuel of Savoy. He showed sympathy for the revolutionaries during the liberal revolts of 1821 and, as Regent, he granted a constitution. However, this was soon annulled by his uncle, Charles Felix, who sent him to join an expedition against the liberals in Spain. Having ascended the throne in 1831, he sought to reinforce the state and to prepare for war against Austria. In March 1848 he granted a constitution and, after the "Five Days of Milan", he declared war on Austria, crossing the borders of Lombardy which was under Austrian rule. After initial victories, he was defeated at Custoza and forced to accept the Armistice of Salasco. In the following year, he resumed the war but, after the defeat at Novara, he abdicated in favour of his son, Victor Emmanuel II, and went into exile in Portugal.

CHARLES MARTEL (689–741). King of the Franks. Illegitimate son of Pepin II of Heristal, he reunited the kingdom subjugating Neustria (717) and Aquitania. He governed as mayor of the palace alongside the last Merovingian King and, in 737, he became sole ruler. He expanded and consolidated the frontiers of the kingdom by winning battles against Saxons, Frisians, Bavarians and Alamanni, and rolled back the tide of Muslim conquest through his important victory at Poitiers (732).

CHIANG KAI-SHEK (1887–1975). Chinese statesman and military leader. He took part in the revolution of 1911 which led to the proclamation of the Chinese Republic. He was an associate of Sun Yat-sen until the latter's death in 1925, when he became the leader of the Kuomintang. Allied with the Communists, he mounted the Great Northern Expedition to destroy the local warlords. In April 1927 he broke abruptly with the Communists and began a long struggle for power. However, faced with the threat of Japanese conquest, he made a further, uneasy alliance with the Communists and became Commander-in-Chief of the army during the Second World War, and President of the Republic from 1943. The end of the struggle with Japan was the signal for the reopening of the long civil war against the Communists. In 1949, losing ground, he moved his government to Formosa where he was President of Nationalist China (now Taiwan, the Republic of China) until his death.

CH'IN. Chinese dynasty of the small Ch'in state which, in 221 BC, subjugated the nearby populations and dominated much of northern China. Although the Ch'in only held sway for a brief period (until 206 BC), they represented a milestone at the beginning of the Imperial period. The founder of the dynasty, Shih Huang-ti, centralized the administration, unified weights and measures, and standardized and simplified the system of writing. He also built the Great Wall as a protection against attacks from northern nomadic peoples.

CH'ING. Last Imperial Chinese dynasty, also known as the Manchu. Of Tartar origin, the Ch'ing were asked for help by the Ming monarchs in 1644 and, within a few years, they had conquered the whole of China and founded a new dynasty (1659). The second Emperor K'ang Hsi (1661–1722) was one of the greatest of Chinese monarchs. He was a capable administrator, favoured the Jesuit missionaries and extended Chinese dominion over Yunnan (1681), Formosa (1683) and Mongolia. The Empire reached the height of its power under Ch'ien Lung (1736–1796) who continued the expansion towards Tibet and further into Mongolia. However, his successors were unable to carry on his policies. Corruption and conspiracies, combined with their isolation from the West, weakened the Ch'ing. Moreover, at the same time, the Europeans were becoming more commercially aggressive (the Opium Wars, 1840–1842) and both Russia and Japan were taking over parts of China in the course of their expansionist policies. Popular discontent and xenophobic feelings burst out in the Boxer Rising (1900) and accentuated the crisis of the dynasty. A further revolt, supported by the army and inspired by the ideas of Sun Yat-sen, led to the fall of the Ch'ing (autumn 1911) and the proclamation of the Chinese Republic (1912).

CHOU. Chinese dynasty. Originating in the valley of the River Wei, they conquered the territories of the Shang Dynasty in about the eleventh century BC. Their lands were organized on feudal principles, and were divided among families linked together by blood ties. The authority of the central government diminished from the eighth century onwards, when the Chou had to move their capital to Loyang in order to defend themselves against invasion from the steppes.

CHOU EN-LAI (1898–1976). Chinese statesman. After studying in Europe and Japan, he became deputy director of the political department of the Whampoa Military Academy in 1924. In 1934 he took part in the Long March, and later worked for satisfactory relations between the Communist Party and the national government. From 1949 he was Prime Minister and Foreign Minister (until 1958) of the People's Republic of China. In 1966 he supported the Cultural Revolution. He worked for the entry of China into the UN (1971), and for detente with the West, symbolized by the visit to China in 1972 of the American President Richard Nixon.

CHRISTINA OF SWEDEN (1626–1689). Daughter of Gustavus Adolphus, she ascended the throne in 1644 after a period of regency which had started at the time of her father's death in 1632. She gained territories in the Peace of Westphalia of 1648. Having become a Catholic, in 1654 she abdicated in favour of her cousin, Charles X Gustavus. She then travelled throughout Europe, finally settling in Rome, after unsuccessful attempts to regain the throne of Sweden (1660) and obtain that of Poland (1667).

CHURCHILL, WINSTON (1874–1965). British statesman. Under-Secretary for the Colonies (1908–1910), he was successively President of the Board of Trade, Home Secretary and First Lord of the Admiralty (1911–1915). On the outbreak of the First World War, he planned the Antwerp and Dardanelles expeditions. Joining the Conservative Party in 1924, he was Chancellor of the Exchequer until 1929, when he went into opposition for ten years. In September 1940 Chamberlain appointed him First Lord of the Admiralty, and he organized naval defences against Germany. He became Prime Minister in 1940 and came to epitomize the British will to resist during the Battle of Britain and the long world conflict. Shortly after the defeat of Germany, the general election of 5 July 1945 returned the Labour Party to power, and led to Churchill's resignation. He regained office as Prime Mimister in 1951 but retired into private life in 1955.

CLAUDIUS, DRUSUS NERO GERMANICUS (10 BC–AD 54). Fourth Roman Emperor, appointed by the army after Caligula's assassination (AD 41). He put an end to a critical period for the Empire, giving authority back to the Senate and reorganizing adminstration. In 43 he conquered southern Britain. His fourth wife, Agrippina, poisoned him to secure the throne for her son, Nero.

CLEMENCEAU, GEORGES (1841–1929). French journalist and statesman. Member of Parliament from 1876 to 1893, and again from 1902, he fought many battles for the secularization of the state and for justice in the Dreyfus case. Prime Minister from 1906 to 1909, and again from 1917 to 1920, he led the French government during the First World War and presided over the Versailles Peace Conference. He left active political life in 1920.

CLEMENT V (?–AD 1314). Born Bertrand de Got, he was elected Pope in 1305 with the support of the King of France, Philip IV the

Fair. In 1309, he transferred the Papacy to Avignon. In obedience to the wishes of Philip IV, he absolved those responsible for the attack on Boniface VIII at Anagni, and he suppressed the Knights Templar (1312).

CLEOPATRA (c.70–30 BC). Queen of Egypt, she ascended the throne in 51 BC, together with her brother Ptolemy XIV. Dethroned by her ministers, she rose to power again with the support of Julius Caesar, whom she then followed to Rome, having become his lover. After Caesar's assassination, she returned to Alexandria where, in 41 BC, she planned the establishment of a universal monarchy with Mark Antony. After the defeat at Actium (31 BC) and Mark Antony's death, she committed suicide.

CLIVE OF PLASSEY, ROBERT (1725–1774). British general and politician. An official of the East India Company, he fought French penetration in India and, with the defeat inflicted on the Francophile Nawab of Bengal at Plassey in 1757, he secured British control of northern India. Govenor of Bengal until 1767, he was accused of corruption and, although cleared, he committed suicide.

CLOVIS I (c.466–511). King of the Franks from 481 and founder of the Merovingian monarchy, he drove out the last Romans and unified Gaul. Having conquered the dominions of the Roman leader Syagrius (486), he occupied the territories along the Loire and the Seine and, by his victory at the Battle of Vouillé, he conquered the Kingdom of the Visigoths as far as the Pyrenees. Having become a Christian, he laid the basis for a unitary state of Gallo-Romans and Franks.

COLBERT, JEAN-BAPTISTE (1619–1683). French statesman. Having become Controller-General for Finance to Louis XIV in 1665, he reorganized the administration and simplified the collection of taxation. He encouraged the development of industrialization and colonial expansion, based on protectionist principles (with high tariffs on foreign imports) and state subsidies.

COLUMBUS, CHRISTOPHER (1451–1506). Italian explorer. In 1478, he settled in Lisbon and, convinced of the possibility of reaching the East Indies by sailing west, he presented his project to King John II of Portugal. Moving to Spain, he persuaded the monarchs, Ferdinand and Isabella, to give him their support and, having prepared a small fleet of three ships, the *Santa Maria, Niña* and *Pinta*, he sailed from Palos on 3 August 1492. Three months later, he landed on a small island in the Bahamas (Guanahani, the modern Watling Island), which he called San Salvador. On his return to Spain, he was received in triumph. He made three further voyages, reaching Cuba, Jamaica, Trinidad and the American mainland near the delta of the Orinoco. He died in poverty at Valladolid, not knowing that he had discovered a new continent.

CONFUCIUS (551–479 BC). Chinese philosopher, by name K'ung-fu-Tzu. He was born into an aristocratic family in the small state of Lu. He worked in public administration until, at the age of 50, he was appointed Minister of Justice by the ruler of Lu. His enlightened work aroused the envy of neighbouring monarchs and he decided to resign from political life and go into exile with some followers. He embarked on a life of wandering, working for different princes, teaching and — according to tradition —compiling the five classics of Confucianism. His philosophy had a profound influence on Chinese society for more than 2000 years.

CONRAD II THE SALIAN (c.990–1039). King of Germany from 1024, in 1027 he was crowned Emperor in Rome by Pope John XIX. He conquered Burgundy and made the lesser fiefs hereditary and inalienable (*Constitutio de feudis*, 1037), aiming at weakening the great feudatories, both lay and clerical. In the struggle between Archbishop Aribert of Milan and the vavasours, or lesser feudatories, he supported the latter, and besieged Milan.

CONRAD III (1093–1152). Son of Frederick I, Duke of Swabia, he fought for the Imperial title against Lothar II, whom he succeeded in 1138 when he was elected by the Diet of Coblenz. Supported by clerical feudatories, he struggled against their powerful lay equivalents, especially Henry the Proud of Bavaria and Welf VI, whom he defeated in the Battle of Weinsberg (1140); during his reign, rivalry began between the Guelphs and the Ghibellines (Hohenstaufen). Persuaded by St Bernard to take part in the Second Crusade (1147), he saw his army defeated at the siege of Damascus.

CONSTANTINE I (280–377). Acclaimed Emperor by the legions in 306, he contended for power with his several rivals. At this time, there were no fewer than six Emperors at once: Galerius, Licinius and Maximin in the East; Maximian, Maxentius and Constantine himself in the West. At first, Constantine was allied with his father-in-law, Maximian; but later he had him murdered after Maximian swore an oath against him. In 311, on the death of Galerius, Constantine allied with Licinius and Maximin and left the government of the East to them, while he fought against Maxentius. Having defeated Maxentius at the Milvian Bridge (312), he was recognized as Augustus by the Senate. In 313 he issued the Edict of Milan granting religious toleration to Christians. On the death of Maximin and the defeat of Licinius in 323, he became sole Emperor at last. In 326 he transferred the capital of the Empire to Byzantium which he renamed Constantinople. He introduced sweeping reforms in the army, administration and legislation. He died near Nicomedia during an expedition against the Parthians.

COOK, JAMES (1728–1779). British explorer. He led three scientific expeditions to the Pacific. He reached Antarctica, Alaska, the Pacific Islands, the coasts of eastern Australia and New Zealand. He died in Hawaii, killed by a native.

CORTÉS, HERNÁN (1485–1547). Spanish *conquistador*. Having reached America in 1504, he began the conquest of the Aztec Empire in 1518. He allied with local populations and succeeded in occupying Tenochtitlán in 1521. In the following year, Charles V made him Governor of Mexico (New Spain), and during the next four years he completed the conquest of the Aztec Confederation. In 1535 he explored the coasts of California but, after the appointment of a Viceroy, he returned to Spain and lived his last years in disfavour.

CRASSUS, MARCUS LICINIUS (115–53 BC). Roman politician. After contributing to Sulla's victory (82), he crushed the slave revolt, led by Spartacus, in 72. In 70 he was made Consul with Pompey and then Censor; in 60 he joined the first triumvirate with Pompey and Caesar. He was assigned the province of Syria. He died at Carrhae while fighting against the Parthians.

CRISPI, FRANCESCO (1818–1901). Italian statesman. He was active in republican agitation, and held ideas similar to those of Mazzini. He worked with Garibaldi after the landing of the Thousand in Sicily (1860), and was a member of Parliament from 1861. In 1865, he abandoned his alliance with Mazzini, became a monarchist and an advocate of strong policies, both domestic and foreign. He was President of the Camera in 1876, Minister of the Interior from 1877 to 1878, and Prime Minister from 1887 to 1891 and from 1893 to 1896. He started Italian colonial expansion, brutally crushed socialist risings in Sicily (by the *fasci*, workers' leagues) and reinforced the alliance with Germany. However, he was compelled to resign after the disaster at Aduwa in Abyssinia.

CROMWELL, OLIVER (1599–1658). English statesman. Member of Parliament in 1628, he became a leader of the opposition to the religious and political aims of Charles I. After the outbreak of the Civil War (1642), he led the Parliamentary armies in England to many victories, including Naseby (1645), and later crushed royalist support in Ireland and Scotland. Following the execution of Charles I (1649), he headed the Republic (the Commonwealth) and later assumed the title of Lord Protector. During these years, the Navigation Act of 1651 contributed to the growth of English maritime supremacy over the Dutch. Cromwell refused the offer of kingship, made in 1657, but the nature of his rule and the accumulation of power in his hands aroused discontent at various social levels.

CYRUS THE GREAT (?–529 BC). King of Persia. He was one of the early rulers of the Achaemenid Dynasty and founder of the Persian Empire. Succeeding his father, Cambyses, in 558 BC, he freed the small Persian state from the rule of the Medes (550), conquered the eastern provinces of Iran (540), and later Babylon (539) and the Greek towns of Asia Minor. He freed the Jews from Babylonian rule, allowed them to return to

Palestine, and permitted the rebuilding of the Temple in Jerusalem. He died while fighting the Massagetae in eastern Iran.

DALMATIANS. Natives of Dalmatia, of Illyric origin. Subjugated by the Romans, they settled along the coast and on the islands. Under Venetian rule they were influenced by Italian culture; later, they were overwhelmed by the Slavs.

DANTON, GEORGES-JACQUES (1759–1794). Outstanding personality during the French Revolution; member of the Convention and the Committee of Public Safety, of which he was the first President. He was a talented orator, one of the strongest opponents of the monarchy, and a supporter of the War Party. He founded the Club des Cordeliers (1790), was Minister of Justice (1792) and organized the national defence forces. Later, believing some social developments to be too radical, he tried to oppose the Terror. Thwarted by Robespierre, he was accused of treason and guillotined.

DARIUS I THE GREAT (?–485 BC). Achaemenid King of Persia. Coming to the throne in 521 BC, he reorganized the empire dividing it into twenty satrapies — fairly autonomous, but subject to his direct superivision. He introduced a system of annual taxation, created efficient postal and transport services, and built a canal connecting the Nile to the Red Sea. He consolidated his frontiers in India and Turkey, declared war on Athens which had supported the rebellion of the Ionian towns (493), but suffered a heavy defeat at Marathon (490). He died while preparing a new expedition against Greece.

DAVID (c.1038–c. 973 BC). King of Israel, member of one of the principal families of Bethlehem belonging to the tribe of Judah. When still a youth, he killed Goliath, the famous Philistine giant; his resulting popularity aroused the envy of King Saul who exiled him. On Saul's death, he was chosen as King of Judah. Having been recognized by the northern tribes and having subdued the Philistines, he re-established the Kingdom of Israel from the Euphrates to the Mediterranean. He carried out important administrative and military reforms, choosing Jerusalem as his political and religious capital.

DAYAN, MOSHE (1915–1981). Israeli general and politician. He played an important role in the war against the Arab League (1948), and commanded the army in the Sinai campaign against Egypt (1956). Defence Minister during the Six Day War (1967), he was reappointed to the same post in 1969, but was heavily critized for failing to foresee the Arab attack during the Yom Kippur War. After Golda Meir's resignation in 1974, he was excluded from the new coalition. Foreign Minister, 1977–1979.

DE GASPERI, ALCIDE (1881–1954). Italian statesman. Elected in 1911 as a representative of the Popular Union to the Austrian Parliament, he worked hard to have Trentino annexed to Italy. Having joined the Italian People's Party, he became a member of Parliament in 1921 and succeeded Don Sturzo as Party Secretary. Imprisoned for four years by the Fascists, he retired from political life altogether until 1943, and worked as a librarian in the Vatican. Foreign Minister in Bonomi's second government (1944) and in Parri's administration. In 1945, he became Prime Minister and held office until 1953 in seven successive ministries, devoting himself to the task of postwar reconstruction.

DE GAULLE, CHARLES (1890–1970). French general and statesman. Educated at the Military College of Saint-Cyr; captain during the First World War, promoted general in 1940. After the Franco-German Armistice, he fled to London and led the French Resistance movement. Prime Minister after the Liberation (1944), he resigned in 1946 under left-wing pressure. Recalled to power in 1958, he was elected President of the Fifth Republic, enjoying extensive powers under a new constitution that he had drawn up himself. After ending the long crisis over Algeria (1962), he led France until 1969 when he resigned over the negative result of a referendum which would have increased his powers to introduce new constitutional reforms.

DIAZ, BARTHOLOMEW (c.1450–1500). Portuguese explorer. In command of three ships, he was the first European to round the Cape of Good Hope (1486–1487), thus opening the passage to India. He died on the return voyage of the expedition which, led by Cabral, discovered Brazil.

DIDEROT, DENIS (1713–1784). Man of letters and philosopher, he was the chief editor of the major work of the Enlightenment, the *Encyclopaedia* (consisting of seventeen volumes and eleven plates) which was the most advanced work of thought and scientific discovery of the time. While preparing it (1751–1752), he had to face bitter criticism and numerous polemical attacks.

DIOCLETIAN (c.243–313). Roman Emperor. He came from humble origins in Dalmatia, and was proclaimed Emperor by his army in 284. He struggled to solve the problems of the succession and of frontier defence against Barbarian incursions. He divided the Empire into four administrative divisions, ruled by a tetrachy of two *Caesares* and two *Augusti*. He organized many military campaigns, subjugating Egypt in 294, and Britain in 297. He introduced institutional and financial reforms, and tried to curb inflation by means of the Edict of Prices (301). He persecuted Christians, regarding them as subversive, and his Triumph in Rome in 303 marked the pacification of the Empire and the culmination of its power. He abdicated in 305.

DISRAELI, BENJAMIN (1804–1881). British statesman, Jewish by birth. Elected as a Conservative member of Parliament in 1837, he served as Chancellor of the Exchequer several times (1852, 1858–1859, 1866–1868). Despite his political leanings, he supported the Second Reform Act of 1867, which gave the vote to about two million working class electors. As Prime Minister (1868, 1874–1880), he promoted reform at home and British prestige abroad: he bought Egypt's shares in the Suez Canal Company (1875), compelled Russia to cede territory to Turkey, and acquired Cyprus for Britain at the Congress of Berlin (1878).

DOMITIAN, TITUS FLAVIUS (51–96). Roman Emperor, son of Vespasian, he succeeded his brother Titus in 81. He worked to expand his Empire and to consolidate his power. Having conquered the whole of Britain (84), he led a successful expedition against the Chatti, and started building the Danubian *limes*. To begin with, he attempted to win support at home through good administration, and in the provinces by grants of offices. However, he later turned to despotism, and was assassinated during a conspiracy. The Senate passed a decree damning his name.

DRAKE, FRANCIS (c.1540–1596). English explorer. As a young man, he fought a privateering war against Spanish shipping off the coasts of Mexico. He was the first Englishman to circumnavigate the world. During his voyage he attacked Spanish possessions in Peru and Chile, enriching himself with booty, and receiving a knighthood from Queen Elizabeth I (1581). He fought the Spaniards again in 1585 and 1587, and in 1588 he contributed to the destruction of the "invincible" Armada of Philip II.

DREYFUS, ALFRED (1859–1935). A Jewish artillery captain in the French army, he was the subject of an infamous judicial prosecution. Charged with treason for allegedly communicating military information to the German government, he was sentenced to life imprisonment on Devil's Island (1894). France was shattered by anti-Semitism, scandals and political turmoil, and passions were further heightened by the famous letter, *J'accuse*, written by Emile Zola, one of Dreyfus' main supporters. The evidence against Dreyfus was found to have been forged, and members of the army were deeply implicated in the conspiracy. In 1899, he was pardoned, the case was retried, the verdict reversed, and he was readmitted into the army.

EDWARD III (1312–1377). King of England. After the death of his father, Edward II, in 1327, he continued his policies of expansion, defeating the Scots (1333, 1347), and advancing his claim to the French throne as grandson of Philip IV the Fair. This provoked the outbreak of the Hundred Years' War, during which he took part in the Battle of Crécy (1346) and besieged Calais (1347). By the Treaty of Calais (1360), he obtained Calais, Ponthieu and Acquitaine.

EINAUDI, LUIGI (1874–1961). Italian economist and statesman, he was professor of public finance at the University of Turin and the Brocconi University in Milan. As a journalist, he campaigned against protectionism in both industry and agriculture. He took no part in political life under Fascism, but later became a deputy, Governor of the Bank of Italy (1945–1948) and President of the Republic (1948–1955). He supported a liberal economic policy and the concept of European federation.

EISENHOWER, DWIGHT DAVID (1890–1969). American general and statesman. During the Second World War he was the Commander-in-Chief of the Allied forces in North Africa and in 1944 he was in charge of the victorious offensive in Normandy as Supreme Allied Commander. In 1948, he left the army and was for two years President of Columbia University. Recalled to military service shortly after the signing of the North Atlantic Treaty (1949), he became Commander of NATO land forces from 1950 to 1952. In that year, as candidate of the Republican Party, he was elected President of the United States and re-elected for a further term in 1956. One of the most important developments during his Presidency was the civil rights and anti-segregationist legislation of 1957 and 1960. In foreign affairs, attempts at detente with the Communist world were combined with a massive build-up of Western defences.

ELAMITES. Descendants of Elam, son of Shem. According to Biblical tradition, the Elamites populated Susiana. Historically, the Elamites who lived in the area to the east of Babylon were of little importance until the twelfth century BC, when they attempted expansion towards eastern Assyria, in the region of the River Diyala. Assyrian links with the Chaldean tribes and the constant interference of the Elamites in Babylonia, induced Assyria to invade and annexe Elam in the seventh century BC.

ELIZABETH I (1533–1603). Queen of England. Daughter of Henry VIII and Anne Boleyn, she ascended the throne in 1558 on the death of her Catholic half-sister Mary; she was the last Tudor monarch. By the Acts of Supremacy and Uniformity (1559), and by the promulgation of the 39 Articles of Religion (1563), she renewed the breach with the Catholic Church and began the consolidation of the Anglican Church. She was excommunicated by Pope Pius V (1570), and persecuted the Catholic missionaries who attempted to win England back to the Papacy. During her reign, England enjoyed a period of cultural splendour and some economic stability, and became a commercial and maritime power sufficient to provoke the hostility of Spain. The outbreak of war (1587) and the destruction of the Spanish Armada (1588) brought victory to England. Elizabeth remained unmarried and, having no children, secured the future of Protestantism in England by permitting her throne to pass to James VI of Scotland (James I of England). He was the son of her cousin, Mary Stuart, who had been executed in 1587 with Elizabeth's tacit approval. His accession to the English throne assured the peaceful union of Scotland and England.

EPAMINONDAS (c.420–362 BC). Theban general. Advocate of the independence of Thebes from Sparta, following the victory at Leuctra (371 BC), he succeeded in spreading the anti-Spartan movement to the Peloponnese. This led to the formation of the Arcadian League. Reopening the war, he was killed during a confrontation with the Spartans at Mantinea (362).

ERIK THE RED (c.940–1010). Norwegian warrior and seaman. He reached Iceland and founded colonies there; around 985, he discovered Greenland and colonized it. His best-known settlement was at Brattahlid, near the modern Julianehaab.

ETRUSCANS. Peoples who, from the earliest times, lived in Tuscany, part of Latium and Umbria. According to recent research, they originated from the fusion of Italic ethnic groups with groups from the eastern Aegean. They were organized in independent city states, and frequently associated in leagues on religious, rather than political, lines. They exercised strong control over central Italy in the pre-Roman period (from the seventh to the fourth centuries BC), and traded with the Greeks and Phoenicians, founding many colonies. Threatened by peoples on their borders, they were finally absorbed by Rome during the First Punic War. From 80 BC they became totally romanized and disappeared as a separate entity.

EUGENE OF SAVOY (1663–1736). Austrian prince. Commander of the imperial army from 1683, he fought against the Turks, distinguishing himself at Zenta (1697), and imposing the Peace of Carlowitz (1699) on the Sultan after this victory. In the War of the Spanish Succession, he was victorious at Oudenarde (1708) and Malplaquet (1709). Later, his greatest victory, he defeated the Turks at Peterwardein (1716), compelling them to sign the Peace of Passarowitz (1718). He died after taking part in the War of the Polish Succession (1733–1735).

FAISAL IBN ABD AL-AZIZ (1906–1975). King of Saudi Arabia from 1964, when he took the throne after overthrowing his brother Ibn Saud II. He implemented a programme of social reforms aimed at modernizing the country. In foreign policy, he adopted a more moderate, pro-Western stance than many other Arab countries, although he supported them during the war against Israel in 1973. He was killed by one of his nephews in March 1975.

FATIMIDS. Muslim dynasty which claimed descent from Fatima, Muhammad's daughter. Founded in North Africa by the Syrian Obaidallah, its power was extended with the help of the Berbers. Moizz, the fourth Caliph of the dynasty, conquered Egypt (969) and founded the capital, Cairo. Egypt enjoyed considerable prosperity under the dynasty, which was overthrown by Saladin in 1171.

FERDINAND I (1793–1875). King of Hungary as Ferdinand V from 1830. He became Emperor of Austria on the death of his father, Francis II, in 1835. He was advised by Metternich, an advocate of absolutism, who persuaded him to adopt a conservative stance. Faced with the revolt in Vienna in 1848 and the flight of Metternich, he at first permitted the formation of a liberal government, but later used the army to restore order. In the same year, he abdicated in favour of his nephew Francis Joseph.

FERDINAND II OF HABSBURG (1578–1637). King of Bohemia from 1617 and of Hungary from 1618, he was crowned Emperor in 1619. In 1618, as a consequence of the outbreak of revolt against the rule of the Catholic Habsburgs in Protestant Bohemia, he became involved in the Thirty Years' War. Following the victories of Wallenstein and Peace of Lübeck (1629), Ferdinand gained many territories in northern Germany. By the Edict of Restitution he forced Protestants to return to the Catholic Church all property seized since 1552. In 1635 he signed the Peace of Prague with Saxony and in the following year he reopened hostilities with France.

FERDINAND I OF BOURBON (1751–1825). King of the Two Sicilies, he ascended the throne of Naples in 1759 as Ferdinand IV. In 1798 and again in 1805 he had to leave Naples, following the French invasions, and retire to Palermo where he remained from 1806 to 1815. In 1812 he was compelled to grant a constitution. The Congress of Vienna (1815) restored his dominions in Sicily and Naples which he then united into the Kingdom of the Two Sicilies, taking the name Ferdinand I. As a result of the *carbonari* risings of 1820, he was forced to grant another constitution, but this was annulled in the following year when the Holy Alliance intervened. He founded the University and the Astronomical Observatory at Palermo.

FERDINAND II OF BOURBON (1810–1859). King of the Two Sicilies, he succeeded his father, Francis I, in 1830. He was strongly opposed to the liberal movement, and sentenced the Bandiera brothers to death in 1844. Forced to promulgate a constitution in 1848, he annulled it a few months later, and bloodily suppressed the revolts in Naples and Sicily.

FERDINAND II OF ARAGON (1452–1516). Known as Ferdinand the Catholic, he became King of Aragon and Sicily on the death of his father, John II, in 1479. His marriage with Isabella of Castile led to the union of Castile and Aragon. In 1492 he conquered the Kingdom of Granada, so freeing Spain from its last Muslim rulers. He expelled the Jews, and reinforced his power through economic and legal reforms. He financed Columbus's voyages. To secure his supremacy over the Mediterranean, he adopted an anti-French foreign policy. Having gained the Kingdom of Naples (1502) and the regency of the Kingdom of Castile (on Isabella's death in 1504), he occupied the Spanish part of Navarre (1512).

FERDINAND VII (1784–1833). King of Spain. He ascended the throne in 1808, following Charles IV's abdication. However, he himself was forced to abdicate in the same year following an invasion by the French troops of Napoleon, led by Murat. He returned to power in 1814 and introduced a reign of terror. Revolts in Cadiz in 1820 compelled him to reintroduce the constitution of 1812. In 1823 he was able to abolish it with the support of the Holy Alliance. To permit his daughter to succeed him on the throne as Isabella II, he amended the Salic Law, causing civil war — the Carlist Wars.

FOCH, FERDINAND (1851–1929). French Marshal. During the First World War, he was first in command of the northern armies, then Commander-in-Chief (May 1917), President of the Inter-Allied Committee and, from March 1918, Generalissimo of the Allied armies on the Western Front. As such, he was in charge of the Battle of France (July–November 1918).

FRANCIS II (1768–1835). Holy Roman Emperor, he succeeded his father, Leopold of Habsburg-Lorraine, in 1792. Repeatedly defeated by France, he was deprived of the title of Holy Roman Emperor by Napoleon in 1806, and became Emperor of Austria as Francis I. His daughter, Marie-Louise, married Napoleon in 1810. He was at first allied with Napoleon in the war against Russia. Then he turned against Napoleon and contributed to his defeat at Leipzig (1813). Francis regained his lost lands at the Congress of Vienna and became a strong advocate of the Holy Alliance, harshly crushing liberal movements.

FRANCIS I (1494–1547). King of France. Son of Charles of Orleans and Louise of Savoy, he succeeded Louis XII in 1515. Aspiring to become Holy Roman Emperor in 1519, he was unable to prevent the election of Charles V of Spain, and they became enemies for many years (from1521 to 1544) in the fight for the supremacy of Italy. Imprisoned by Charles V at Pavia (1525), he later regained his freedom and sided with Henry VIII of England and the Italian states in the continuing struggle against Charles. However, the Treaty of Cambrai (1529) left Italy in the hands of the Emperor, and when Francis invaded Piedmont in 1536, he was defeated and was forced to sign the Peace of Crespy (1544).

FRANCIS JOSEPH (1830–1916). Emperor of Austria, he ascended the throne in 1848 on the abdication of his uncle Ferdinand I. Hostile towards the national and liberal revolts which broke out in Europe, he continued the traditional absolutist and military policies of Austria. Having lost Lombardy in 1859 and the Veneto in 1866, he had to accept the establishment of the Dual Monarchy, under which his territories were divided into two equal states: Austria and Hungary (1867). In 1882 he joined the Triple Alliance, and in 1902 he annexed Bosnia-Herzegovina. Following the assassination of his nephew, Francis Ferdinand, at Sarajevo in 1914, he declared war on Serbia, so starting the First World War.

FRANCO, FRANCISCO (1892–1975). Spanish general. Dictator from 1939. Supported by Nazis and Fascists, he led the Falange Party and the Nationalist army in the Spanish Civil War (1936–1939), defeating the Republican forces and overthrowing the democratic Republic. He remained neutral during the Second World War, and partially relaxed his totalitarian rule after it, although he retained all power in his own hands. In the late 1960s he revived dictatorial methods in the struggle against a growing opposition. In 1969, he chose Juan Carlos of Bourbon as his successor, a decision ratified by the *Cortes*. Juan Carlos became King on Franco's death.

FRANKLIN, BENJAMIN (1706–1790). Statesman, scientist and American writer. A representative from 1751, he was a key supporter of the autonomy of the colonies and signed the Declaration of Independence (1776). He was a member of the diplomatic missions to Paris which obtained French support for the colonists in the American War of Independence from Britain, and he helped negotiate the Treaty of Paris with Britain (1783). President of Pennysylvania and delegate to the Constitutional Convention (1787), he advocated the autonomous rights of the states within a federal structure, and took part in drawing up the Constitution of the United States.

FRANKS. Germanic peoples who appeared in the third century AD in the area of the Lower Rhine. At the end of the fourth century, the Romans allowed them to settle along the borders of the Empire as *foederati*. As the Roman Empire became weaker, the Franks established themselves in the region of Cologne (the Ripuarian Franks) in Belgium and northeastern France. The latter (under the Merovingian Dynasty, and especially under Clovis) took over the greater part of France and, having become Christians, formed the most powerful Christian Kingdom in the West. After Clovis's death, they went through a period of decline which ended with Pepin the Elder, founder of the Carolingians.

FREDERICK I BARBAROSSA (1125–1190). Hohenstaufen Emperor, he succeeded his uncle Conrad III in 1152. In Germany he put an end to the wars between the Guelphs and the Ghibellines. He was later crowned Emperor in Italy by Pope Adrian IV (1155), but failed in his attempt to extend his power over the Italian cities. In conflict with Pope Alexander III and the civic republics of Lombardy (he conquered and destroyed Milan in 1162), he supported the Anti-Pope Victor IV, who in turn supported the Imperial side. Defeated by the Lombard League at Legnano in 1176, he was forced to seek a reconciliation with Alexander III and, in the Peace of Constance (1183), he acknowledged the autonomy of the civic republics of Lombardy. He died in Cilicia while taking part in the Third Crusade.

FREDERICK II (1194–1250). Son of Henry VI and Constance, the heiress of Sicily, he was the last great Hohenstaufen monarch. King of Sicily (1198), he was elected King of Germany in 1212, after promising Pope Innocent III that he would give up the Kingdom of Sicily in favour of his young son Henry. Crowned King of Germany a second time in 1215, at Aix-la-Chapelle, he received the imperial crown from Pope Honorius III in Rome in 1220. In Sicily, he worked at the centralization of the state and made Palermo an important centre of culture and patronage. He led the Fifth Crusade in 1228, gaining Jerusalem without bloodshed. Hoping to restore the Imperial power over the Italian civic republics, he defeated the Lombard League at Cortenuova in 1237. Excommunicated by Gregory IX and Innocent IV (1239 and 1245), he was finally defeated by the civic republics at Parma, while his son Enzo was captured at La Fossalta (1249). Frederick died soon afterwards.

FREDERICK II THE GREAT (1712–1786). Son of Frederick William I, he quarrelled with his father at an early age. He was sent away from Berlin in 1730 and spent some years in study. When he succeeded his father in 1740, he implemented a policy of renewal and of enlightened despotism. Allied with France in the War of the Austrian Succession (1740–1748), he occupied Silesia and his possession of it was confirmed by the Peace of Aix-la-Chapelle (1748). In 1756, an anti-Prussian coalition of Austria, Russia and France plunged Europe into the Seven Years' War, during which Frederick won the important Battles of Rossbach and Leuthen (1757), and established Prussia as a European power. In 1772, he expanded his territories by annexing West Prussia and Danzig.

FREDERICK WILLIAM (1620–1688). He succeeded his father as Elector of Brandenburg in 1640. Known as the Great Elector, he was the true founder of Prussian power. By the Peace of Westphalia (1648), which ended the Thirty Years' War, he gained eastern Pomerania and in 1657, by the Treaty of Wehlau, he obtained Polish recognition of his sovereignty over East Prussia. In 1675, he won the important Battle of Fehrbellin against Sweden. Having re-established good relations with France, he ruptured them after the revocation of the Edict of Nantes (1685) and accepted Protectant refugees. He augmented his power by creating a permanent army, and by establishing efficient administration in his Electorate.

FREDERICK WILLIAM I (1688–1740). King of Prussia, he ascended the throne in 1713. He continued the work of expansion and unification, begun half a century previously by the Great Elector Frederick William, and annexed western Pomerania and Stettin at the end of the Northern War (1729). He dedicated himself to strengthening Prussia, raising the size of the army to 80,000 highly trained men, and centralizing the administration.

FREDERICK WILLIAM III (1770–1840). King of Prussia from 1797. In 1806 he joined the Fourth Coalition and declared war on the France of Napoleon. He was defeated at Jena and, at the Peace of Tilsit (1807), compelled to surrender most of the land Prussia had acquired in the Partitions of Poland, and all territory west of the Elbe. He also had to accept a type of Napoleonic protectorate. Between 1807 and 1813, his ministers began a number of important reforms. In 1813 he joined the Sixth Coalition, which defeated Napoleon at Leipzig, and in 1815 his armies took part in the Battle of Waterloo. After 1815, he joined the Holy Alliance and adopted a more conservative policy at home. In 1817, he united the Lutheran and Calvinist Churches under him.

FUGGERS. Family of German merchants and bankers, whose fortunes were founded in the fourteenth century. In the fifteenth and sixteenth centuries, the Fuggers became the richest family in Europe, capable of financing the Habsburg Emperors. It was with the support of 500,000 florins provided by Jacob Fugger the Rich (1459–1525), that Charles V was elected Holy Roman Emperor (1519).

GAMA, VASCO DA (1469–1524). Portuguese explorer, he opened the commercial route between Western Europe and Asia. In his first expedition (1497–1498), with four ships, he rounded the Cape of Good Hope, crossed the Indian Ocean and reached Calicut, an important Arab commercial centre in India. Returning home, he was appointed Admiral of the Indies, Persia and Arabia, and set out on a second expedition in 1502. Sent to the Indies as Viceroy by King John III, he signed a treaty with the princes of the Malabar coast, giving Portugal a type of commercial monopoly.

GANDHI, INDIRA (1917–1984). She was the first woman Prime Minister of India. Daughter of Nehru and educated in the Western tradition, she married the journalist and member of Parliament, Feroze Gandhi, in 1942. She was President of the Congress Party (1959) and Minister of Information (1964). She was elected Prime Minister in 1966 and re-elected subsequently, despite the serious divisions within the Congress Party, the failure of many measures and the increasingly problematical situation at home. In 1973, she signed a pact of economic cooperation with the USSR. She was strongly criticized following the testing of an atomic bomb. A few months later, she authorized the annexation of Sikkim (1975), so eliminating the buffer state between India and China. Then, charged with electoral abuses, she declared a state of emergency and silenced the opposition. Defeated in the election of 1977, she regained power in 1980. Following disorders in the Punjab, which her government had tried to suppress, she was assassinated by Sikh members of her bodyguard.

GANDHI, MOHANDAS KARAMCHAND (1869–1948). Indian statesman, known as "the Mahatma" — the noble-hearted. He graduated in law in London and, from 1893, spent 21 years in South Africa, working with the Indian community on the themes and methods of the struggle for civil, social and political rights. He developed the principles of *Satya* (the ideal truth) *Ahinsa* (non-violence) and civil disobedience. On his return to India (1915), these methods, when applied to matters of general interest, proved very effective against both the British administration and Hindus of superior castes. He was persecuted, arrested and imprisoned; he fasted repeatedly but never abandoned his struggle or beliefs. He was assassinated by a Hindu extremist a few months after the proclamation of Indian independence (1947), while he was devoting his last energies to establishing peace between Hindus and Muslims.

GARIBALDI, GIUSEPPE (1807–1882). Italian patriot and leader of the *Risorgimento.* Because of his role in the unsuccessful revolts organized by Mazzini (1833–1834), he had to flee to South America. There he became involved in the revolts in Brazil and Uruguay, leading a troop of Red Shirts. Returning to Italy, he fought against the Austrians in 1848. He defended the Roman Republic, set up in 1849, but again had to flee the country. He took part in the renewed fighting in Italy in 1854 and 1859, and in 1860 he organized the expedition of the Thousand, which freed Sicily and Naples from Spanish rule; he then handed over the conquered lands to Victor Emmanuel of Savoy. In his attempts to take Rome, he was blocked by the French (Battle of Mentana, 1867). He was elected to the Italian Parliament in 1874 and retired in 1876.

GAULS. Peoples who came from the upper regions of the Danube. In the second millennium BC, they settled in the country which was called Gaul after them. They constituted the principal branch of the Celts. In the course of the first millennium BC, they invaded Spain and Italy, and in 380 BC, occupied and sacked Rome. They pushed on into the Danube valley, Greece and Asia, where they settled in Galatia. They were divided into several branches which gave rise to tribal units and warlike monarchies, but all shared the same traditions, language and religion. The Druids — priests recruited from the aristocracy — were the most important social group. They were farmers and traded with the Mediterranean world. The main group of the Gauls was subdued by Caesar in 58–50 and romanized.

GEISERICH (?–AD 477). King of the Vandals, he succeeded his brother, Gunderic, in 428. He led the Vandals from Spain into Africa, where he took Carthage, but formally acknowledged the power of the Western Roman Emperor Valentinian III. On the death of the Emperor, considering himself independent, he sacked Rome (455), conquered the Mediterranean islands and devastated the coasts of Italy and Greece, repelling all attempts by Roman Emperors to defeat him.

GENGHIS KHAN (1115–1226). Founder of the Mongol Empire, one of the largest in history. His name was Temujin and he was the son of Yesügei, tribal leader of the Kiyat. With great skill and cunning, he succeeded in unifying and dominating the nomadic tribes of eastern Mongolia (1203) and western Mongolia (1206), compelling them to acknowledge him as Genghis Khan (supreme ruler). He invaded northern China as far as Peking (1215), and conquered Turkestan, Iran, Afghanistan and southern Russia (1218–1225). His vast empire, divided into semi-autonomous states, stretched from the Caucasus to the Indus, from the Caspian Sea to Peking. A shrewd politician, he was tolerant towards the various religions, and employed the peoples he conquered in the organization of his empire. He died before being able to complete the conquest of China.

GEORGE III (1738–1820). Ascending the British throne in 1760, he entered into conflict with the Whigs who held power in Parliament. During his reign, Britain lost the American colonies (Treaty of Paris, 1783), conquered most of India, and fought Napoleon who retaliated by imposing the Continental System. In 1788 illness began to affect his mind, his condition deteriorated and from 1810 onwards periods of regency became necessary.

GERMANIC PEOPLES. A large population group of Indo-European origin who spread from Scandinavia and northern Germany, where they may have settled as early as the third millennium BC. During the fourth millennium, they occupied the whole of the area of modern Germany, then inhabited by the Celts, either pushing them out or mixing with them. They were organized into monarchies, where all the power was in the hands of the warriors. They considered land a commodity for use, and not for exchange or inheritance. Among the Germanic tribes were the Cimbri, the Teutones, the Lombards, the Saxons, the Vandals, the Goths and the Franks. The Nordic legends perpetuate the names of their divinities — Odin, his assistants the *valkyries*, and his son Thor — and their seat, Valhalla.

GIOLITTI, GIOVANNI (1842–1928). Italian statesman. Member of Parliament from 1882, Minister at the Treasury under Crispi in 1889, he was Prime Minister in 1892–1893. Compelled to resign after the scandal of the Banca Romana, he was again Prime Minister for most of the period from 1903 to 1914. At home, he aimed at broadening the basis of his government by inviting the socialists to join it; he introduced universal male suffrage, and favoured the north of Italy, which made rapid economic and industrial progress, but left the problems of the south unsolved. Abroad, while maintaining the alliance with the Central Powers, he improved relations with France and England but waged war in Libya (1911–1912). He returned to power in 1920, in conditions completely changed by the war. Later, despite the rise to power of Fascism in 1922, he retained his seat in Parliament but moved into opposition in 1924 and remained politically active until his death.

GLADSTONE, WILLIAM EWART (1809–1898). British statesman. He was Prime Minister four times, from 1868 onwards. At first a supporter of the Conservative Party, he became Leader of the Liberals in 1867. From the time of his entry into Parliament in 1832, he worked to introduce various reforms, including the widening of the franchise and improvements in education and administration. He supported Home Rule for Ireland, and opposed the pro-Turkish policies of Disraeli although he continued the latter's programmes of colonial expansion in Africa. In fact, it was his determination to achieve Home Rule for Ireland that brought about his fall in 1886 and again in 1894.

GODFREY OF BOUILLON (1060–1100). He inherited the County of Bouillon from his uncle, and obtained the Duchy of Lower Lorraine as a reward for the help given to the Emperor Henry IV in the civil war in Germany. He joined the First Crusade, together with Alexius Comnenus, fighting at Nicomedia, Dorylaeum and Antioch. After the conquest of Jerusalem in 1099 he was rewarded with the title Protector of the Holy Sepulchre. He died while trying to consolidate the conquest.

GOMULKA, WLADYSLAW (1905–1982). Polish statesman. He participated in the Polish Resistance to the Nazi occupation during the Second World War, and held government office until 1949. Accused of deviationism, he was imprisoned (1951–1954). Rehabilitated in 1956, and having become First Secretary of the Central Committee of the Communist Party, he contributed to diplomatic detente between Germany and Poland, while maintaining close relations with the Soviet Union. He resigned following the workers' riots in December 1970. In 1971 he was suspended from membership of the Central Committee.

GONZAGA. An old family, from the town of the same name, which established itself in Mantua at the end of the twelfth century, imposing its rule there in 1328. The Gonzaga controlled Mantua until 1708, at first through their main branch which died out in 1627, causing a war of succession, and then from 1631, through the cadet branch of Gonzaga-Nevers. Marquises from 1433 and dukes from 1530, they ruled Guastalla from 1539 to 1748 through another branch.

GORBACHEV, MIKHAIL SERGEYEVICH (born 1931). Soviet statesman. He joined the Communist Party of the Soviet Union in 1952, rising to the rank of the First Secretary of the Stavropol region party organization in 1970. He was coopted to the central Party apparatus (1970–1980), becoming a full member of the Politburo in 1980. His election to the office of the Secretary General of the Party (1985) marked the beginning of major economic and social reforms in the USSR. These were hailed as the new policies of *glasnost'* — openness in political and public life, and *perestroika* — restructuring of the economy.

GOTHS. Germanic peoples, originating in Scandinavia, who started to migrate southward at the end of the second century AD. The main body divided into two distinct groups: Ostrogoths (Goths of the east) and Visigoths (Goths of the west). The Ostrogoths invaded the Roman Empire, assimilated its culture and, under King Theodoric, assumed the role of defenders of the Western Empire; having settled in Ravenna, they were dispersed in the sixth century by the armies of Justinian. The Visigoths occupied northern Italy and then marched on Rome which they sacked in 410. Moving on into France, they founded a kingdom which lasted until 511. Defeated by the Franks at Vouillé, they retired to Spain where they remained until the Muslim invasions.

GRACCHI, TIBERIUS (c.162–133 BC) and GAIUS (c.154–121 BC). Roman statesmen, sons of the Proconsul Tiberius Sempronius Gracchus and his wife, Cornelia, daughter of Scipio Africanus. They attempted to resolve the political, economic and social crises brought about by the rapid development of the Roman Republic in the Mediterranean. They held many offices and each was Tribune of the *plebs*, Tiberius in 133 and Gaius in 123 and 122. As reformers, they favoured smallholders against the Senate oligarchy and the great landowners, and were responsible for introducing agrarian laws designed to produce a more equal distribution of the *ager publicus* and a precise delimitation of property. Gaius founded new colonies and promoted public works to solve the problem of urban unemployment. Both died in armed clashes with their opponents.

GREGORY I THE GREAT (c.540–604). Elected Pope in 590, he became the supreme political, military and religious authority in Italy, and made Rome the centre of Christianity for the first time. He set out to convert the Lombards and the Anglo-Saxons, founding the Archbishopric of Canterbury in 597. He modified the liturgy and intervened actively in the life of the Church. His mediation was decisive in leading to the truce between the Lombards and Byzantium in 599. He wrote many books, and was made a saint.

GREGORY VII (1015–1085). Also known as Hildebrand, he was elected Pope in 1073. His reforms and prohibition of lay investiture of bishops (at the Council of 1075) provoked the oppostion of the King of Germany and Emperor Henry IV, who declared the Pope deposed at the Diet of Worms, 1076. In retaliation, the Pope first excommunicated Henry, then pardoned him (at Canossa, 1077), but subsequently recognized another King of Germany (1080). Nevertheless, he was unable to prevent Henry from marching on Rome and occupying it in 1083, imprisoning the Pope in the Castel Sant' Angelo, and setting up Clement III as Anti-Pope. Gregory was released by Robert Guiscard, but spent the remainder of his life in confinement at Salerno, near Naples.

GUEVARA, ERNESTO CHE (1928–1967). Revolutionary leader. Originally from Argentina, he started a revolutionary movement in Bolivia, then in Peru, Guatemala, Costa Rica and Ecuador. Having met Fidel Castro in Mexico in 1955, he landed with him in Cuba. After the flight of the dictator Batista in 1959, he became Minister of Economics and Industry in the revolutionary government. Entering Bolivia secretly, he organized underground warfare there and developed the "theory of guerilla focus" which made armed struggle an instrument of permanent action. Taken by surprise, he was captured by the Bolivian army and killed.

GUPTA. Indian Dynasty which ruled in the Ganges Basin between the fourth and the fifth centuries AD. Founded and consolidated by Chandragupta (c.320) and Samudragupta (335–375), the dynasty completed the unification of India which then enjoyed a period of exceptional prosperity, liberty and cultural achievement. The Gupta collected tribute from defeated peoples, but permitted their rulers to retain their thrones. Their tolerance led to the rebirth of all the old mystical and religious traditions. The dynasty was crushed in 455 by an invasion of Altaic Huns.

GUSTAVUS II ADOLPHUS (1594–1632). King of Sweden from 1611. Backed by a well-organized state and possessing exceptional military ability, he embarked upon a series of victorious campaigns which gave him almost complete control of the Baltic coasts. Invited by the German Protestants, he invaded Germany during the Thirty Years' War. Allied with France (1631), he won many battles, defeating Wallenstein at Lützen (1632) but dying during the fighting.

HABSBURGS. German feudal dynasty, of Swiss origin. The name means "hawk's castle" in German. The Habsburgs were the most important ruling family in Europe from the fifteenth to the twentieth centuries. The first Habsburg to rule over the Holy Roman Empire was Rudolph I who became Emperor in 1273. The dynasty held this postion uninterruptedly from 1437 to 1740 and reached its zenith under Charles V. After his death, the House divided into the two lines of Austria and Spain. The latter became extinct in 1700. In 1740 the main Austrian branch also died out and the thrones of the Empire and of Austria passed to the cadet branch of Habsburg-Lorraine which ruled until 1918.

HADRIAN, PUBLIUS AELIUS (76–138). Roman Emperor, successor to Trajan in 117, he moved to Rome in 118 from Syria, where he had been Governor, after ending the war against the Parthians. In 121 he embarked on a series of journeys to inspect the provinces. He visited Gaul, reinforced the German and Danubian frontiers, and arranged for the building of a huge wall (Hadrian's Wall) in Britain. He also travelled through Spain, Africa, the East, Egypt and Greece, leaving evidence of his work everywhere. Back in Rome in 134, he distinguished himself by his talent in literature, music and architecture. He was also a great admirer of Greek civilization.

HAILE SELASSIE (1891–1975). Emperor of Ethiopa. A close relative of Emperor Menelik II, he was declared heir to the throne and

Regent to Menelik's daughter, the Empress Zauditu, in 1916. In 1930, he became Emperor, proclaimed a constitution and introduced a penal code based on European models. In May 1936, after the Italian conquest, he was compelled to leave the country and he took refuge in England. Returning home in 1941, he worked for the development of his country, often using dictatorial methods. In September 1974 he was overthrown in a coup and arrested.

HAMMURABI (c.1728–1686 BC). King of the first dynasty of Babylon, he was the main figure in Babylonian history and one of the most important rulers of the ancient Orient. He tried to unite the Sumerians and the Accadians; he declared Accadian the official language but allowed the Sumerian language to be used for religious and liturgical purposes. He employed the same energies in organizing and unifying the law: his name is for ever associated with the Code of Hammurabi, the oldest body of known laws, of great maturity and judicial complexity.

HAN. Dynasty which ruled China from 206 BC until AD 220. Having taken power in the aftermath of a revolt against the Ch'in, the Han further enlarged the Chinese Empire to govern a land which stretched from Korea to Vietnam and Uzbekistan. During their supremacy, China enjoyed one of its periods of greatest splendour: there was trade with the Roman Empire and internal government was grounded on efficient local administration. Under the Han, Confucianism became the state religion, a university to train high officials was founded, and the arts and letters were held in high esteem.

HANNIBAL (247–183 BC). Carthaginian general, he became Commander-in-Chief in Spain at only 26 years of age. When the Second Punic War broke out (218), he crossed the Alps with an army of 20,000 men and attacked the Romans in Italy, defeating them at the Ticinus, on Lake Trasimene (217) and at Cannae (216). Compelled to leave Italy in order to defend Carthage, he was defeated at Zama by Scipio Africanus (202) and outlawed by his fellow citizens. At first he took refuge at the court of King Antiochus III of Syria; later he sheltered at the court of Prusias, King of Bithynia, where he poisoned himself to avoid falling into the hands of his enemies.

HANOVER. German royal family which occupied the British throne as a result of the Act of the Settlement (1701) from 1714 until 1901. The dynasty began with George I (1714–1727) and continued under George II (1727–1760), George III (1760–1820), George IV (1820–1830) and William IV (1830–1837). Because of the operation of Salic Law, Queen Victoria was debarred from succeeding to the German throne of Hanover and this was therefore inherited by Ernest Augustus, Duke of Cumberland. When Queen Victoria ascended the British throne the two branches of the dynasty separated. Victoria was succeeded by her son Edward VII, who inherited the paternal surname of Saxe-Coburg.

HARUN AL-RASHID (766–809). Fifth Abbasid Caliph, he ascended the throne in 786. He conducted victorious wars against the Byzantine Empire and exchanged ambassadors with Charlemagne. Commemorated in the *Thousand and One Nights*, he was the most famous of the Abbasid caliphs and his territories stretched from North Africa to the Indus River.

HATCHEPSUT (c.1520–1482 BC). Queen of Egypt of the Eighteenth Dynasty. She ruled jointly with her husband, Thutmoses II, and on his death, in 1504 BC, she became Regent for her son, Thutmoses III. Her reign marked a period of prosperity for Egypt. Apart from the building of the Terrace Temple at Deir el-Bahri, near Thebes, she sponsored a commercial delegation to Punt.

HATTUSIL III (?–1250 BC). King of the Hittites from 1275 BC, he usurped the throne, ended the war with Egypt and made an alliance with Ramses II, confirming it by marrying his daughter to the Pharaoh.

HENRY IV (1050–1106). Holy Roman Emperor. Son of Henry III, he was crowned King of Germany in 1054, and Emperor in 1056, under the regency of his mother, Agnes of Poitou. For a long time he struggled against Pope Gregory VII who wished to remove eccesiastical investitures from lay authority. Excommunicated, he was overthrown by the German princes who elected Rudolf of Swabia in his place (1076). Nevertheless, Henry rose to power again with his submission at Canossa (1077) and his victory over Rudolf. After a second excommunication (1080), he went to Italy, appointed an Anti-Pope, Clement III, and had himself crowned Emperor. Following Gregory VII's death (1085), his position was weakened again, by the struggle against Urban II and the Lombard League, and by conflict with his sons, Conrad and Henry. The latter succeeded his father as Henry V, after declaring him dethroned in 1104. Henry IV died in exile at Liège.

HENRY VII (c.1270–1313). Holy Roman Emperor, also known as Henry of Luxemburg. He was unanimously elected King of Germany in 1308, and carried on the Hohenstaufen policy of intervention in Italy. Called to Italy as a liberator (by Dante, among others) in 1310, he was crowned King in Milan in the following year. Soon afterwards, the Guelph towns of Lombardy and Tuscany, united in a league under Robert of Anjou, rebelled and Henry had a hard struggle to have himself crowned Emperor in Rome in 1312. He died suddenly in the following year while preparing to fight Robert.

HENRY II (1519–1559). King of France, he ascended the throne on the death of his father, Francis I, in 1547. He continued his father's opposition to the Emperor Charles V: allied with the German Protestants, he succeeded in taking control of the three bishoprics of Metz, Toul and Verdun (1552). After Charles V's abdication, he continued the struggle against Philip II, but was defeated at Saint-Quentin (1557). By the Peace of Cateau-Cambrésis, he was forced to give up his possessions in Italy, but he managed to retain the English town of Calais and the three bishoprics. He died after being wounded in a tournament.

HENRY IV (1553–1610). The first Bourbon King of France. Brought up as a Protestant, he succeeded his mother, Jeanne d'Albert, on the throne of Navarre (1572), and led the Protestants in the French religious wars. Reconciled with King Henry III after the assassination of the Catholic Henry of Guise (1588), he was designated his successor on the throne of France. After Henry III's murder (1589), and only following successive military victories and his conversion to Catholicism, he was able to enter Paris and receive recognition as King (1595). After the Peace of Vervins with Spain, and the promulgation of the Edict of Nantes (1598) which granted freedom of worship to Protestants, he devoted himself to the reorganization of the state. He was assassinated by a fanatical Catholic.

HENRY VIII (1491–1547). King of England, succeeding his father Henry VII in 1509. Through victories over the French and Scots (1513) he restored England's position as an important European power — a position which was consolidated through the diplomacy of Cardinal Wolsey. In 1529 he began a struggle with Rome because of the refusal of Pope Clement VII to annul his marriage with Catherine of Aragon. He obtained legislation from Parliament enabling him to discard Catherine and marry Anne Boleyn (1533), and the Act of Supremacy (1534) declared him Supreme Head of the English Church, now split from Rome. He crushed his opponents, among them Thomas More, suppressed the monasteries and confiscated their wealth. He also made himself head of the Irish Church and King of Ireland (1541). He married six wives (Catherine of Aragon, Anne Boleyn, Jane Seymour, Anne of Cleves, Catherine Howard and Catherine Parr) and had one son, Edward, and two daughters, Mary and Elizabeth.

HENRY THE NAVIGATOR (1394–1460). Portuguese prince, son of John I, King of Portugal. He devoted his life to organizing overseas expeditions, hoping to break the monopoly of the Mediterranean powers over trade with the Orient. He founded a research centre for seamen, cartographers and astronomers. He financed expeditions which explored the northwestern coasts of Africa, reached Madeira and the Azores, and rounded Cape Verde.

HEROD THE GREAT (c.73–c. 43 BC). Son of a minister of Hyrcanus II. Governor of Galilee in 47, he was appointed Tetrarch of Judea by the Roman Senate in 40 BC, following the Roman victory over the Parthians. Neutral in the fight between Antony and Octavian, he sided with the latter after the Battle of Actium, receiving Octavian's support in consolidating his state and enlarging his borders. He ordered the killing of many relatives in the course of bitter family struggles, and was also responsible for the slaughter of the innocents at Bethlehem. These events gave Octavian an excuse to intervene as a peacemaker. One of Herod's most remarkable works was the building of the new Temple at Jerusalem in 10 BC.

HINDENBURG, PAUL VON (1847–1934). German field marshal and statesman. Commander of the Eastern Front during the First World War, he defeated the Russians at Tannenberg and on the Masurian Lakes (1914). Nominated Commander-in-Chief, he directed military operations until the end of the War. In 1925, he was elected President of the Republic, at the head of a conservative coalition, and was reappointed in 1932; in the following year, he nominated Hitler Chancellor of the Reich, and thus brought the Nazis to power.

HINDUISM. An old religion which derived from the Vedic beliefs of the Aryan-speaking peoples of northern India, in the second millennium BC. It embraces numerous cults and rites, and offers contrasting routes by which to attain an understanding of the Prime Mover or Supreme Being. The apparent polytheism of Hinduism is, in fact, a deep representation of the various forms in which the Prime Mover may be manifested. The trinity, composed of Brahma, Vishnu and Shiva, is the fundamental personification of the different aspects of the Supreme Being. Hinduism, whose priestly caste is the Brahmins, has about 500 million followers.

HIROHITO (born 1901). Emperor of Japan. He became Regent in 1921 due to the poor health of his father, Yoshihito. In 1926 he ascended the throne, thus starting the Showa period. He pursued an active policy of expansion in Manchuria and China, and in 1941 entered the Second World War with the attack on the United States at Pearl Harbor. Following the defeat of Japan in 1945, the future of Hirohito became uncertain: however, his prerogatives survived (although subject to Allied authority during the American occupation), even though he renounced the divine attributes of the imperial office.

HITLER, ADOLF (1889–1945). German politician. Having joined the German National Socialist Party in 1919, he became its leader in 1921. After the failure of the Munich *Putsch* in 1923, he was arrested and imprisoned. On his release he reconstituted the Party and added a military organization to it. Sustained by the years of acute economic crisis in Germany, he attracted substantial popular support in the election of 1930. Stepping up violence against the Communists, and continuing his subversion of democratic institutions, he secured a decisive electoral advantage in 1932. Appointed Chancellor of the Reich in January 1933, he imposed a ruthless dictatorship, liquidating all possible rivals. In the following years, he rearmed Germany and, by invading Poland in September 1939, he plunged Europe into war. He extended to the countries he overran his policy of extermination of already disadvantaged minorities (Jews, gypsies, homosexuals and the handicapped — all denigrated as *Untermenschen*). He committed suicide on 30 April 1945, when the Second World War ended in the total defeat of the Nazis and the entry of Soviet troops into Berlin.

HITTITES. Indo-European peoples originating in the Balkans, who settled in the Anatolian highlands in the twentieth century BC. Archaeological evidence has established that their empire conquered Syria and Mesopotamia between the nineteenth and the seventeenth centuries, under the leadership of sovereigns and military hierarchies of a feudal type. In the course of their expansion, they contended with Egypt for the supremacy of Asia Minor, winning the Battle of Kadesh in 1236 BC, but collapsed completely in the twelfth century. The Hittites based their miliary success on the use of light chariots drawn by horses. They were the first to discover how to work iron.

HO CHI MINH (1890–1969). Revolutionary Vietnamese statesman. Having left Vietnam in 1911, he lived in France where he joined the Socialist Party and, later, the Communists. Then, after spending some time in Russia, in 1941 he returned to Vietnam, and organized guerilla warfare against the Japanese invaders and the representatives of the French Vichy government. In 1945, he founded the Vietminh in order to continue the struggle against French colonialism, and became President of the Republic of Vietnam which was recognized as autonomous within the French Union in 1946. However, when this arrangement failed to work, he intensified his campaign for the expulsion of the French. After the Geneva Agreement of 20 July 1954, which confirmed the independence of North Vietnam, Ho Chi Minh as president dedicated himself to the reconstruction of the country which became a People's Republic. During the Vietnam War, he gave the support of North Vietnam to the nationalist movement in the South.

HOHENSTAUFEN. German dynasty which ruled in Sicily (1194–1268), and in Germany (1138–1254) as Holy Roman Emperors. Conrad III was the first of the Hohenstaufen Emperors; he was succeeded by Frederick I Barbarossa (1152–1190), Henry VI (1190–1197), Frederick II (1220–1250) and Conrad IV (1250–1254). The family began its decline on the death of Frederick II and it faded out when Conradin died in 1268.

HOHENZOLLERN. German dynasty which ruled in Brandenburg-Prussia (1415–1918), and as Emperors of Germany (1871–1918). The dynasty started with Frederick VI who received the title of Elector and the Mark of Brandenburg from the Emperor Sigismund in 1415. In 1701, Frederick I was made King of Prussia. In 1871, William I became Emperor of Germany. In 1918, following the defeat of Germany in the First World War, William II, the last Emperor, abdicated and was exiled in Holland.

HONORIUS III (?–AD 1227). Born Cencio Savelli, be became Pope in 1216 and tried, unsuccessfully, to continue the work of Innocent III. He reopened the struggle against the Albigensians, and gave approval to the Dominican and the Franciscan Rules (1216 and 1223). At one time tutor to Frederick II, he crowned him Emperor (1220) and granted him the administration of Sicily provided that he kept it separate from the Empire; he also tried in vain to persuade him to go on crusade.

HONORIUS, FLAVIUS (384–423). First Western Roman Emperor. He succeeded his father, Theodosius, in 395. Weak and indecisive, he had to face constant Barbarian invasions and the dissolution of the Empire. At first, he accepted the assistance of the Barbarian general, Stilicho, who was also his tutor and administrator, and a keen supporter of the empire. However, in 408, Honorius had Stilicho killed. After the sack of Rome by the Visigothic King Alaric (410), he turned to another general, Constantius, who succeeded in partially restoring the Empire and made a treaty with the Visigoths.

HORTHY VON NAGYBANYA, MIKLÓS (1868–1949). Hungarian politician. Commander-in-Chief of the Austro-Hungarian fleet at the end of the First World War, he led the Hungarian opposition to the Communist Republic of Béla Kun in 1919, and in the following year he took power in a coup. Nominated Regent of Hungary in the same year, he sided with Hitler and Mussolini and in 1941 he joined the war against the Soviet Union. In 1944 he tried to open peace negotiations but was accused of treason by the Germans and imprisoned at Munich. At the end of the war he retired to Portugal.

HUASCAR (?–AD 1532). Inca King, son of Huayna Capac. On the death of his father, he inherited the southern part of the empire, based on Cuzco (1527). He was soon involved in a war of succession against his half-brother Atahualpa, who defeated and killed him.

HUAYNA CAPAC (?–AD 1527). Penultimate King of the Incas. Under him, the Inca Empire reached the height of its power, extending its territory as far as modern Ecuador. Before his death he arranged for the empire to be divided between his sons, Huascar and Atahualpa, and the war for the succession, which broke out, facilitated the conquest of the empire by the Spaniards.

HUGUENOTS. Generic name of French Protestants, followers of Calvin. It derives from the assimilation of the German *Eidgenosz* (confederate), with the name of the Frenchman, Hugo de Besançon, leader of the Reformers who fought against the Duke of Savoy in Geneva. Persecuted by the French monarchs, the Huguenots obtained freedom of worship by the Edict of Nantes (1598), which was later revoked by Louis XIV in 1685.

HUNS. Nomadic peoples, originating in the Asiatic steppes, who at the end of the fourth century and in the fifth century AD, devastated Europe under leaders such as Attila. On the death of Attila (453), the unity of the various tribes collapsed.

HURRIANS. Ancient population which migrated from northern Mesopotamia in the second millennium BC and formed the Kingdom called Mitanni. For a brief period, they dominated most of Syria and northern Iraq but were then subjugated by the Hittites in the fourteenth century.

HUS, JAN (1369–1415). Bohemian religious reformer. Priest and Rector of the University of Prague, he held doctrines similar to those of Wycliffe and, despite being excommunicated, continued to preach against the sale of indulgences. While attending the Council of Constance (1415), he was arrested and condemned to be burnt as a heretic.

HUSSEIN I (born 1935). King of Jordan, he ascended the throne in 1953. Educated in Britain, he followed a pro-Western policy and adopted a moderate stance towards Israel. Nevertheless, in 1967, the presence of Palestinian refugees in the country induced him to side with Egypt in the war against Israel, resulting in the loss of his lands on the West Bank of the Jordan. In 1973, he again took part in military action against Israel.

HYKSOS. Asiatic invaders who overran northern Egypt in the eighteenth and seventeenth centuries BC, so ending the Middle Kingdom. The Hyksos established their capital at Avaris on the delta of the Nile, and are credited with having introduced the horse and the war chariot into Egypt. They were expelled by the kings of the Eighteenth Dynasty in about 1570 BC.

IBN BATTUTA (1304–1368). The greatest Arab traveller in the Middle Ages. In 25 years, he travelled throughout the Muslim world — North Africa, the Middle East, Persia (Iran) —and reached as far as southern Russia and China. His writings are one of the few historical records of the Orient in this period.

IGNATIUS OF LOYOLA (1491–1556). Spanish priest. Founder of the Society of Jesus. Wounded by the French in the Battle of Pamplona (1521), he decided, while recovering, to lead the life of an ascetic. After attending the University of Salamanca, he studied at the University of Paris where he gathered together his first followers and, in 1534, swore vows of poverty and chastity. Ordained priest in 1537, he was unable to fulfil his intention of travelling to Palestine and so embarked on missionary work with his associates. In 1540, the Jesuits obtained approval from the Pope (in the bull *Regimini militantis*) and in the following year he was appointed their first Superior. From Rome, he supervised the military organization and the ascetic and theological training of the Society, which was destined to become the most effective force in the Counter-Reformation. He was canonized.

INCAS. Peoples of South America who, in the thirteenth century AD, founded a kingdom (with Cuzco as capital) in the region of modern Peru. At the time of the Spanish conquest, the Inca Empire extended from Ecuador to northern Chile, and inland to include the Andean highlands. Although knowing nothing of writing, the wheel or the use of animal power, the Incas developed a very advanced civilization which possessed an efficient road system, fine architecture in stone, and exquisitely worked objects made of gold and silver. Their government was strongly centralized, no private landownership was permitted, and the Inca — the Emperor — was venerated as a descendant of the Sun God.

INNOCENT III (1160–1216). He was elected Pope in 1198. Determined to affirm the supremacy of the Papacy in the Investiture Struggle with the Empire, he crowned the Emperor Otto of Brunswick in 1209. Later, he deposed Otto and supported Frederick II in his place, obtaining acknowledgment of the supremacy of the Church from many monarchs. He summoned the Fourth Crusade which ended in the conquest of Constantinople and the foundation of the Eastern Latin Empire (1204), and worked to restore the unity of the Church. He fought hard against heresy: he supported the Albigensian Crusade (1208–1209), condemned the Waldensians, and supported the establishment of the new orders of Franciscan and Dominican friars. In 1215 he summoned the Lateran council which marked the climax of papal theocracy in the Middle Ages.

ISABELLA OF CASTILE (1451–1504). Queen of Castile. After lengthy conflicts with the nobility, she ascended the throne of Castile (1474) and put an end to the civil wars. Her husband, Ferdinand (whom she married in 1469) became King of Aragon in 1479, thus uniting the two kingdoms. Together, they embarked on a war against the Moors whom they finally ejected from Spain in 1492. She reorganized the administration of her kingdom and sought religious conformity, by either expelling or forcibly converting the Jews. She supported Christopher Columbus whose voyages opened up America to colonial expansion.

ISMAIL PASHA (1830–1895). Governor of Egypt (1864), he started a policy of independence and westernization of the country. In 1867, he received the title of Khedive from the Ottoman Sultan. Financial bankruptcy caused by the expense of modernization of the state compelled him to hand the control of the Suez Canal (which has been opened in 1868) to the British in 1875. He also had to accept Anglo-French control over Egyptian finances. He abdicated in 1879 in favour of his son.

IVAN III (1440–1505). Grand Duke of Moscow, he succeeded his father, Vassili II, in 1462. He married Sophia, the niece of the last Byzantine Emperor, and gave unity to Russia, making it the spiritual heir of the Eastern Roman Empire. Profiting from the collapse of the power of the Golden Horde, he subdued Novgorod between 1478 and 1480, conquered the cities of northeastern Russia, and reaffirmed his supremacy over the other Russian princes. Having attacked Lithuania in 1492, he secured recognition for himself as monarch of all Russia in 1494. He rebuilt and enlarged his residence, the Kremlin.

IVAN IV THE TERRIBLE (1530–1584). First Tzar of Russia, he succeeded his father, Vassili III, in 1533. However, his mother acted as Regent until 1547 when he took power himself. He consolidated his absolutism, ruthlessly stamping out revolts by the great feudatories (the boyars), confiscating many of their properties and rewarding the lesser nobility with the compulsory labour of the peasantry. He was unable to secure a permanent port for himself on the Baltic due to the opposition of Poland (1562) and Sweden (1567). After a series of military failures, he had to give up Livonia and Finland. However, he fought successfully against the Tartars, taking Kazan (1552) and Astrakhan (1554), and incorporated part of Siberia into his dominions (1582).

JAMES I (1566–1625). King of England, and the only son of Mary Stuart, Queen of Scotland (who was compelled to abdicate). Crowned James VI of Scotland in 1567, he tended to side with Elizabeth I in the struggle between the latter and his mother, and obtained the succession to the English throne in 1603, unifying the crowns of England, Scotland and Ireland for the first time. His ambiguous attitude in religious matters led to the hostility of both Catholics (Gunpowder Plot, 1605) and some Protestants, whose divisions over matters of faith and practice remained unresolved. Important royal policies encountered opposition in Parliament, leading to friction among the various interest groups.

JAMES II (1633–1701). King of England and second son of Charles I. Educated in France, he returned to England after the Restoration (1660), and, despite his overt Catholicism, he succeeded to the throne in 1685, on the death of his brother, Charles II. He appointed Catholics to office in place of Protestants, and he used his prerogative to remove legal disabilities against his co-religionists. He shared the pro-French sympathies of his brother. The combined effect of his policies mobilized both Whigs and Tories in Parliament against him. Their opposition led to an invitation to William of Orange, his son-in-law, who was Protestant and anti-French, to come to England. When he landed in 1688 James II offered no resistance and fled to France.

JEFFERSON, THOMAS (1743–1826). Statesman and third President of the United States. One of the authors of the Declaration of Independence (1776), Governor of Virginia (1779–1780), member of the Continental Congress (from 1783), ambassador to Paris and advocate of friendship with Revolutionary France, and first Secretary of State of the United States of America. He founded the Republican (later Democratic) Party in opposition to the Federalists who had conservative and pro-British tendencies. President from 1801, he favoured the colonization of the West, purchased Louisiana from Napoleon (1803), abolished the slave trade, and kept the United States out of the Napoleonic Wars. In 1809, he retired to private life, but continued to exert an influence on American politics.

JEWS. Semitic people originating in Mesopotamia. They spread into Syria, Palestine and Egypt in the third and second millennia BC. In 70 BC, the Roman Emperor Titus conquered Jerusalem (their capital), and from then until 14 May 1948, when the State of Israel was proclaimed, the Jews were scattered around the world without a home of their own. During this Diaspora, or dispersal, they frequently had to live — sometimes accepted, but more often heavily persecuted — in distinct communities within the countries where they had settled. The vicissitudes of the Diaspora have led to the distinction between the Sephardim (or Jews of the Levant) and the Ashkenazim (or Jews of the West). In Israel, the former are more numerous.

JOAN OF ARC (1412–1431). French heroine of the Hundred Years' War. The daughter of peasants, she heard "voices" which told her of her mission to free France from English rule. In 1429, the Dauphin Charles permitted her to ride at the head of his forces, and she played a major role in the liberation of Orleans. Despite having a position of honour at the side of Charles VII during his coronation at Rheims, she did not receive his wholehearted support and did not succeed in lifting the English siege of Paris (1429). Imprisoned by the Burgundians and handed over to the English, she was tried at Rouen by a court presided over by the Bishop of Beauvais, Pierre Cauchon. She was condemned to die at the stake for heresy. She was rehabilitated in 1456, and canonized in 1920.

JOHN XXII (1245–1334). Born Jaime Duesa, he was elected Pope in 1316, and became the second of the Avignon Popes. An able administrator, he persecuted the Franciscans, and condemned the doctrines of the absolute poverty of Christ and the apostles (1323). He also attacked the idea that the empire should be independent of the Church. He excommunicated (1324) Emperor Louis the Bavarian, who had accused him of heresy. He imprisoned the Anti-Pope Nicholas V (nominated by the Emperor at Rome at 1328), and received his submission two years later.

JOHN I (1167–1216). King of England and known as Lackland. Youngest child of Henry II, he succeeded his brother Richard and was forgiven for his attempt to usurp the throne while Richard was away on crusade (1191). During his reign he contended with the opposition of the barons who were supported by the clergy. Excommunicated (1209) for not having accepted the papal nominee as Archbishop of Canterbury, he later submitted to the Pope. After the loss of Normandy (1204) to the French under Philip II Augustus, the continuing war against France further weakened his position in relation to the nobility: in 1215, they forced him to accept *Magna Carta*, the charter which established remedies if their privileges were ignored. However, the struggle with the barons continued until his death in the following year.

JOHN III SOBIESKI (1624–1696). He became King of Poland in 1674 after his victory against the Turks in the Battle of Chocim. Allied with Emperor Leopold I and with Pope Innocent XI, he again crushed the Turks while they were besieging Vienna (1683), and was acclaimed a hero of Christianity. His death signalled the virtual end of the independence of Poland, which was ruled by foreign kings for the next 66 years.

JOHNSON, LYNDON BAINES (1908–1973). American statesman. He served as a Democratic member of the House of Representatives from 1937 until he was elected as one of the Senators for Texas in 1949. A leader of the Democrats in the Senate from 1953, he was chosen by John F. Kennedy in 1960 as candidate for the office of Vice-President. After the assassination of Kennedy, he took over as President (1963) and was re-elected in 1964. He continued the liberal policies of Kennedy, and implemented many social reforms. Abroad, he extended American military involvement in the Vietnam War, a policy which made him increasingly unpopular and which contributed to the student protests of 1968. The stress of the political situation persuaded him not to seek a further term as President, and he retired from politics (1968).

JOSEPH II (1741–1790). Holy Roman Emperor. Son of Francis I, he succeeded him in 1765 and ruled jointly with his mother, Maria Theresa, until her death in 1780. His method of government is known as "enlightened despotism". Aiming at confronting Prussia with the reality of Habsburg power, he worked to establish a strongly centralized state. He carried out ecclesiastical reform in the Church, and regulated its internal structure. He made German the sole language of the empire — a measure which provoked opposition. His constant aim, never realized, was the conquest of Bavaria. He died without sons.

JULIAN THE APOSTATE (331–363). Roman Emperor, nephew of Constantine, he renounced Christianity and was therefore given the name apostate. He was appointed Caesar and Prefect of Gaul (335) by Constantius II whose sister he married and whom he succeeded in 360. He tried to restore paganism, abolishing the privileges of the Catholic Church and compelling the Church to pay for the reconstruction of the old temples. He also denied education to Christians, so that they reacted strongly against him. Administrative reforms and a reduction in royal extravagance improved the economic condition of the empire. He died while fighting the Persians.

JULIUS II (1433–1513). Born Giuliano della Rovere, he was elected Pope in 1503, and dedicated himself to the recovery of the Papal States. In order to regain Ferrara and Rimini, he fought vigorously against the Republic of Venice (1508–1510), joining the League of Cambrai (1509) with the Emperor Maximilian and the King of France, Louis XII. Later, worried about French domination in Italy, he made peace with Venice, and built up the Holy League (Venice, Switzerland, Spain and England). He succeeded in winning over the Emperor (previously a supporter of a French-backed council to depose the Pope) to recognize the authority of the Lateran Council of 1512–1517. He died while preparing an attack on Spain in pursuit of his never-abandoned aim of ending all foreign interference in Italy.

JUSTINIAN (482–565). Eastern Roman Emperor. He ruled jointly with his uncle, Justin I, from 527 until the latter's death in the following year. He pursued a vast programme of political and administrative reorganization and of the restoration of imperial authority. In the *Corpus Iuris Civilis*, he reformed Roman law. He favoured industry, commerce and relations with the West, but he opposed the Papacy. His generals, Belisarius and Narses, reoccupied North Africa (533–534), Italy (536–552) and southern Spain (554). He fought against the Bulgars, Slavs and Huns, and against the King of Persia, Chosroes I.

KENNEDY, JOHN FITZGERALD (1917–1963). Thirty-fifth President of the United States, and the youngest ever to have been elected. A member of one of the richest American families, he was elected to the House of Representatives as a Democratic member in 1947 and to the Senate in 1953. Known for his reformist and anti-racist policies, he was elected President in November 1960, taking up office at the beginning of 1961. In foreign affairs, he achieved his most spectacular success when he forced the Soviet Union to remove the missile bases which it was constructing in Cuba (1962). He pursued dynamic policies of international detente, of economic aid to the underdeveloped countries, and of greater federal involvement in the fields of civil rights, education and health — policies which earned him both popularity and hostility. He was assassinated in Dallas in 1963, in circumstances not yet fully explained.

KENYATTA, JOMO (c.1890–1978). One of the most influential of African statesmen. From 1920, he fought for the rights of the Kikuyu population of Kenya against colonialism. Among the founders of the Pan-African movement (1945), he was accused of responsibility for the violence carried out by the secret Mau Mau organization, and was imprisoned from 1953–1961. Later, as President of the Kenya African Union, he went to London to present the case for his country's independence. He became President of the Republic in 1964, and held office until his death.

KERENSKY, ALEXANDER (1881–1970). Russian socialist revolutionary. Member of the Duma (1912), he led a provisional government after the February 1917 Revolution. Overthrown by the October Revolution and defeated by the Bolsheviks at Gatchina, he fled to France and then New York where as a writer he took up anti-Soviet activities.

KHMER. Ancient civilization which flourished in central and southern Cambodia between the sixth and the fourteenth centuries AD. It was a result of a fusion between Hindu influences and fundamental elements of Buddhism. The decline of the Khmer Kingdom began in 1218 with the death of Jayavarman VII, and was completed with the destruction of the capital Angkor by Siam in 1431. Khmer is the language of eighty per cent of the population of Cambodia (Kampuchea), and has given its name to the people who speak it.

KHRUSHCHEV, NIKITA (1894–1971). Soviet statesman. Political commissar at Stalingrad during the Second World War and a member of the Presidium from 1952, he joined the collective leadership of the Communist Party after Stalin's death (1953). He launched the de-Stalinization campaign, and condemned him openly at the Twentieth Party Congress (1956). However, the Hungarian Revolution, which followed it, was still repressed militarily. Freeing himself from internal opposition (1957) and reinforcing his own power, he assumed the Chairmanship of the Council of Ministers (1958) and sponsored initiatives in favour of disarmament and detente with the West, obtaining significant personal successes. Economic and political failures (especially in the Cuban Missile Crisis with the USA and in his Virgin Lands Policy), and the decisive deterioration in relations with China led to his fall in 1964.

KING, MARTIN LUTHER (1929–1968). Black Baptist pastor, he started a movement for the emancipation of Black Americans, and became one of its most important leaders. The use of methods of non-violence, such as passive resistance, civil disobedience and huge marches (for example, Washington in 1963), enabled him to obtain the passage of two laws of benefit to the civil rights of black people (1965). He won the Nobel Prize for Peace (1964). Taking a stand against the Vietnam War, he was assassinated while launching a national campaign against poverty.

KOŚCIUSZKO, TADEUSZ (1746–1817). Polish patriot and national hero. Educated in Paris, he went to America (1776) where he fought in the War of Independence, becoming a general. He returned home in 1784, and fought to secure Poland's autonomy from Russian rule (1792). After a period of exile in France, he led an insurrection by the nobility to achieve Polish independence and unity (1794). Imprisoned by the Russians, he was freed two years later. He spent his last days in exile, continuing to struggle for Polish liberty.

KOSSUTH, LOUIS (1802–1894). Hungarian statesman and patriot. He fought against Austrian domination and led the Hungarian Revolution (1848). When independence was proclaimed, he became President of the provisional revolutionary government (1849). Defeated by the armies of Austria and Russia, he fled to Turkey (where he remained until 1851) then to the United States, and finally to England where he met Mazzini. He devoted himself to attempts to provoke uprisings against the Habsburgs. He refused the amnesty offeed to him by the new Austro-Hungariarn regime (1867), and died in Italy. He received an honourable burial in Budapest.

KOSYGIN, ALEXEI (1904–1980). Russian statesman. He joined the Communist Party in 1927 and became a member of the Central Committee in 1939. From 1959 he was Vice-President and then President of Gosplan (the Committee for Economic Planning). Vice-Chairman of the Council of Ministers (1960) and member of the Presidium, he succeeded Khrushchev in 1964, ruling jointly with Brezhnev. He worked for the modernization of agriculture and industry. He retired in 1980, and died soon afterwards.

KUBLAI KHAN (c.1216–1294). Mongol Emperor, nephew of Genghis Khan. He completed the conquest of China (1279) and attempted the invasion of Japan. He founded the Yuan Dynasty which governed China until 1368, gave a solid base to his empire, began a policy of tolerance, reopened old trade routes and introduced some social reforms. Marco Polo visited his court at Peking.

KUSH. African Kingdom on the Upper Nile, founded in about 1000 BC. In 725 BC Kush conquered the whole of Egypt and founded the Twenty-fifth Dynasty. The Assyrian invasions (676 and 663 BC) pushed it southwards, and the capital was transferred to Meroe. As the greatest producer of iron at the time, Kush traded with Egypt, Arabia and India. In 350 BC the Kingdom of Kush collapsed under an invasion from the nearby Kingdom of Axum.

LAFAYETTE, MARIE-JOSEPH (1757–1834). French general and statesman. A hero of the American War of Independence, he returned to France in 1781 and became one of the leaders of the liberal bourgeoisie. A member of the States General and then of the National Assembly, and Commander of the National Guard after the fall of the Bastille (1789), his popularity declined when he ordered his troops to fire on a crowd which was calling for a Republic (1791). Having left France for Austria (1792) he stayed out of politics during the Napoleonic period, but was a member of the opposition after the restoration of the Bourbons (1814). Later, he was a key figure in the July Revolution (1830) and in the proclamation of Louis Philippe as King of the French.

LANCASTER. English royal family. Founded by Edmund, second son of King Henry III of England, and Earl of Lancaster from 1267. On the death of his son Henry, first Duke of Lancaster (1361), the title and the fee (lands) passed to Henry's daughter Blanche and her husband John of Gaunt (son of Edward III) who, for a short time, was the most powerful man in the kingdom. Their son, having deposed his cousin King Richard II, ruled as Henry IV from 1399 to 1413. He was succeeded by Henry V (1413–1422) and Henry VI (1422–1461), whose weakness and incapacity led to the Wars of the Roses between Lancaster and York (1455–1485).

LAO-TZU (c.604–c.531). Chinese philosopher. According to tradition, he was the founder of Taoism — a mystic religion which developed in reaction to the moral and political teachings of Confucianism. Lao-tzu is reputed to have been the author of the *Tao-te Ching*, one of the most important sacred books of Taoism.

LEE, ROBERT E. (1807–1870). Commander of the Confederate army in the American Civil War (1862). He had previously refused the command of the troops of the Union, offered to him by Lincoln, because of his loyalty to his native Virginia. Although he was opposed to slavery and secession, he defended Richmond, won numerous victories against the North, and invaded Pennsylvania. He was defeated by General Grant in the Battle of Appomattox (1865), which ended the Confederate military effort. Retiring from politics, he spent the last years of his life as a school principal.

LENIN, VLADIMIR (1870–1924). Russian revolutionary and statesman, born Vladimir Ilyich Ulyanov. Imprisoned (1897) and deported to Siberia for three years, he lived abroad from 1900 to 1917 (except for a brief return during the 1905 Revolution), studying and writing about Marxism. He went home in 1917, and gave decisive impetus to the Bolshevik left. With the support of the Petrograd soviet and garrison, he led the October Revolution which proclaimed the Union of Soviet Socialist Republics. Assuming power with Trotsky, Sverdlov and Stalin, he signed the harsh Treaty of Brest Litovsk (1918), and faced civil war, foreign intervention and severe economic crisis. At the same time, he dedicated himself to laying the basis of a socialist state. In 1919 he founded the Third International, focal point of the international workers' movement. From 1922 he was seriously ill and became less able to take a full part in affairs.

LEO I THE GREAT (?–AD 461). Pope from 440, he defended the unity of the Church and proclaimed the complete supremacy of the Papacy. He fought the heresy of Manichaeism, and had the Monophysites condemned at the Council of Chalcedon (451). As a result of the absence of Imperial authority in the West, he intervened in person in order to stop the invasion of Italy by Attila's Huns (452) and to limit the destruction of Rome during its sack by the Vandals of Geiserich (455). He was later canonized.

LEO X (1475–1521). Born Giovanni de' Medici, son of Lorenzo the Magnificent, he was made a cardinal when still adolescent, and became Pope in 1513. Although not dissolute himself, he permitted corruption among priests and courtiers, and was inclined to nepotism. However, he was also a sincere believer and a lavish patron of the arts. At first undecided in the conflict between Francis I and Charles V, he cured the split with France (Concordat of Bologna, 1516) although he had to agree that the King should appoint to ecclesiastical office. Later he sided with Charles V. He ended the Lateran Council in 1517, but was ineffective in dealing with the Reformation which he barely understood, thus contributing indirectly to its development.

LEO XIII (1810–1903). Born Gioacchino Pecci, he was elected Pope in 1878, the first Pope to possess no sovereign territory. He succeeded in putting an end to the anti-Catholic measures (*Kulturkampf*) in Germany, and encouraged the French bishops to accept the Third Republic. More uncompromising in his dealings with the Kingdom of Italy, he refused to accept the Law of Guarantees, and continued the ban forbidding Catholics from participating in elections. In the period of social unrest, he defined (in the encyclical *Rerum Novarum*, 1891) the position of the Church in relation to the limited intervention in politics which was permitted to Catholics. A learned man, he opened the archives of the Vatican to researchers, encouraged the use of a modernized catechism and the establishment of new schools.

LEO III THE ISAURIAN (c.675–741). Acclaimed Eastern Roman Emperor on the death of Theodosius III (717), he opposed the expansion of Islam, first by lifting the siege of Constantinople (August 718) and then by victory over the Arabs at Afyonkarahisar (740). With the promulgation of a code of law (*Ecloga*, 740), he carried out political, social and judicial reforms, aimed at the protection of the poorest sections of society. The reforms included two decrees against image worship (726 and 730), a cult which contributed to the wealth and immense power of the aristocracy, clergy and monasteries. These decrees began the struggle over iconoclasm.

LEOPOLD I (1640–1705). Son of Ferdinand II, he was King of Hungary from 1655, Holy Roman Emperor from 1657, and King of Bohemia from 1658. He was in almost perpetual conflict with the Turks and with France. The Imperial armies lifted the Turkish siege of Vienna (1683), and finally crushed the Ottomans at Zenta (1697). By the Peace of Carlowitz (1699), Leopold I obtained Hungary and Transylvania.

LEOPOLD II (1747–1792). Son of Francis I of Habsburg-Lorraine, he was Grand Duke of Tuscany from 1765, and then Holy Roman Emperor on the death of his brother Joseph II (1790). He turned Tuscany into a modern state, making use of the typical methods of enlightened despotism: he promoted administrative, legislative and financial reforms, looked after the interests of the middle and lower sections of society, and tried to reform the Church in accordance with Jansenist principles. In the empire, he made peace with the Turks and the Netherlands, and carried out mild reforms. Faced with the French Revolution, he made a defensive treaty with Russia, and was opposed to armed intervention in France.

LEOPOLD II (1835–1909). King of the Belgians, he succeeded his father, Leopold I, and ruled as a constitutional and liberal monarch. In his newly founded state, he had to face problems of linguistic and ethnic dualism (French and Flemish), controversy about religion in education, and difficulties arising from economic development. Abroad, he defended his independence against the two neighbouring powers of France and Germany. He started commercial and colonial expansion, gaining personal possession of the Congo (Congress of Berlin, 1884) which he then surrendered to the Belgian state in 1908.

LEWIS I THE GREAT (1326–1382). King of Hungary and Poland. He succeeded his father, Charles Robert of Anjou, in 1342, and tried to unite Hungary, Poland and Naples under one crown. Following the murder of his brother, Andrew (husband of Joanna I of Anjou), he went to Italy (1346) and conquered the Kingdom of Naples but later had to abandon it (1350) owing to the opposition of Pope Clement VI. He was victorious against the Bohemians (1345), the Lithuanians (1351–1352) and the Tartars (1354), and embarked upon a number of wars against Venice, obtaining the Dalmation coast and islands (treaties of Zara, 1358, and Turin, 1381). He became King of Poland in 1370, but the union with Hungary lasted only until his death.

LINCOLN, ABRAHAM (1809–1865). Sixteenth President of the United States. Of humble origin, he became a well-known lawyer and started his first battles against slavery as a member of the Whig Party in Congress (1847–1849). Returning to politics in 1854, he opposed the slavery legislation proposed by Douglas, and engaged him in a series of open debates. He joined the newly formed Republican Party in 1856 and stood as a candidate for President in 1860, on an anti-slavery platform. His election provoked the secession of the southern states and the outbreak of the Civil War, in which Lincoln led the Union (the North) against the Confederacy (the South). In 1863 he proclaimed the emancipation of the black population of the South and in 1864 was re-elected as President. He was assassinated by a fanatic southerner, John Wilkes Booth, a few days after the end of the war (16 April 1865).

LIUTPRAND (?–AD 744). King of the Lombards from 712, he consolidated the kingdom and tried to extend it to the whole of Italy, pushing out the Byzantines. He carried out reforms to strengthen his bonds with the Romans. From 726, profiting from the struggle over iconoclasm between the Papacy and Byzantium, he attacked Pentapolis and the Exarchate of Ravenna on many occasions. Opposed by Pope Gregory II, he left Rome after giving him Sutry, the nucleus of what was to become the Papal States (728). Having made an agreement with Pope Zacharias, he defeated and deposed the Dukes of Spoleto and Benevento (742). Shortly before his death, he began diplomatic contacts with Byzantium to discuss a new settlement of Italy.

LIVINGSTONE, DAVID (1813–1873). Scottish missionary, he was sent to southern Africa as a doctor and explorer. He was the first European to cross the Kalahari Desert (1847–1849), and he then sailed up the Zambesi, discovering the (then unknown) Victoria Falls, and exploring the Congo basin (1853–1856). With an expedition financed by the British government (1858), he discovered Lake Nyasa and, in the course of a journey (started in 1866) searching for the sources of the Nile, he met Stanley near Lake Tanganyika in 1871.

LOLLARDS. English preachers, followers of the religious reformer, John Wycliffe (1320–1384). They denied the doctrine of transubstantiation, and upheld a belief in poverty as a way of life, inspired by the Holy Scriptures. Their radical preaching contributed to the Peasants' Revolt (1381), which was ruthlessly suppressed. The movement, which became clandestine after its condemnation by the Council of Constance (1415), contributed to the Protestant Reformation.

LOMBARDS. Germanic peoples, in origin a tribe of Suevi, who migrated to northwestern Germany in the second century AD and then to Pannonia and Noricum (modern Austria). Under pressure from the Avars, they descended on Italy in 568, forming the Lombard Kingdom and consequently restricting the Byzantines to the coasts and the islands. Converted to Christianity by Gregory I, they quickly merged their culture with that of the Romans. However, they later quarrelled with the Papacy and, in 774, were defeated by Charlemagne who was answering Pope Adrian I's call for help.

LOTHAR II OF SUPPLINBURG (1060–1137). Emperor. Leading the Saxon opposition to the Franconians, he was elected King of Germany by the papal party on the death of Henry V (1125), the last of the Franconian Dynasty. After a long struggle against his German opponents, he was crowned Emperor by Pope Innocent II (1133) and received the confiscated estates of the Empress Matilda as a reward for solving the dispute between the Anti-Pope Anaclectus II and Roger II the Norman. In Germany, he obtained the definitive submission of his Swabian adversaries (1135) and then returned to Italy where he reimposed imperial power on the free cities and drove Roger II back to Sicily.

LOUIS I THE PIOUS (778–840). King of the Franks and of Aquitania. In 813, he was summoned by Charlemagne to assist in ruling the empire, and in 814, he succeeded him as his sole heir. Continuing his father's project to create a unified Christian Empire, he issued the *Ordinatio Imperii* (817) by which his eldest son, Lothar, became co-Emperor and the younger sons received land and royal titles. At first he granted full independence to the Papacy. This was later rescinded by the *Constitutio Romana* (824), compelling the popes to swear loyalty to the Emperor. The birth (by a second marriage) of a fourth son, Charles the Bald, and the grant to him of the territories held by Lothar, twice brought about Louis' deposition (830 and 833–834) and led to wars over territory which lasted until after his death.

LOUIS IV THE BAVARIAN (1287–1347). King of Germany and then Emperor, he was the son of Louis II, Duke of Bavaria. On the death of Henry VII, he defeated his rival, Frederick of Habsburg. Threatened with excommunication for having assumed the title of King of Germany without the Pope's approval, he started a long conflict with the Avignon Papacy. When he was finally excommunicated, he accused Pope John XXII of heresy. He took the Imperial crown in Rome (1328), adopting the position of Marsilius of Padua who taught that the people, and not the Pope, had the right to proclaim the Emperor. He deposed John XXII and chose another Pope. At the Diet of Rheims (1338), he obtained official recognition from the German princes of the legality of his rule. However, he was later abandoned by his supporters and, failing to reach a settlement with the Papacy, he had to accept the preferment of Charles IV of Luxemburg as King (1346).

LOUIS IX (1214–1270). King of France, he took power in 1235 after the regency of his mother, Blanche of Castile (1226–1235). Having stamped out a number of revolts by feudal lords, he obtained Normandy and Anjou from Henry II of England (Peace of Paris, 1258). He remained neutral in the fight between the Papacy and the Emperor Frederick II, and extended French influence in Provence as a result of the marriage between his brother, Charles of Anjou, and Beatrice of Provence. He also exerted his influence in Italy by backing Charles' expedition to help Pope Clement IV against the Ghibellines (1265). He supported both the Seventh Crusade (1248), during which he suffered a lengthy imprisonment, and the Eighth Crusade to Tunisia, where he died of plague. He was canonized in 1297.

LOUIS XIV (1638–1715). King of France from 1643. On the death of the Regent Mazarin (1661), he took power into his own hands. Known as the Sun King, he was the outstanding representative of absolutism. Having reduced the powers of the nobility and the *parlements*, he ruled through an efficient bureaucracy. Advised by the ministers Colbert and Louvois, he led France to the cultural, economic and political supremacy of Europe. He enlarged France's European territories and made it a maritime and colonial power. Absolutist and intolerant in religious matters, he issued the Declaration of the Four Articles of the Gallican Church (1682), persecuted the Jansenists and revoked the Edict of Nantes (1685). The crisis, begun in 1685 by the rigidities of his system of government, the effects of the Wars of the League of Augsburg and the Spanish Succession, and the territorial losses suffered by the Treaties of Ryswick (1697), Utrecht (1713) and Rastatt (1714), left France exhausted and in decline on his death.

LOUIS XV (1710–1774). King of France, he was the great-grandson and successor to Louis XIV. At first, Philip of Orleans (1715–1723), Louis of Bourbon (1723–1726), and Cardinal Fleury (1726–1743) acted as Regents, while later the King was also influenced by his mistresses, among them the Marquise de Pompadour. During his reign, the monarchy was weakened by the increasing opposition of the *parlements* (dominated by aristocratic elements), by a ruinous financial policy, and by the loss of Canada and the Indies at the end of the Seven Years' War (Peace of Paris, 1763). Although he attempted to reassert absolutism and to dispense with the *parlements* (1771), he was unable to halt the economic and political decline of the state.

LOUIS XVI (1754–1793). King of France. He inherited a corrupt and nearly bankrupt country from his grandfather, Louis XV. He was unable to carry out the reforms of his ministers Turgot, Necker and Calonne because of the hostility of the Queen and the privileged social groups. However, in order to placate the bourgeoisie, he summoned the States General (1789) to its first meeting since 1614. His actions, in relation to the National Assembly and in calling in troops, led to the uprising in Paris and the fall of the Bastille. The abolition of the monarchy (21 September 1792) and the execution of the King and Queen were the consequences of many factors: Louis' indecisive attitude to the Revolution, his failure to move towards a constitutional monarchy, his attempted flight (1791) and his agreement to war against Austria.

LOUIS PHILIPPE (1773–1850). King of the French from 1830, following the insurrection in Paris and the exile of Charles X. He gave a liberal slant to French policy, widening the suffrage, and supporting the principle of non-intervention abroad. Later, confronted by domestic difficulties, he reinforced his links with conservatives, both at home and abroad: he ended ties with England, completed the occupation of Algeria and became pro-Austrian. Overthrown by the 1848 Revolution, he fled to England where he died.

LUDOVICO *IL MORO* (1452–1508). Having become *de facto* Duke of Milan (1480), he acted as guardian to the young Gian Galeazzo after the murder of his elder brother, Galeazzo Maria Sforza. He intervened in the wars for supremacy in Italy. At first he allied with the Aragonese of Naples, but when Ferdinand I tried to compel him to cede power to the legitimate heir Gian Galeazzo, he supported the expedition of Charles VIII of France against Naples (1494). In the following year, he took part in the anti-French league which defeated and expelled Charles VIII. His unscrupulous alliances prevented him from winning support against Louis XII of France when he claimed the Duchy of Milan as a descendant of a Visconti (1499); betrayed, he became a prisoner of the French in Novara (1500), and died at Loches in France.

LUMUMBA, PATRICE (1925–1961). Congolese patriot and statesman. Founder of the *Mouvement National Congolais*, he was imprisoned by the Belgians (1959). After independence, he became Prime Minister of Zaire (1960). He worked to secure the unity and the democratic development of the country, in conflict with the shifting colonial and tribal alliances which led to the secession of Katanga. After quarrelling with President Kasavubu, he was arrested by General Mobutu, handed over to the Katangese police and murdered.

LUTHER, MARTIN (1483–1546). German religous reformer. An Augustinian monk, he became a priest in 1507. While a teacher of philosophy and theology at the University of Wittenberg, he evolved the doctrine of justification by faith, the fundamental basis of his theology. Opposing the sale of indulgences, on 31 October 1517, he nailed his 95 theses to the main door of Wittenberg Cathedral. Refusing to retract them, he was excommunicated (1520) and outlawed by the Emperor (Worms, 1521). Given protection at Wartburg by the Elector of Saxony, he translated the Bible into German, and established the organizational and theological basis of the new Church. From Wittenberg, he directed the reformist movement which, spreading rapidly in Germany, had both political and social implications whose more radical tendencies he tried to curb. He supported the power of the princes against the Church of Rome, and he justified their actions in bloodily suppressing the Peasants' Revolts of 1525.

MACARTHUR, DOUGLAS (1880–1964). American general, Commander-in-Chief of the Allied forces in the Pacific during the Second World War. He directed all operations against Japan and accepted its surrender on 2 September 1945. Commander of the occupation forces in Japan, he was appointed Commander of the United Nations troops at the outbreak of the Korean War (1950). However, after making unacceptable demands in this role, he was dismissed by President Truman in 1952.

MAGELLAN, FERDINAND (1480–1521). Portuguese explorer. In 1519, he organized a Spanish expedition to the Moluccas. Setting out with five ships, he reached Brazil and then sailed south in search of a passage westwards. In November 1520 he passed through what are now called the Straits of Magellan and entered the Pacific Ocean. In March 1521 he reached the Philippines and was killed there in a fight with the local people. The only surviving ship, *Victoria*, returned to Spain in September 1522, having completed the first circumnavigation of the world.

MAMELUKES. Mercenary soldiers originating in the Caucasus. During the medieval period, they were employed by Egypt and other Muslim states. Then, from 1252 to 1517, the Mamelukes ruled Egypt and Syria, successfully blocking the invasions of Tamerlane's Mongols, and driving out the Franks from Syria. In 1517, having made Egypt the main Mediterranean power, they were defeated by the Ottoman Turks and forced to become their vassals.

MANSUR, AL- (?–AD 1002). Effective leader of the Omayyad Caliphate of Cordoba from 978, he conducted numerous campaigns against the Christians of northern Spain, occupying Barcelona and Santiago de Compostela. A capable administrator, he provided Muslim Spain with an excellent system of government.

MAO TSE-TUNG (1893–1976). Chinese statesman. Son of a small landowner, he was one of the founders of the Communist Party in Shanghai (1921) and became its President in 1931. To escape the Nationalists, he led the Communists in the Long March (1934–1935) to Shaanxi. With the government he had established there, he conducted the struggle against Chiang Kai-shek and, from 1937 onwards, against the Japanese invaders. At the end of the Second World War, during which the Communists had united with the Nationalists to fight against the Japanese, Mao Tse-tung reopened the offensive against Chiang Kai-shek. After taking Peking, he proclaimed the Chinese People's Republic on 1 October 1949, and became its first President. He carried out a policy of collectivization and rapid industrialization, trying to follow a different path to socialism from that pursued in the Soviet Union. In 1958 he resigned as President but retained office as Party Secretary. In 1966 he launched the Cultural Revolution. His death, and the problems of the succession, opened a new era in China.

MARAT, JEAN-PAUL (1743–1793). French revolutionary and journalist. At the outbreak of the French Revolution, he founded the newspaper *Ami du Peuple*. Later, he became head of the Jacobin Club. He took part in the fall of the Girondists. He was murdered in his bath by Charlotte Corday.

MARATHAS. Hindu peoples of western India. In the seventeenth century, under the leadership of Shivaji (1627–1680), they offered armed resistance to the Muslim Mogul emperors, and formed a confederation of states in central and northern India. In the eighteenth century, the Maratha Confederation fought bravely against the British.

MARCUS AURELIUS (121–180). Roman Emperor. He succeeded Antoninus Pius in 161. Philosopher and man of learning, he ruled the state with uncommon ability and energy. Having restored peace to the eastern frontiers by means of a campaign against the Parthians in Syria (166), he defeated the invading Marcomanni and Quadi, who had crossed the Alps and destroyed Aquileia (167–169). He died at Vindobona (Vienna) while preparing a third expedition against the Marcomanni.

MARIA THERESA (1717–1780). Daughter of the Emperor Charles VI, she became heiress to the throne by virtue of the Pragmatic Sanction (1713). On the death of her father (1740) she ascended the thrones of Austria, Hungary and Bohemia. The claims of the major European states to the imperial throne gave rise to the War of the Austrian Succession (1740–1748). By the Peace of Aix-la-Chapelle, which ended the war, she obtained the acknowledgement of her husband, Francis of Lorraine, as Emperor, in return for her surrender of Silesia to Prussia, and of Parma and Piacenza to Spain. She attempted to recover Silesia during the course of the Seven Years' War (1756–1763) against Frederick II of Prussia. Both Maria Theresa and her son, Joseph, who ruled in association with her from 1765 onwards, followed the ideals of enlightened absolutism, carrying out administrative and political reforms.

MARIE ANTOINETTE (1755–1793). Daughter of the Emperor Francis I and Maria Theresa of Austria. In 1770 she married the Dauphin of France, the future Louis XVI. Her extravagant and frivolous lifestyle alienated public opinion and, during the French Revolution, she suffered the fate of her husband. Recognized at Varennes while trying to escape with the King, she was arrested and later guillotined.

MARY STUART (1542–1587). Queen of Scotland, daughter of James V. She married Francis II of France and, on his death, returned to Scotland (1560) where, in 1565, she married Lord Darnley, a prominent English Catholic. As a result of this union, she lost the support of most Protestants and many nobles. After the mysterious assassination of Darnley and her new marriage with Bothwell, she sought refuge in England under the protection of her cousin Elizabeth. However, she was kept prisoner in England for many years and was eventually sentenced to death for her part in plotting against Elizabeth.

MARY II STUART (1662–1694). Queen of England, Scotland and Ireland. Daughter of James II, in 1677 she married her cousin William of Orange, and ruled jointly with him after the overthrow of James II (1689), following the Glorious Revolution. The two monarchs governed with ability and energy, trying to balance the various factions among the Whigs and Tories, and undermining the position of the Jacobites.

MATTHIAS CORVINUS (1440–1490). Elected King of Hungary in 1458, he reinforced the frontiers, defeating the Turks at Jajce (1463). In the hope of obtaining the German throne, he intervened in European politics. Taking advantage of the conflicts between the Papacy and the King of Bohemia, George Podebrady, he overran Moravia, Silesia and Lusatia. Later, he turned against the Habsburgs, occupying Vienna (1485), Lower Austria, Carinthia and Styria. Frustrated in his imperial ambitions following the election of Maximilian (1486), he again took up his project of a campaign against the Turks, but died before being able to carry it out. He was a great patron of letters, founding the Corvina Library in Budapest and the University of Bratislava.

MAURYA. Indian dynasty founded in 313 BC by Chandragupta Maurya, who ruled in northern India until about 180 BC. The greatest monarch of the dynasty was Asoka (273–232); he subjugated the whole of India with the exception of the extreme south, and introduced Buddhism as the official religion.

MAXIMILIAN I (1459–1519). Holy Roman Emperor. Son of Frederick III. In 1477 he married Mary of Burgundy, and inherited her territories. However, he had to fight Louis XI and Charles VIII of France before he could take control of them. Nominated King of the Romans in 1486, he added Flanders and the Tyrol to his dominions and, having become Emperor (1493), he recovered Artois and Franche—Comté from France. In 1495, after the death of his wife, he married Bianca Maria Sforza, and supported Ludovico *il Moro* against Charles VIII. Militarily, his policies achieved little, but his dynastic achievements were more considerable and prepared the way for the great Empire of Charles V.

MAXIMILIAN OF HABSBURG (1832–1867). Archduke of Austria, he was appointed Governor of Lombardy (1857) by his brother Francis Joseph. In 1864, he accepted the crown of Mexico offered to him by Napoleon III, but his reign lasted less than three years: when the French troops left Mexico, he was executed by the republican followers of Benito Juarez.

MAYA. Peoples of Central America who, between the third and the ninth centuries AD, created a flourishing kingdom in southern Mexico and in Yucatan. The Maya were farmers and lived in communities, scattered in the jungle. Their main centres, such as Copán, Palenque and Tikal, were ceremonial places inhabited only by nobles and priests. Among the characteristics of such cities were the great stone pyramids, surmounted by temples. The Maya attained a remarkable understanding of astronomy and mathematics, worked out a precise calendar, and evolved a type of ideographic writing still partly undeciphered. In about the ninth century, they migrated — for reasons still partly unknown — towards northern Yucatan. Here they mixed with another Mexican people, the Toltecs, and founded a new kingdom whose main centres were Chichén Itzá, Uxmal and Mayapan. By the time of the arrival of the Spaniards, Maya civilization was in decline: Yucatan was divided into many rival states which were easily conquered.

MAZARIN, JULES (1602–1661). Cardinal and French statesman. Papal diplomat, he became secretary and adviser to Richelieu and on his death (1642) succeeded him as First Minister to Louis XIII. During the minority of Louis XIV, he was the chief collaborator of the Regent, Anne of Austria. Carrying on Richelieu's anti-Habsburg and anti-Spanish policies, he added to the territories of France by the Treaties of Westphalia (1648) and the Pyrenees (1659). At home, he stamped out the Frondes (1648), thereby strengthening monarchical absolutism and retaining effective power until his death.

MAZZINI, GIUSEPPE (1805–1872). Italian patriot and statesman. A leading figure in *Risorgimento*, he joined the *Carbonari* in 1827, and then left them to found the "Young Italy" movement (1831), with a programme of unification and republicanism. After the failure of the risings which he had organized in Piedmont in 1833, he went to Switzerland where he founded the "Young Europe" movement (1834). Later, he lived in London. On the outbreak of the 1848 revolutions he returned to Italy where he became one of the triumvirs of the Roman Republic. In exile again from 1849, he played a more minor role in the latter insurrections which led to Italian unity, and pursued republicanism as opposed to the prevailing monarchism of leaders such as Cavour.

MEDES. Ancient peoples who, from the second millennium BC, lived in the north-western area of what is now Iran. In the eighth century BC, they were subdued by the Assyrians, but after frequent rebellions, they established an empire in the seventh century with its capital at Ecbatana. Under King Cyaxares, in about 625 BC, they expelled the Scythians from northern Iran and then, allied with Babylon, conquered and destroyed the Assyrian cities (612 BC). The Empire of the Medes was eventually overthrown by Cyrus the Great (550 BC) and incorporated into the Persian Empire.

MEDICI. Italian family who ruled Florence and then Tuscany fron the fifteenth to the eighteenth centuries. Already famous in the thirteenth century as bankers and merchants, they obtained *signoria* of Florence in 1435 under Cosimo the Elder (1389–1464). His nephew was Lorenzo the Magnificent (1449–1492), great patron of the arts and shrewd politician. Expelled from Florence twice (1494 and 1527), the Medici regained power on both occasions after the failure of the republican experiments. In 1569, Cosimo I (1519–1574) received the title of Grand Duke. The Medici ruled the Grand Duchy until the death of Gian Gastone (1737). The family then died out. The Medici family provided three Popes — Leo X, Leo XI and Clement VII.

MEIJI. Japanese term (meaning enlightened) applied to the Emperor Mutsuhito (1852–1912), whose long reign (from 1867) marked a period of rapid modernization in Japan. Having abolished feudal practices and the *samurai* class, he promulgated a constitution (1889), fought successfully against China (1894–1895) and Russia (1904–1905), and annexed Korea (1910). By his death, Japan had become a world power.

MENELIK II (1844–1913). Emperor of Ethiopia. *Ras* of Showa, through able diplomacy, he succeeded in 1889 in taking power on the death of the Emperor John IV. In the same year, he made the Treaty of Uccialli which acknowledged Italian sovereignty over Eritrea. The controversial interpretation of this agreement gave rise to the Italo-Abyssinian War (1896) which ended in the complete defeat of the Italians at Aduwa, and compelled Italy to recognize the full independence of Ethiopia. Menelik then began a policy of modernization of the country, building railways and schools, and establishing a new capital at Addis Ababa.

MENES (4th millennium BC). Egyptian Pharaoh, the first of the First Dynasty. He unified Lower and Upper Egypt, and founded the Old Kingdom. He is credited with the foundation of Memphis.

MENTUHOTEP (3rd millennium BC). Egyptian Pharaoh. He re-established the unity of Egypt at the end of the First Intermediate Period, and transferred the capital to Thebes. He is considered to be the founder of the Middle Kingdom (2050–1780 BC) and the originator of the Eleventh Dynasty.

MEROVINGIANS. Royal dynasty of the Franks, founded by Clovis I (466–511) who conquered most of the territory which consitutes modern France. The fact that all his sons possessed similar hereditary rights led inevitably to the division of the kingdom and to wars for supremacy. In 639, on the death of Dagobert I (the last effective monarch), new territorial divisions occurred, and the mayors of the palace became the real rulers. One of these, Pepin the Short, deposed the last Merovingian King, Childerich III, and in 751 became the first Carolingian King.

METTERNICH, KLEMENS VON (1773–1859). Austrian statesman. Ambassador to Paris from 1806 to 1809, he negotiated the peace after Wagram, and arranged the marriage between Napoleon and Marie Louise of Austria. He became Chancellor and Minister of Foreign Affairs (1810) and devoted all his energies to the defeat of Napoleon. At the Congress of Vienna (1815), he successfully imposed his conservative settlement, restoring legitimate monarchs to their thrones. He formed the Holy Alliance with Prussia and Russia with the object of maintaining the *status quo* and of crushing any sign of liberal protest. However, the death of Francis I (1835) reduced his power at home, and the insurrections of 1848, in Vienna and Milan, compelled him to retire. He fled to London but returned home in 1851.

MILTIADES (c.540–489 BC). Athenian statesman and general. He defeated the Persians at Marathon (490), thus preventing them from marching on Athens. However, after the failure of successive naval expeditions against the island of Paros in the Cyclades, he was imprisoned, and died before being released.

MINAMOTO. Japanese *samurai* family. In 1185, their head, Yoritomo (1147–1199), became unofficial monarch of Japan after defeating the rival family of Taira. He received the hereditary title of *shogun* from the Emperor (1192), and founded a military government in Kamakura, leaving only formal authority to the Emperor in Kyoto. On the death of Yoritomo, the Minamoto were eliminated by the Hojo family.

MING Chinese dynasty founded by Emperor Chu Yuan-chang who defeated the Mongol dynasty of the Yuan in 1368. Under the Ming, China became a commercial power whose fleets reached Indonesia, India, the Persian Gulf and Eastern Africa. In 1409, Emperor Yung-lo transferred the capital from Nanking to Peking, which he embellished with wonderful monuments. During the Ming period, the first Portuguese merchants settled in Macao (1557). Soon afterwards, the Jesuits arrived (1582). At the beginning of the seventeenth century, several revolts weakened the empire and induced the Manchu, a population who lived along the northeastern frontier, to intervene. From 1659 the whole of China was ruled by the Manchu (also known as the Ch'ing).

MINOS (2nd millennium BC). Monarch of the Minoan civilization. He ruled Crete in about the middle of the second millennium BC as a priest and legislator. According to tradition, it was Minos who built the Labyrinth, in which he kept the Minotaur.

MIRABEAU, HONORÉ (1749–1791). French statesman. Member of the Third Estate in the States General of 1789, he advocated a political programme based on monarchy and a representative system, in which the privileges of the nobility and clergy would be abolished.

MITHRIDATES VI (132–63 BC). King of Pontus. Ascending the throne in 111 BC, he began an intense programme of conquest. Having made an agreement with the King of Bithynia, he attacked the Roman territories in the East, and penetrated Asia Minor and Greece, stirring up a revolt against Rome. However, he was defeated by Sulla at Chaeronea (86) and at Orchomenus (85), and was compelled to agree to the Peace of Dardanus by which he had to hand over all the conquered territories. Reopening the war, he was defeated by Licinius Lucullus (74) and then, finally, by Pompey on the Euphrates (66).

MOGUL. Indian dynasty founded by Babar, a direct descendant of Tamerlane. In 1526 he defeated the Sultan of Delhi and established the Mogul Empire. The conquests of Baber were enlarged by his nephew Akbar (1556–1605), and especially by Aurangzeb (1658–1707), in whose reign the Empire reached its maximum size. However, weakened by Hindu revolts and threatened by European commercial penetration, the empire had already started to disintegrate by the end of the eighteenth century. After 1803 the Mogul monarchs became subject to the British. The last monarch was Bahadur Shah II who was deposed by the British in 1858.

MONGOLS. Generic name which is applied to various nomadic peoples originating in the steppes of Central Asia. Unified by Genghis Khan (1155–1226), they attacked and conquered China, where they started the Yuan Dynasty (1260–1368), and southern Russia, where the monarchs of the Golden Horde (1237–1480) established themselves. In the fifteenth century, Tamerlane tried to revive the empire of Genghis Khan, but his conquests did not survive him. One of his descendants, Babar, founded the Mogul Empire in northern India in the sixteenth century.

MUHAMMAD (c.571–632). Prophet and founder of Islam. Born in Mecca, he endured poverty as a youth, but then married a rich widow and became a merchant. In about 610 he started to preach a new monotheistic religion, different fron the traditional cults. Forced to flee from Mecca in 622, he and his followers moved to Medina. (This event, the *Hegira*, is the first day of the Muslim calendar.) At Medina, he founded a theocratic state: this won him great support among the Arab tribes, and enabled him to return to Mecca in triumph in 630, and to consecrate the city to the new religion. Muhammad is venerated by Muslims as the Prophet of Allah (the only God), who received the revelations which are collected together in the Quran, the holy book of Islam.

MUHAMMAD II (c.1429–1481). Ottoman Sultan, he succeeded his father Murad I in 1541. Two years later, on 29 May 1453, he took Constantinople and made it the capital of the Ottoman Empire. During his reign, he reinforced Turkish power throughout the Mediterranean, conquering the Peloponnese, part of Albania and Serbia, as well as the Crimea and Trebizond.

MUHAMMAD ALI (1769–1849). Officer in the Turkish army. Sent to Egypt to fight against the Napoleonic invasion, he was appointed Viceroy. After defeating the Mamelukes (1811), he dedicated himself to the modernization of Egypt, embarking on ambitious public works, building up a modern army and fleet, and attempting to throw off Turkish control. In 1823, he conquered the Sudan and then Syria (1831–1840), and was only prevented from attacking Turkey by the intervention of the European powers. However, they were prepared to permit him to hold the sovereignty of Egypt and to make his title there hereditary.

MONTESQUIEU, BARON DE (1689–1755). Philosopher of the Enlightenment. He was a shrewd critic of the French society of his time and an admirer of English institutions. In his book *De l'esprit des lois* (1748), he advocated a government based on the separation of powers.

MONTEZUMA (1466–1520). King of the Aztecs, he ascended the throne in 1503. On the arrival of the Spaniards, he offered no resistance, believing them to be gods, and was imprisoned by Cortés. Wounded during a rebellion against the Spaniards (1520), he died soon afterwards.

MONTGOMERY, BERNARD LAW (1887–1976). Commander of the British Eighth Army in Africa during the Second World War, he defeated Rommel at El Alamein (1942). After leading the British armies during the Normandy landings (1944), he advanced into the heart of Germany where he remained as a commander of the occupation forces after the end of the war. From 1951 to 1958 he was Deputy Commander of the military forces of NATO.

MOSES (13th century BC). Lawgiver of the Jews. According to the Bible, Moses was chosen by God to liberate the Jewish people from slavery in Egypt, and to lead them towards the Promised Land. Leaving Egypt and reaching Mount Sinai, Moses gave the Tablets of the Law (the Ten Commandments) to his people and laid down the principles of monotheism. However, because he doubted God's word, Moses was not permitted to set foot in the Promised Land, and died before reaching it.

MURAT, JOACHIM (1767–1815). One of Napoleon's generals and King of Naples (1808). In November 1799 he took part in the coup which brought Napoleon to power. In the following year, he married Napoleon's sister, Caroline. Supporting Napoleon in all his campaigns, he became King of Naples as successor to Joseph Bonaparte. After the Battle of Leipzig (1813), he tried to negotiate a separate peace with Austria and Britain in the hope of retaining his dominions. Disappointed by his failure to do so, he again allied himself with Napoleon during the Hundred Days. Defeated by the Austrians at Tolentino in 1815, he fled to Corsica, from where he organized an expedition to regain the throne of Naples. However, when he landed at Pizzo Calabro, he was arrested and executed.

MUSSOLINI, BENITO (1883–1945). Italian dictator. Active as a socialist propagandist and editor-in-chief of *Avanti!* (the Socialist Party newspaper), he was expelled from the Party for his support of Italy's intervention in the First World War. On 23 March 1919, he founded the Fascist Party in Milan. In October 1922 he organized the march on Rome. The King, Victor Emmanuel III, incapable of controlling the situation, gave in to Mussolini's threats and appointed him Prime Minister. Between 1922 and 1925 he installed a dictatorship, stamping out all opposition either through the violence of his Black Shirts, or by means of sweeping laws which gave him absolute power. On 11 February 1929, he signed the Concordat with the Pope. Determined to build an empire as glorious as ancient Rome, he attacked Ethiopia (1935) in violation of the requirements of Italy's membership of the League of Nations. He also supported the dictator Franco in the Spanish Civil War, and allied with Nazi Germany and Japan in the Three-Power Pact (1940). In the same year, although unprepared, he entered the Second World War. The subsequent military failures led the Fascist Grand Council to dismiss him on 25 July 1943. He was then arrested on the orders of King Victor Emmanuel III. Freed by the Germans, Mussolini established a puppet government at Salò. After the defeat of the German armies in Italy, he was taken prisoner by the partisans and executed on 28 April 1945.

NABOPOLASSAR (?–605 BC). King of Babylon. Allied with the Medes and the Scythians, he crushed the Assyrian Empire which had been weakened since the death of Assurbanapal, and destroyed Nineveh (612 BC). He was the founder of the New Babylonian Empire and the Chaldean Dynasty.

NAPOLEON I (1769–1821). French Emperor. Born in Corsica, he studied at the military academy at Brienne, and came to prominence in the siege of Toulon (1793). In 1796, he took command of the armies in Italy and won important victories against Austria, compelling it to sign the Peace of Campo Formio (1797). Returning to France, he overthrew the Directory in the coup of 18–19 Brumaire (9–10 November 1799) and became Consul (from 1802 Consul for life). He reorganized finances, promulgated the Napoleonic Code, and concluded the Concordat with the Holy See (1801). Having defeated the Austrians at Marengo and signed the Peace of Amiens with Britain, he crowned himself Emperor (1804) in the presence of Pope Pius VII. He was then victorious against Russia and Austria at Austerlitz (1805), and Prussia at Jena (1806), and reorganized the German states into the Confederation of the Rhine. He also installed members of his own family on the thrones of Spain, the Netherlands and Naples. In 1812 he began the disastrous invasion of Russia which led to the defeat at Leipzig (1813). Forced to abdicate, he retired to Elba. In March 1815 he escaped and returned to France where he regained power as Emperor for the Hundred Days. Defeated at Waterloo, he was eventually exiled to St Helena where he died.

NAPOLEON III (1808–1873). French Emperor. Third son of King Louis of the Netherlands, he tried to revive the Napoleonic Empire. After the failure of two attempts at a coup against King Louis Philippe (1836 and 1840), he fled abroad. Returning to France during the 1848 revolutions, he was elected President of the Republic on 10 December. In 1851 he secured a ten-year term. In the following year he proclaimed himself Emperor, and implemented a policy of authoritarianism at home and prestige abroad. He took part in the Crimean War, supporting Piedmont during the struggle for Italian independence, and Maximilian of Habsburg in his expedition to Mexico. He was deposed after the French defeat in the Franco-Prussian War of 1870, and retired to England where he died.

NASSER, GAMAL ABDEL (1918–1970). Egyptian statesman and army officer. In 1952 he took part in the coup which overthrew King Farouk and proclaimed the Republic. Following a power struggle with General Neguib, he became Prime Minister in 1954 (President in 1956). He began a programme of Arab socialism, promoting agrarian reform, nationalizing the Suez Canal, and working for the social and economic development of the country. Hostile to Israel, he aimed at the leadership of the Arab world and distinguished himself as one of the major spokesmen of the "non-aligned" countries.

NEBUCHADNEZZAR II (?–562 BC). Son of Nabopolassar and King of Babylon from 605. Under him, the empire reached its greatest heights, and Babylon became a wealthy and beautiful city. He fought against the Egyptians; he also occupied and destroyed Jerusalem (587), deporting its population.

NEHRU, JAWAHARLAL (1889–1964). Indian statesman. Follower of Gandhi, he joined the struggle for Indian independence from Britain in 1919. In 1923 he became Secretary of the Congress Party. He conducted the final negotiations for independence and, in 1947, became Prime Minister and Foreign Minister. Internationally, he supported the Colombo Pact which was signed by the countries of Southeast Asia, and the Bandung Conference (1955) which brought together the Afro-Asian states. He remained independent of the two superpowers.

NELSON, HORATIO (1758–1805). British admiral. He fought against Revolutionary France. In 1798 he commanded the fleet which crushed Napoleon's navy at the Battle of the Nile. From 1803 to 1805 he blockaded the French fleet in Toulon. In the Battle of Trafalgar, he fought bravely against the French and the Spaniards, gaining the victory but losing his life.

NERO, CLAUDIUS CAESAR (37–68). Roman Emperor. Adopted son of Claudius, he succeeded him in 54 after marrying his daughter, Octavia. At first, he ruled sensibly and justly under the guidance of Seneca; later, he killed his wife, his mother Agrippina, and Britannicus, the son of Claudius, believing that they threatened his supremacy. His reign became increasingly despotic and dissolute: he accused the Christians of the fire which destroyed Rome in 64, and embarked on a cruel persecution which may have included the killing of Peter and Paul. In the following year, he discovered a plot against him and sentenced many of his advisers, including Seneca, to death. As discontent spread, he was deposed in a Praetorian conspiracy and killed himself.

NICHOLAS I (1796–1855). Tzar of Russia. He ascended the throne in 1825 and at once crushed the Decembrists Revolt, led by young officers who demanded the introduction of a constitutional monarchy. Advocate of strict absolutism, he was the inspiration behind the Holy Alliance. He stamped out the revolts in Poland (1830–1831) and Hungary (1848–1849). To reinforce the Russian protectorate over the Orthodox peoples of the Balkans, he started the Crimean War (1854–1856) against the Turks who were supported by the British, French and Italians.

NICHOLAS II (1868–1918). Last Tzar of Russia. He succeeded his father, Alexander III, in 1894 and continued his absolutist policies. The failures in the Russo-Japanese War (1904–1905) and the bloody repression of the uprising in St Petersburg (1905), increased his unpopularity and compelled him to concede some reforms, such as the election of a legislative assembly, the Duma. He was forced to abdicate during the 1917 Revolution, and was imprisoned at Ekaterinburg, where he and his family were executed by the Bolsheviks.

NIXON, RICHARD (1913–1994). Thirty-seventh American President. Elected to the House of Representatives in 1946 and to the Senate in 1950, he was Vice-President under Eisenhower (1953–1960). After being defeated in the election of 1960 by Kennedy, he was elected President in 1968, and re-elected in 1972. He resigned in 1974 over the Watergate Affair. He was the first American President to pay an official visit to China, and a strong advocate of withdrawal of American troops from Vietnam.

NORMANS. The name means "men of the north." It was given to the Scandinavians (also called Vikings) who, in the ninth century AD, sacked and sometimes settled on the coasts of Europe. Some of the Normans established themselves on the French coast. In 911 they were enfeoffed by Charles the Simple with land along the lower reaches of the Seine. Converted to Christianity under Rollo, the Normans extended their lands and established the foundations of the Duchy of Normandy. It was from Normandy that William the Conqueror invaded England in 1066. Others, such as Robert Guiscard, set out for southern Italy where in less than a century they formed a united kingdom covering southern Italy and Sicily, which (especially under Roger II) developed a unique culture.

ODOACER (c.434–493). Barbarian general. He was acclaimed king by his armies, following the refusal of Orestes (Regent and father of Romulus Augustulus) to compensate him with a third of Italy. He then occupied the peninsula, and so ended the Western Roman Empire. Having sent the imperial insignia to Zeno, the Eastern Roman Emperor, he received in return the title of *patricius*, and the right to rule Italy. He consolidated the borders, was tolerant in his dealings with the population, and respectful towards the Church. For a long time, he withstood (489–493) the Ostrogothic invasion. When he was finally compelled to surrender, he was betrayed and assassinated.

OLMECS. Peoples of Central America who, from the eleventh century BC, developed one of the most ancient pre-Columbian cultures on the southeastern coasts of Mexico. Many relics of their civilization still survive: huge basalt heads three metres (nine feet) high, small sculptures made of jade, amethyst, rock crystal and other materials, the large pyramid and artificial mounds at the ceremonial centre of La Venta, and the terraced pyramid at Monte Albán.

OMAYYADS. First Islamic dynasty, founded by Mo'awiya in 661 after the deposition of Ali, son-in-law of Muhammad. Mo'awiya paid much attention to both administration and finance, moved his residence to Damascus, and made the caliphate hereditary. Under the Omayyads the Arabs extended their influence in the Orient (conquering Kabul, Bukhara and Samarkand), in North Africa (taking Carthage, 698) and in Spain, where they defeated the Visigoths. Halted at Poitiers (732), the Omayyads were overthrown by the Abbasids (750). A branch of the dynasty founded the Emirate of Córdoba, which later became a caliphate (756–1030).

OSTROGOTHS. Germanic peoples, also referred to as "Goths of the East." They originated from the division of the Goths into two branches, the other being the Visigoths. Having occupied the Ukraine (in the fourth century AD), they were pushed further westwards by the Huns (in about 370) and settled in Moesia (Bulgaria). The withdrawal of the Huns allowed them to move on into Greece (in about 455). Later, under their King Theodoric, they settled in Italy (493). After defeating Odoacer, they founded an Ostrogothic Kingdom with Ravenna as its capital. They adopted the role of defenders of the Roman Empire and its culture. Later again and despite their strong resistance (536–552), they were dispersed by the reconquests of Justinian.

OTHMAN (?–AD 656). Third Caliph of Islam, a member of the Omayyad Dynasty. Elected in 644, although not without opposition, he subdued the Persian Empire, part of Cyrenaica, Tripolitania and Tunisia. He organized an expedition against the Byzantine Empire, prepared a fleet and took Cyprus (649). He sponsored the official compilation of the Quran but, in the worsening feuds among the followings of Ali (Muhammad's son-in-law), he was killed in a conspiracy which marked the beginning of the civil wars of Islam.

OTTO I THE GREAT (912–973). Emperor and King of Germany. Succeeding his father, Henry I of Germany, he crushed the opposition of the great feudatories (938) and extended his influence over Lotharingia and Burgundy. He advanced into Italy, defeated Berengar II, married Adelaide (widow of the Emperor Lothar), and assumed the rights of the imperial crown. He suppressed the revolt of his son (953) and defeated the Hungarians at Lechfeld (955). He was called back to Italy by Pope John XII who needed his help against Berengar, who had been given possession of Italy (Diet of Augsburg, 952). Crowned Emperor (in Rome, 961), he restored imperial control over the Popes, compelling them to swear loyalty, and firmly established the supremacy of the Saxon Dynasty and its right to expand into and Christianize the Slav East. He installed Pope Leo VIII (963), had his son, Otto, crowned as co-Emperor (966), and tried unsuccessfully to acquire the Byzantine lands in southern Italy (967–972).

OTTO II (955–983). Emperor and King of Germany. He married the Byzantine princess Theophano, and succeeded his father, Otto I, in 973. After annexing Bavaria, and coming to terms with Lothar, King of France (who had occupied Lorraine), in 980 he marched into Italy and invaded the Byzantine lands, seemingly to fight against the Muslims. Seriously defeated by the Arabs in Calabria (982), he narrowly escaped death. He had his son Otto elected as King of Germany (Diet of Verona, 983). He died in Rome while planning new campaigns in southern Italy and against the Slavs who had risen in revolt and crossed the Elbe.

OTTO III (980–1002). Emperor and King of Germany. He succeeded his father, Otto II, while still a child, but only took power in 994, after periods of regency under his mother, Theophano, and his grandmother, Adelaide. After leading victorious campaigns against the Slavs (997), he made many expeditions to Italy to defend the Papacy against the Crescentius family (996–998). He devoted himself to the *renovatio imperii*, a policy designed to unite the temporal power of the empire with the spiritual power of the Church. The policy was sealed by the removal of his capital to Rome, the administrative unification of Italy and Germany, and the election (999) of his teacher and spiritual adviser, Gerbert of Aurillac, as Pope Silvester II. However, his policies were terminated by resistance in Germany and Italy, and by his early death.

OTTOCAR II (1233–1278). Margrave of Moravia and Archduke of Austria (1251), he became King of Bohemia in 1253, succeeding his father Wenceslas I. He enlarged the dominions of Austria, occupying Styria (1261), Carinthia and Carniola (1269). In the imperial election of 1273 he was defeated by Rudolf I of Habsburg who compelled him to surrender all the occupied territories. He refused and, outlawed, was killed in the Battle of Marchfeld.

OTTOMANS. Turkish Islamic dynasty founded by Osman I, who freeing himself from the control of the Seljuks, founded the Ottoman Empire in 1307. Sustained by religious fanaticism, the Ottomans crossed the Dardanelles (1356) and advanced unopposed into the Balkans. Having halted the invasion of Tamerlane in the East, the Ottomans renewed their expansion in Europe. In 1453 they took Constantinople (renamed Istanbul). Their empire reached its zenith under Suleiman I who reached the gates of Vienna in 1529. However, the first signs of crisis appeared with the Turkish defeat at Lepanto (1571). Later, in the seventeenth and eighteenth centuries, a long series of wars against Austria and then Russia led to the decline of the empire, which was replaced with a republic by Mustafa Kemal Atatürk in 1922.

PARTHIANS. Semi-nomadic people of Iranian origin. Under Arsaces, they freed themselves from the Seleucids (250 BC) and established a kingdom to the east of the Caspian Sea which soon stretched from Afghanistan to the Euphrates, and included Persia, Media and the Babylonian region. After centuries of fighting against the Romans, they were finally defeated by the Sassanids (224), but an independent principality survived in northern Chorasmia. They were skilled horsemen and archers, famous for their tactics of simulating flight and then suddenly turning round and firing arrows at their pursuers.

PAUL III (1468–1549). Born Alexander Farnese, he was elected Pope in 1534 on the death of Clement VII. To stop the spread of the Reformation, he reconciled himself with Charles V, began the internal reform of the Catholic Church, approved the foundation of the Society of Jesus (1540), re-established the Inquisition (1542) and summoned the Council of Trent (1545).

PAUL IV (1476–1559). Born Gian Pietro Carafa, he became Pope in 1555. In conjunction with Cajetan of Thiene, he founded the Theatins (1523) and fought with great vigour against the Protestant Reformation. He augmented the power of the Inquisition and published the Index of prohibited books (1557). Hostile to Spain and supported by the Duke of Guise, he tried to prevent Philip II from becoming King of Naples (1580).

PAUSANIAS (?–468 BC). Spartan general from 480 BC. He defeated the Persians at Plataea (479), and occupied Cyprus and Byzantium (478), where he acted as monarch (471–470). His power and prestige aroused suspicion both in Sparta and among its allies. Recalled home, he was accused of attempting to overthrow the oligarchic government with Persian and Athenian support. Condemned to death for treason, he was walled up in the Temple of Athena where he had taken refuge.

PEISISTRATUS (c.600–529 BC). Tyrant of Athens in 560 BC. Although he was exiled by his enemies in 555, he was able to profit from the disagreements among the opposing factions, and in 546, he returned to Athens and regained supremacy. In domestic policy, he treated the peasants favourably, beautified Athens, developed trade and, through able diplomacy, secured a dominant position over the Aegean and the Hellespont, laying the basis for the future maritime Empire of Athens.

PELOPIDAS (c.420–364 BC). Theban politician and general. During the period of Spartan domination, with Athenian assistance, he overthrew the oligarchic government and Spartan military domination of Thebes (379 BC). In cooperation with Epaminondas he reorganized the army and joined him in a series of wars designed to develop the supremacy of Thebes. He took part in the victory at Leuctra (371), but, after taking Larissa in Thessaly (369), he was defeated and imprisoned by Alexander of Pherae. Freed in 368 in return for surrendering Thessaly, he died while winning the Battle of Cynoscephalae.

PEPIN III THE SHORT (c.715–768). King of the Franks. Son of Charles Martel, he was a powerful mayor of the palace under the Merovingians. From his father, he inherited vast territories in Neustria, Burgundy and Provence (741), and shared effective power with his brother Carloman. He strengthened his kingdom and obtained Austrasia after the abdication of his brother (747). He was supported by Pope Zacharias, and was elected King by the Franks at Soissons, deposing Childerich III (751). Allied with Pope Stephen II against the Lombards, he defeated them twice (754 and 756) and compelled them to hand over to the Pope the Exarchate of Ravenna, Pentapolis and Rome. In his last years, he expanded his kingdom and divided it between his son Charles (the future Charlemagne) and Carloman.

PERICLES (c.495–429 BC). Athenian statesman. As a demagogue (popular leader), he was elected as *strategos* every year from 461 to 429. He introduced democratic reforms, and made Athens the cultural centre of Greece. He consolidated the power of Athens by means of a series of wars, and ran the Delio-Attic League as an empire. After the Peace of Callias with Persia (449) and the Thirty Years' Peace with Sparta (446), he reinforced and beautified Athens, extending its influence in Thrace, Pontus and Magna Grecia. He provoked a new war with Sparta and the Peloponnesian League (431) and, in doing so, began the decline of Athens. In the following year, Athens was overwhelmed by the plague, which may have been the cause of his death.

PERÓN, JUAN DOMINGO (1895–1974). Twice President of Argentina (1946–1955) and 1973–1974). He was supported by the army and the workers' unions (with whom he had become associated while he was Minister of Labour). This backing enabled him to set up a regime which combined social reform with economic direction, together with elements of economic self-sufficiency and corporatism. However, his government also became known for repression, corruption and anti-clericalism. In 1955 there was a political revolt by the army and the regime collapsed. After a series of military governments, Perón returned from exile in Spain (1973) and was re-elected President.

PÉTAIN, PHILIPPE (1856–1951). French general. He fought in the Battles of the Marne (1914), Artois and Champagne. He was appointed Commander-in-Chief of the French forces in 1917 after his successful defence of Verdun, and was made Marshal of France in 1918. Commander in Morocco in 1925, general inspector of the army in 1931, Minister of War in the government of Doumergue in 1934, and ambassador in Spain in 1939. Deputy Prime Minister in the government of Paul Reynaud (1940), he became Prime Minister after the German victory (16 June 1940). He signed the armistice with Germany, and set up the Vichy government with Nazi support. He was tried and sentenced to death at the end of the Second World War, but the sentence was commuted to one of life imprisonment.

PETER I THE GREAT (1672–1725). Tzar of Russia, he succeeded his half-brother Feodor in 1682, ruled jointly with another half-brother, Ivan IV, and took sole control in 1689. After travelling incognito in Europe, he returned home and introduced many reforms in an attempt to bring Russia up to the standard of the most advanced countries. He reorganized the army and the bureaucracy, moved the capital to St Petersburg (1712) which he had founded in 1703, and suppressed the Orthodox Patriarchate of Moscow, taking over its religious authority (1721). He fought against Sweden, causing its collapse through his victory at Poltava (1709), and extending his dominions over Livonia, Estonia, Karelia and part of Finland (Peace of Nystad, 1721). He died without heirs, having executed his son Alexis (1718), and left his throne to his wife, Catherine I.

PETER I (1798–1834). First Emperor of independent Brazil and son of John VI, King of Portugal. After the invasion of Portugal by Napoleon (1807–1811), the royal family fled to Brazil where Peter remained as Regent after his father returned home in 1821. Having become a symbol of Brazilian independence, he was proclaimed emperor when independence was gained in 1822. Ascending the throne of Portugal on the death of his father (1826), he arranged for his young daughter, Maria II, to take his place there and appointed his brother Miguel as Regent. In 1831 he abdicated the Brazilian throne in favour of his son Pedro II and returned to Portugal, where Miguel had abolished the constitution and proclaimed himself absolute monarch (1828). Receiving a warm welcome, he marched on Lisbon, compelled Miguel to go into exile and reinstated Maria on the throne.

PETER III (c.1239–1285). King of Aragon, Count of Catalonia and King of Sicily. He was a shrewd politician and diplomat. He allied himself with Alfonso X of Castile, Denis of Portugal and the Eastern Roman Emperor, Michael Palaeologus. He claimed the throne of Sicily as husband of Constance, daughter of King Manfred. However, he had a rival in Charles of Anjou who had settled in the island in 1266. Taking advantage of the Sicilian Vespers (1282), he landed in Sicily, defeated his rival and was crowned King in Palermo. He was excommunicated by Pope Martin IV but succeeded in repelling the troops sent against him, led by Philip III of France (1285).

PHILIP II AUGUSTUS (1165–1225). King of France. He ascended the throne in 1180, succeeding his father Louis VII. In 1191, he took part in the Third Crusade and, from 1199, he fought against King John of England, depriving him between 1202 and 1206 of many of his French possessions — Rouen, Normandy, Brittany, Poitou and Aquitaine. With his victory at Bouvines (1214) over Otto of Brunswick, John and the feudatories of Flanders and Boulogne, he completed his plans of territorial unification, and gained all English land north of the River Loire.

PHILIP IV THE FAIR (1268–1314). King of France, successor to his father Philip III. He engaged in war against Edward I of England (1294–1298) and crushed a revolt in Flanders (1302–1305). In conflict with Pope Boniface VIII for having imposed taxes on ecclesiastical property, he was excommunicated, and reacted by sending an expedition which led to the Pope's imprisonment at Anagni (1303). After Boniface's death, he secured the election of Pope Clement V (1305), and the Holy See was transferred to Avignon (1309). He also suppressed the Knights Templar and took possession of their properties.

PHILIP II (c.382–336 BC) King of Macedon. He reigned from 359 BC, at first as Regent for his nephew Amyntas IV, and then as King himself from 356. He strengthened his borders and eliminated domestic unrest. He then devoted himself to the conquest of the Greek cities. After occupying Thessaly (352) and Thrace (342), he defeated the Athenians at Chaeronea (338). In 337 he organized the Corinthian League under the leadership of Macedonia, and including all Greek towns except Sparta. He aimed at a war with Persia but was murdered before he could carry out his plan.

PHILIP II (1527–1598). Son of the Emperor Charles V, he was crowned King of Spain in 1556. He unified the Iberian Peninsula and ruled over an empire which included the Low Countries, part of the New World, Milan, Naples and Sicily. He married Mary Tudor in 1554, and was a strong supporter of Catholicism and the Counter-Reformation. He reinforced the Inquisition and tried to achieve European supremacy but his policies led Spain into financial difficulties (despite the flow of gold and silver from the colonies). He met strong opposition from England, which defeated the Spanish Armada (1588), and also from the Protestant rebellion in the Low Countries.

PHILIP V (1683–1746). First Bourbon King of Spain. With the support of Louis XIV of France, he ascended the throne in 1700 on the death of the last of the Spanish Habsburgs, Charles II. His accession led to the War of the Spanish Succession (1701–1713). By the Treaties of Utrecht and Rastatt (1713–1714) he was confirmed as King of Spain but had to give up the Low Countries, the Milanese, Naples, Sardinia, Sicily, Gibraltar and Minorca. His policies were influenced by his wife Elizabeth Farnese, and especially by his First Minister, Alberoni, who was finally dismissed following pressure by the European powers. In 1724 Philip V abdicated in favour of his eldest son, Louis, but when the latter died a few months later, he returned to the throne. In 1738, by the Peace of Vienna, he was recognized as King of Naples, which his son, Carlos, had conquered.

PHOENICIANS. Semitic peoples who, from the earliest times, settled in the narrow coastal strip of land to the west of Syria, between the Anti-Lebanon Mountains and the Mediterranean. The geography of the area allowed the formation of a series of city-states (Byblos, Beirut, Sidon and Tyre) rather than a unitary state, and this made it easier for invaders — Assyrians, Arameans, Egyptians, Babylonians and Persians. The Pheonicians were great sailors and merchants: they voyaged as far as the Canaries, and founded colonies all around the Mediterranean.

PIUS II (1405–1464). Born Enea Silvio Piccolomini, he was a scholar and humanist. Among the most distinguished advocates of Conciliar theory at the Council of Basle (1431–1449), he was elected Pope in 1458. He tried to persuade the Christian princes to embark on a great crusade against the Turks, first by summoning the Congress of Mantua (1459) and then by launching a new appeal for a holy war (1463). He is also remembered for his wide-ranging literary activities.

PIUS V (1504–1572). Born Antonio Ghislieri, he was a Dominican. Head of the Inquisition in 1558, he was elected Pope in 1566. He was an inflexible defender and propagator of the integrity of Catholic doctrine as defined by the Council of Trent. He published the Roman Catechism (1566), a breviary and a missal, fought against the Huguenots, and compelled the Jews to live in ghettos. He excommunicated Elizabeth I of England (1570), and organized the Holy League which defeated the Turks at Lepanto (1571).

PIUS IX (1792–1878). Born Giovanni Maria Mastai Ferretti, he was elected Pope in 1846, and reigned longer than any other Pope. He granted a constitution (1848) but came out against Italian nationalism, fleeing to Gaeta when the Roman Republic was established. Napoleon III helped him to return to Rome (1850), where he was able to re-establish his absolute power. He lost the Papal States (1859–1860) and, when Rome was annexed to the Kingdom of Italy, he retired into the Vatican (1870) and refused to accept the Law of Guarantees (which, among other matters, severely limited his territorial sovereignty). During his pontificate, he promulgated the dogma of the Immaculate Conception (1854), attacked liberalism and progressive thought (1864), opposed the anticlerical laws passed by Bismarck in Germany (1875) and proclaimed the doctrine of Papal Infallibility (Vatican Council, 1870).

PIZARRO, FRANCISCO (c.1474–1541). Conqueror of Peru. Illegitimate son of a Spanish soldier, he took part in two expeditions to South America (1524–1526) to seek his fortune, and then obtained — in conjunction with Almagro — financial support from Charles V for a new expedition which aimed at the conquest of the Inca Empire. Having landed at Tumbes (1531) with about 300 companions, including his brother Hernando, he reached Cajamarca in November and, through a plot, captured the Inca Atahualpa. He completed the conquest of Peru in 1533, founded Ciudad de los Reyes (modern Lima) in 1535, and fought and killed Almagro in 1538. He was killed in retaliation by followers of Almagro.

POLO, MARCO (1254–1324). Venetian traveller. His father and uncle were famous merchants who had visited the Chinese court, and Marco joined them on their second expedition to the East from 1271 to 1295. During this period, he lived for seventeen years at the court of Kublai Khan, who gave him important duties and titles. On a subsequent voyage he was captured and imprisoned by the Genoese at the Battle of Curzola (1298) and while in prison, dictated *Il Milione*, his memoirs and a description of his voyages. After being set free, he died in Venice.

POMPEY THE GREAT (106–48 BC). Roman general and politician. He distinguished himself in the Civil War (89) and was one of the supporters of Sulla, who gave him important commands in Sicily and Africa. He was rewarded with the honour of a Triumph. On the death of Sulla (78), he defeated Lepidus and Sertorius. With the help of Licinius Crassus, he completely crushed the slave rising led by Spartacus, and became joint Consul with him in 70. In 67, armed with full powers, he crushed the Mediterranean pirates and succeeded Licinius Lucullus as commander in the war against Mithridates, King of Pontus. In consequence, he extended and consolidated Roman dominions in Asia (62). Failing to obtain the expected rewards from the Senate, he formed the first triumvirate with Caesar and Crassus (60). After the death of Crassus and while Caesar was in Gaul, he tried to secure extraordinary powers. When civil war broke out because of Caesar's refusal to give up the command of his legions (49), he fled to Greece, as Caesar crossed the Rubicon to march on Rome. Defeated by Caesar at Pharsalia (48), he then fled to Egypt where he was betrayed and murdered by a hired killer of Ptolemy XIV.

PTOLEMIES. Dynasty founded by Ptolemy, son of Lagos, a general of Alexander the Great, who took Egypt after the death of its monarch and proclaimed himself ruler in 305 BC as Ptolemy I Soter. The dynasty died out in 30 BC, with the deaths of Cleopatra and her son Caesarion.

PUGACHEV, YEMELYAN (c.1740–1775). Leader of major Cossack rebellion in eighteenth-century Russia. Deserting from the army after being engaged in various wars, he took charge of the Cossacks of the Urals who rebelled because Catherine II was trying to limit their autonomy. He claimed to be Tzar Peter III (who had been assassinated in 1762 to provide Catherine with the succession). He gained great support from the peasants, gathered a large army of more than 25,000 men, and led a revolt which spread as far as the Volga. Defeated in 1774 near Tzaritzyn, the Cossacks themselves handed him over to General Suvorov. After a brief period of imprisonment, he was executed in Moscow.

PURITANS. Followers of an English Protestant movement which developed in the sixteenth and seventeenth centuries. As Calvinists, they advocated rigid moral standards and believed in the doctrine of predestination. They opposed episcopal hierarchies and demanded new forms of church government, such as the Presbyterian system, based on elected synods, and the Separatist (later Congregationalist), which believed in maximum local autonomy for individual communities of believers. Their religious innovations, transferred to the political level, contributed to the Parliamentary struggle against the Stuarts in the seventeenth century. The Independents among them brought Oliver Cromwell to power, and generated radical political and religious movements, such as the Levellers. In 1660, Presbyterianism became the official religion in Scotland. However, in Restoration England it was largely defeated in the struggle with Anglicanism, and many Nonconformist clergy were ejected from their livings. Despite the Toleration Act (1689) of William III, Nonconformity retained its separate identity. The first English colonists in North America were Puritans, many of them going there to escape persecution.

PYRRHUS (318–272 BC). King of Epirus. He ascended the throne in 306 on the death of his father. After a period of conflict with Neoptolemus which ended in 297 BC, he interfered in the struggle among the successors of Alexander the Great (the *Diadochi*), with mixed results. Aiming at extending his dominions, he turned to Italy where the inhabitants of Tarentum had asked him to help them against the Romans (280). He gained important victories at Heraclea (280) and at Ausculum (279), although suffering great losses, and then freed Sicily from the Carthaginians (278–276). Incapable of taking political advantage of his victories, he was defeated by the Romans at Beneventum (275) and returned home to Epirus. Here, he renewed his attempt to obtain supremacy over Macedon and Greece. He died at Argos.

RADETSKY, COUNT JOSEF FRANZ (1766–1858). Austrian field marshal. Having joined the imperial army in 1784, he distinguished himself against the Turks (1788–1789), and in the wars against Napoleon. Military adviser to the imperial court, he was sent to Italy in 1831 as military Governor of Lombardy. He suppressed the Milanese revolt of the "Five Days" (March 1848) and organized the Austrian counter-offensive which led to the victories of Custoza and Novara (1848 and 1849). He was Governor of Lombardy from 1849 to 1856.

RAMSES II (c.1301–1235 BC). Pharaoh of the Nineteenth Dynasty, who reigned for 66 years. After many victorious campaigns in Nubia, Libya and Syria, he fought the Hittites under King Muwatallis in the Battle of Kadesh (1299). The result was indecisive. He then made an alliance with the new Hittite King, Hattusil III, and later married his daughter. During his reign Egypt enjoyed a period of prosperity and power, when wonderful monuments such as the Temples of Abu Simbel and the Ramesseum at Thebes were built. There were ten further pharaohs who took the name of Ramses. The most important was Ramses III (c. 1198–1166 BC), founder of the Twentieth Dynasty. He was the last great monarch of ancient Egypt which, by then, was already threatened by the Libyans and the "Sea Peoples".

RAYMOND IV (1042–1105). Count of Toulouse. He fought in support of Gregory VII against the Normans in Italy (1074). In 1096 he answered the call of Pope Urban II, took part in the First Crusade and reached Constantinople in 1097. Having quarrelled with Godfrey of Bouillon after the conquest of Jerusalem (July 1099), he withdrew to Constantinople (1100), and continued to fight against the Muslims. He died during the siege of Tripoli in Syria.

REAGAN, RONALD (born 1911). American statesman. Governor of California (1967–1974), he became Republican presidential candidate. His terms of presidency, after the successive landslide victories of 1980 and 1984, were marked by a consistent policy of lowering taxation and increasing military spending, especially on the "Star Wars" project. A committed opponent of Communism, he engaged financial and military aid in Latin America, as well as sending a task force to Grenada (1983), and bombing the Libyan coast (1986) in protest against Libya's support of international terrorists.

RHODES, CECIL (1853–1902). Financier and imperialist. He emigrated to South Africa in 1870 for health reasons, and made a fortune from the diamonds and gold of Kimberley and the Transvaal. He became a member of the Cape Colony Parliament, and supported the need for British expansion in South Africa. As Prime Minister of Cape Colony (1890–1895), he negotiated the annexation of Bechuanaland, and colonized the area which later constituted Rhodesia. Faced with Boer resistance to his expansionist policies and held responsible for the Jameson Raid into the Transvaal (1895), he was forced to resign in January 1896. He then continued his work with the British South Africa Company.

RICHARD I (1157–1199). King of England, known as Lion-heart. He succeeded his father, Henry II, in 1189, and in the following year he left for the Third Crusade. During it he distinguished himself at the siege of Acre (1191) and made an armistice with Saladin (1191). He was forced to return home because of the scheming of his brother, John, who was trying to usurp the throne. However, on the journey back he was taken prisoner by Leopold of Austria and the Emperor Henry VI and was only freed in exchange for a large ransom (1194). When he reached England, he defeated his brother and the rebellious lords. He then declared war on Philip II Augustus of France, defeating him at Ypres (1197) and Courcelles (1198). He died during the siege of Châlus.

RICHELIEU, ARMAND DUPLESSIS DE (1585–1642). Cardinal and French statesman.

Bishop of Luçon in 1606, and confidant of Maria de' Medici in 1615. He was nominated First Minister by Louis XIII (1624) and for the next two decades he exercised an unchallenged influence over French politics. He defended royal absolutism, defeated the Huguenots at La Rochelle (1628), and suppressed the aspirations of the nobility. Abroad, he aimed at restoring the political supremacy and prestige of France. He allied with Gustavus Adolphus of Sweden against the Habsburgs in the Thirty Years' War, and then intervened directly against Austria. Before his death, he appointed Cardinal Mazarin as his successor, to prepare the way for Louis XIV.

ROBERT OF ANJOU (1278–1343). King of Sicily. Son of Charles II of Anjou, he succeeded his father in 1309. At the head of the Guelph towns of Lombardy and Tuscany, he carried out a policy hostile to the Emperor Henry VII. Although he obtained the *signorie* of Florence (1313), Genoa (1318) and Brescia (1319), he was unable to consolidate his position. Faced with the threats of the Emperor Louis IV of Bavaria, he was eventually reduced to exercising influence only in those areas of Sicily which lay outside Palermo (1333).

ROBERT GUISCARD (c.1015–1085). Duke of Puglia, son of Tancred of Hauteville. In 1059 Pope Nicholas II created him Duke of Puglia, Calabria and Sicily, areas still occupied by the Arabs and Byzantines. Having conquered Calabria (1059–1061) and having ceded Sicily to his brother Roger, he took possession of Salerno (1077) and made it his capital. Asked for help by Pope Gregory VII, who was besieged in Castel Sant' Angelo by the Emperor Henry IV, he interrupted a brilliant offensive against the Byzantines (at Durazzo, 1082). After sacking Rome, he took the Pope as a virtual prisoner to Salerno. After Gregory's death, he returned eastwards and died during the seige of Cephallenia.

ROBESPIERRE, MAXIMILIEN (1758–1794). French politician, and one of the leading figures in the French Revolution. A lawyer in Arras from 1781, he was a member of the Third Estate in the States General (1789). He became one of the most important radicals of the period and dominated the Jacobins. A member of the Committee of Public Safety (July 1793), he became in practice the arbiter of the political situation, keenly defending the Republic from all threats, both domestic and foreign. The Reign of Terror, which he introduced, was overthrown in the coup of 9 Thermidor (27 July 1794). He was then arrested and executed together with some of his supporters.

ROGER II (1095–1154). King of Sicily. In 1101 he succeeded his father, Roger I, as Count of Sicily. In 1127 he purchased Puglia, gaining recognition from Pope Honorius II. On the death of this Pope, he supported the Anti-Pope Anacletus II against the legitimate Pope Innocent II. In 1130, Anacletus made him King of Sicily and of Calabria, Puglia and Capua. He conquered Tripoli, Djerba and Corfu, thereby extending his authority in the regions around the Central Mediterranean. He made Palermo his capital, giving his court a cosmopolitan character and making it a meeting point of Arab and Christian cultures.

ROMANOVS. Russian aristocratic family which took royal power in 1613, under Tzar Michael III (1613–1645), and held it until the Revolution of 1917. The direct line of the family died out in 1730, after the reigns of Alexis (1645–1676), Feodor III (1676–1682), Ivan V (1628–1696) who ruled jointly with Peter I (1682–1725), Catherine I (1725–1727), and Peter II (1727–1730). The dynasty continued with Anna Ivanovna (1730–1740), Ivan VI (1740–1741), Elizabeth (1741–1762), Peter III (1762), Catherine II (1762–1796), Paul I (1796–1801), Alexander I (1801–1825), Nicholas I (1825–1855), Alexander II (1855–1881), Alexander III (1881–1894) and Nicholas II (1894–1917).

ROMMEL, ERWIN (1891–1944). German field marshal. In the Second World War, after fighting in Poland and France, he was appointed to command the *Afrikakorps* in Libya in 1941: the capture of Tobruk was among his successes. Pushing on to El Alamein, he was defeated by the British Eighth Army and forced to retreat into Tunisia (October 1942 to April 1943). As commander of the German armies in France, he fought in Normandy where he was seriously wounded on 17 July 1944. Accused by the Gestapo of having taken part in the July Plot against Hitler, he killed himself on 14 October 1944.

ROMULUS AND REMUS (8th century BC). Legendary founders of Rome. Sons of Mars and Rhea Silvia, they were abandoned soon after their birth by order of Amulius, King of Alba Longa. According to tradition they were rescued by a she-wolf and brought up by the shepherd Faustulus and his wife Acca Larentis. They restored the throne of Alba Longa to their grandfather, after they had killed Amulius. Quarrelling with each other over the building of Rome, Romulus killed Remus and became the first King. To populate the new town, he welcomed adventurers of all types and organized the rape of the Sabine women, so starting a long war. According to the legend, Romulus disappeared mysteriously during a thunderstorm and was made a god.

ROMULUS AUGUSTULUS (5th century AD). Last Western Roman Emperor. He ruled from 475 to 476, gaining the throne because his father Orestes had deposed the Emperor Julius Nepos. He was then overthrown by Odoacer, who transferred the imperial insignia to the Eastern Roman Emperor Zeno.

ROOSEVELT, FRANKLIN DELANO (1882–1945). Thirty-second President of the United States. He became a Democratic Senator for New York State in 1910 and was elected its Governor in 1929, despite suffering (since 1921) from poliomyelitis which severely limited his movements. In 1932 he stood for election as President as a candidate of the Democratic Party, and defeated his rival Hoover. He took office on 4 March 1933 and, to combat the economic crisis, he introduced a vast programme of social and other reforms, named the New Deal. In 1933 he inaugurated a policy of good relations with Latin America and also recognized the government of the Soviet Union. He was re-elected in 1936 and again in 1940 and 1944 — the first American President to serve for more than two terms. On the outbreak of the Second World War, he tried to keep America out of the conflict, even though he helped Britain (through Lend-Lease and the Atlantic Charter). However, after the Japanese attack on Pearl Harbor (7 December 1941), he declared war on Japan, Germany and Italy. With his Allies, he participated in the conferences at Casablanca, Teheran and Yalta.

ROTHARI (?–AD 652). King of the Lombards. After the death of Arioald, he married the former's widow Gundeberga, and reigned from 636 to 652. He completed the campaigns against the Byzantines, conquering Genoa and the Ligurian coast. He also promulgated the famous Edict of 22 November 643 — a fundamental codification of Lombard Law, which reflected the strong influence of Roman law. A believer in Arianism, he gave the Church a firm organization.

ROUSSEAU, JEAN-JACQUES (1712–1778). French philosopher, born in Geneva. In his main writings, such as *Émile* and *The Social Contract* (both 1762), he advocated a return to the state of nature when man was happy and uncorrupted by civilization and progress. As a political thinker, he outlined a society based on direct democracy, in which the citizens would submit voluntarily to the "general will".

RUDOLPH I (1218–1291). King of Germany and of the Romans. Son of Albert IV of Habsburg, he inherited his father's lands in Alsace in 1239. In 1273, his election as King of Germany and of the Romans put an end to the interregnum of 1254–1273. Rudolph laid the basis for the fortunes of the Habsburgs, acquiring considerable territories himself. In wars between 1276 and 1278 he took Bohemia, Austria, Styria, Carinthia and Carniola from Ottocar of Bohemia. In the West, he defeated the Count of Savoy and the Duke of Burgundy, although in Italy he gave up the Kingdom of Naples and the Romagna. He was unable to secure the succession for his son Albert because of the opposition of the German princes to his increasing power, and Adolf of Nassau was chosen instead.

SADAT, ANWAR (1918–1981). Egyptian statesman. One of the authors of the coup which overthrew King Farouk in 1952, he was Vice-President from 1957 and became President on Nasser's death in 1970. He helped to create a federation of Arab Republics, and became its President in 1971. He also tried, without success, to regain from Israel the territories lost in 1967 (arguing on the basis of the United Nations resolution passed in 1971). In 1972 he expelled Russian advisers and technicians, and, together with Syria, he started an offensive against Israel with the support of an Arab embargo on oil exports to the West (1973). He then developed greater links of friendship with the United States, which led to a peace treaty with Israel in 1979. He was assassinated during a military parade.

SAFAVIDS. Shia Islamic dynasty of Persia. It took its name from Safit al-Din (1253–1334), one of the descendants of Ali. The dynasty was founded by Sheikh Ismail (1487–1524), who took the title of Pasha in 1501 and imposed the Shia faith on the regions he had conquered. Having defeated the Sunni Ottomans and the Uzbeks, he extended his control over most of Persia. The dynasty reached its zenith under Abbas I the Great (1587–1629), but began its decline under his successors — Safi I (1629–1642), Abbas II (1642–1667), Suleiman (1667–1694) and Husain I (1694–1722). Unable to withstand Afghan attacks, the dynasty died out in 1736.

SALADIN (1138–1193). Muslim hero. Sultan of Egypt and Syria. After overthrowing the Fatimid Dynasty (1171), he founded the Ayyubids, and extended his control over Egypt, Palestine, Syria, Mesopotamia and Yemen. He inflicted serious defeats on the Crusaders and conquered Jerusalem (Battle of Hattin, 1187). In the Peace of Damascus (1192) which concluded the Third Crusade, he confined the Christians to a strip of coastal land.

SALAZAR, ANTONIO DE OLIVEIRA (1889–1970). Dictator of Portugal from 1933. Minister of Finance in the government of Carmona (1928), he was elected Prime Minister in 1932 and set up a corporate and totalitarian regime, based on a new constitution (1933). He supported the Nationalists in the Spanish Civil War and remained neutral in the Second World War, although favouring the Allies. He restored the economy, but faced increasing opposition both at home and in the colonies owing to widespread poverty, the brutal methods of his secret police (PIDE) and the restrictions imposed on freedom. He left public life in 1968, and was succeeded by Marcelo Caetano.

SAN MARTÍN, JOSÉ DE (1778–1850). Argentine general and liberator. Together with Simon Bolivar, he led the struggle for South American independence from Spain. After fighting in the Spanish army in Europe against Napoleon, he returned to Argentina in 1812 to serve the revolutionary government, and his work contributed greatly to the proclamation of Argentinian independence (at Tucumán, 1816). He then fought to drive the Spaniards from Peru. Making an adventurous crossing of the Andes with his army (1817–1818), he freed Chile and then Peru (1820–1821), assuming the title of Protector of Peru. However, in the following year he resigned after quarrelling with Bolivar. He retired to France in 1823 but continued working for the South American cause.

SANTA ANA, ANTONIO LÓPEZ DE (1794–1876). Mexican general who, in 1824, overthrew the Emperor Iturbide and proclaimed the Republic. He was chosen as President several times (1831, 1841 and 1846), winning a famous victory at Fort Alamo (1836), but suffering the secession of Texas. In 1845 he declared war on the United States which had taken Texas into the Union, but he suffered a heavy defeat. Returning to power as a dictator from 1852 to 1856, he was finally defeated by his rival Juárez in 1863. He lived his last years in exile.

SARGON I (end of 3rd millennium BC). First ruler of the Semitic dynasty of Accad. After the initial victory over Lugalzaggisi, Sumerian King of Erech, he mastered the whole of Mesopotamia, and extended his frontiers to establish what is considered to be one of the world's first empires: it stretched from the Mediterranean coasts of Syria and Palestine to the Zagros Mountains of Iran. He divided his empire into administrative districts which were governed semi-autonomously.

SARGON II (?–705 BC). King of Assyria, he took power in 721 through the support of the army. He completed the conquest of Israel and, in accordance with Assyrian custom, deported the population: 30,000 Jews were taken to Mesopotamia. After obtaining control of Mediterranean trading routes through the possession of Cyprus, he subdued Babylon. He then proclaimed himself King (709), deported part of the population, and began a victorious campaign against the Egyptians.

SASSANIDS. Zoroastrian dynasty which governed the Persian Empire from 224 to 640. It was founded by Ardashir I, nephew of Sassan, who overthrew the Parthian Dynasty founded by Arsaces. He ruled a vast empire which stretched from the frontiers of the Eastern Roman Empire to Central Asia, where he conquered the Kushana Empire. The Sassanids fought a series of almost uninterrupted wars against the Eastern Empire: from the beginning of the fourth century, these became increasingly religious in character. The Sassanids reached their greatest power in the reigns of Shapur I (241–272), Shapur II (309–379), Chosroes I (531–579) and Chosroes II (590–628), but later, under Yezdigird III, they were defeated by the Arabs who took possession of Persia.

SAUL (11th century BC). First King of Israel. He belonged to the tribe of Benjamin, and according to the Bible, was chosen as King (c. 1040 BC) by the Judge Samuel to lead the revolt against the Philistines. Having freed Israel, he increased its military power by defeating his enemies abroad. However, he quarrelled with the priesthood who chose David in his place. Abandoned by the people who had appointed him, he committed suicide after being defeated in the Battle of Mount Gilboa against the Philistines.

SAVONAROLA, GIROLAMO (1452–1498). Dominican friar. Prior of the Convent of San Marco, Florence, he won great popular support by advocating radical religious and political reform. He contributed to the fall of the Medici (1494) and replaced them with a theocratic republic. Excommunicated (1497) by Pope Alexander VI for his strong criticisms of the corruption of the papal court, and opposed by the Florentine mercantile interests, he was arrested. After three trials, he was condemned as a heretic and schismatic; he was hanged and then burnt at the stake.

SAVOY. Italian royal family. Descended from Umberto Biancamano, first Count of Savoy (11th century AD). In 1416 Count Amadeus VIII was created a duke by the Emperor Sigismund. In the sixteenth century, the family became involved in the wars between France and Spain and, following these, Dukes Emmanuel Philibert (1528–1580) and Charles Emmanuel I (1562–1630) were able to consolidate their dominions. By the Treaty of Utrecht (1713), the title of King of Sicily, later changed to King of Sardinia (1720), was conferred on the family. In the course of the movement for Italian liberation, the House of Savoy adopted various positions. Following the exile of Charles Albert after the 1848–1849 revolutions, King Victor Emmanuel II took a major part in the subsequent struggles which led to Italian unification, and was crowned King of Italy on 17 March 1861. He was followed on the throne by Umberto I (1878–1900) and Victor Emmanuel III (1900–1945). Later, the royal family was accused of supporting Mussolini and was overwhelmed by the disasters of the Second World War in Italy, which culminated in the collapse of Fascism. After the Armistice of 8 September 1943, the king fled to Brindisi and later abdicated in favour of his son Umberto. However, the monarchy proved unable to survive and lost the vote in the referendum of 2 June 1946 when Italy chose to become a republic.

SCIPIO AFRICANUS, PUBLIUS CORNELIUS (235–183 BC). Roman general. During the Second Punic War, he fought alongside his father in the Battle of the Ticinus (218). Nominated Proconsul in Spain when he was still very young, he defeated the Carthaginians under Hasdrubal (at New Carthage in 209 and at Baecula in 208) and imposed Roman control over Spain. As Consul in 205, he went to Africa, conquered Tunis (204) and defeated Hannibal at Zama (202), thus ending the Second Punic War and earning the nickname Africanus. Consul again in 194, he led the campaign against Antiochus III of Syria and was the chief architect of the Roman victory at Magnesia (190). Returning home, he was forced to retire from public life because of the hostility of the Senate.

SCYTHIANS. Nomadic peoples, probably of northern Iranian origin. In the seventh century BC, they settled in the plains of southern Russia, and temporarily gained influence in the Balkans and Greece. They pushed on into Syria and Egypt but were forced back. At the beginning of the fourth century, they were attacked by the Macedonians, the Celts and, above all, by the

Sarmatians who destroyed them during the second century BC (after establishing an independent state in the Crimea). Famous as horsemen and archers, the Scythians were expert craftsmen in gold and silver, and created original forms of art.

SELEUCIDS. Dynasty founded in 305 BC by Seleucus I Nicator (304–281 BC), general of Alexander the Great. The Seleucids governed Syria and the greater part of Asia Minor until 64 BC, but, fighting with the Ptolemies of Egypt for possession of northern Syria and Palestine, they were unable to crush the aspirations for greater independence among the subject peoples. In the course of the third century, they lost Cappadocia, Pontus and Pergamum which had already formed themselves into independent kingdoms by the time of Antiochus I (281–261). Antiochus III (223–187), the most important of the Seleucid monarchs, was defeated by the Romans at Magnesia and compelled to give up Asia Minor (Peace of Apamea, 188). Confined to northern Syria and weakened by internal quarrels, the kingdom was finally conquered by Pompey (64) who overthrew Antiochus XIII and Philip II, and made it a Roman province.

SELIM I (1467–1520). Ottoman Sultan, son of Bayazid II. He ascended the throne in 1512 and conducted a number of successful campaigns which led to an enlargement of his kingdom. Having defeated the Safavid Shah Ismail I, he conquered western Anatolia and Armenia (1513–1514). His victories provoked the hostility of the Mamelukes of Egypt but, in a series of further campaigns in 1516–1517, Selim conquered Syria and Egypt. He deposed the Mameluke Sultan and usurped the title of Caliph, previously held by the last of the Abbasids who was sent into exile in Cairo.

SELJUKS. Turkish Islamic dynasty, founded by Seljuk who, in the eleventh century AD, led his people into Corasmia. The Seljuks defeated the Ghaznevids in 1037. In 1055 they occupied Baghdad and proclaimed their leader, Tughril Beg (1037–1063), as Sultan. In 1071, under the leadership of Alp Arslan (1063–1072), they founded an empire in Asia Minor with its capital at Iconium. In the following year they defeated the Byzantines at Manzikert. The empire reached its zenith with the conquest of Damascus (1078) under Malik Shah (1072–1092). However, the Seljuk Dynasty began to decline in the twelfth century when the kingdom broke up into several parts, the most important of which was the Sultanate of Rum.

SENNACHERIB (?–681 BC). Assyrian King from 705, he succeeded Sargon II. He fought against the Kassites in Syria and Palestine, besieging Jerusalem and compelling King Hezekiah to pay tribute. He then attacked and destroyed Babylon (689). He was assassinated by his sons.

SEPTIMUS SEVERUS (146–211). Roman Emperor. Governor of Pannonia under Marcus Aurelius, he was proclaimed Emperor by his legions on 13 April 193 and marched on Rome, defeating his rivals. He strengthened the northern borders which were menaced by the Barbarians and pushed back the Parthians. At home, he reformed the law and reduced the power of the Senate in favour of the equestrian ranks. He introduced oriental customs to Rome.

SFORZA. Princely family founded by the adventurer, Muzio Attendolo Sforza, whose son, Francesco I (1401–1466), succeeded the Visconti and obtained the Duchy of Milan in 1450. The dynasty ruled in Milan until 1535—Galeazzo Maria (1466–1476), Gian Galeazzo (1476–1494), Ludovico *il Moro* (1494–1500), Massimiliano (1512–1515) and Francesco II (1521–1535). On the death of Francesco II, the Duchy of Milan went to the Emperor Charles V.

SFORZA, FRANCESCO (1401–1466). Duke of Milan, son of Muzio Attendolo Sforza. A soldier of fortune, in 1431 he defeated the Venetians on behalf of the then Duke of Milan, Filippo Maria Visconti, and occupied Ancona and some papal possessions in Umbria. After his marriage to the Duke of Milan's daughter (1441), he again defeated the Venetians who, on Visconti's death, claimed the Milanese. Having conquered Milan, he was proclaimed Duke (1450). By the Peace of Lodi (1454) he inaugurated a period of political stability among the Italian states.

SHAH JAHAN (1592–1666). Mogul Emperor of India. Son of Jahangir, he came to the throne in 1627 on the death of his father, against whom he had rebelled four years previously. He is remembered primarily for his building of the Taj Mahal at Agra, which he constructed as a memorial to his wife Mumtaz Mahal; but he also completed the conquest of the Deccan, and consolidated the frontiers with Persia. In 1658 his son Aurangzeb, took advantage of his father's ill health, seized power and imprisoned him in the Fort at Agra.

SHALMANESER III (?–824 BC). King of Assyria, son of Assurnasirapli II, whom he succeeded in 858 BC. He continued his father's expansionist policy, aiming at control of Middle Eastern trading routes. He conducted a series of victorious compaigns against the Syrians and Arameans, occupying Damascus and compelling the Kingdom of Israel to pay tribute. His primary objective was the stability of his kingdom in the face of repeated revolts against his harsh rule. He defended his northern borders against the growing power of Urartu, and his western frontiers by sending expeditions to the Zagros Mountains. He also reinforced his political control over Babylon.

SHANG. First recorded Chinese dynasty (1650–1027 BC). According to tradition it was founded by Tang the Victorious in succession to the legendary Hsia Dynasty. The technique of working in bronze was developed to a high level during this period.

SHINTOISM. The "way of the Gods", the original religion of Japan. It was at first based on a belief that the Emperor was descended from the Goddess of the Sun, Amaterasu, but then (at the beginning of the fifth century AD) Shintoism absorbed many aspects of Buddhist thought. In the seventeenth century, this led to a reaction, also provoked by nationalism, which restored Shintoism and revived the belief in the divinity of the Emperor. Shintoism also venerates some aspects of the landscape, certain animals and the spirits of ancestors.

SIGISMUND (1368–1437). Son of the Emperor Charles IV of Luxemburg, he became King of Hungary in 1387 after marrying Queen Mary. He fought hard against the Turks but was defeated at Nicopolis in 1396. Imperial Vicar for his brother Wenceslas, who was deposed in 1400, he defeated the pretenders Robert III of Wittelsbach and Jobst, Margrave of Moravia, in 1411. He summoned the Council of Constance which put an end to the Great Schism. On the death of Wenceslas (1419), Sigismund succeeded him on the Bohemian throne, and had to contend with the Hussites. He summoned the Council of Basle (1431), was crowned in Rome (1433) and became a close ally of Pope Eugenius IV.

SILVESTER I (?–AD 335). Successor to Miltiades in 314, he may have received the so-called Donation of Constantine. During his pontificate the Council of Nicaea (325) met and condemned Arianism.

SOLOMON (c.990–931 BC). King of Israel, son and successor of David (970 BC). He strengthened his kingdom and protected his frontiers by allying with his most powerful neighbours, at the same time increasing trade. Despite material prosperity, cultural achievements and the renowned wisdom of Solomon, a crisis developed which, on his death, ruptured the unity of his kingdom. This was caused by the heavy taxation necessary for the building of great public works, such as the Temple at Jerusalem, the oriental extravagance of his court, and his excessive religious tolerance (although this was combined with restrictions on the automony of the various tribes).

SOLON (c.640–560 BC). Athenian legislator. Appointed Archon in 594–593 BC. He was the author of constitutional and legislative reforms which reduced the privileges of the aristocracy and admitted other citizens to various offices according to their wealth.

STALIN (1879–1953). Soviet politician, born Joseph Vissarionovich Dzhugashvili. Educated in the seminary at Tiflis in Georgia, he joined the revolutionary movement against the Tzar in 1898, and was arrested and deported on many occasions. A member of the editorial board of *Pravda*, he became People's Commissar for Nationalities in 1917, and General Secretary of the Communist Party of the Soviet Union in 1922. On Lenin's death, he allied himself with Kamenev and

Zinoviev to neutralize Trotsky, and in the 1930s he eliminated all his rivals in a series of spectacular purges — the victims included Kamenev, Zinoviev, Rykov and Bucharin. During the Second World War, he led the Soviet Union against Germany. At the end of the conflict, relations with the West deteriorated, and the years of Cold War began. In this period, he used every means he could to exercise control in those countries occupied by the Red Army where people's republics were created, modelled on Soviet lines. At home, he continued to give priority to heavy industry, maintained rigid control of the economy through the system of Five Year Plans and pushed forward the collectivization of agriculture. After his death, the "cult of personality" and other aspects of his policies were denounced by the new leaders, especially Khrushchev.

STANISLAS I LESZCZYŃSKI (1677–1766). King of Poland from 1704. Opposed by August II and August III of Saxony, he had to give up his prerogatives between 1711 and 1733. In 1736 he was forced to abdicate and retreated into the Duchies of Bar and Lorraine, which he had received at the end of the War of the Polish Succession by the Treaty of Vienna (1738).

STANISLAS II PONIATOWSKI (1732–1798). Last King of Poland. Polish aristocrat, and ambassador in Moscow at the court of Catherine II. (He became her lover.) He ascended the Polish throne with the help of Russian troops in September 1764, but was unable to prevent the progressive break-up of his kingdom — by the First (1772), Second (1793) and Third (1795) Partitions. He abdicated on 25 November 1795 and went into exile at Grodno and then St Petersburg.

STEPHEN II (?–AD 755). Pope from 752 (sometimes referred to as Stephen III, although his predecessor, another Stephen, died before being crowned). From Pepin the Short, his ally against the Lombard Aistulf, he obtained the donation of the Byzantine territories of the Lombards (*Promissio carisiaca*) which formed the nucleus of the Papal States. As a reward, Pepin was re-consecrated in the Abbey of St Denis in July 754 and obtained the title *patricius* of the Romans.

STEPHEN I (c.969–1038). King of Hungary. Son of Geisa, Duke of Hungary, he succeeded his father in 997 and received the title of King from Pope Silvester II (1000). He organized the Hungarian Church (for which he was canonized), and reformed the structure of the state, dividing his dominions into counties. He successfully defended the kingdom against the claims of the Emperor Conrad II the Salian and against the Bulgars.

STILICHO, FLAVIUS (c.365–408). Roman general of Vandal origin. A relative and tutor of the Emperors Theodosius and Honorius, he defeated Alaric at Pollenza (402) and Radagaisus at Fiesole (405). Falling into disgrace, he retired to Ravenna where he was killed in a plot.

STUARTS. Scottish Dynasty. Kings of Scotland, 1371–1714, and of England, 1603–1714. The name derives from the post of steward, given by King David I of Scotland to Walter Fitzalan, whose descendant Walter married Mary, daughter of King Robert I the Bruce, in 1315. The son of this marriage, Robert II, was King of Scotland from 1317 to 1380. Later Stuart monarchs were Robert III (1390–1406), James I (1406–1437), James II (1437–1460), James III (1460–1488), James IV (1488–1513), James V (1513–1542), Mary (1542–1567), and James VI (1567–1625). The last of these rulers became King of England in 1603 as James I, and his Stuart successors were Charles I (1625–1649), Charles II (1660–1685), James II (1685–1688), Mary II (1689–1694) and Anne (1702–1714).

STURZO, LUIGI (1871–1959). Italian statesman. Ordained priest in 1894, he joined many Catholic cultural, social and political movements. Advocating the need for Catholics to be an organized political force, he founded the *Partito Popolare*, and was its Secretary until 1923. He was in exile during the period of Fascism but returned to Italy in 1946. In 1952 he was appointed a life member of the Senate.

SUCRE, ANTONIO JOSÉ DE (1795–1830). Venezuelan statesman. Lieutenant to Bolivar, he assisted him in the foundation of Columbia, uniting Venezuela and New Granada (1819), and in the wars of liberation in Ecuador and Peru. President of Bolivia from 1826 to 1828, he resigned in order to return to Colombia where he was later assassinated.

SUHARTO (born 1921). Indonesian statesman. He fought against the Dutch in the liberation struggle in 1945. General and Commander-in-Chief in 1960, he played a decisive role in the failure of the Communist coup of 1965. He superseded Sukarno in March 1967.

SUKARNO, AHMED (1901–1970). Founder of the Indonesian Nationalist Party in 1927, he made himself first President of the Indonesian Republic in 1945. After leading the opposition against the Dutch attempt to restore colonial rule in the postwar period, he proclaimed the independence of the country in 1950. A neutralist, he was among the promoters of the Bandung Conference (April 1955) to bring together the countries of the Third World. Deprived of effective power by a coup in 1965, he retained only formal responsibilities for the next two years. He was succeeded by Suharto.

SULEIMAN I THE MAGNIFICENT (1494–1566). Ottoman Sultan, he succeeded his father Selim I in 1520. Having taken Belgrade and conquered Hungary (winning the Battle of Mohács, 1526), he took advantage of the rivalry between Francis I and Charles V to make an alliance with the French and to besiege Vienna (1529). He conducted many campaigns against the Christians (sieges of Corfu, 1537, and Malta, 1564). In the east, he strengthened the frontiers which were threatened by the Persian Safavids. A patron of letters and the arts, he promoted financial reform and the construction of many buildings, employing the famous architect Sinan. He died in Hungary while besieging Sziget.

SUMERIANS. Early inhabitants of southern Mesopotamia. Their origins are uncertain. They produced one of the first civilizations, in the third millennium BC. Their autonomous city-states (Kish, Lagash, Ur, Umma and others) were ruled by priest-kings. Below these, there was a sacerdotal caste who controlled all activities connected with the temple (*ziggurat*) and its enrichment. The Sumerians are credited with the invention of cuneiform writing and the wheel, the introduction of written laws, the study of astronomy and the development of irrigation systems. The last dynasty died out in 2006 BC.

SUN YAT-SEN (1866–1925). Chinese statesman. He entered politics in 1884, and was active in various anti-Manchu organizations. He advocated the modernization of China and, exiled in 1885, he returned during the upheavals which led to the fall of the Manchu (Ch'ing) Dynasty. Elected in Nanking as provisional President of the Republic (1912), he yielded power to General Yuan Shih-kai and founded the Kuomintang — the Chinese Nationalist Party. After the period of reaction under Yuan and the warlords, he was elected President of the Kuomintang government in Canton (1921). He died in 1925 without having realized his dream of a united and republican China.

TALLEYRAND, CHARLES MAURICE DE (1754–1838). French diplomat and statesman. Bishop of Autun before the Revolution, he was a deputy of the clergy in the States General (1789). Two years later he was excommunicated for having voted in favour of the civil constitution of the clergy. Foreign Minister under the Directory, the Consulate and the Empire, he left office in 1807 after quarrelling with Napoleon. In 1814, at the request of the victorious powers, he formed a provisional government which prepared for the return of the Bourbons. French representative at the Congress of Vienna, he continued to be politically active after 1815, and became prominent in 1830 as a supporter of the new King Louis Philippe. He concluded his career as ambassador in London (1830–1834), and wrote his memoirs.

TAMERLANE (1369–1405). Mongol leader. His name is a European corruption of Timur Lang ("the lame one"). He proclaimed himself King of Transoxiana in 1369, after eliminating the other claimants. He then led an almost continuous series of expeditions, conquering a large part of Asia (first Corasmia, then Persia, Azerbaijan, northern India, Syria and Mesopotamia). In 1402, after defeating the Turks under Bayazid I at Angora, he reached Smyrna. Returning to Samarkand, his capital, he organized an expedition against China but died while conquering Turkestan.

TANG. Chinese dynasty which ruled from 618 to 907. Founded by an able soldier, Li Shih-min, who conquered China while it was convulsed by civil war, and proclaimed himself Emperor under the name T'ai Tsung. Other important monarchs of this dynasty were T'ai Tsung's son, Kao Tsung (650–683) and Hsuan Tsung (712–756). The dynasty presided over a period of great splendour in China but it was weakened by attacks from Tibet and the steppes.

TARTARS. Nomad peoples of Turkish-Mongolian stock, originating in Central Asia. A tribe of Tartars followed the armies of Genghis Khan and settled in the Crimea and the Urals. Their descendants remained there after the Russian reconquest, partly mixing with Slavs and Caucasians.

TASMAN, ABEL JANSZOON (1603–1659). Dutch explorer, in the service of the Dutch East India Company. On the instructions of Governor Van Diemen, in 1642 he set out to explore the South Seas. He discovered the island which he named after the Governor and which was renamed Tasmania in 1853. He also found the southern island of New Zealand, and touched the islands of Tonga, Fiji and Bismarck on his way home. He led a second expedition along the Australian coasts in 1644.

TELL, WILLIAM (?–AD 1354). Legendary Swiss hero of the time of the war of liberation against Albert I of Austria (fourteenth century). Because he refused to bow to the hat of the Austrian Governor Gessler (which was mounted on a post), he was sentenced to shoot an arrow at an apple balanced on his son's head. He passed the test and later killed Gessler.

THATCHER, MARGARET (born 1926). British Conservative politician. After election to Parliament (1959), she became Minister of Education (1975) in Edward Heath's government. Replacing him as the leader of the Conservative Party in the same year, she won three consecutive general elections in 1979, 1983 and 1987. During her term of office a range of economic reforms was introduced, focusing heavily on privatization of nationalized industries, reduction of inflation, lowering of taxes and high defence spending. As a result, her government was often criticized for lack of attention to health, education and welfare, and inability to reduce high levels of unemployment. Her popularity reached its peak during the 1982 Falklands War against Argentina.

THEMISTOCLES (528–462 BC). Athenian statesman, general and popular leader. He embarked upon a major ship-building programme which enabled him to defeat the Persian fleet of Xerxes at Salamis (480). He rebuilt the city walls of Athens and connected the town to the port of Piraeus. Accused of treason and embezzlement, he was exiled (471) and, after much wandering, he arrived at the court of King Artaxerxes I of Persia. He died in the Orient in mysterious circumstances.

THEODORIC I (c.454–526). King of the Ostrogoths. Son of King Theodemir of the House of Amals, he spent his youth as a hostage at the Byzantine court in Constantinople. He became King of the Ostrogoths on the death of his father (474) and was sent by Emperor Zeno to Italy with the task of defeating Odoacer. He won victories at Verona (489) and on the River Adda. After compelling Odoacer to surrender at the end of a long campaign, he ordered his assassination (493). Recognized as master of Italy, Theodoric established himself in Ravenna and Verona, and worked to improve relations between Romans and Ostrogoths. However, in the last years of his life he was angered by the persecution of Arians, instigated by the Emperor and the Pope, and decided to put to death some of his Roman advisers, including Boethius and Cassiodorus.

THEODOSIUS I (c.347–395). Roman Emperor. He distinguished himself as an army leader in Moesia, and was nominated *magister equitum* by the Emperor Gratian after the defeat at Adrianople (378). In the following year he was appointed Governor of the Orient. He used coercive methods to enforce the conversion of Arians and pagans to Catholicism but was compelled to accept penance from Bishop Ambrose of Milan for the massacre at Thessalonica (390). On many occasions he defeated the Barbarians, but also made settlements with them and encouraged them to live within the frontiers of the empire. He also reorganized the empire, and on his death, it was divided between his sons Honorius (the West) and Arcadius (the East).

THIERS, ADOLPHE (1797–1877). French statesman. Prime Minister in 1836 and 1840, he held office again after the French defeat in the Franco-Prussian War, and was in charge of the suppression of the Paris Commune (1871). He was the first President (1871– 1873) of the Third Republic.

THUTMOSIS. The name of four Pharaohs of the Eighteenth Dynasty in Egypt. Thutmosis I (c.1530–1520 BC) extended his kingdom southwards, conquering part of Nubia. Thutmosis II (c.1520–1504) continued the work of strengthening the kingdom and laid the basis for his successor, Thutmosis III (1504–c.1450), who led no fewer than seventeen campaigns, and conquered Asia as far as the Euphrates. The military expeditions of his successor, Thutmosis IV (1425–c.1405) are less well-known.

TIBERIUS, JULIUS CAESAR AUGUSTUS (42 BC–AD 37). Son of Livia and, by adoption, of Augustus, he became Emperor in AD 14. A courageous general, he strengthened the frontiers of the empire by means of a number of victorious campaigns, mostly led by Germanicus. In AD 26 he retired to Capri, entrusting the government of the empire to the Prefect Sejanus. He ferociously persecuted the emperor's adversaries but was eventually executed.

TIGLATHPILESER (?–1074 BC). Assyrian King, he ascended the throne in 1112 BC. He was the architect of Assyrian predominance in Asia, and extended his kingdom from the Black Sea to the Phoenician cities of Sidon and Byblos. He was succeeded by two further Assyrian rulers of the same name. These were Tiglathpileser II (965–933) and Tiglathpileser III (745–725); the latter absorbed both Syria and Palestine into his empire and succeeded in unifying the crowns of Assyria and Babylon.

TITO (1892–1980). Born Joseph Broz, he was President of the Republic of Yugoslavia from 1953. A socialist militant in Zagreb from 1910, he was a prisoner of the Russians in 1915 and then became a soldier in the Red Army after the Bolshevik Revolution. From being a trade unionist, he became Secretary of the Yugoslav Communist Party in 1937. He led the partisan resistance following the German occupation in 1941. Prime Minister after the liberation, he gave a decisive lead to his country both in breaking with the Cominform (1948) and in following a policy of neutrality between the two power blocs.

TITUS, FLAVIUS VESPASIAN (39–81). Roman Emperor, son of Vespasian. Having led the Roman legions in the Jewish War (which ended with the destruction of the Temple at Jerusalem in 70), he returned to Rome and became co-ruler with his father. He ascended the throne in 79 and ruled with wisdom. The great eruption of Vesuvius occurred during his reign. It buried Pompeii, Stabiae and Herculaneum.

TOKUGAWA. Japanese *shogun* dynasty, founded in 1603 by Ieyasu Tokugawa (1542–1616). He moved the capital to Edo (Tokyo) and ruled the state on behalf of the Emperor, pursuing a policy of isolation. The most important members of the dynasty (which ended in 1868 when the fifteenth *shogun*, Yoshibonu Tokugawa, surrended power to the Emperor Mutsuhito) were Iemitsu (1623–1651), Genroku (1687–1709) and Yoshimune (1716–1745). (*Shogun* is a Japanese word for general).

TOLTECS. Ancient peoples who settled in the central areas of Mexico and, in particular, around Tula in the eighth century BC. In the tenth century, the Toltecs came into contact with the Maya. In 1168 Tula was conquered and sacked by the Chichimecs. As the Toltecs declined, the Aztecs rose to power in Mexico.

TOTILA (?–AD 552). King of the Ostrogoths from 541, when he succeeded Hildebad. He led his armies to Cumae and Naples (543), occupied Rome for the first time in 546 and again in 549. In the same period he fought with Belisarius. He later campaigned in southern Italy. Defeated by Narses at Tadinae, he died in battle.

TRAJAN, MARCUS ULPIUS (53–117). Roman Emperor, son of a general of the same name. He distinguished himself fighting against the Jews and the Parthians in Syria, and was acclaimed Emperor in 98 in place of Nerva, by whom he had been adopted. Under him, the Roman Empire attained its greatest size: he subjugated Dacia (101–106), Armenia, Mesopotamia and part of Arabia. A good administrator, he constructed important public works — the *Forum*, the baths, and the aqueduct named after him. He died in Cilicia while campaigning against rebels.

TROTSKY, LEON (1879–1940). Born Leon Bronstein, he was a Russian revolutionary agitator as early as 1898. He collaborated with Lenin on the newspaper *Iskra* (1904) and was one of the leaders of the 1905 and 1917 Revolutions. He was People's Commissar for Foreign Affairs after the October Revolution, People's Commissar for War from 1918 and organizer of the Red Army. He was compelled to resign in 1925 after disagreements with Stalin, expelled from the Communist Party in 1927 and exiled in 1929. He continued to criticize Stalinism and proclaimed the necessity of permanent revolution. He was assassinated in Mexico, probably on Stalin's orders.

TRUMAN, HARRY SPENCER (1884–1972). Democratic Senator for Missouri from 1934. Vice-President under Franklin Roosevelt in 1944, he became President of the United States in April 1945 on Roosevelt's death. He was re-elected for a further term in 1948. In foreign affairs, he came to believe in the necessity of containing Communism as early as the Potsdam Conference (July–August 1945). For this reason, he approved the Marshall Plan in 1947, favoured the formation of the Atlantic Pact (NATO) in 1949 and, in June 1950, intervened on the side of the South Koreans when they were attacked by the North. In domestic affairs, he opposed isolationism and the excesses of the anti-Communist witch-hunts conducted by Senator McCarthy.

TUDORS. Anglo-Welsh dynasty. The family's associations with the English throne developed in 1428, when Owen Tudor married King Henry V's widow, Catherine, who then gave birth to Edmund, later Earl of Richmond. Edmund's son, Henry, was half-brother to Henry VI through their mother: he became king as Henry VII (1485–1509), following his victory at the Battle of Bosworth (1485) which ended the Wars of the Roses. Other monarchs of this dynasty were Henry VIII (1509–1547), Edward VI (1547–1553), Mary I (1553–1558) and Elizabeth I (1558–1603).

TURATI, FILIPPO (1857–1932). Italian statesman. He graduated in law and was one of the founders of the *Lega socialista milanese* and of the magazine *Critica sociale*. In 1892 he started a party for Italian workers which, three years later, took the name *Partito Socialista Italiano*. A member of Parliament from 1896, he was the leader of the moderate wing of the Party against the radicals. As an anti-militarist, he opposed Italian intervention in the First World War. In 1922, he started the *Partito Socialista Unitario* and was later among the most uncompromising opponents of Fascism. In 1926 he was compelled to go into exile in France.

TUTANKHAMEN. Pharaoh of the Eighteenth Dynasty, who restored the ancient cults which had been threatened by the monotheistic reforms of Amenophis IV (Akhenaton). In 1922, the Englishmen Carnarvon and Carter discovered his tomb, practically intact and containing a large number of objects of outstanding artistic value.

UGUDEI KHAN (c.1186–1241). Son of Genghis Khan, he became Emperor of the Mongols in 1229 and established his capital at Karakorum. A wise ruler, he conquered the Chinese Empire of the Ch'in (1234) and Korea (1241), while his armies invaded southern Russia, Poland and Hungary, but were halted on the Adriatic by defeat at Liegnitz (1241).

URBAN II (c.1040–1099). Born Otto de Lagery, he became Pope on the death of Victor III (1088). He carried on the policies of Gregory VII, and summoned the First Crusade at the Councils of Piacenza and Clermont-Ferrand (March and November 1095).

VANDALS. Germanic peoples who emigrated from the Baltic regions towards Central Europe near the end of the second century AD. Having invaded Gaul (406) under King Gunderic, they moved to Spain (409) and, finally, under the pressure of the Visigoths, into Africa. Under the leadership of King Geiserich (428–477), they founded an Arian Kingdom. However, this was weakened by the inability of the Vandals to integrate with the local populations or to moderate their ferocity in dealing with them. The kingdom collapsed in 534 in the face of the Byzantine armies of Belisarius, general of Justinian.

VARANGIANS. A branch of the Vikings who, in the ninth century AD, moved across Russia in the direction of the Black Sea and Byzantium, and contributed to the formation of the Principalities of Novgorod (c.860) and Kiev (882).

VESPASIAN, TITUS FLAVIUS (9–79). Roman Emperor. Son of Flavius Sabinus, a tax collector, he held various offices under Caligula, Claudius and Nero, and fought in Germany and in Britain. Leader of the legions in Judea where a revolt had broken out, he was besieged in Jerusalem when he heard of Nero's death and of the subsequent upheavals. He was acclaimed Emperor by his soldiers on the death of Vitellius (69). He left his son, Titus, in Judea, while he returned to Rome. There, he reorganized administration and taxation, and cleared the huge deficits (of over 40,000 million sesterces) caused by his extravagant predecessors. He also reformed the Senate and the equestrian ranks.

VESPUCCI, AMERIGO (1454–1512). Italian explorer, secretary and diplomat in the service of the Medici. He left Florence on missions to France and Spain, and then settled in Seville. He may have made a first voyage to the Caribbean in 1497. Two years later, accompanied by Juan de la Cosa and Alonso de Hojeda, and on the instructions of King Ferdinand, he set out to verify the findings of Columbus. He reached the mouth of the Amazon River and the coasts of Brazil. During a later voyage on behalf of the Portuguese monarch, he explored the bay of Rio de Janeiro and pushed on southwards as far as Patagonia. In 1507 the German cartographer Martin Waldeseemüller, convinced by Vespucci's reports that the land he had just explored was a new continent, and not Asia, called it America in Vespucci's honour.

VICTOR AMADEUS II (1666–1732). Duke of Savoy. Son of Charles Emmanuel II, he came to the throne at the age of nine, under the regency of his mother, Maria of Savoy-Nemours. He took part in the War of the Spanish Succession, first as an ally of France, and then (1703) as its enemy. He was besieged in Turin (1706), but by the Treaties of Utrecht and Rastatt he regained Nice, Savoy and Monferrato. He also gained Sicily (1713), of which he became King. In 1718 he exchanged Sicily for Sardinia, and dedicated himself to the reorganization of his dominions. He abdicated in 1730 in favour of his son, Charles Emmanuel III.

VICTOR EMMANUEL II (1820–1878). King of Italy. Eldest son of Charles Albert, he took over on the abdication of his father after the defeat by the Austrians at Novara (1849). In 1852 he appointed Cavour as his First Minister, supporting him in his decision to participate in the Crimean War and in his determination to seek the alliance of Napoleon III with a view to reopening the struggle with Austria. When war began in 1859, the support of France and the expeditions of Garibaldi and the Thousand led to victory. He became King of Italy on 17 March 1861. Following Cavour's death (1861), he frequently interfered in the policies of his ministers. In 1865 he moved his capital to Florence, and later completed the unification of Italy by annexing the Veneto from Austria (1866) and taking Rome (1870).

VICTOR EMMANUEL III (1869–1946). Son of Umberto I, he ascended the throne in 1900 on the assassination of his father. He supported the policies of his Prime Minister, Giolitti, which led to the Italian conquest of Libya (1911–1912), and intervention in the First World War. An indecisive monarch in the postwar period, he failed to take a firm stand when Mussolini marched on Rome (October 1922) and entrusted him with the formation of a government. Pushed out of active political life by the Fascists, he became Emperor of Ethiopia (1936) and King of Albania (1939) following the conquest of both countries. Even if he was opposed to Italy's participation in the Second World War, he failed to frustrate Mussolini's decision to ally with Germany. After the fall of Mussolini on 25 July 1943 he regained an active place in politics when he appointed Badoglio as Prime Minister. He left Rome for Brindisi on 8 September 1943 and, in April 1944, he appointed his son Umberto to act in his place. In May 1946 he abdicated in Umberto's favour and went into exile in Egypt.

VICTORIA (1819–1901). Queen of Great Britain. The only daughter of Edward, fourth son of King George III, she ascended the throne on 20 June 1837 on the death of King William IV. She married Albert of Saxe-Coburg in 1840 and ruled with the help of a number of great Prime Ministers, from Peel to Palmerston and from Disraeli to Gladstone. During her reign, Britain greatly extended its colonial possessions and formed its Indian Empire, of which she was made Empress in January 1877.

VIKINGS. Name given to Scandinavian peoples, also known as Varangians or Normans. Between the eighth and the tenth centuries AD, they sailed along the coasts of Europe searching for plunder, and reached Iceland, Greenland and, perhaps, the American coast.

VILLA, PANCHO (1887–1923). Mexican revolutionary. In 1910, he allied with Francisco Madero to lead the peasantry against Porfirio Diaz, and won control of the region of Chihuahua. After the assassination of Madero (1913), he joined Carranza in the struggle against the reactionary Victoriano Huerta. Allied with Emiliano Zapata, he took Mexico City (December 1914 to January 1915), but was forced to abandon it. In 1920, during the presidency of Adolfo de le Huerta, he gave up the guerilla war and retired to a farm at Durango where he was later assassinated.

VISCONTI. Princely family who sided with the Ghibellines. They ruled Milan from 1277 to 1302, and from 1311 to 1447. The family's fortunes were founded by Uberto, whose son Ottone (1207–1295) was acclaimed *signore* in 1277 after defeating Napoleone della Torre at Desio. The Visconti regained power under Matteo I (1250–1322) and continued to hold it under his sons Galeazzo I and Marco, who was succeeded by Azzonde (1302–1339). They then strengthened their position under Luchino (1292–1349) and Archbishop Giovanni (1290–1354), and the dominions of the Visconti passed to Matteo II (1319–1355), Galeazzo II (1320–1378) and Bernabó (1323–1385). The last great members of the dynasty were Gian Galeazzo (1351–1402), first Duke of Milan, who succeeded his uncle Bernabó after poisoning him, and Gian Galeazzo's son, Giovanni Maria (1389–1412), who was assassinated during a conspiracy. The title then passed to Giovanni Maria's brother, Filippo Maria (1392–1447), before the dynasty died out. The Duchy of Milan passed to Francesco Sforza, the army leader who had married Bianca, Filippo Maria's daughter.

VISIGOTHS. Germanic peoples, also known as Goths of the West. In the fourth century AD they settled in the region between the Rivers Dnieper and Danube, where they were converted to Arian Christianity by Ulfilas. They defeated the Emperor Valens at Adrianople (378) and obtained the status of *foederati* of the Empire from Theodosius. There then followed a largely peaceful period, but after the death of Theodosius (395) they invaded Greece, Macedonia and Thessaly, and devastated Italy (sack of Rome by Alaric, 410). Under Athaulf (410–415), they invaded Gaul, conquering Aquitania and Toulouse; under Euric (466–484), they extended their dominions in Gaul and took Spain; and under Alaric II (484–507) they had to face the Franks of Clovis who defeated them at Vouillé, 507. They were confined to Spain until July 711, when they were defeated at Guadalete by the Arabs who then overran the Iberian Peninsula.

VLADIMIR THE SAINT. (c.956– 1015). Son of Svyatoslav, Prince of Novgorod from 970. He gained the Principality of Kiev by fratricide, and unified Russia from the Ukraine to the Baltic. He strengthened his links with Byzantium, marrying Anna Porphyrogenitus, sister of the Emperor Basil II. In 988, he and his subjects were converted to Christianity.

WALLENSTEIN, ALBRECHT VON (1583–1634). Army leader of Czech origin. He served the Emperor Ferdinard II of Habsburg during the Thirty Years' War and led his armies, which he often financed himself, into battle in many parts of Europe. However, his ambitions aroused the suspicions of the Emperor and the hostility of a number of German princes; he was therefore dismissed from his supreme command (Diet of Ratisbon, 1630) and retired to the dominions he had received on his creation as Duke of Friedland in 1625. On the defeat of Tilly at Breitenfeld (1631), he was recalled to his post to fight against Gustavus II Adolphus of Sweden. He succeeded in halting his enemies at Lützen on 16 November 1632 and defeated them at Steinau (October 1633). While he was negotiating with the enemies of the Emperor in the hope of obtaining the crown of Bohemia, he was assassinated by a high-ranking member of his entourage.

WALPOLE, ROBERT (1676–1745). First Earl of Orford. Whig member of Parliament. He was Prime Minister from 1721 to 1742, under George I and George II. He undertook the effective management of Parliament and made government increasingly more answerable to Parliament than to the monarch. He laid the base for the colonial expansion of Great Britain.

WASHINGTON, GEORGE (1732–1799). First President of the United States of America. A Virginian landowner, he fought in the Seven Years' War against the French (1756–1763). He became commander of the rebel colonists in June 1775 and led them, with varying fortunes, throughout the War of American Independence, to the final defeat of the British at Yorktown (1781). In December 1783 he gave up his military command and retired to Mount Vernon. He returned to active politics, representing Virginia at the Constitutional Convention in Philadelphia (1787) which approved the Constitution. He was unanimously elected President of the United States on 4 March 1789, and was re-elected in November 1792 for a further four-year term.

WATUSI. Tall people of Nilotic stock. Originally nomads, they settled (probably in the seventeenth century AD), in the areas of Lake Victoria and Tanganyika where they established powerful kingdoms.

WELLINGTON, ARTHUR WELLESLEY, DUKE OF (1769–1852). British general and statesman. He joined the army in 1787 and served in India from 1796 to 1803. In 1808 he was appointed to command the British forces in the Peninsular War, during which he defeated the armies of Napoleon (Battles of Vimeiro, 1808, Talavera, 1809, and Vitoria, 1813). He was ambassador to Paris and British representative at the Congress of Vienna, and he led the Allied forces in the Battle of Waterloo (June 1815). Commander of the forces of occupation in France after the decisive defeat of Napoleon, he returned to England in 1818 and devoted himself to politics as a member of the Tory Party. He was Prime Minister from 1828 to 1830 and briefly in 1834, and Foreign Minister from 1834 to 1835. He was appointed Commander-in-Chief for life of the British army in 1842.

WELSER. Family of Augsburg bankers whose fortunes were founded in 1476. Their wealth reached its climax during the reign of Charles V when they received the right to exploit the copper deposits and trade of Santo Domingo and Venezuela.

WENCESLAS IV (1361–1419). Son of the Emperor Charles IV of Luxemburg, who gave him nominal powers relating to the throne of Bohemia when he was only two years of age. He was elected King of the Romans on the death of his father (1367), but he was never crowned Emperor. He was deposed in 1400 in the course of the struggle which shattered the Empire and the Papacy during the Great Schism, but he continued to rule in Bohemia. He died in Prague during the conflicts surrounding Hus.

WESLEY, JOHN (1703–1791). English theologian, son of an Anglican minister. He went to America in 1735. After his return home in 1738, he founded the Methodist movement with his brother Charles and with George Whitefield. The movement advocated a return to the spiritual origins of Protestantism and the purity of faith, and minimized the importance of ritual.

WILLIAM I (1797–1888). King of Prussia and Emperor of Germany. Son of Frederick William III of Prussia, he was Regent from 1858 and succeeded his unstable brother Frederick William IV in 1861. With a major contribution from the Chancellor Bismarck, he transformed the army into an invincible machine of war, and waged a series of victorious campaigns (against Denmark 1864, Austria 1866 and France 1870) which led to his coronation as Emperor (Versailles 1871). As a result of this, he brought together under his control a confederation of 25 German states dominated by Prussia. Until his death, William supported Bismarck, whose policies lay at the root of the great economic and colonial development of Germany.

WILLIAM II (1859–1941). Nephew of William I, Emperor of Germany from 1888. He dismissed Bismarck in 1890 and abandoned his balanced system of alliances. He reinforced the army, created a large fleet, and formed a vast colonial empire: his expansionist ambitions led to friction with Britain, France and Russia, and contributed to the tensions which provoked the outbreak of the First World War. Germany's defeat in the war and the consequent domestic problems forced him to abdicate in 1918.

WILLIAM I THE CONQUEROR (1027–1087). Duke of Normandy from 1035, he consolidated his position and enlarged his dominions towards Maine and in part of Brittany (1065). Claimant to the throne of England, he inherited it on the death of his cousin, Edward the Confessor, but took possession only after defeating a rival claimant, Harold, at Hastings (1066). He imposed the Norman feudal structure, reinforcing Anglo-Saxon institutions of central government and limiting the autonomy of his greater vassals. He spent most of his time in France.

WILLIAM III OF ORANGE (1650–1702). King of England. Stadtholder of Holland, 1672, he halted the invasion of the Netherlands by Louis XIV. He married Mary, daughter of James II of England, and was invited by the English Parliament to take the place of his father-in-law. He became King in 1689. He continued to fight against French expansionism until the signature of the Treaty of Ryswick in 1697.

WILSON, HAROLD (born 1916). British statesman. Professor of economics at Oxford. Labour member of Parliament from 1945, he became leader of the Labour Party in 1963 and was Prime Minister from 1964 to 1970 and from 1974 to 1976.

WILSON, THOMAS WOODROW (1856–1924). American statesman. Twenty-eighth President of the United States. A member of the Democratic Party, he was elected Governor of New Jersey (1910) and, in the presidential election of 1912, he defeated Roosevelt and Taft. In domestic affairs, he championed the concept of progressive taxation and opposed monopolies; in external affairs, he kept the United States out of the earlier years of the First World War. Re-elected in 1916, he took America into the war against Germany and Austria-Hungary on 7 April 1917. At the end of the war, he favoured a peace based on principles of equity, which he elaborated in the Fourteen Points, but he was disappointed with the peace settlements. He advocated the formation of the League of Nations but the preponderance of isolationists in the Senate prevented the United States from joining. One of his final acts was the approval of the nineteenth amendment to the Constitution which gave women the vote.

WITTELSBACHS. German princely family. It derived its name from Otto von Scheyern who owned Wittelsbach Castle, near Augsburg, from 1214. Bavaria was another possession of the family: it was a duchy from 1180 to 1806, and then a kingdom until 1918. Two of the best-known members of the dynasty were the Emperors Louis IV the Bavarian (1328–1346) and Charles VII Albert (1742–1745).

WYCLIFFE, JOHN (c.1320–1384). English theologian and teacher at Oxford. He translated the Bible into English and advocated religious and social egalitarianism. His ideas were spread by his followers, the poor preachers or Lollards. He denied the supremacy of the Papacy over civil authority (*De officio regis*, 1378) and the doctrine of transubstantiation, and opposed the sale of indulgences. He was condemned by a council in London (1382) and his teachings were suppressed.

XERXES I (?–465 BC). King of Persia, son of Darius I. He succeeded his father in 485. Having suppressed a rebellion in Egypt, he organized an expedition against the Greeks. He defeated the Spartans under Leonidas at Thermopilae (480), invaded Attica and took Athens which he destroyed by fire. He returned home after the defeat of his fleet at Salamis (480).

YAMAMOTO, ISOROKU (1884–1943). Japanese admiral. He fought in the Russo-Japanese War (1904–1905) and was Japanese representative at the London Naval Conferences of 1929 and 1934. He was Deputy Minister for the Navy in 1936 and its Commander-in-Chief from 1939. He prepared the plans for the attack on Pearl Harbor and directed the Japanese conquests in the Pacific.

YORUBA. African peoples settled in the regions of Nigeria, Togo and Benin. From the beginning of the first millennium BC they developed a variety of cultures and formed kingdoms such as the Kingdom of the Oyo which was established round the holy city of Ife, and survived until the eighteenth century AD.

YOUNG, BRIGHAM (1801–1877). Carpenter and glass-maker. He joined the Mormon sect and became its leader on the death of Joseph Smith in 1844. He led the Mormon community westwards as far as the shores of the Great Salt Lake, Utah, where Salt Lake City was founded.

YPSILANTI. A Fanariot family of Byzantine origin. Three brothers from this family, Alexander (1792–1828), Demetrius (1793–1832) and Nicholas (1798–1834), were heroes of the Greek War of Independence (1821).

ZAPATA, EMILIANO (1883–1919). Mexican revolutionary. He was one of the leaders of the Indian peasant movement. He first joined the revolution of Francisco Madero against the dictatorship of Porfirio Diaz (1910). He sided with Pancho Villa in the struggle for agrarian reform; together they took Mexico City (December 1914 to January 1915). While continuing the struggle on behalf of the Indians in the region of Tlatizapán, he was ambushed and assassinated.

ZAPOTECS. Pre-Columbian peoples, settled in the region of modern Oaxaco, Mexico, from the first millennium BC. Their religious capital was Monte Albán. From the ninth century AD onwards, they were invaded and subdued by successive waves of Miztecs, Chichimecs and Aztecs.

ZENO (c.426–491). Eastern Roman Emperor. A general under the Emperor Leo I whose daughter, Ariadne, he married. He came to the throne in 474 on the death of Leo II and succeeded in freeing his dominions from the threat of the Goths under Theodoric, by sending the Goths to fight in Italy.

ZHDANOV, ANDREY ALEKSANDROVICH (1896–1948). Soviet politician. Communist militant from 1919, he collaborated with Stalin as Party Secretary in Leningrad from 1934 onwards (the period of the great purges). He advocated the annexation of the Baltic countries and played a major role in defending Leningrad against the Germans. In 1947 he was among the founders of the Cominform, the official information bureau.

ZINOVIEV, GRIGORII EVSEYEVICH (1883–1936). Soviet statesman. Born Hirsch Apfelbaum, he was an ally of Lenin from 1903 and one of the leaders of the 1905 Revolution. Exiled in 1908, he returned to Russia with Lenin in April 1917 and took part in the October Revolution. President of the Executive Committee of the Third International (1919–1926), he made an alliance with Stalin and Kamenev (the so-called *troika*) which led to Stalin's rise to the post of Party Secretary. He quarrelled with Stalin and was in disgrace from 1927. In 1936 he was accused of the assassination of Kirov, and was tried and executed during the great purges.

ZOROASTER (between 1000 and 600 BC). Religious reformer of ancient Iran, he is also known as Zarathustra. After having a vision while in a state of ectasy he began to preach a new religion, revealed to him by Ahura Mazda, "the Wise Lord". These beliefs, based on the concept of the conflict between Good and Evil, required followers to take sides and to struggle for Good against Evil, while awaiting the triumph of the former. The principles of this religion are contained in the *Gathas*.

ZOSER (27th century BC). Pharaoh of the Third Dynasty. He was one of the founders of the Old Kingdom. He is remembered, together with his architect Imhotep, as the builder of the stepped pyramid of Sakkara.

ZWINGLI, HULDREICH (1484-1531). Swiss religious reformer. He started preaching in 1519 at Zurich and, within a short time, succeeded in giving the city a rigid theocratic organization. He led the fight against the Catholic cantons and was killed in the Battle of Kappel. He expounded his teachings (which were based on a rigid adherence to the Scriptures) in *De vera et falsa religione* (1525).

Index

(Page numbers in italics refer to illustrations)

Acknowledgements
This book was designed by Fernando Russo. The maps are from the archives of Vallardi Industrie Grafiche, and the illustrations are reproduced with permission of the following agencies and organizations:

Agache; Apostolo; Archivio Vallardi; Archivio 2P; Bayerische Staatsbibliothek, Munich; Bibliothèque Nationale, Paris; Borromeo; British Museum, London; Civico Gabinetto Numismatico, Milan/Saporetti; G Costa, Milan; Hans Hubert, Garmisch-Partenkirchen; Harding; Landesmuseum Joanneum Graz/Hofstetter Dia; Lores Riva; Marka; Museo Archeologico, Milan; Museo Arqueologico Nacional, Madrid; Museo Cristiano, Cividale del Friuli; National Gallery, London; Naturhistorisches Museum, Vienna/Salmer Barcelona; Nimatallah; Oesterreichische Nationalbibliothek, Vienna; Pedone; Pellegrini; Pinna; Pucciarelli; Scala, Florence; Schweizerischer Landsmuseum, Zurich/Marka; SEF di Regaldi Angelo; Shostal Associates Inc., New York; Staatsbibliothek Bildarchiv, Berlin; Staatsbibliothek Kunstbibliothek, Berlin; Three Lions Inc., New York; Titus, Turin; Württembergisches Landsmuseum, Stuttgart/Marka.